Perspective:

The Golden Rule

To My Dear Friends
Wilfred & Adele

David Meakes
Jan - 2019

by

David Meakes

Perspective: The Golden Rule

Library of Congress Control Number: 2017951656

ISBN-13:	Paperback:	978-1-64045-820-8
	PDF:	978-1-64045-821-5
	ePub:	978-1-64045-822-2
	Kindle:	978-1-64045-823-9

Printed in the United States of America

LitFire LLC
1-800-511-9787
www.litfirepublishing.com
order@litfirepublishing.com

Contents

This bookis dedicated with loving memories of
James Meakes,1877-1943
and
Elsie Buthcher Meakes, 1883-1968

My parents, James and Elsie Meakes.

Preface

My unfocussed intention was to drift through my 90th year leaving it to others to decide how, or if, they would prefer to remember me when I made my Final Exit. I had always felt that I would be viewed as presumptuous to make any suggestions. That is why I am only now leaving a personal account which will allow judgment by others. In October 2011, my daughter-in-law Maria Estrada brought me some printed forms intended to lessen the post-passing stress to others at the time of my Final Exit, and they included, as the final question, "How do you wish to be remembered?" Outside of my life-example, I had planned nothing! That is how my family members had all done it. But I also remembered the long list of questions, that I later wished I had asked my father, when I last saw him at my age of less-than-eighteen years. Wouldn't it be appropriate to answer some similar queries in advance? That question became the initial stimulus for this effort.

The logical answer to the same question was the observation made by Benjamin Franklin and recorded in *Brilliant Quotes*: "If you would not be forgotten, as soon as you are dead and rotten, either write things worth reading, or do things worth the writing." Thus a possibility came to my mind. I had never done anything worth writing about, but, for no apparent reason I was living an unexpectedly long life which would allow me miniscule doing time, and an inevitably uncertain, diminishing amount of writing time. But maybe there would be enough time in which to prepare an educational account of my life-errors; an account of my previously under-emphasized concern regarding world peace; the futility of war; my despair at the blind public preparation and acceptance of war; and the resultant "money-pit" now known as "National Security," where our education, health, and social welfare dollars are squandered.

I have come to realize that the Golden Rule was a fundamental principle that my parents had impressed into my consciousness at an early age. At that time, I had deemed it to be a simplistic thing for a kid to learn, but I now think that it is of major importance; that it is an attribute, that learned by all children of every country, could be an influence on world peace. So this book is subtitled *The Golden Rule,* and you will hear much about it in this account.

In the ocean of past peace history and commentary, this book will be just a perishable, floating leaf. However, it is important to me that it brings clear understanding. I wish it to be historically educational, and simultaneously convincing. I will be quoting some history and historical commentary to improve understanding. To make an important point I will quote some authors in some length, and my reliance on their apt aphorisms, historical commentaries and wise analyses , suggest that this book could also have been aptly sub-titled *Commentary by the Sages of the Ages.*

As there are 6 parts, to this book, many readers may be tempted to read only the portion in which they think they are interested, or decide to *read no more* of something with which they do not agree. The topics, though not interlocked, are interlinked, making full understanding possible only when the whole topic or the whole book is read. I think that you will find interest in the least expected topics. It is suited to be read in chapters, or parts, but I earnestly implore you to read all, as that is the only way that the reader will gain full understanding. You will not easily understand Part #2 unless you have first read Part #1. The same is especially true of #3, unless you have first read #2. Please get understanding by reading the parts sequentially.

In writing this book, I have now become much more aware of the pronounced need of a liberal arts education which I never had; or the use of the 54 volume set of the *Great Books of the Western World,* which I owned but thoughtlessly gave away. Because my limited remaining lifetime will not allow adequate time to purchase contemporary books, and for adequate time to read and study, I will have to rely on my limited, ageing, home library with its addition of a few post-1990 books. To make my point of view clear, I want to let the reader savor the freshness of similar opinions phrased in different cultures; in earlier eras; and so in different ways enriching and strengthening the end result. I hope that my choice of references will bring maximum understanding.

The flowing panorama of events during a long life should help one to achieve an insightful perspective on life's important and challenging questions. That is the hopeful reason for naming this book *Perspective.* At an earlier age, I lacked the introspection, the inspiration, and the perspective to write this account. For example, I was probably in my 60s by the time I took time to ponder thoughtfully how some of my life's major decisions and actions, taken in my 20s, were heavy on impulse, bereft of thoughtful analysis, and how because of that, the following years were overly demanding of my time, effort, money and emotional tears; and how those same factors pursued me all the way into retirement. That self-analysis is what is meant by Virginia Woolf, English author (1882 - 1941), *The Arizona Republic, Thought of the Day,* who was quoted as having said that, "The compensation of growing old was simply this: that the passions remain as strong as ever, but one has gained -- at last the power which adds the supreme flavor to existence, the power of taking hold of experience, of turning it around, slowly, in the light."

A thoughtful quotation of Kierkegard , also from the Arizona Republic applies to us all, "Life must be lived forwards, but can only be understood backwards." That is why perspective comes later in life. One more appropriate, but modified, observation on growing old by Benjamin Franklin, "Too soon old; too late smart." Perspective on life is an acquirement that should improve as one ages. Surprisingly, I have also found philosophy to have an important place in a fulfilled life. That may be evident in future pages.

The guideline question, "How do you wish to be remembered?" compels me to write an I oriented account with which I am not comfortable, but which is necessary. Studs Terkel in his book *The Great Divide*, quotes Carlos Fuentes," We must go forward, but we cannot kill the past in doing so, for the past is part of our own identity and without our identity we are nothing." Our past experience molds our present person.

Is there a fundamental purpose for this wordy effort? Of course! I dream that my different presentation; my associated timeline, commentary and analysis; and that of some insightful quotations, will help to produce a uniquely different and more understandable concept of attainable world peace. I dream that this commentary on religious and political opinions, and on historical events, will provide the tiny seed, or one of a number of tiny seeds, that culminates in a global, peaceful society.

The achievement of global peace envisioned above, requires, in my view, three major criteria for unshakeable stability. The first is to try to impart to the reader, the importance of the *Golden Rule* in the future of mankind. Please, think this through. Implanting in the malleable minds of children the perception that people are kind, just, and that primarily good things can be expected from them, will make it easier for the Golden Rule to become wholly accepted and employed.

So, strive for a global educational mandate: Teach the Golden Rule Obligation so deeply to all children, that it becomes the primary response to all situations. This positive impression by the child would make it easier to do to others as they would want others to do to them. Your response could well be, "Oh! Come on Dave! There is evil out there! The child will get taken advantage of by the bullies of the world." Abuse of the timid personality will occasionally occur. However, the way I have reacted to others has made me view myself as having been somewhat timid and yet I am certain that I have never been bullied.

My experience has been that the trusting approach is the way to go. Yes, you will occasionally have your benevolence tested, but the great majority of people are trust worthy. The rare exceptions hurt, but trusting others will usually produce trustworthy people. The Golden Rule added to the immense reservoir of global, human, compassionate intelligence would produce a better world. Naïve? And utopian? That may be. Let's talk about the possibility later.

The second criterion is the concept of the *brotherhood of man. Utopian* again! But again it is attainable. There is usually a unifying influence from contemporary religion; from international organizations; from United Nations outreach; from the growing experiences of helping each other; and by the development of global educational institutions, especially the United World College. The trend is, and will be to automatically move towards togetherness (brotherhood), a necessity for world peace.

The third criterion of this concept is to discuss the *founding of world government* which will promote the elimination of international rivalries and the fostering of international cooperation for the betterment of all peoples. The word international would be replaced by global or universal. Global government will come through the Golden Rule, and the trend toward a cooperative, togetherness of the world's peoples.

The intent is to make clear that the combination of these three principles will, by removing the causes of war, arrive at the ultimate goal of world peace. They are symbiotic. Each helps the other two. All of the rest of the topics discussed are of lesser importance, or are stage-setting, in relation to those main messages.

However, as an incentive to produce that sort of outcome, we must first remove roadblocks to that goal. The major one is the money to be made when waging a war. We must promote an awareness of the excessive profit-in-war, and how it destroys the pursuit of happiness and the well-being of mankind. Just think of the number of schools and hospitals that could be built by each of the $133-million-dollar F-35 exotic fighter planes that are currently under production. Added to that is the cost of the fuel, the ongoing maintenance and the education of the pilots and crew to operate it, and to the lack of positive progressive use to which their time could be put. The Communist collapse in 1990 should have produced a gigantic peace-dividend, but failed to so when the terrorists arrived. There are myriads of social welfare needs to which those saved dollars could be put, and which would provide jobs for all.

The five years I spent in the military during World War II, gave me plenty of time to realize that the bloodshed, the money spent, and the early youth-years wasted, were all permanently lost to *WAR!* They were irreplaceable! It was all stupidly cruel! It is far beyond the time to assert my convictions. This thought is clearly stated by James Hillman , author of *A Terrible Love of War,* "My having been witness only to war's remnants and saved from war's actions, has perhaps saved this theme for my late life. Whatever earlier gave me pause, now gives me cause." What irritated me before, I now find enraging.

In some countries, especially the USA, abhorrent, immoral, obscene profits are being made in the manufacture, use, and sale of the military hardware used in the slaughter of our fellow humans. This militaristic economy is, of course, supported by *MIPUGU* (my acronym for the Military, Industrial, Political, Union, Government, University complex), in the name of "full employment." My despair deepens when I realize that even if the armament industry was operated on normal, legitimate profits *without* the ever-present graft and profit over-runs, it would still be so expensive that it would sacrifice the health, education, and social lives of our populace. Even operated as a non-profit enterprise, that sacrifice of the nation's well-being would occur. The obvious solution is global abolition of war.

Our national paranoia is stirred in the phrase national security which, of course, brings fear, super charges our patriotism, demanding evermore *secure* security. *I contend that our security lies not in our strength of arms but, in the long term, our easy-to-build, cooperative, caring, compassionate society that our international neighbors would then admire, trust, and try to emulate. With an open, welcoming society , enemies would become friends.*

The Cold War was totally within my timeframe but the ill-defined insanity of international relationships, left an equally ill-defined target for general, contemporary understanding or of *specific effective protest.* The chapter 'Paranoia, Personalities, Politics and War' is intended to illustrate how the contagion of the paranoid personalities of a handful of people can affect the policy, and consequently the history, of a country. It is not intended to be comprehensive, only illustrative. If the U.S. and Russia had been led by men with benign sensibilities, there might have been no Cold War. It would probably have avoided the consequential, simultaneous Korean War, Vietnam War, Gulf War, Afghanistan War and the Iraq War etc. It would have saved a multitude of lives and oceans of tears, and much of the world's precious resources. Earlier in life, my feelings were of a "gut-level" and unvoiced nature , but, the abysmal stupidity of the Vietnam War occurred during my forties; I was 75 when I wrote my unpublished manuscript, *American Citizenship Reconsidered;* 81 when The Vietnam War's immoral equivalent, the Iraq War, came along; and about 86 when I wrote another unpublished manuscript, *Debacle at Dieppe.* This book could now be an opportunity to pass some more memories and opinions into someone else's memory, and so maybe my past reading, study, thought and action would not disappear without a trace. Naming it *Perspective,* using a dated personal narrative or timeline, and using some cogent history, and an abundance of the incisive thoughts of wise historians, I could mount a potent anti-war discussion. It could also become evident how the philosophical, religious, political, and social environment of my early years influenced my war concern - and everything else in life, including my major mistakes. The dearth of my father's earlier memories is an example to be avoided! My primary concern being the prevention of war, I will suppress the discussion of battles and routine military memories but, recount in some detail the lives of my parents and their beliefs; my juvenile environment and contacts with anything military; my religious orientation; my political views; my military experiences and concurrent military events. It should become apparent how these factors influenced my hatred of wars' perceived inevitability.

The Bible, Mathew 24:6 said that, "you will be hearing of wars and rumors of war." That resigned, expected inevitability must end. Concerted, united efforts against militarism, are desperately needed.

In *The Great Quotations* Bernard Baruch, financier and presidential advisor (who probably took much profit from WW1 war-oriented investments), said it simply, *"TAKE THE PROFIT OUT OF WAR!"*

That is the idea. That is the hope. That is the goal. That is the primary reason for this book. I have the hope that some thinking, concerned person will respond to the goal of this book. I have the hope that someone, - any *Someone,* - has the spark to move the idea into reality; has the insight and ability to insert the unoriginal idea into public policy; which could then make war profitless and be followed by world peace.

To place it on the cover, Toni Morrison the author of *Brilliant Thoughts* chose the following comment of Oliver Wendell Holmes, Supreme Court Justice, out of 2190 quotations in her book. "A person's mind stretched to a new idea never goes back to its original dimensions." I hope that the idea that lives forever is of a world without war. The idea comes first, and - in time, its' fulfillment.

Mitch Albom in *Tuesdays with Morrie* quotes Professor Morrie Schwartz, "The little things I can obey. But the big things - how we think, what we value - those you must choose for yourself. You can't let anyone - or any society - determine those for you." Using my skeleton narrative this account will be primarily about those big things - religion, politics, war and peace. Eleanor Roosevelt recognized the same thing and commented in Great *Quotes from Great Leaders,* "In the long run we shape our lives, and we shape ourselves. The process never ends until you die. And the choices we make are ultimately our own responsibility." Both writers tend to make this character formation process into a very deliberative, selective process. So it should be, but in the average life, because of lack of earlier-life focus, I think that it probably happens more unintentionally and imperceptibly.

If I believed in a specific religion, I would only have to say so, and I need say no more. However, I have written over 50 pages on religion! That is because I wish to explain my rational thinking and *why*. That *why* is true of my discussion about politics, war, world peace and what we can do about each of them. Stating opinions must come with good reasons, explanations, and conclusions, thus more commentary. I devoutly hope that this book brings understanding.

I feel that my lifetime of avoiding speaking out on those major issues needs some explanation about why I have the conscientious impulse to do so now. Steve Allen, author and TV-host provided me with self-recognition when he was quoted in *The Arizona Republic* newspaper as having said, "I am not a leader, a joiner or a follower."

Even more aptly, in *Brilliant Thoughts,* I felt indebtedness to Terry Josephson whose plain phraseology described a three dimensional concept that has helped me to see, and understand, myself from when I was an awkward gangly youth to the present. "No matter where you go, or what you do, you live your entire life within the confines of your head," she had reflected.

In 1932, my tenth year, my father and mother were in their subdued, not-so-frolicking, ages of 55 and 49 years; Dad's stressful job as the Secretary and Treasurer of a bankrupt, depression-wracked municipality kept him tied under-communicatively to his job for long hours; by my intimate experience, my brother Frank 5 years older than I, was never bullying, but was assertively domineering; not a natural student, I had to struggle valiantly to pass my English class; was always in failure mode with my Mathematics classes and my Grammar class; was uninterestedly in reverie-mode through my history class - and I stuttered*!*

Stuttering, by itself, puts one into a reluctant-to-speak mode. Respect for authoritative, always-female teachers was automatic, but easy communication by this sister-less, shy, reluctant kid, was not possible. The reality was that it was safer not to let others know that

I was even in my 'confines .' Better to just pull the shutters and keep quiet. And offer opinions? That would mean I would have to open my mouth and then everybody would recognize dumb Dave was in there! So, especially when around adults, I kept myself deliberately, and unobtrusively, withdrawn in my confines.

Guess what? In the military I found a hierarchical stream of graded authority from me *UP!* That was even worse. The ranks above me all exuded military authority to be respected. My peers, and presumed-superiors, were City-Kids, which I knew had to make them brighter, smarter, and certainly more sophisticated than me, and they all talked endlessly about many unfamiliar things -- most especially how they knew all about girls. I could only remain mute.

When I transferred to the airforce and was commissioned in aircrew, I sensed some loosening restraints though my confines remained very familiar territory - and always have. My reluctance to impose my opinions on others also came from thinking I would appear preachy and pushy, and, that I was trying to appear more important or wise than others. Perceiving myself as barren of worthwhile ideas, I seldom spoke about politics or religion, and if at all, only with intimate friends.

Using discretion, I later adhered to the sensible admonition that when in a medical practice, one should not comment on religion, politics, or controversial social affairs. I felt a kinship with one-time New York state governor Herbert H. Lehman who, in *This I Believe* said, "So many things affect a man's philosophy and his life that I found it difficult to put into words my personal beliefs. I hesitate to speak of them publicly for fear of giving the appearance of preaching." To a marked degree I also extended that discretion into family and social affairs. I emphasize this confession because that past reticence, and lack of assertiveness, has left me with a continuing feeling of being a no-show on important affairs. One result is that I have now developed a feeling of regret at my failure to leave much of a mark on my family and friends regarding my beliefs on important issues. So this book is an attempt to 'state my piece' and remedy the problem.

My grandniece Naomi McIlwraith, in her 2012 book *Kiyâm,* wrote, "I asked how speech and words give you power. You said, "words and speech are power but they're not power if there ain't no-one listening." Now I read your words as you wrote them. Your great grandfather Mistahi Maskwa (Cree native language) said, "words are power." You say, "If no-one ever speaks the words that should be spoken the silence destroys you."

How perfectly appropriate! To repeat again, my past silence *is* destroying me. Ellen Wood, English playwright, 1813-87, referenced in 2012, in *The Arizona Republic,* said it simply, "It is not so much what we have done amiss, as what we have left undone will trouble us looking back." That applies to me. Only now in my 90s, after a lifetime of reticence, I feel the obligation to leave some of what is in my head as an imprint on other people's minds. The Native American proverb fits, "We will be known forever by the tracks we leave." My entity, variously known as Dave, Dad, Grandpa Dave, Big D, Uncle Dave and Doctor Meakes, wouldhave faded from this earthly scene with barely a ripple to denote his departure. Maria's, "How do you want to be remembered?" caused me to consider that few would remember me! That was another genesis of *Perspective.* I recognized that I had an obligation to be remembered for what I *actually thought,* rather than for someone else's perception *of what they thought I thought.* That need had developed because of my failure to express my opinions to others and will doubtless result in some surprise, some consternation, and maybe even anger among those who I know. Albert Schweitzer in his autobiography, *The Light Within Us,* wrote that, "The only essential thing is that we strive to have light in ourselves. Our strivings will be recognized by others, and when people have light in themselves it will shine out from them." Descriptive words! As mentioned earlier, previous members of my family who died, left only life examples, which Dr. Schweitzer is saying is sufficient. However, those quotations I use in this book are from people who had brilliant and widely known lives, whose lights shone brightly, and are thus, remembered. Many nameless people leave exemplary, courageous, productive lives, but live them in isolation thus unlit and thus - unremembered. We all leave a life example, but I feel that I never let that inner aspect of my life show adequately to others. Having kept myself vocally inarticulate, I now need this written vehicle of words.

Though I didn't readily voice my anti-Vietnam war view to my patients, I did so by mail to Presidents Johnson and Nixon and to many other prominent and influential Americans. A substantial amount of correspondence and related materials resulted, and formed a large part of my 1989 presentation to the University of California in Santa Barbara. Also my 85 page, unpublished manuscript entitled *American Citizenship Reconsidered,* was sent to them in 1998.

During our lifetimes a multitude of events are experienced, and even if only mildly introspective, it becomes clear, that you find that you have frequently modified your opinion. Everyone, including politicians , should be able to change their mind. What you are reading, and will be reading, in this account is "where-I-am-at" in my 90s. There is still plenty of room for me to change. I'm ready! I think it is so very important to teach our children to think study, learn, grow, and to feel free to change their opinions.

Edward R Murrow, author of *This, I believe* which is a book of "the beliefs and opinions of 101 prominent American citizens," wrote in his book introduction, "The beliefs of the men and the women in this book will change importantly over the years. Very positive beliefs of young people change through experience so that in later years they look back and say, "How could have I thought that so important?" But that is natural and good. The only wrong is not letting your beliefs grow as you grow." That last sentence is crucially important! Please ponder!

Murrow phrased it well. Opinions and beliefs are just present-day opinions and beliefs. They can be expected to modify with time. We all have a right to our opinions, even when they are not the generally-accepted societally-traditional opinions. The ones I object to, are the ideas that come from people who:

- do not do their own thinking those who say, "It was good

enough for my Dad and Mom (or for Senator X), so it's good enough for me." Parents' ideas may have been good, but only for their time and place. Do you agree with what they said? Think it through carefully. *Your* opinion, not theirs, is the most important!

- those who say, "I like Senator X, so I will vote for him." You may like him but listen to his words. Is he also talking good sense? Is it something you can believe? Most importantly, what is *your* opinion?
- or those who say "I don't like Senator Z because he flip-flops in his opinions." That may be true. But he may genuinely have changed his opinion. Try to clearly understand his new opinion. Check with his staff. You have a right to be suspicious because sometimes it is obvious that he has done it just to secure the votes of a specific voting bloc. Think through your opinion of him.

On the same point John Maynard Keynes, in *Brilliant Thoughts* challenges the speaker, "When the facts change, I change my mind. What do you do, Sir?" I find that the, "slam-dunk" arrival of an immediate opinion comes more rarely than it used to. I find myself probing for more facts; or nuances of interpretation that bring a different conclusion. Do not fear slowing down, rethinking, and maybe changing your opinion. Be flexible. Basic principles should remain consistent. Tactics may change. Also saying it clearly was Brooke Astor, President of the Vincent Astor Foundation, *Los Angeles Times*, Aug. 18th 1963, "Constant change is weakness, but change at the right time is strength."

For family-interest, *Perspective* is intended as a military time line of my life; as my commentary on my most important beliefs; and, at some points, a simple military history of the follies of war. The format is probably not what a traditional author would recommend, but the sequence of events and their retelling, has directed what came next. The description of the family religion in which I developed, probably led towards my present beliefs. The description of the Great Depression of the 1930s probably led to my political point of view. My exposure to the brutal obscenities of World War II certainly began my trek to hatred of the physical and emotional suffering caused by war. The blend of the three has led to my visceral loathing of many things to do with our arms industries and to some U.S. foreign policies which still nurture hatreds. Our still-necessary military services need full support and appreciation, but, as will be proposed in this book, at a probably - distant date, they should be reduced to a ceremonial force.

I understand very clearly that dull, too academic, and too wordy, writing will make the reader's eyes glaze over and interest fade. The daunting, and complex nature of the topics of war, peace, education and world government are nevertheless so critical that no worthy comment should be excluded. I'm a simple guy who is trying to convey to others in my simple way, but still do so efficiently. If the account is to be informative and of lasting value, I must also be free to describe or explain at length.I promise to keep my chain-saw handy to eliminate what I think is excessive wording.

Aldous Huxley-Author, *The Great Quotations,* "However, elegant and memorable, brevity can never do justice to all the facts of a complex situation. On such a theme one can be brief only by omission and simplification." So I will strive to be brief, but I must still say what I feel is necessary in order to explain fully and make my point clear.

I have lived in the United States for 60 years, and during the administrations of 12 consecutive presidents (1947-50 and 1958 to 2015), and I have visited 49 of the 50 states by car. Though I remain a Canadian citizen I have loved the United States; have lived an American-life experience; paid American taxes; have been apprehensive while my American son served in the U.S. Marines, and was adversely affected by war the same as all American citizens. I know very well what I have missed by not being a citizen in the country in which I have lived, and will explain *why* in this book. I write about my abhorrence of war and what I hope can be done about it, but also how I relish the freedom to speak specifically of my disillusionment of how, in the attempt to provide world leadership, the post-WWII U.S. administrations have exhibited, what I have perceived as, a militaristic foreign policy. That is the only reason that I am not a U.S. citizen.

The perception by the U.S. that it should help lead the world to a US-based form of democracy was gestated in good will, good intentions , and an altruistic belief that all the world desired the same form of democracy as the U.S. But, in my view, it is a too-impatient foreign policy. A country with a differing history, will have a different road in mind, to improve its' situation. We need to be patient. The world's sluggish trend to democracy has produced a generalized U.S. disillusionment comparable to my own.

The dominance of European, especially British, world leadership was greatly diminished post-WWII, and the power and might of the U.S. filled that vacuum. By its' very existence, the necessary U.S. world-wide leadership appeared heavy-handed. In Canada the comment used to be, "It is like being in bed with an elephant." The U.S. could not easily avoid bruising their friend Canada's feelings of pride in their comparable history of gaining independence from Great Britain (in 1867); their pride in a 140-year period of comparable freedom and democracy; their leap to fight for our mutual freedom over two years before the U.S. did, in both WWI and WWII. The later unnecessary and immoral wars, thought by U.S. Administrations to be defensive, remain the reason I have felt a moral repugnance, and moral reluctance, to pledge allegiance to the USA. An injection of the Golden Rule into U.S. foreign policy would improve my perception.

So the following discourse may have an aura of anti-Americanism. That is not intended. I love the U.S. and its' dramatic story of the birth of independence and freedom, which Canada duplicated without a War for Independence about 90 years later. Both of which I have relished too the maximum. I identify with those American multitudes who wish to improve whatever faults they see that their country has, and wish to go about repairing it wherever possible.

I will write this account as though I am an American citizen; with deep heart-felt affection, and appreciation, of the United States and its' classic constitution and bill of rights; with deep appreciation for the opportunity for the modest professional success I've had; with eternal love for Olga, nee, Ortega, my Mexican-American wife; with love for her seven sons and their descendants and with reciprocal affection for the loving, warm friends I've made. I hope the reader's understanding of my actions will come from reading *all* of *Perspective.*

I admired my sister-in-law, English teacher, author, peace-activist, and Vice President of the Canadian Peace Council, Edna Williams-Meakes (Mrs. Arthur Meakes). As she did, I had a long standing hatred of war, its abuses, and its futility. However, she developed it earlier and did something about it. She spent over 50 restless years on a relentless quest for world peace. She travelled to many countries, organized and lectured in many peace conferences, and published a book named *A quest for Peace and Alternatives to War.* During the mid-Cold War years she was criticized and misunderstood by many, including many of her friends and family. She resolutely persisted. She was intensely focused. I was not - until the Vietnam War began.

I am gratefully thankful for the ready assistance bestowed on me by my grand-niece and author, Naomi McIlwraith, PhD in Literature, of Edmonton, Alberta, Canada. As a professor in English, she utilized infinite tact in teaching me some badly needed basic grammar, and, as an author, she employed great sensitivity with her needy great-uncle when giving him her sage advice regarding the complexities of manuscript development. Thank you Naomi, I love you. Then she selflessly referred me into the equally attentive, capable hands of my Arizona editor-neighbor, Marta Schmitz. I especially appreciated Marta's good- humored tolerance of my irritating frequent insertions into an already "final-final" manuscript.

I have an immeasurable amount of appreciative admiration for my son, Michael G. Meakes, astronomer and now director of IT at Living Classrooms, Baltimore, Maryland, for the ready use of his technical "know-how"; for his cheerful and magical performances in an endless number of manuscript rescues; how, by using the technical miracle, the "Team Viewer," he was able to literally peer over my Arizona word processor shoulder; how he has soothed my panic attacks from immobile text production, impotent cursors, and the frustration of seeing pages of manuscript fade into ghostly, empty screens. Early and late, he has been readily available to rescue his despairing father from still another impending disaster. This four-year effort would not have been possible without him! My appreciation and love are boundless, Mike. Thank you! I love you!

This preface is much longer than planned because I wish the reader to have the information necessary to be able to better understand my thought processes as they relate to the topics discussed.

PERSPECTIVE

The Golden Rule

PART ONE
FORMATIVE YEARS

Timeline: Life of David Meakes

Sept 10, 1922:	Born to James Meakes and Elsie (Butcher) Meakes. Youngest of five brothers; born in a log house; on a farm; in Saskatchewan, Canada; no running water; no electricity; no gas; none in the 3-mile-distant *Westmoor* one-room country school; where one teacher taught Grades 1 through 8; Saskatchewan depression era budget made no allowance for payment for high school teachers for country kids so took Saskatchewan government correspondence course for Grades 9, 10 & 11 without a teacher;
Jul 8, 1940	Volunteered for Canadian Army Medical Corps.
Dec 1940	Shipped overseas on SS Pennland to Great Britain;
Aug 1942	Minor action with disastrous *DieppeRaid* (France)
Oct 12, 1943	Met future wife Joan Doe
Oct 31, 1943	Embarked on the SS Andes, returning to Canada for Canadian Air Force Aircrew training
Nov 1943	Began training
Nov 1944	Graduated as Pilot Officer (army equivalent is Second lieutenant)
Jul 1945	Discharged
Aug-Oct 1945	As member of horse crew on the U.S. SS Mexican,

	took load of horses from Montreal to Rotterdam, Holland
Oct 1945	Traveled to England
Nov 24, 1945	Married Joan Doe
Apr 1946	Returned by SS Ile De France to Canada
Dec 1946	Finished high school in Saskatoon, Saskatchewan, Canada
Dec 1946	Traveled by train to Chicago
Dec 1946	Began a four-year Podiatry course in an accelerated three-year schedule for WWII home-coming U.S. veterans (minimal vacation time)
Dec 1949	Graduated with degree of Doctor of Surgical Chiropody (later replaced with Doctor of Podiatric Medicine)
June 1950	Established Podiatry practice in North Vancouver, BC Canada
Apr 1955	Divorced Joan
Apr 1955	Married Marguerite (Peggy) McLaughlin, nee Young
Apr 1955	Moved to Mexico City, Mexico
Jul 1955	Returned to Toronto, Ontario, Canada
Jul 1955-Jun 1958	Practiced in Toronto, Ontario, Canada
Jul 7, 1956	Son, Michael Glenn Meakes born
Jun 1958	Moved to California
1958-1992	Practiced in Torrance California
Sept 1992	Retired
Feb 1997	Peggy died
Nov 14 1998	Married Olga Consuelo Estrada, nee Ortega
2004	Moved to Mesa, Arizona
Oct 2011	Started writing this book
Nov 2015	Completed book

Orientation of region of birth: Extend the Montana/North Dakota border north about 200 miles beyond the Canadian border, and that is about where I grew up. The location was near Lestock, Saskatchewan, Canada. More direct highways have since shortened inter-city distances and populations have grown. The following figures are my approximate estimates. *Using 1930s figures,* we were about 110 miles north of our capital city of Regina, Saskatchewan, population about 30,000; from Saskatoon, 180 miles, population 35,000; from Punnichy, 18 miles, population 275; our nearest town, Lestock, 7 ½ miles, population 220; from Wishart 13 miles, population 75; from Bank End 18 miles, population (estimated) 65; Westmoor country school 3½ miles; nearest neighbor, one mile.

My Parents

Norman Cousins wrote in *This, I Believe,* "Something I heard in India. Free will and determinism are like a game of cards. The hand that is dealt you represents determinism. The way you play your hand represents free will." I think that my parents played their hands in superb fashion. In my opinion, lives cannot be fulfilled in any manner more completely than in service to others. Theirs were fulfilled lives. Regretfully, I cannot claim the same measure of lifelong fulfillment.

I have realized that there were several factors in my life that impelled me toward my present state of mind. Some of these were my family influence including my religious indoctrination (some of you will say the lack thereof); the 1930s Great Depression and Saskatchewan's response to it; my 5 year WW II experience; and, of course, the political and military events of the subsequent 70 years. As the blend of our parent's genes and our environment are usually credited for one's life foundation, I will start with them, first commenting that I am so grateful for their gentle, tolerant, by-example method of teaching.

My mother, Elsie Butcher, was born in Tunbridge Wells, Kent, England in 1883. She had nine brothers and sisters, of which eight and herself, simultaneously with her parents, courageously immigrated to the undeveloped North West Territories (future province of Saskatchewan), Canada in 1904; at her age of twenty-one. She and my father married in 1908 and they produced a family of five brothers James (Jamie), 1909; Henry (Harry), 1911; Arthur (Art), 1912; Frank, 1917 and David, 1922 (Me). Mom died in 1968 at age eighty-five.

For some time, before her age of 21 she worked as a cashier in an English store, describing a system that I saw myself in only one store, in England, in WWII. The cashier was located on a balcony and the money and bill (receipt or invoice) were, by some non-electrical means, sent "whizzing" (her word) up a wire to the cashier, who quickly made the change, sending the cup whizzing back with change and receipt. She was always interested in music; played the pump organ (foot pedal organ) and piano; and the auto-harp. On the 1943 death of my father she moved from the farm to the city of Saskatoon where she sang in a church choir; participated in a country music group; sang in the annual symphonic chorale; and at about 75 years of age, took informal lessons to be able to play the pipe organ. In her early 80s she used to play the piano for her retirement home friends each evening. She was interested in Archaeology, and for some unremembered reason she was studying Latin in both pre-WWII and post war years. I did not know what her level of education was, but my brother Art told me she "had not had much more" than Grade 3 because she had to go to work to help her parents with the medical costs of her older, greatly handicapped sister, Hilda.

My father was born in Little Marlow, Buckinghamshire, England in 1877. He had two younger brothers, Charlie and Tom, and one sister, Louisa ("Louie"). His father, James Meakes, died in 1890 and as a result Dad and his brothers, after testing, qualified with a "Foundational Scholarship" for education in the *Sir William Borlase* School, a privately endowed school for poor children. J. C. Davis in *A History of Borlase School* relates that when a son died in 1612, Sir William Borlase endowed the school in memoriam saying in his will, "My will is the said house and other houses and lands shall wholly be employed forever for the benefit of the poor."

There are 16 of Dad's report cards existing in which his behavior is rated good for the first 4 month period; very good for the next 10 periods and excellent for five periods. In that same time-span he won annual scholastic first prizes, acquiring a prize-book each year. From about age 16 to 22 he worked as a book-keeper for Thomas Wethered & Sons Brewery Ltd., Marlow, England. He appears to have stayed quite involved in the community, winning first prizes in boxing, fencing and gymnastics. He also developed a life-long stamp-collecting hobby and also the skill of wood carving on top-quality hard wood, several decorative examples remaining on family display about 120 years later.

An 1893 (school?) newspaper clipping reads, "James Meakes, in the place he took in the Cambridge Local (Exams for Juniors) and Thomas (Uncle Tom) Meakes two more boys who have conferred credit already on their school as well as on themselves." At age 16 my Dad had qualified for Cambridge University entrance, but could not go because of lack of money.

The following are some letters of recommendation that he acquired at about the age of 22, before his immigration to Canada.

Feb 10th 1900, Michael Graves, Headmaster of Sir William Borlase School, "I have known Mr. James Meakes for many years, and have a high opinion of his character and capabilities. He was for some years under my charge when I was Head Master of Sir W. Borlase's School, Great Marlow, so that I can speak from intimate knowledge of him, and since he has left school I have had many opportunities of watching his work. He will, I am sure, do any work that maybe entrusted to him with painstaking care." Michael Graves wrote the introduction to *A History of Sir Wm. Borlase School* in 1932.

March 17th 1900, Francis C. Wethered, Vice Chairman of *Thomas Wethered and Son's Brewery Ltd,* "Mr. James Meakes has been a clerk in this brewery from Jan 17th 1894, and is now leaving at his own wish. During the whole of this time he has done his work in a most satisfactory manner and I have had, as a director of the company, every reason to be well pleased with his general conduct. I consider that he is well suited for any position of trust. His influence among the young men of the town, I have reason to know, has been in several directions for the good."

Hecler Rectory, Wooburn, Maidenhead, March 16th 1900, "I am sorry to lose you from my ward as you have always been an exemplary associate. Hoping you find in Canada what you wish."

Little Marlow Vicarage, Marlow, March 16th 1900, "The Rev. A. J. Thompson has known for about 12 years James Meakes, whose character as a consistent churchman and a man of the highest principle, genial temper, and most loyal and helpful spirit, he has his very highest opinion. He commends him most cordially to the care and good will of any priest or churchman in Manitoba within whose range of oversight, or intercourse he may come in his new home." The term "priest" was normal for the Church of England (Anglican, Episcopalian). Dad described his later religious affiliation as non-denominational.

Canadian Immigration

In 1900 Dad emigrated from England to Boissevain, Manitoba, Canada where he worked for about 4 years as a farm-hand, learning how to farm; saving money for his later homestead and developing a hobby of collecting plants of the area.

Not known where, but probably at the Sir William Borlase School, he acquired a superior level of knowledge in botany. He developed an album of compressed wild flowers in the 4 years he was in Boissevain, Manitoba, left it with his employer, and it now resides in the Boissevain Community Archives. Its value lies in the fact that for the years 1900 to 1904, it is a definitive record of the indigenous flowers of the region before the purity of the local strains were infiltrated by the introduction of European flowers brought by settlers.

A mystery developed in 1998 in Boissevain, when a question arose as to the identity of the author James Meakes. Quotation from the Brandon Sun July 31st 1998, "Perhaps the most impressive fact, is that James Meakes seems to have had no formal education in the field of botany. One would not guess as much from his scrapbook. It includes 54 orders containing 244 varieties and 261 flowers, all with their common English names, proper Latin terms, and the date they were picked. All are sorted according to division, and most were picked on the Johnstone property. Sage brush, Buttercup, Red Clover, Canada Thistle - all just a handful of the example of plants preserved in these pages representing a goodly portion of the flora of southwestern Manitoba circa 1907." It would be more accurate to say circa 1900 to 1904. "His penmanship is excellent, and everything is obviously properly pressed, as almost all of the specimens have survived with color intact despite existing more than 90 years." The archives director located my son Michael living in Baltimore, Maryland.

Two similar albums, donated by my mother and brothers, are in the Agricultural Department at the University of Saskatchewan, Saskatoon, Saskatchewan, and one at the University of Manitoba in Winnipeg, documenting approximately 1904 to 1920.

1905: James Meakes Log Shack

In 1904, using a newly purchased wagon and team of horses, Dad moved about 500 miles north west to the Touchwood Hills, a pioneering community in the North West Territories of Canada (to be formed into the province of Saskatchewan in 1905). He acquired 160 acres of land for $10, built his homestead shack, acquired the needed ranch animals and farmed simply. Cars had just been invented, and were only a fantasy, not yet a reality, in that horse-dependent, remote region with only wagon trails. The railroad had not developed that far west, but would be constructed by 1909-1910, then creating the towns of Lestock and Punnichy. In 1904-5 there were no schools, no towns, very few fences, no businesses (only a couple of distant trading posts), and very few neighbors. He met, and in 1908 married, my mother Elsie Butcher; raised a family of five sons, (the youngest me); established a weekly Sunday school service; was appointed Secretary and Treasurer of the Emerald Municipality in 1928; made one room his office, served until his death in 1943.

The community, non-denominational Stone Church, built in 1888 (now a 'heritage site') was about 6 miles away but there were no formally educated preachers in the near-area. Dad felt the "call" (the spiritual desire), to initiate a non-denominational Sunday school. On the completion of the construction of the one room, 3 ½ mile distant Westmoor country school in 1908, he moved the service he had been leading, from neighbor Earl Richardson's living room, into the school, where there-after, almost all community events took place. Not used since 1959 the dilapidated derelict building still stands. For 35 years, until his death in 1943, he conducted a Bible-oriented Sunday-School service to which those of all religious persuasions came, including the less-expected Greek Catholics and Roman Catholics. The lack of theological formality may have been a deterrent to some, but there was no alien dogma to deter anyone. The following is a description of that statement.

It is with the utmost caution that anybody should attempt to analyze , or interpret, the religious beliefs of another. Nuances of thought can probably not be easily perceived by another, most especially a juvenile son. I emphasize that I now enter this arena of thought, with some trepidation, but, from his words and actions I will be as complete and accurate as I can be regarding his Biblical stance.

My father spoke of it every morning of my life before I joined the military, and with that daily exposure I think that my understanding of his beliefs is basically correct. At home, every day, following breakfast, Dad would read to all the family, a chapter, or episode, from both Old and New Bible Testaments, and then, following a short kneeling-prayer, conclude with the Lords' prayer. I think Dad had felt fettered by the rigid theology of the Church of England (Anglican or Episcopal) church, in which he had been raised. He appears to have decided that, for him, most of the rituals were unnecessary for simple pure belief; that those rituals only tended to clutter and divide the beliefs of all religions; and that that was why each religious denomination had developed their own individual, dogmatic, Biblically-interpreted, requirements. He sought undiluted, basic Christianity, which, coincidentally, would be more appropriate in his Sunday-school homilies to our multi-cultured neighborhood, with its diverse faiths and beliefs.

At the weekly Sunday school that Dad founded, there were no essential (consequentially debatable) requirements of belief. The Lord's Prayer was usually used, and so could be said to be a simple ritual. There was no priestly robe, surplice or reversed white collar. There was no choir. There was no affirmation (no required declaration of belief), no confirmation, no communion, no baptism, no salvation, no conversion, no purgatory, no catechism, no confession, no penitence, no atonement, no transubstantiation of bread and wine, no liturgy, no litany, no sacramental rites, no religious icons, no symbolism (such as crucifix, candles, incense), no compulsion, no exhortation, no messianic theology, no complex rigid interpretations and nothing that could be called membership. His homilies were heavy on Jesus' teaching of brotherly love and forgiveness - and of the selected wisdom of the Old Testament. For example, Proverbs, 10-12, "Love covers all transgressions." Essentially that is the Golden Rule.

Though it was never mentioned, I often wondered if my Dad's religious beliefs had been influenced by Native Cree Indian beliefs. Especially in the 1904 to 1908 period, before his marriage to Mom, Dad knew, and "sat-with," several of the older members of the local

Muskowekwan Indian Reservation. I remember Dad telling about their accounts of their lives prior to the establishment of reservations; of their buffalo hunting days, that had ended about 20 years earlier; and of their wisdom-of-living. I noticed the parallel of Dad's simple belief of prayer to the Heavenly Father and the Native belief in prayer to the Great Spirit. That simple dogma-free belief of the Indians, and that of my father, coincided with the spiritual needs of our religiously diverse community.

Very similar to my father's changing view of theological dogma is this quotation by Gabriel Langfeldt from the book *Albert Schweitzer.* "For Schweitzer, dogma was an intellectual obstacle in the way of arriving at the meaning of life. It was only when he freed himself from it that he was able to develop his ethical talent to the full." However, Albert Schweitzer's beliefs were clearly developed through his father who, in Germany, conducted a weekly worship service. Langfeldt continues "This view of divine service is due first and foremost by the sermons conducted by Schweitzer's father which were full of the gospel of love, and of simple quiet devotion. At these times" he writes, "his father's simple way of preaching, really came into its own."

From Albert Schweitzer's autobiography *The Light within Us,* "The sermons used to make a great impression on me because I could see how much of what my father said in the pulpit 'was of a piece' with his own life and experience. I came to see what an effort, I might say what a struggle, it meant for him to open his heart to the people every Sunday. I still remember sermons from him while I was in village school. In the deep and earnest devotion of those services, the plain and homely style of my father showed its real value." I do not recognize that "struggle" in my father's sermons, but I am so very glad to have the simple eloquence of Schweitzer's own words to speak for me. His observations of his father were otherwise precisely true of my father.

When Dad died in June 1943, I was overseas in WWII. An account appeared in the *Touchwood Times* of Punnichy, Saskatchewan, Canada. July 1st, 1943, and in 1980 it was reprinted in the history book *Emerald: In Past, in Prose, Poetry and Pictures.* Quotation: "However, to speak of

Westmoor (the country school and surrounding district), or to think of its activities, it is impossible to the average person who knows the place, without at the same time connecting it with its most outstanding inhabitant, James Meakes. Jim was Westmoor, and when the minister, who, conducting Jim's funeral service a few years ago chose as his text the words of David uttered over the body of Abner, "Know ye not that there is a prince and a great man fallen this day in Israel," all felt that no more appropriate text could be found to describe the man whose upright unselfish life has been an example to all of us. For some thirty years he conducted a Sunday school at Westmoor. But it was far more than a Sunday school; adults from near and far gathered on a Sunday afternoon, for Jim, with his well stored mind and gifts of speaking and singing, was well worth going to hear, and no-one went away empty."

During each service there were about 3 hymns for which my mother would play the pump (foot pedal) organ. Dad's homily was usually based on the wisdom and morality of both the Old and New Testament. The school consisted of only one room and Mom taught the children's Sunday school out on the grass, or necessarily indoors in the winter, but before the main sermon. Dad presided over many funerals (Brother-Frank's estimate *in Emerald Past, in Prose, Poetry and Pictures,* "hundreds of people") for which he would never accept any payment. For him, his religion was simply his love and concern for his neighbors, and helping their families in their time of physical and emotional stress. Dad and Mom's example was high-lighted by their unfailing respect for all people of all ethnicities, all religions, and all points of view. In *Emerald Past, in Prose, Poetry and Pictures* and in *Memories of Lestock,* there are many references to my father's good influence. I feel so grateful to my parents for their Golden Rule life examples.

I retain several, fond, anecdotal memories which reinforce my perceptions of the free-thinking tolerance of my parents, which, became their teaching by example. Here are a few examples. Care of the horses, cows, pigs and chickens was the only work allowed on Sundays, regardless of urgency, such as very time-sensitive autumn threshing (the year's work could be ruined by a Sunday or Monday-rain). They approved my 1938 one-week Perryville Church of Christ Bible School. Dad laughed at my confusion of religious identity when on my August 1940 army leave I showed him my army Pay-book where I stated I was a member of the Church of England. I wasn't. Dad and Mom readily allowed the Nazarenes (Apostolics, Penticostals, Holy Rollers) to hold their annual summer "big-tent" revival in our pasture, at the south end of our lake. They had to pass through our yard and they used the lake for baptism. We occasionally, courteously, attended. The very loud music and shouts of, "Praise the Lord" were easily heard the half-mile from our home causing Mom to say "We prefer much quieter worship." Dad and I attended the Roman Catholic funeral of Bill Bovine in Lestock, and the priest sprinkled holy water and used incense. Dad's comment was, "We don't find that necessary." Dad's old Bible, which I think my nephew Rev. "Al" Meakes has, showed a great deal of use in the New Testament portion though he commented, and read, liberally from the Old Testament. If I remember correctly, his prayers were directed to God. There was absolutely no swearing allowed in our home. Being nondenominational meant that there were no negative comments made about others or about their religious beliefs etc. Itinerant Jehovah Witnesses used to come and they were invited to feed their horses and come in for a coffee and some respectful conversation. I remember my Dad's criticism of "whoever was the driver" of the Jehovah Witness sleigh in the village of Bankend, who had left his horses tied to a hitching post in a frigid winter blizzard, without horse blankets and without a nose-bag of food - but no criticism of his religious beliefs. Among our closest and most respected friends were three Atheist brothers and their families. Dad's copy of the Moslem Koran was underlined, bracketed and contained extra clippings showing his wide ranging interests.

Mom, Harry and I, periodically attended Wednesday prayer meetings at the S or H homes. Mrs. S, a Nazarene, believed in prophecy and talked avidly about the return of the Jews to Palestine, the rebuilding of the Temple in Jerusalem, and the later coming of the Messiah. I know how thrilled she must have been (my brother Harry was also) when in 1948 the country of Israel was founded, and in her view, the first step was completed. She interpreted the "beast" in the Book of Revelations in apocalyptic terms as being the Soviet Union, the "great bear of the north." From her I probably heard my first taste of anti-Communist rhetoric, and realized how religion can influence wars. In the early 1960s, I remember angrily disposing of an evangelistic record that came to our California household, which was based on the Revelations-revealed inevitability of war between the atheistic Russian Communists and our "Western-World" righteous believers. The focus was incorporating religious belief into rigid militaristic politics! I was livid. It was the only time I interfered in the religion of my wives.

Neither of our parents ever urged us to participate in prayers, either at the Sunday school, or at home. Belief was strictly voluntary, and free will or free thought prevailed. You were not urged to "testify," as some of the children of the Nazarene churches had to do. I loved my parents for that freedom of choice. They lived their lives superbly, as examples of their beliefs. Dad may have taught the same message in words, but in retrospect, their life examples were even more compelling than the spoken words.

Grandparents are often noted to have had great influence on their grandchildren, but that was not true in my case, except only by the indirect route of the teaching of their kids, my parents. Paternal Grandpa James Meakes, Sr. died in 1890; Maternal Grandpa Henry Latham Butcher died in 1919; both before my birth. Grandma Emily Butcher did not live near us and died in 1929 when I was seven and I have no memories of her. Grandma Eliza Meakes/Marshall lived in Vernon, BC, Canada, about 1500 miles from my home and I only remember seeing her on one occasion. In my formative years, they were remote in location and time and I know nothing of their inter-racial attitudes. But I feel I must mention them because two of their children were my parents and I can only assume that my parents also developed their attitudes to others in their own formative years and while still under their parent's influence.

Apocalyptic religious movements flourish in times of human stress and they successfully did so in our area in the 1930s Great Depression. When times are bad, the marvelous "promised land" of heaven is a wonderfully comforting vision. The book *Bad Land* by Jonathon Raban chronicled similar conditions in Montana some 450 miles south of us. "On Sundays, roving evangelists with accordions (the letters: "Jesus Saves" on the side), commandeered the local school house for revivalist "hymn-sings" and Sunday School. But they got few takers."

Our setting was similar, and the number of takers in our area also appeared to be limited. The presentation of the Nazarene evangelist's concept of salvation tended to leave most of our serious, theologically-anchored and analytical neighbors unmoved. To the chagrin of the evangelists, many of the younger generation of our theater-less community, looked on their revivalist, religious services as entertainment rather than seriously considered religion. The community-built, primarily-Protestant *Stone Church* made any religious groups welcome. Therefore, the Nazarene group qualified. The Nazarene denomination was pastored by Rev. "X" who preached Sundays, and in never-ceasing revival-mode, as many week evenings as possible, some in the form of prayer-meetings in someone's home. Music was loud; religious appeals demonstrative and beseeching; and conversions were exuberantly dramatic.

Rev. X was a good carpenter, built several pews, many still in use 78 years later. However, the sturdy "prayer-bench" was the focus of the congregation. That is where a former convert prayed passionately over a potential convert to, *"Come, to the Lord."* All converts were asked to testify what God had done in their life. On more than one occasion, Jesus was demonstrated as riding into Jerusalem on a donkey, by the minister straddling the back of a chair. Frenzied appeals were given when the preacher would lower a standing person to the floor, supposedly in a trance mode. This, usually occurred when healing was attempted by prayer. It was imaginatively rumored that the preacher knew what areas in a person's neck to press to facilitate a trance.

A frequent maneuver was for a preacher, or a convert you knew, to come from behind you - between you and the guy next to you - put his arms over each of your shoulders, and appeal for you to come forward to the prayer bench. The pressure was intense because the community was small; you knew everyone at least a little; some of your peers were among the converted; and at those tender years few of us had developed a resistance-mode or pro-and-con method of judgment. When someone allowed their name to be added to the salvation roll, the 10 to 40 people in the congregation erupted into rapturous shouts of, "Praise the Lord!" and "Hallelujah!"

Rev X stayed in a private home and drove an unusual car, a bright yellow coupe with glass windows, not the floppy fabric curtains with isinglass windows to be found on all older, local cars. Both color and model were not seen amongst our local farmers. On one occasion, someone daubed red paint (the "color of the Devil"), all over his car. That, rather non-Golden-Rule episode, was matched by another, potentially more serious event.

Reverend X frequently called on church neighbors for physical help and my amiable brother Jamie, living on his rented farm only a mile or two away, was an easy "Yes." For some specific task Jamie met Rev. X at the church and putting his tools on the ground, Jamie unlatched the always-unlocked shed door which covered the entrance to the church, pushing it in, and bending to pick up his tools. That momentary delay saved Jamie from injury. As he pushed in the door, an immense block of wood fell from above, big enough to kill or maim. The religious hatred of whoever set the trap for Rev. X almost "nailed" my brother Jamie. The religious hatreds of the Crusaders had seeped through to a tiny rural community in another continent, and in a later millennium. But then religious hatreds don't have to migrate, because they are always with us. Look at the anti-Moslem hatreds of today, and in return, their hatred of the "Infidel-West!"

About 1938, his ministry was followed by that of Rev. "Z." My memory of him was that, following a scientific geological estimate that the earth was a composed of molten liquid 18 miles below the crust, his telephone pole poster announced that next Sunday's service would inform you (and curiosity would bring you in) about, "Hell - 18 miles from Wishart."

Thanks to my parents tolerance of others is one of the most visceral of feelings that I have. In the negative sense of the word, to tolerate evil is wrong. For example, one cannot tolerate murder, robbery, cruelty, abuse of others or the milder forms of the same, such as bullying, falsification of taxes, (robbery of our pockets and our neighbors' pockets and our shared national treasury), etc. But intolerance of others because of color, ethnicity, religious belief, political belief, etc. is intolerable. I so appreciate the fact that there was never a judgmental attitude, or reference, by my parents, to other races, ethnicities, religions, political view-points, etc. They were supremely tolerant of others.

Even on simple situations such as the time that I was reprimanded, when I made a mildly mocking comment about the ever-present drop of drainage on the end of our neighbor's nose. "David! Don't make fun of him. It might be because he has tuberculosis. In any case, in winter months, most of us, when outside, have the same." A boy's insensitivity was transformed into understanding, and to Golden Rule compassionate awareness of his neighbor's potential for the then-dreaded scourge of tuberculosis. My parents taught as they reprimanded.

Derogatory jokes and terms due to physical appearance were taboo. The common pejorative terms used by a few, when speaking of our neighbors, the Russians, Ukrainians, Polish, Rumanians, Hungarians and Yugoslavians were, "Slavs," "Ukes" or "Bohunks," but never in our home. Not being used at that time was the term "Metis," for part native Indian and part French. The term "half-breed" now sounds very crude, but at that time it was thought of as identifying and informative, and in our home it had zero pejorative, connotation.

PERSPECTIVE

With laughter, my Dad would relate having seen an earlier-in-the century advertisement for a laborer in the Winnipeg paper which said, "No Englishmen need apply."

A few very germane quotations, all which suggest my parent's beliefs, follow.

- Nelson Mandela said in *Great Quotes from Great Leaders,* "No one is born hating another person because of the color of his skin, or his background, or his religion. People must learn to hate, and if they can learn to hate, they can be taught to love, for love comes more naturally to the human heart than the opposite."
- Harry Bridges, Communist and Labor Leader of the San Francisco stevedores, 1950s-60s. *The Great Quotations,* "No man has ever been born a Negro-hater, a Jew-hater or any other kind of hater. Nature refuses to be involved in such suicidal practices."
- In *The Great Quotations,* U.S. President Thomas Jefferson is quoted, "My answer to a letter from a mutual friend was: Say nothing of my religion. It is known to God and my-self alone. Its evidence before the world is to be sought in my life." Again he said, "I never told my own religion, nor scrutinized that of another. I never attempted to make a convert, nor wished to change another's creed. I have ever judged of other's religions by their life - for it is from our lives and not from our words, that our religion must be read." Could it be said any better! I could not quote anything more relevant to my father, than to make clear that as a lay preacher, he was neither a proselytizer nor an evangelist.
- Samuel Johnson, English author 1709-1784, in *A Thought for Today* said, "A life that will bear the inspection of men and God is the only certificate of true religion."

- John L. Roth, A *Quiet and Peaceful Life,* "There is a variously told story of a plain dressed Dunkerd (Amish) accosted on the street of a Pennsylvania town by an evangelical young man, who asked, "Brother, are you saved?" The long-bearded Dunkerd did not respond verbally immediately. He pulled out a piece of paper and wrote on it. 'Here' he said, 'are the names and addresses of my family, neighbors, and people I do business with. Ask them if they think I am saved. I could tell you anything'," These quotations all suggest the religious attitude of my parents.

Our community had an interesting character, by the name of Alfred Thibault. "Fred" was born in Quebec, Canada, and came west to Saskatchewan in 1880 at 20 years of age. He was powerfully built and I will spare you many stories telling of his strength. His Bible knowledge was said to be prodigious, Dad saying that it appeared he could quote spontaneously, profusely, and appropriately. His grandson later said that "he knew the Bible by heart." He used to carve Bible texts into large tree trunks to "let others know that Thibault had been there." When the CPR railroad was being built into Wishart in the 1920s, he used to go and preach to the railroad workers.

Fred told Dad that once, when he was deeply in debt, God told him to get on a train to Winnipeg, which he did. He played poker on the 800 mile round trip and won enough money to pay off his debts and his taxes. Wonderful faith! The oldest second-family son was named Isaac. He became Canada's heavy weight boxing champion, and changing his name to Jack Tebo he became a sparring partner for the U.S. world champion heavy weight Joe Louis, as well as for Max Schmelling.

The Five Meakes Brothers

Dad benefited very well from the teaching he received at The Borlase School, and his apprenticeship at the Wethered Brewery, carrying his knowledge of bookkeeping into his Canadian life. During the teens, twenties and thirties he audited the financial statements and books of about a dozen rural school districts. I think that the country school accounts must have been fairly simple because his annual fee was said to be only "$2.00 or $3.00." Then in 1928 he was offered the job of secretary-treasurer of the rural municipality of Emerald (an area approximately 30 miles by 30 miles). After his death in 1943, an accountant's degree was required. He thus helped our family survive the Great Depression, and the dry years more easily than some of our neighbors. I thank Sir William Borlase, who, in the 1600s endowed that school, and through that action my Dad's free education, in turn allowing me to remain in my country school, while my Dad could pay for a hired man, when I was really needed on the farm.

Our home was geographically located in the Marlow SchoolDistrict, and Dad was its first resident. When the school was built in 1916, they turned to my Dad for secretarial-treasurer services. In *Memories of Lestock,*

Milton Halliday recorded, "Marlow (rural school) was indeed fortunate to have for many years, in the person of James Meakes, secretary-treasurer as meticulous in keeping records as he was capable in administering the affairs of the school district. More than anyone else Mr. Meakes made possible the glimpse into Marlow's early history. For twenty-seven and a half years until his death in 1943, entries in the Marlow minute books appear in his careful and precise script." Occasional cars were seen on the main Lestock-Wishart road, and as our school horses were easily spooked, we attended Westmoor School.

Paul Pearsall in *Pleasure Prescription* describes his Hawaiian ancestors' system. "Our ancestors did not parent (actively raise their children) they created a mutually responsible family based on reciprocity of care giving. Children were not "raised", they lived, worked, and absorbed their values from within the family system. They were expected to contribute to the family and were obligated to help their parents, grand-parents, and siblings to develop even as they themselves were cared for into maturity. In Polynesia this is still the approach to parenting. Hawaiians call it "familying" or "ohana."

For me, that concept epitomized the concept of cooperation. Our family functioned with in itself in similar fashion. Even at age 16 or 17, I never received any payment for work, including our harvesting-time 60-hour work weeks. I received only a small depression-accentuated, "two bits," or less, of spending money on those occasional visits into our town, Lestock. Of course, food, clothes, medical care, and habitation were automatically provided.

In early 1941, I had been in the military and overseas, for at least 8 months, when, I remember the elation and astonishment I felt when I received a mailed payment of thirty dollars from my brother Art. I had worked for him for a dollar a day in the fall of 1939, and by the next spring, he had sufficient money that he could pay me. My astonishment came from my thinking of Art as a part of our family unit, and that therefore I rated no payment. Art perceived that, though married and living close by, he was only cooperatively working with the family unit, and that he, by leaving our home unit when he married, had formed his own separate family unit. He understood which I had not yet understood, that he was not an integral part of that home family unit any more, and so he felt the obligation to me to pay my wages. Positively, I know, that never even once did I wonder about our family arrangement. It probably had never occurred to me that some individuals in some family units were individually paid, thus not so likely developing the cooperative, family-unit obligation feeling in the manner that I had. I'm describing this arrangement in detail, as a prelude to my later description of how family-unit thinking can fit into the political cooperative movement.

We had three rifles, but only the .32 rim-fire functioned. We had a much-used 10-gauge shotgun - which had already been outlawed for new sale, but for which we could still purchase shells. It would blow the head off of a duck and it had the kick of an elephant, and I remember experiencing a black and blue shoulder when I failed to press the gun butt firmly to my shoulder. Dad's secretary-treasurer job came with a .32 center-fire revolver for which he never had any shells. As each of my four brothers left farming (1943 to 1965), none continued to own guns.

There were never any military influences, pro or con, in our home or our neighborhood. When my Dad was a youth he had briefly considered enlisting for the British "Boer War," but "the timing being off, he did not do so." I remember admiring the rousing sound of the French national anthem La *Marsillaise,* when I heard it on the battery-operated radio at the time of the defeat of the French by the Nazis in early 1940.

Depression era life focused on survival. There were no glorified patriotic remembrances of wartime valor in our neighborhood. There were no marching bands, no local statues (only Punnichy had a 3-foot WWI memorial stone monument), no rousing victory remembrances, no jingoistic fervor, no boasted bravado, and no stirring patriotic oratory. I guess you don't need any of that because I eventually volunteered without it. My only remembrances were the November 11th one-minute silences, and the artificial red poppies to commemorate those who died in WWI and, simultaneously, the Nov 11th 1918 cease fire agreement. I am certain that in my growing years I never saw anyone in military uniform.

MY PARENTS

Our small community had its short list of WWI veterans. The most prominent was Colonel James Hollis wearing his rancher/farmer clothing but still maintaining his military crispness of speech and demeanor; six foot 5-inch "Shorty" Richardson minus one arm; George Noble, his marksman reputation marred by shooting the tip off his finger while shooting a sick cat; Randall McRae and his quiet modesty about trench warfare; Fred Bagnall, Westmoor school teacher, and his slender book *Not Mentioned in Dispatches*; and my Dad's close friend Jack Matley, postmaster at Punnichy. Except for Col. Hollis, these would be considered a normal cross section of neighbors anywhere. My oldest cousin, Reg. Longley from Brandon, Manitoba, Canada, was killed on Vimy Ridge in France in 1918.

But one moving war story was told at our home. Jon Tubeck was a Polish immigrant, who came to live at our home as a farm-hand, when my older brothers Jamie and Art moved off the home farm. He was such an integral part of our family that many neighbors referred to him as Jon Meakes. Only a couple of times in the 1933 to 1940 period, his melancholic nostalgia overwhelmed him, and, needing to unload, he would relate the story of seeing his father, mother and seven brothers and sisters, "killed by the Germans" in WWI.

Horse-pulled, homemade toboggans.

I attended Westmoor, the 1-room country school which had nothing martial about it in any way. My later passion for reading history was, in no way, engendered there. It was a dull subject, consisting of remembering foreign wars with strange names, and all with dates to remember. Not the only poem taught, but the only poem still remembered, are 16 lines from Horatius defending a bridge in the Etruscan war of antiquity - not too important! More dramatic and memorable was the account of "The charge of the 600" in the 1854 British/Russian Crimean war, and of Florence Nightingale, the courageous, humanitarian nurse and martyr of that conflict.

I remember my parent's humanitarian concern about the Italian invasion of Ethiopia, possibly accentuated because Emperor Haille Sellasie was a "Christian." The nearby Allenby country school was named after WWI General Allenby. It had a young men's softball team comprised of seven Thibault brothers and their two cousins, which was nicknamed the Ethiopeans, because they were shirtless and darkly tanned. One of our neighbors who clearly knew little of the immensity of the world was sure that the Italian bombing in Ethiopia was giving us our bad weather.

A book named *The House of the Spaniard,* written by British Intelligence Corps Colonel Arthur Behrend, was sent to Dad and Mom by the author's mother, Mrs. Keats-Behrend, (with whom I visited 5 years later when in England). As a novel it brought a fictional look at the intrigues prevalent in the Spanish Civil War. The English newspapers and magazines, sent monthly by the same lady, brought a closer look at the British concern regarding the growing Nazi menace. There was no television at that time, our radio was very inefficient, but those English newspapers, Dad's Winnipeg Free Press newspaper, some of the government high school correspondence materials, and home discussions were giving me a limited awareness of world events.

Canada's territorial military history was limited to the 1600s - 1700s war with France for possession of the country. Canada had never allowed slavery and was fortunate not to have endured the tragedy of civil war; but did have the minor 1885 Riel Rebellion, which involved legitimate land concerns of the French and Metis residents of Batoche, a north western Saskatchewan community. It involved a few deaths and Colonel Hollis had served in a humanitarian way for participants and for residents of the area. World War I was the only other military memory. Though not without friction and not without subsequent criticism, governmental relationship with the Natives of Canada had been mostly peaceful, and suffered none of the Indian Wars that occurred in the United States.

In the world of today most people get their news from TV or the Internet. But I have inherited my Dad's need for a daily newspaper, having now subscribed to one daily for most of 70 years. In the 1930s Dad subscribed to the *Winnipeg Free Press,* and accepted the at-least-two-days-later train delivery. The news, even in that remote region, seemed essential. The famous U.S. comedian Will Rogers, in The LA Times March 17th, 1963 was quoted, "Take my ham away, take my eggs away, even my chili, but leave me my newspaper."

We had the *Books of Knowledge*, a set of about 10 books for younger teenagers; the monthly *National Geographic Magazine*; a few teenage books; a basic library of about 125 books. Brothers Harry and Frank signed up for a monthly mail delivery of about 4 books, loaned from a provincial lending library. Radio required a major aerial, a car battery, two dry cell A batteries, and one dry cell D battery. Then reception consisted of one static-laden Regina station with its minimal amount of interesting content; there was no television yet; there were our northern Canadian long winter evenings; all of which, tended to encourage reading. Family discussions about specific books did the same.

With no TV or radio to compete, books were a central focus of our lives. Both Dad and Mom read a lot; bought books at auction, (occasionally Dad's own previously-loaned books), and talked a lot about reading. Brother Frank was the non-stop reader of all time. A 1989 eulogy given in the Saskatchewan legislature by Roy Romanov, a later premier (governor), said: "Frank was educated formally to Grade 8, and then he took grades 9, 10 and 11 by correspondence course, back in another time. - Frank Meakes was indeed a very well-read and very well-educated person. This was a person who read through life, right to his dying hours, I'm sure to his dying days; a person who was active not only beyond (sic) reading but in the promotion of books, the library system. He was given an honorary recognition by the Saskatchewan Library Association for his contribution to the libraries."

Frank probably read more than any of us and I remember him reading particular books two and three times. He was particularly fond of the American author Zane Grey, who wrote mainly on idealistic early Western stories. Much later in his life, I recall Frank saying how he thought that when he had acquired about 37 of Zane Grey's books he was making good progress on his pursuit of attaining *all* of the Zane Grey series of books, only to determine that Zane Grey had authored over 140 books. Later in life, when Frank came to California for his semi-annual visit, he would make an immediate trip to my bookshelf to find what I had acquired since he had last visited. He also visited Zane Grey's home near Payson Arizona.

Living in a remote, sparsely populated, scenically limited, region with depression limited travel, books became the most interesting part of our daily existence. They gave us a mind's window into places, people and things that we could only imagine. There were some very prominent people who, we later found, were inveterate readers. These four represent many others.

Abraham Lincoln was described by the Durants in *Pictorial History of American Presidents,* as an intense lover of books. He gained his education from incessant reading, bringing his knowledge to the presidency of the USA. "Abraham Lincoln was a self-educated man who read and studied many books without the prompting of teachers." "The things I want to know are in books" he said. "My best friend is a man who'll get me a book I ain't read." Dennis Hanks, Lincoln's cousin said "Abe made books tell him more than they told other people."

Albert Schweitzer German physician, philosopher, theologian. He must have toted trunks filled with books into his remote African mission-hospital. He already had a broad, classical education but that was not enough! In his biography, *The Light Within Us,* "My craving for reading was limitless. I still have it. I am quite unable to put down a book I have begun. I would rather read all night. At the very least I must have skimmed through it to the very end. If I like it, I may well read it two or three times."

Winston Churchill, *Painting as a Pastime* 1932. Churchill writes lovingly about books and reading. "Nothing makes a man more reverent than a library --. As one surveys the mighty array of sage, saints, historians, scientists, poets and philosophers whose treasures one will never be able to admire - still less enjoy- the brief time of our existence here dominates mind and spirit." He was already supremely educated, but his appetite for more reading and education was insatiable.

President Thomas Jefferson in *Brilliant Thoughts* said, "I cannot live without books." Though I loved books, just surviving life dominated everything else until about age 37. War, marriage, travel, professional studies, office establishment, all brought major residential changes between 1940 and 1959. After five years in the military, I had resided in Great Britain, Saskatoon Saskatchewan, Chicago, North Vancouver British Columbia, Mexico City, Toronto and California. My reading was strictly educational and medical and the newspaper.

About 1953, at age 31, I acquired the *Outline of History* by H.G. Wells, authored in 1920. Will Durant in *The Story of Philosophy* in 1953, and speaking of the writing by H.G. Wells of *The Outline of History*, thirty-three years earlier said, "It was an astonishing and stimulating performance for one mind."

"History became popular, and historians became alarmed. Now it would be necessary for them to write as interestingly as H.G. Wells." Seventy-six years after the publication of the book, and over 40 years after my purchase - on Jan 24, 1996, *The LA* Times book reviewer, Michael Foote, commented that the *Outline of History* was, "written with zest - and it was optimistic. His humane and vibrant prose is indeed a tonic for the heart and mind." Those raves tell you I had "lucked out." I have been hooked on history ever since.

PART TWO
RELIGIOUS OPINIONS

Now you know about my parents and their religion - how about me? Schopenhauer in Will Durant's *A study of Philosophy* comments, "First one must live. Then one may philosophize." I think maybe, at age 93, that my time has come. I had the occasion to think about my religious beliefs about 19 years ago. What follows is the entire text of my '*Religion, as I view it, in 1996.*' Though wordy, I felt the necessity for making my opinion clear. This is the complete text.

My Religious Opinions in 1996.

"That is where I am at now." Simple direct words! But they meant more to me than many years of mainline religious sermons, because they brought some understanding to the drifting, chaos pre-existing in my secular-leaning, religious thinking. I first heard them at the Pacific Unitarian Church in Palos Verdes, California in 1964. They were used by many whose thinking about philosophy, religion, and ethics, etc. was also not static but was always evolving. I realized that I wasn't alone in my shifting religious thinking. I was at the Unitarian Church because I identified with their opposition to the Vietnamese war, but, I was also finding a psychological home.

Because they didn't espouse mainline theology, I quickly felt at home at PUC. No messianic theology, no sacramental rites, no religious dogma, no esoteric Biblical interpretations -- just a plain language concern for the here-and-now, and no scriptural language about the here-after. I was initially signed in by a former Roman Catholic and then given an orientation by a former Jew. The minister Reverend Al Hendricksen was formerly a Lutheran. All had joined the Unitarian Church because of their feeling of lack of fulfillment in their traditional denominations. There appeared to be few adults who had been Unitarians from birth. Their concern with the Here-and-Now, at that time obviously included the Vietnam War. I felt that I could not have found a more appropriate place.

So the essay on religion that follows reflects my flexible 1996 views which may shift, so ask me again next year. Obviously this is very unlike the theologically rigid straitjackets imposed by the mainstream religions and most especially, the fundamentalist ones, whose faith is in a timeless, never-changing God.

I sense that I could well be the archetypical horror of every fundamentalist minister in America. The guy…

- …who has been married to a devout Bible-believing pillar of the church for the last 42 years.
- …who has spent the last 20-plus years, routinely, every Sunday, seated in the 4th seat from the left aisle, in the 8th row.
- …who has always dressed in a conservative, conventional suit, tie, and shirt, and always carried a Bible.
- …who never grew a beard, had long hair, sported tattoos or any other deviant appearance traits.
- …who has never voiced any controversial opinions on religion, politics, or ethics,
- …who has listened attentively to the weekly sermons.
- …who has helped babysit for parents doing visitation.
- …who, accompanying his wife, made Sunday rounds of the church shut-ins.
- …who at the annual Mission church boutique, and the annual bazaar, has sold his hand-crafted jewelry, deducting nothing for the semi-precious stones, findings (settings), time, or work and gives the entire proceeds to the church.
- …who annually helped build the stage props for the Christmas cantata and Christmas play.
- …who has routinely served as pall-bearer for all, including believers;
- …who has been an apparent financial supporter.

- But also the guy…
- ...who has never been an official church member.
- …who now, in the most unguilty, unrepentant manner states that he is an Atheist.
- …who states that he once took the American Humanist Leadership study course.
- …who says that the best sermons; the most well-reasoned arguments; the most evangelical appeals; the most Biblically-proven truths; the most dramatic emotional conversions; and the most reverence-inspiring, group-solemn, communions, delivered by a broad spectrum of the 'Faith'; has not changed his Atheistic viewpoint even a little.

To every mainline theologian, I know that what I have to say will be viewed as untrue, foolish, false, absurd, super-conceited, sacrilegious, fallacious, irrational, illogical, and anything but the Gospel-Truth. It is most unpopular to say what one thinks negatively about religion, but by stating what I believe, and what I don't believe, I will be maintaining my integrity not necessarily my popularity. I see myself as an Agnostic- Atheist, if there is such an entity. The main argument I can see for gods, a god, or God, is the profound awe that one has to have when considering the beauty, the precision, and the mystery of the universe. Most especially the life processes on our planet, not the least being the human body. We cannot currently understand causative or formative processes involved in the spark-of-life. I know that many would call it misplaced assurance, even vanity when I say that the steady growth of human accomplishment, gives us confidence that in time (maybe a long time) the human race will arrive at a point where they will finally fathom the laws of nature sufficiently to be able to understand the initiation of life.

Using new scientific equipment and new knowledge, there have been discoveries made, which in the past would have defied common sense. Numbers three through seven of these listed happened in my lifetime. Here are just a few:

- The falsity of an earth centered universe.
- The universe of microscopic life.
- The ability to determine the composition, orbit and orbital speed of distant stars.
- The discovery of deep ocean life that needs no sunlight to live.
- The knowledge and technology to be able to measure 'continental-drift.'
- The ability, knowledge, and technology to enter, travel, and exist in space.
- Recent discovery of the probability of past microscopic life in Martian rocks, and the overwhelming logic of abundant life in the universe. The existence of distant galaxies, have been found in my lifetime. The Andromeda galaxy, the only galaxy visible from earth was considered only as a gas cloud in the 1930s. *2013 insert;* Since 1996, starting with sheep, life has been cloned. I acknowledge that a 'blue-print' was necessary; and that life was not initiated from 'scratch.' Another is the science of DNA identification.

The fundamentalist minister would point to all of these as demonstrations of the power of the almighty God. I would say that our understanding of these demonstrations indicates our steadily growing knowledge of the universe. Space probes, even our local solar system, are frequently bringing us information on cosmic events some of which appear to be challenging the natural laws as we know them on this planet. I think that in time, the mystery of the initiation and evolution of life will become clearly known. In the interim, I do not understand the need to worship a supposed creator - just in case the Biblical theology is true. I think that position is an atheistic one, with a nod in the direction of agnosticism.

We may have scientific answers to many more of the natural phenomena of this earth than did our ancestors, but I think that religiously, we have not progressed beyond their belief in the mystic faith of the unknown and in prayers and praise to an imaginary deity.

I see little difference between the ancient sun-worshippers and the present-day main-line religious believers, except that those ancients could physically see the object of their worship.

The Bible is tremendous in its volume of words, and is unique in its authorship, said to having been compiled over 40 generations (1500 years), and by about 40 different authors (all unproven figures that I am willing to accept). It is a stupendous creation and the Old Testament (the Jewish Bible) is accepted to a degree, by even the secular Israelis, as a history textbook. But I do not view the Bible as sacred. I see it as being the oral history, oral biography, and oral philosophy of the thoughtful Israelites with contemporary (2000 B.C. to about 80 A.D) theological input by the Israelites and the early Christians.

I should at this point state again where I am located in the spectrum of belief. Hopefully, I can use a quote from the book *Evidence that demands a verdict* by Josh McDowell, and published, I think, by Christian Book.com. I fit the quote, "For many today, the study of history is incorporated with the ideas that there is no God, miracles are not possible, we live in a closed system and there is no supernatural." If I believe that there is no possibility of miracles, then the mystical aspects of religion will never make any sense. And they don't. The same quotation continues and indicates that that position (my position) is not, "critical, open and honest," and that the resurrection of Christ is ruled out in advance. To the latter statement - I agree! I would also comment that the belief that there are no miracles, also rules out all the mysticism and sacredness of the Bible.

The Pentateuch, the most ancient, first five books of the Old Testament, were written by, and for, the ancient Hebrews of about 2000 BC to about 1000 BC. The Hebrews had been a semi-nomadic people and during that period were undergoing the difficult process of changing from the freedom and lawlessness of desert life. They were evolving into a more stationary and sedentary people, to who, the leaders were teaching new concepts. Neighborhood concerns, such as property rights, laws of justice, laws of social behavior, and the controls exercised by the evolving religious practices, were examples of these new controlling laws. Automatically, their religion also involved their oral history, as they both came in the same package.

This is described in the book *Life and Language in the Old Testament* authored by W.E. Chase: "History to the Hebrew mind was inseparable from religion. There was no history without religion, no religion apart from history. The two were one, an entity, indivisible. The active manifestation of the presence of God through historical events in the Old Testament is not only at the very root of the Hebrew religion, there is no religion without it." The priests (theologians) were also the political leaders. I believe there is probably some basis in truth to many of the political and military stories of peoples and events in the Old Testament. However, in every generation, as in mine, oral histories are often inaccurate in time, garbled and exaggerated in content, and distorted again, and again, and again, in the retelling.

National Geographic Dec 1996, Page 12, there is an article about Genghis Khan by Mike Edwards who comments on an ancient (1162-1227 AD) authoritative book, written by a contemporary Mongol civil servant about Genghis Khan. Quote: "Historians consider his book an important account of Genghis Khan's campaigns, but he was writing in part to please his masters and like other chroniclers of the time, he never met a fact that couldn't be hyperbolized." End of quote. This statement could be applied to some of the questionable facts, as well as the theological interpretations to be found in the Old Testament.

As the political, historical, military and social events took place, the Israelite priesthood (the political leaders and intellectuals of the time) added their theological-spin or interpretations of the events,and then used these stories as teaching tools to better control their illiterate followers. In time, frequently many generations later, the stories, with emphasis on the theology, were inscribed in tablet, parchment and papyrus thus fixing those accounts in a multi-millennial, sacred deep-freeze where each phrase and each word thought to have portentous sacred theological meaning, is made unchangeable! Some ultra- orthodox Jews have been known to spend painstaking months on one word, one phrase, or one verse from the Old Testament. I have personally heard many Christian fundamentalist preachers who have spent entire sermons, with intense emphasis, on the import of individual words and phrases, thought to be of profound consequence. An untethered evangelical orator can spend a very long sermon considering a very short Biblical quotation.

Political and theological control, were intertwined in the Old Testament. Taking the forty-year saga of Moses and the Israelites in the wilderness as fact, then it was a natural progression from the theological tablets of Mount Sinai to the physical and political, and religious control of the rebellious Israelites. The no-longer existing tablets (Ten Commandments) were probably inspired, and made by Moses himself. However, the control resulted from the wisdom and leadership of Moses though the theological interpretation that he used got the credit. (Inserted in 2014) - In other words, the Israelites would not easily believe the *human,* Moses, about whom, according to the Bible, many were disbelieving and bad-mouthing; but they *could* believe and, *consequently be controlled,* by Moses's presentation of the tablets as being delivered on Mount Sinai by *God.* End of insert.

That brilliant theological concept then became the ongoing new creed of The Ten Commandments. The new standard of behavior immediately helped to create a more acquiescent and controllable people or society. Moses would be thrilled to find it being used today! If those violently mal-adjusted members of our present-day society were amenable to the mystical power of the tablets from on High we would still view the results as worthwhile, even though we might believe there was no theological reality. The result is dependent on what is *believed* by the individual or the people.

Probably many of the doubters in our congregations (like me), and also those disposed to crime and malfeasance, are comparable to the rebellious Israelites of Moses' time. *Control,* is still the desirable and beneficial result. Frequently, in Old Testament times, the leaders further controlled the Israelites by new revelations from On High. They continued to embellish the record, by continuing to invoke the input of the Deity in every event and then record it in their ongoing historical narrative. The next step in the strengthening of the theological base was by declaring the collection of pre-Biblical writings to be sacred, and then control was further enhanced by declaring the evolving Bible to be The True Word of God. The political-priests sought control!

Quite a lot of the physical Old Testament history of Israel has been authenticated by archaeological artifacts, old structures, etc., a considerable amount of which I have fortunately been able to see (having spent 3 trips and 68 days in Israel). But archaeological evidence to confirm the psychological thoughts or beliefs of the builders can only rely on the ancient scrolls, stone-carvings, etc. God, speaking from a cloud, doesn't leave any archaeological trace of his voice. Specific structures, places, and events have been confirmed, but the mental processes of those involved in ancient events can only be inferred by what the prophets-priesthood left in the form of depicting and writing on stone. An Old Testament archaeologist and scholar, writing in the 1996 Sept/Oct issue of BAR (Biblical Archaeological Review) magazine comments about the Old Testament writers of a later date (about 450 BC), "- certainly the writers recast the whole story to suit the theological needs of the Exile and post-exilic period." I think it was really Old Testament theological and political *"spin"*.

The New Testament I view as primarily a biography of Jesus Christ and his influence, with theological input by the apostles, but without the political support of the *national* theocracy (the Israelites) that existed in the Old Testament. I believe that there was a historical figure called Jesus Christ, but I believe none of the associated theology.

I view the historical Jesus Christ as a young, brilliant, wise, philosophical, very charismatic, and very religious, Jewish rabbi, who, because of his profound immersion in the Jewish faith believed, or said he believed, that he was the long-prophesied Messiah.

One explanation of the many Old Testament prophecies fulfilled in his lifetime could be that because of his great knowledge of the Old

Testament scriptures, he was able to stage some events, and also that he was able to quote exactly from the ancient scriptures at critical moments, in both ways arranging prophecy fulfillment. Here is one example from the Bible, Zechariah 9:9, written about 520 BC, "- he is just and endowed with salvation, humble, and mounted on a donkey. Even a colt, a foal, of a donkey." Written in the first tense it should not, in my view, be considered as a prophecy, as it is by fundamentalist theologians. But if considered as such, it could have been fulfilled by Rabbi Jesus, knowing of the quotation from over 500 years beforeand asking for a donkey as in Luke 19:30, "- Go ye into the village --ye shall find a colt tied--." There were doubtless many colts tied in all villages at that time.

It appears that many of the so-called prophecies are not prophecies at all. Some appear so non-specific and vague that calling them prophecies is stretching it. Even a major prophecy from Micah-5:2 (written about 735 BC to about 730 BC), which is quoted so frequently as predicting Jesus' birth in Bethlehem refers to the birth of one that, "is to be a ruler in Israel." I don't think that Jesus qualified as a, "ruler in Israel", and in 700 BC a ruler would have indicated one of those theocratic-politicos, not Jesus, a theologian. It appears to be a failed prophecy. I have not heard the theological explanation of why Old Testament prophecies being discussed, are written in the present tense (1500 BC to 450 BC), and not in the future tense. How do they qualify as prophecies?

In the over-twenty references to the disciples/apostles witnessing Jesus after his resurrection, only one person uses the pronoun "I". That person was Paul, and everyone who is aware of New Testament narrative knows that Paul was *not* there, - that he was still a member of the ruling opposition party - the Romans, and that he justifies *seeing* Jesus because it was in a vision (*dream*) and that it was later when he "*saw it.*" About six of the total say, "you saw" or "we saw", which could be part of an apostolic conspiracy or maybe an apostolic group hysteria. Another three were visions (*dreams).* Finally, Acts - 10: 39-42, relates that: "(God) granted that He (Jesus) should become visible, *not to all the people,* but to witnesses who were chosen before by God, that is to us, who ate and drank with Him after he arose from the dead --." So he was said to be invisible to *non-witnesses. They were there but couldn't see him.* Once again, in my *closed* system, it is not a possibility.

There are many theories regarding the resurrection which I will not pursue. However, there is one more thought which I have not heard mentioned anywhere. To Jesus Christ who was deeply immersed in his religion, and who was actually convinced that he was the Jewish Messiah and the Son of God, but also wouldn't be allowed by his Father to undergo crucifixion, - what more natural exclamation would there be than the one that the Bible records, "My Father, why hast thou forsaken me?"

Miracles, by their very nature, cause skepticism. Clearly there were those that could be given valid explanations and weren't miracles at all. Some of Jesus' enthusiastic followers (the apostles), believing in the ancient prophecies may have had their eye on cabinet posts in the expected Jesus theocratic administration. They may have promoted, or even invented, some of his more dramatic miracles. These followers may have had the desire to provide the new creed modern day (28 to 33 AD) miracles to equate with Old Testament, much revered, ancient Hebrew miracles of 500 to 1500 years earlier; such as the burning bush, Red Sea crossing, manna, and the Lord's frequent conversations. The *modern* miracles would bring reinforcement belief to the new Christian creed.

There were a few indirect 1st century AD references to Christians, and Flavius Josephus, a Jewish historian (33 AD to 100 AD), was the main regional and independent historian (disregarding the not-so-independent Apostles). About 80 to 100 AD, while in Rome, he wrote a 2-volume history entitled *The Antiquities of the Jews* and the *History of the Jews.* In the 1000 page Whiston edition the Christians are acknowledged in one paragraph. A.B. Whiston was a British Mathematics professor who translated the writings of Josephus from Greek to English in 1737 AD. You can compare his translation with the one that follows his translation.

Whiston translation: "There was about this time Jesus, a wise man, if it be lawful to call him a man; for he was a doer of wonderful works, a teacher of such men as receive the truth with pleasure. He drew over to him both many of the Jews and many of the Gentiles. He was (The) Christ. And when Pilate, at the suggestion of the principal men amongst us, had condemned him to the cross, those who loved him did not at first forsake him, for he appeared to them alive again on the third day, as the divine prophets had foretold these, and ten thousand other wonderful things concerning him. And the tribe of Christians, so named from him, are not extinct this day." End of quote.

To illustrate the variations that can occur from one translation to another (maybe because of the agenda, and prior beliefs of the translator). Here is the Arabic translation of the same passage as translated from the original. (About 600 years previous to the Koran) - Quote: "At this time there was a wise man who was called Jesus. And his conduct was good, and was known to be virtuous. And many persons from among the Jews and other nations became his disciples. Pilate condemned him to be crucified and to die. And those who had become his disciples did not abandon his discipleship. They reported that he had appeared to them three days after his crucifixion and that he was alive; accordingly, he was perhaps the Messiah concerning whom the prophets have recounted wonders."

Flavius Josephus also stated (Whiston translation) " - so he, Ananus, assembled a council of judges, and brought before it the brother of Jesus the so-called Christ, whose name was James, together with some other, and having accused them as law-breakers, he delivered them over to be stoned." Josephus also has a longer paragraph in which he speaks of John the Baptist and his death by decree from King Herod.

Regardless of my disbelief, I have an unshakable conviction of the need for freedom, tolerance, and respect, for all devout people and their religions. However, religious intolerance can produce a similar psychological and emotional trauma to that produced by other bigotries. Consequently, we must have unlimited freedom of belief, but careful restriction of religious intolerance.

There are positive aspects to devoutly-held religious beliefs that I think are indisputable, though in no way do I think they are mystical or miraculous. In number 1 and number 2 that follow, the same results may be obtained by secular groups, political groups and community groups, etc.

1. Though done for religious reasons, the harnessing of religious belief to humanitarian service to the needy, can not only help the needy, but bring the usual sense of fulfillment to the giver. Two outstanding exponents of this religion based concern were Dr. Albert Schweitzer and Mother Theresa.
2. Initiated by religious beliefs, the believers of a community can unite, and can together achieve large community projects, unlikely of fulfillment without the cooperative effort. If their efforts incorporate the brotherhood of man (all races) then their religious community effort may help overcome local racism and bigotry.
3. For this religious positive, I think that one must have that mystical belief in 'things unseen.' I think that a deep emotional peace can come to those who believe in whatever *their* religion teaches - no matter how primitive, or even how aberrant from the mainline religions. Religious beliefs, devoutly held, can bring hope to the holder. It is, at this point, that it approaches the opiate of the masses referred to by Karl Marx. The point was, that a Russian serf of the 1880s, the American slave of the earlier 1800s, a depression era despairing person, and many others in hopeless circumstances, could only look forward to the promise of eternal life when all pain, illness, hunger, loneliness, inequalities are swept away (as the 1940s Black Golden Gate Quartette used to sing, "there are no restrictive

signs in Heaven"). At this time, I cannot see, or even try to present, a secular equivalent to #3. One would need a complete submission to the unknowable (faith) for this unlimited acceptance of God's Divine Will. I can discern a psychiatric component at work here that could also induce faith healing.

4. Number three leads us to number four, the Power of Prayer which also requires total trust and the fully "surrendered belief in things unseen." In my closed opinion, if one is being prayed for, he must know about it, or he can't be helped. One might be moved to envy the tranquil minds of those who have that absolute, immovable conviction that indicates the non-freethinkers, the unquestioning minds of the zealots; those individuals that have unshakable trust and blind faith in their omnipotent, omniscient, omnipresent God. I would expect them to be as at peace with their faithful state of mind, as I am, with myclosed mind.

Healing Words, subtitled *The power of prayer and the practice of medicine, Larry Dossey M.D.* My view remains unchanged though author Larry Dossey presents several anecdotal examples, and some statistics and investigations, which he claims support a much greater role for prayer, even to change *past* events! That's stretching it while weakening his argument!

However, I believe that there is also a secular equivalent. There are many medical conditions that are amenable to psychological input. The many aches and pains connected with negative thinking, depression, and mental illness can evaporate when the psychological input of a positive outlook is established. Many unexpected recoveries of the major illnesses of both churched and the 'unchurched,' have been recorded.

I believe that somewhere 'down the centuries,' that the psychology of religious belief and prayer will be harnessed for mental, psychological, and also physical needs. At that point religions could fade away subject to the status of number 5 the most important of the religious positives.

5. The Golden Rule is taught in many of the religions, and in my view, is the most important of the positives. In essence it is the treating of others as we would wish them to treat us (the Golden Rule). I wish I could foresee a future where there was a systematic comprehensive, teaching plan based on that one concept, but I cannot. Teaching the Golden Rule as part of religion would be dropped and teaching it would be based on intelligent common sense and the emerging awareness of mutual self-interest. *The Bible* - Matthew 7:12 "Therefore, however, you want people to treat you, so treat them, for this is the Law and the Prophets."

   Currently, the Golden Rule is randomly taught, and is secondary in emphasis, because it is submerged into each denominations religious code. Dogma dominates, and in the denominational view, the dogma is the moral code. Nevertheless, that is the main reason I can think of for maintaining religious observance - and so as to develop that trait in early life the emphasis should be on the teaching of children.

   I think it would be wonderful if from kindergarten right through university the Golden Rule would be taught according to the level of student comprehension. For example, in later years it could enter into the courses on psychology and especially on the myriad of relationships in personal life, family, sexual, marital, work, play, social organizations, political organizations, corporations and in international relations as a universally accepted concept. It seems to me that there would be no disagreement by religious organizations, school authorities, teacher unions, and individuals. In time, probably several generations, there would be a positive influence on all families and their home life. Gradually this should permeate, through school teaching, to even the most dysfunctional families. That can only lead to greater sympathy and respect of others; greater appreciation for the richness of all peoples and cultures, thus edging toward a time where the "brotherhood of man" would be real, and not simply an empty platitude.

In Judaism's Babylonian Talmud, Shabbat 31, there is the story of a man who wanted to learn the entire Torah while standing on one foot. The Talmud is an immense encyclopedic body of learned rabbinic studies centered on the Pentateuch - the first five books of the Old Testament, also called the Torah. The greatly respected Rabbi Hillel said to him, "What is hateful to you do not do to your neighbor - this is the Torah. The rest is commentary, now go and study."

Insertion in 2013-2015: The teaching concept received reinforcement with six encouraging headlines 16-18 years after my 1996 commentary: 2012 *The Arizona Republic.* "Project aim is to spread kindness in classrooms." Founder, Marcia Meyer- thebekindpeopleproject.org

The Arizona Republic, 2013, Laurie Roberts, "Quiet acts of kindness, make impact."

The Arizona Republic, Nov 19th 2012, Steve Zabilski, "Let's try a bold vision: Committing to helping people."

The Arizona Republic, 2013, Roberto Rodriguez, "Cultural studies, teach concept of humanity."

USA Today, Dec 31st 2014, "Airbnb gives $1 million for good deeds."

The Arizona Republic, Sept 30th 2015, "Pope Francis challenges us to show love."

Return to 1996 - Retaining that Golden Rule emphasis in religious training, all the rest could be discarded. I see only a happier world resulting. When the *Golden Rule* is universally established, and the power of prayer has been converted to a philosophical science, then the churches could wither away, or convert to humanitarian organizations. Their current random teaching of the Golden Rule to their small portion of the populace would then be unnecessary. Pending the demise of organized religions, I can dream of some modifications of the current religions starting with the elimination of their tax-free status. I would enjoy seeing them eliminate their dogma, their ritualism, their symbolic practices, their attempts to produce religious awe, their complex theological interpretations, and the elimination of the arrogant certainty and sanctimony of some individuals in their religious "truths."

I do not view the presence or absence of religion in a person's life as being a moral issue. Many religious leaders do view it as a moral issue. I see the most starkly evident example of the lack of the Golden Rule when two religions conflict, as has happened in so many wars; currently most notable to us are the conflicts in Northern Ireland, Israel and the current (1996) war in Yugoslavia. It has always been evident how every society invokes *their* God to bring them victory over their foes, who usually have the same God as themselves.

Feeling as I do about the fundamental importance of the Golden Rule, I would like to say, and be truthful, that I have unwaveringly practiced it. But like all religious adherents, I certainly can't claim perfection. I, too, am a sinner.

How does my respect and tolerance square with talking about religion elimination? That respect and toleration would continue but their elimination would be centuries into the future, and would be achieved by gradual education and a voluntary process, so that no force or mandatory law would be used, as was attempted in the Soviet Union. It would simply be a withering away, which appears to be happening already.

Again, as I see it, the Golden Rule would have a place in all human relationships including the withering religions, politics, commercial relationships, intergovernmental relations, international relations, etc. If indoctrination occurred from the earliest years, these relationships could not help but be more harmonious, more productive, less stressful, and more efficient. The people you met each day would be happier more agreeable and their happiness would exist, not so much because of others being considerate of them, but more because of the internal contentment felt by being considerate of others. Several psychologists attest to the mental happiness, with peace of mind, to be noted in those who give of themselves freely in helping others, and who feel they are doing the Right Thing. The right thing has been gravely distorted at times. For example, the ardent Nazis in their torture of the Jews, thought of it as the right thing. Slavery apologists used Bible quotations to justify their slavery of the Blacks. However, the Golden Rule in this case (doing kindly to others) is the right thing. And everyone would be winners.

This approach is predicated on an optimistic view of mankind. At my age, I have certainly had my share of encounters where human responses reflected a very mistrusting, paranoid view of others. The right wing politician, and the fundamentalist theologian, will not view my scenario as anything near to sanity. I can hear the comment "Get real! Read the newspapers. Listen to the news." But a trusting, open, optimistic approach to others tends to produce a mirror response in them. A positive, optimistic view would gradually bring an improving world. I would much rather error on the side of viewing the human race too optimistically, rather than too negatively. Dream! Coupled with my political utopia, discussed elsewhere, the world would be a much more pleasant place.

Remember at the beginning that this was my Utopia, my reverie. My receding religious utopia would have completed its religious recession (the religious dogma would be gone) and I would then have my psychological utopia. Fuzzy thinking? Maybe, but I hope for it! Next year I may modify this version, but now, in 1996, this-is-where-I-am- at-now in my religious belief and I'm not asking anyone to join me, only to *please use the Golden Rule generously.*

John Wilkerson, author of *Jerusalem as Jesus Knew It,* and subtitled *Archaeology as Evidence,* is a Christian who writes, using archaeology as a buttress of his belief in Christianity. As stated previously, archaeology does indeed confirm many of the physical aspects of the

Bible accounts, especially the Old Testament. The reason is that the Old Testament archaeology reflects permanent stone structures erected by the dominant major political-religious authorities of about 1500 years of Israelite history. The dearth of New Testament archaeology is a result of the New Testament covering only about sixty years of a dominated, secretive sect, and their apostles. In Wilkerson's preface he speaks of the uncertainty of the authorship of the New Testament. "A Gospel is not exactly a "Life of Jesus," for a life or a biography would have to tell us all sorts of personal data about him. Gospels are not biographic. Nor, indeed, are they objective, factual records of the kind that we expect from sociologists, or journalists reporting the news."

Wilkerson continues, John 20:31, "The writer's attitude toward Jesus is one of commitment, and they write with a missionary agenda. The gospels are therefore intended as propaganda. John tells us that he is writing, '- that you may believe that Jesus is the Messiah, the Son of God, and that believing, you may have life in his name.' The concern of the Gospel writers is with the *spiritual belief, rather than a material truth*, even though the material existence of Jesus was to be the means by which the spiritual truth was given its expression. Who were the Gospel writers? Today's equivalent of saying, 'Mathew, Mark, Luke and John' would be, 'John Smith, Peter Jones, David Robinson and Michael Brown,' names that appear by the dozens in every telephone directory. Plenty of Matthews, Marks, Lukes and Johns were about in the first century AD, and merely to have names like these does not tell us who they were." End of his quote.

2015 insertion: Father Bertrand Ruby states in his book *Mary of Galilee*-National Geographic Dec 2015, "The evangelists (Apostles) were writing 45 to 60 years after Christ's death and were not biographical. So don't expect them to have all the elements about Mary. Her life is picked up from hearsay."

It would have added to the reliability of the Gospels if the New Testament would have identified the written Gospels with actual individuals named in the Gospels themselves. That would have established eyewitness accounts, but that was not done and it has remained for later Christian theologians to assume that Gospel writers were identified with Gospel characters. That assumption (or calculated attempt) has been to try to establish Gospel reliability and authenticity. However, to quote John Wilkerson again, "But the New Testament does not make these identifications and one of our earliest witnesses outside the New Testament speaks in a way which makes these identifications unlikely.

This is a writer named Papias who probably died about 130 AD, who tells us that Mark (and he does not say John Mark, see Acts XII 12) became Peter's *translator or interpreter* and wrote down accurately all the *memories* he told him. The impression is that Mark, the Gospel writer, was entirely dependent on Peter for his information and was probably not a member of the same group of the apostles themselves. But if Mark was not an eyewitness, nor we must assume were Mathew and Luke, since they seem to have relied on Mark's gospel for a great deal of their information." End of quote. Wilkinson goes on to say that Mathew and Luke do have some unknown secondary source formuch of their material. He also acknowledges that there are contradictions between the various Gospels - though he says that they are "slight, in comparison to many of those found in other ancient documents." I would wonder why *divinely-inspired writings could vary* in even the smallest details!

My Current Religious Opinions

Thus, ends my long-winded 1996 commentary. Except that I have softened my position on mainline religion, I would reach the same conclusions today (2014) as I did then. Think of this continuing, rambling account as a component part of this-is-where-I'm-at-now method of arriving at a conclusive answer, which of course, with an evolving opinion, will never come. Conclusiveness I really don't need. At this point, I feel the need, of offering a fairly comprehensive view of my admiration of the wisdom to be found in the Bible, but also my continuing disbelief in the theology of the Bible, particularly because it may be in opposition to what is believed by the reader. I apologize in advance, if my comments seem overly wordy, but my position on such a subject should be crystal clear. I plan to allow no pre-existing rigidity of thought. This personal narrative and these opinions are mine, and so probably carry questionable credibility. I feel it will be helpful to quote some of the opinions of those articulate thinkers of the past. My recent surge of reading, study and reflection has done four things for me:

My 1996 point of view has received much reinforcement by many writers, some of whom I will quote, and also, by a large amount of unincluded material.

PERSPECTIVE

1. I rediscovered the exemplary manner in which my parents manifestly lived their lives of Golden Rule observance, always in service to others. I came to realize that it appears that my father went through the same this-is-where-I-am-at-now process that I have experienced. Dad appeared to have shed all his juvenile Episcopal ritual and dogma, retaining only his evident belief in Jesus, and in simple, basic New Testament theology. I have shed all mystical theology down to the uncluttered Golden Rule. I see no divine compulsion to do otherwise. It is a logical and rewarding approach to life.
2. I have, more sensitively, realized that as a pioneering, struggling, neophyte-farmer, he was really *living* the Golden Rule by establishing a living room Sunday service. He was bringing his New Testament Golden Rule based homily to those who wished for it, and maybe some who needed it. At a tiny level, he was establishing what churches do, a community spirit. When his life ended in 1943, his school house ministry also ended.
3. I see more clearly now, than in 1996, that the presence of consideration for others (the Golden Rule), including your adversary, is what produces functional success or failure in all facets of life. I am referring to family relationships, marriage, work relationships, companies, organizations, governments, international relations and agreements, laws, legislation, political movements, and most especially - war. This broad involvement *implies the need for mandatory childhood Golden Rule inculcation.*
4. My current, more intensive reading and study, has brought me to a better level of understanding and appreciation of religion in general. I have come to realize that the doctrine of Jesus Christ was one of love and forgiveness, and was probably intended as a softening effect on the stern, demanding, God of the Old Testament. Love of others is the basis of the Golden Rule. So, drop the superfluous dogma and

concentrate on the Golden Rule itself, and all will be well. Webster's dictionary refers to dogma as a "body of theological doctrines, strictly adhered to." Webster then defines doctrine as the equivalent of dogma. That word "strictly" removes the freedom of thought. Some of those religious doctrines are baptism, communion, confession, atonement, penitence, purgatory, original sin and stated-declaration-of-belief of what is considered correct by predetermined, approved, religious creed. I hope, and intend, that the following segment brings some understanding of the history and development of religion.

Miniscule History of Religious Development

From the dawn of time, the most primitive of people sought fulfillment and imaginative security from fear in the mystical belief of a protective god. The Old Testament (the Hebrew Bible) presents the Israelites as the originators of the one-God-concept of religion during the early B.C. era. Fear of alien gods, and thus of alien neighbors, impelled them to consistently attempt removal of any religious opponents to their one God (Yahweh).

On the defeat of the Israelites and the destruction of Jerusalem in 67AD, the major religious power passed to the Romans, and their many gods, while Christian development was developing "underground." In 27 BC, back at headquarters in Rome, in worship of the Roman gods, the Pantheon, a massively imposing building, had been commissioned. The structure was not completed until 117 AD, 184 years later. I have been fortunate, twice in my lifetime, to stand gaping at the impressive, polished marble tribute to the ancient Roman gods. Its unique nineteen-centuries old architecture, 140 feet wide and 140 feet tall, with its distinctive 30 foot opening at the apex for the rain and sunshine to enter; the niches where a statue of each of the Roman gods was originally placed; has rated at least one book devotedentirely to its architecture. About 370 AD the Roman Catholic pope, Pope Constantine, overcame the Romans and replaced each Roman gods in the Pantheon, with a Christian entity. Yahoo comments that this "magnificent, ancient temple" is now called "the church of Santa Maria and Martyrs."

Roman Catholicism, tracing their pontificate from Apostle Peter, continued to develop; followed by the writing of the Koran about 700 AD, when the prophet Mohammad initiated the religion of Islam; followed by the break-away religion of Lutheranism in the 1500s; then came a flood of lesser Protestant religions. These, added to the multiplicity of cults, and tribal religions developing in all parts of the world, gives some credence to the comment by Earl Lee in *Free Inquiry Magazine*, Oct/Nov 2005, "Looking at today's world it seems that people have an overwhelming desire to believe they are desperate to believe, as if belief were some sort of drug."

One historical, theologically important event occurred during that flood of Protestant denominations which has perpetuated church divisions. Clinton Lee Scott points out the contentious divisions of Roman Catholicism and Protestants in *Religion can make Sense*, "The Catholic Church always believed in the infallibility of the Pope. But at the time of the Protestant Reformation, Protestants substituted for an infallible Pope an infallible Bible." So now the Protestant *truth* is not from the mouth of the Pope but from the pages of the inerrant Bible. I cannot believe either! The headline December 1976, by Peter D. Bunzel, Opinions Section editor, *LA Times* speaks accurately for me, "I cannot, of course will myself to believe." Belief can't be proved, so no-one is right- or everyone is right.

This mini-history is a brief account of only the Jewish and Christian religions

Origins of Religion: Fear

Thomas Hobbes, 1651, *The Story of Philosophy,* "Fear of things invisible is the natural seed of that which everyone in himself calleth religion."

Sept 22nd, 1963, *This Week Magazine, The Los Angeles Times,* published an excerpt called "The Art of Imagination" - *New Book of the Art of Living* authored by Wilfred A. Peterson. Quotation, "Imagination" said Albert Einstein, "is more powerful than knowledge. Imagination enlarges your vision, stretches the mind, challenges the impossible. Without imagination, thought comes to a halt!" But was it able to originate the lofty concept of God? Of course! Anything can be imagined! The human mind is imaginatively unlimited in its capacity to produce new ideas. Imagination can liven up any idle reverie. But if fear is added to the imagination, one is more likely to produce an idea with a security component. There is an old saying, possibly anonymous, - "Necessity is the mother of invention." Think of fear and try a modification: "The perceived necessity of security is also the mother of invention."

Our own imagination about ancient days provides a choice of frightening scenarios: it could be a prowling saber-tooth tiger out there somewhere; or it could be a vindictive, tribal enemy nearby; or it could be a spreading epidemic of the "Creeping Crud" while the witch doctor is on vacation. Someone "mouths" a prayer to an imaginary entity/ deity, that produces a random success; begets a new imaginary god, and, with later embellishment a new religion. Fear can provide the impulse. Fear can be the spark. The one thing that is certain is that it is from the human mind that the concept of a new protective deity, or god, or religion first emerged.

Albert Einstein, *N.Y. Times Magazine,* Nov. 9th, 1930, (Also *Great Quotations),* "With primitive man it is primarily fear that evokes religious notions fear of hunger, wild beasts, sickness, death --. In this sense I am speaking of a religion of fear. This, though not created, is in an important degree, stabilized by the portion of a special priestly caste which sets itself up as a mediator between the people and the beings they fear, and thus produces political control." This, then, becomes *BOTH* priestly *political* control and priestly *spiritual* control of the people, thus a merging of church and state. The transfer of the belief that a god could make no mistakes was retained when the Israelites developed their new One-God religion.

The most concerned citizens of the early leaders were automatically the priest-leaders. It followed naturally that one of those leaders became the religious spokesman, and so became the representative of God here on earth. That applies all the way from the Pope down to your local priest or pastor. They are deemed omnipotent.

Euripides and Plato, circa 400 BC (maybe the first recorded Atheists) both commented in *The Great Quotations* that, "He was a wise man who invented God." Napoleon Bonaparte, also in *The Great Quotations* observed that "all religions have been made by men," and that "religion is excellent stuff for keeping common people quiet." Think! What other reason could all three have when they thought the inventor was wise, than that the societal inventor had learned a better control of those he led.

It may have occurred to the apprehensive, insecure potentate that his lonely position as the leader-at-the-top would be much strengthened *if he could transfer his fear of his own subjects to them,* and he could show more effective result when divine supreme decisions reinforced his own. He needed a noncompetitive mystical, *therefore indisputable,* authority, not just religious input but *authoritative orders.* Eureka! God! The added mystical authority of the priest could not be realistically questioned, and executive actions originated by the rulers and the priests would dominate because they now came from *ONE* entity. That concept emerged automatically when it was realized that *political control* could be enhanced through religious authority and command. (God wills it!). It was the only way a recalcitrant populace could be controlled short of summoning the "palace police." No ruler wanted rebellion! His ideal was an acquiescent and placid kingdom, or tribe. "There was no religion without politics and no politics without religion," is a quote by W. E. Chase in *Life and Language in the Old Testament.* It was clear that the emerging protective entity could be used as a tool of control of unruly subjects. Think of the rebellious subjects of the Biblical Moses.

A ruler's dream! If one could gain control of the developing creed; place into use those rules that would be most helpful to the ruler; justify it for being mandatory because God said so; use personal charisma and leadership to train and imbue the most trusted adjutants in the same belief; a tranquil status quo could be maintained; and then it would be possible to reduce the money allotted to those guys who made the spears (the greedy arms dealers)! The monarch would be wealthier. This concept could be thought of as occurring centuries beforeMoses, but note the masterful, imaginative way in which Moses controlled his rebellious followers, and, how he embellished his religion by the use of the Ten Commandments. Though frequently thought of as only theological; as legendary prehistory; or as only mystical in nature; the Moses account is consistent with the view of religious invention (or modification). You will also find the Biblical account consistent with the above description, though the Bible, of course, emphasizes the event as though it was staged by God.

So the *fear-control* relationship of politics and religion has lingered through the leader-priest to the present time. In both of the Testaments of the Bible, the national political control was administered by the priests, that situation continuing under the gods of the Romans.

Religion was usually part of government during most of the first two millennia AD, bringing with it wars because of the bigotry of fixed belief, the classic example being the bloody Crusades.

David De Leon, Socialist leader (circa 1900) in *The Great Quotations* noted, "The moment religion organizes into a specific creed it becomes a political force. From Moses down to Brigham Young every creed founder has been a state builder." Prior to 1870, the Roman Catholic Popes retained their control of Italy, but then the minor states of Italy formed a central Italian government and the Popes for sixty years lost direct power and political control of Italy. Because of the wealth, power, influence and immense wealth of the Roman Catholic church the restive nation, under the leadership of Benito Mussolini, signed the Lateran Treaty in 1930, allowing for compensation for the church's immense property external to the Vatican; allowing Roman Catholicism to be 'the sole religion of the state' (Italy); and allowing the Roman Catholic territory and property in Rome to have national sovereignty, a country within a country, 'The Vatican' in Italy. In the Vatican, the creed had morphed back into *an official religious and political force.* For sure, there was, and is, no separation of church and state in the Vatican.

I deplore the influence that organized religion plays in politics in many countries. The overt attempts of the "religious right" to dominate national policy in this country, is still based on *fear-control* and is not consistent with freedom of religion and the diverse opinions of the citizenry. The United States is officially a secular nation, not a Christian nation.

Atheism and Agnosticism

The commentary on the previous page by Euripides and Plato, circa 400 BC, ("it was a wise man who invented God") reveal that it had not taken very long for some who were not rulers, to note that religion had a political, non-religious agenda, and used their compulsory, theological, God-driven agenda to support the political authorities. Thus, 2400 years ago, doubt about the validity of the theological component of religion was already being manifested. Doubtless even before this point there were those who were already arriving at the concept of Atheism. But along with Atheism comes a slightly less fundamentalist thought - Agnosticism - an Almost-Atheism. So, how are they different?

My own feelings of disbelief are echoed in the voiced doubts of Alva Edison, the great inventor, *The Great Quotations,* "My mind is incapable of conceiving such a thing as a soul. I maybe in error and may have a soul, but I simply do not believe it." He is willing to show doubt by saying "I maybe in error." I reserve the same margin of doubt. In other words, I believe and think like an Atheist, but will not claim I'm right!

Emerson Hughes Lalonde, author, in his book *and Thy Neighbor as thyself,* also speaks for me when he defines lucidly what he believes: "Today, (1945) nearly two centuries after Thomas Paine wrote *The*

Age of Reason his utterance is more to the point than ever: 'I do not believe in the creed professed by the Jewish church (Judaism), by the Roman(Catholic) church, by the Turkish (Islamic) church, by the Protestant (Christian church), nor by any church I know of. My own mind is my church. All national institutions of churches, whether Jewish, Christian or Turkish (Muslim), appear to me to be no other than human inventions, set up to terrify and enslave mankind, and monopolize power and profit. Human society can only be saved by universalism'." Universalism, to be discussed later, is a concept which includes all people, everywhere.

My misgivings regarding religion are well phrased by Leo Tolstoy, who, in the middle 1800s, probably referring to the Russian Orthodox Church, wrote the following in *The Wisdom of Tolstoy,* "From my childhood, from the time I first started to read the New Testament, I was touched most of all by the doctrine of Jesus which inculcates love, humility, self-denial and the duty of returning good for evil. This to me has always been the substance of Christianity (the Golden Rule*).* The rules of the Church touching articles of faith, dogmas, the observance of the Sacrament, fasts, prayers, were not necessary to me, and did not seem to be based on Christian truth." "I was troubled most that the miseries of humanity, the habit of judging one another, of passing judgment on nations and religions, and the wars and massacres, all went with the approbation of the Church." These are all a negation of the Golden Rule, and his commentary is direct in its message.

Abraham Lincoln in*, The Great Quotations,* "My earlier views of the unsoundness of the Christian scheme of salvation, and the human origin of the scriptures, have become clearer and stronger with advancing years and I see no reason for thinking I shall ever change them." You could also correctly say that I was not oriented toward a mainline religion because my parents never taught me their rituals and their dogmas. They clearly felt that they were not necessary for their limited-dogma religion. And those dogmas are certainly not necessary for mine. I am so very grateful to my parents.

When he wrote *The Outline of History* in 1920, H. G. Wells appears to have viewed Atheism as being as still being "in the closet" (where I was). His comment was: "There are many more believers (in Atheism) than those that speak out because they do not want to offend others, or expose themselves to unpleasantness." As previously described, I have already traversed that road of my life.

Now contrast the openness of contemporary, perceptive comedian George Carlin who, in *The God Delusion,* is quoted by Richard Dawkins, using plain language to illuminate the incongruities of Christian theology. "Religion has actually convinced people that there is an invisible man living in the sky, who watches everything you do, every minute of every day. And the invisible man has a special list of these ten things he does not want you to do. And if you do any of these ten things he has a special place full of fire and smoke and burning and torture and anguish where he will send you to live and suffer and burn and choke and cry and scream forever and ever 'til the end of time. - But he loves you."

The founders of the Christian faith appear to have attempted to retain much of the "fire-and-brimstone" of the Old Testament, while tacking the philosophy of love and forgiveness on top. In doing so they have distorted, and even nullified, much of the doctrine of Jesus Christ himself, who appears to have been a traditional rabbi deeply immersed in fundamental Judaism but preaching a new mellow philosophy of love and forgiveness. Though charismatic, he was just a *human* rabbi. He failed to use his concept of the centrality of individual belief, and his compassionate recommendation to forgive the individual sinner, when he became offended at *all the people* in three villages who did not accept his teaching. To me it appears that Jesus reverted to Old Testament theology and shed his messianic aura when he condemned the villages of Chorazim, Bethsaida and Capernaum.

The Bible, Mathew 11:20-24, "Woe to you, Chorazim! Woe to you Bethsaida! For if the miracles had occurred in Tyre and Sidon which occurred in you, they would have repented long ago in sack cloth and ashes."

"Nevertheless I say to you, it shall be more tolerable for Tyre and Sidon in the day of judgement than for you."

"And you, Capernaum, will not be exalted to heaven will you? You shall descend to Hades (Hell), for if the miracles had occurred in Sodom which occurred in you, it would have remained to this day."

Sending an entire village to hell, the harsh words of Jesus, on that occasion were reminiscent of the vengeful God of the Old Testament. *His words betray his humanness, and do not indicate any divinity.*

In 2003, my wife Olga and I drove to all three doomed villages. Jesus was at least right about their longevity. Chorazim, having a Jewish history, has been made into the *Korazim National Park* by Israel. It is a 25-acre (my estimate) jumble of black basalt stone arches, walls and rubble. Bethsaida is about a 5-acre (my estimate) low hill with unexcavated, extruding portions of buildings, with occasional rock-engravings. Both appeared to be uninhabited. Capernaum is primarily a Palestinian village with a Christian-tourist economy, adjacent to the ruins of a 200 AD roofless synagogue, the tiny, roofless, stonewalled village of Capernaum, and the 'traditional' house of (Apostle) Peter. That house, since my 1980 trip, now has a glass-floored Christian church above its ruins. Sodom, gone long before Jesus' time, appears only as salt-encrusted rocky outcroppings on the southern end of the Dead Sea.

The irreconcilable segments of the merged philosophies, leaves the thinking and questioning Christian with confused disbelief. As I understand the beliefs of today, the *fundamentalist* Jews and Christians both tend to maintain their beliefs in the avenging God, while the milder contemporary forms of both religions, believe more in the justice of, "forgive the sinner but not the sin." The general populace has modified their thinking greatly during my lifetime. Many social taboos, most of them originating in the Old Testament, have become socially acceptable.

So why do I equivocate, and leave wiggle-room, calling myself Agnostic? The dogmatic, fundamental Hebrew or Christian says, "There is a God." The fundamental, dogmatic Atheist says, "There is no God." Either viewpoint suggests an immovable opinion. I can't prove Atheism; I certainly can't prove the existence of God, and I promised *NO* rigidity of thought. So the "wiggle-room" makes me an Agnostic who says, "I think like an Atheist, and, as I cannot prove there is no God, I will react as though I am an Atheist. Atheism suggests the rigidity of thought, the inflexible maligned dogma, which I have always disliked so much. It is too much like some of the religionists I have known, who have always said, "You're wrong, I am right!"

How can one be content with a body of belief that does not make reasonable sense? How can one be led by family tradition, by theological tradition and persuasion, to believe in something that does not obey the laws of nature or the scientific truths of this universe? Human *reason* has to be the criteria by which one is guided. Such an important concept needs some reinforcement.

Tolstoy says it plainly in *The Wisdom of Tolstoy,* "Man has only one instrument wherewith to know himself and to know his relation to the universe - he has no other - and that instrument is his reason."

Benjamin Franklin *in The Great Quotations,* "The way to see by faith is to shut the eye of reason."

William Drummond, historian, in *The Great Quotations,* "He who will not reason is a bigot; he who cannot is a fool; and he who dares not is a slave."

President James Madison 1783, *The Great Quotations,* He holds that religion, "can be directed *only* by reason - must be left to the conviction and conscience of every man; and it is the right of every man to exercise it as these may dictate."

Mohandas Gandhi in his *Autobiography* wrote, "In the matter of religion, beliefs differ, and each one is supreme for himself. If all had the same belief about all matters of religion, there would be only one religion in the world."

Pope Pius IX-*The Great Quotations,* "Every man is free to embrace, and profess, that religion by the light of reason he considers to be truth." "All the truths of religion proceed from the innate strength of human reason; hence reason is the ultimate standard by which man can and ought to arrive at the knowledge of truths of every kind." Such an eminent theologian acknowledges reason rises above religion! Weighty words from a weighty source!

Thomas Hager in *Force of Nature,* speaking of Linus Pauling said, "Like many Enlightenment philosophers, he had replaced God with Reason, and he believed in the steady upwards progress of society based on the application of Rational thought and the scientific method. Knowledge was the key. Pauling's morality grew out of what he knew to be true; he knew that he was a rational person, and he believed that other rational persons would, with sufficient knowledge, come to similar conclusions." Pauling received a Nobel Prize in Chemistry and subsequently a Nobel Prize in Peace. He believed passionately in the freedom of speech, having survived Senator Joe McCarthy Black List. Hager continues, "In politics the underlying information, the received wisdom, he believed, was the U.S. Constitution and the Bill of Rights, documents which he revered as monuments to the philosophy of the Enlightenment."

However, I am aware that many feel they are being rational when they look at the universe and say, "there is a God." That is one reason that I respect all beliefs.

Secularism

The concept of freedom of thought, especially religious and political thought, was a superb and wonderful vision of what our founders thought a free-thinking future populace could enjoy. The genius of the founding fathers of the United States was that they carried that thought further by understanding that without that freedom, traditional religious beliefs would still bind the country in archaic, political and theological constraints. Only unrestrained thought would suffice. They were knowledgeable men who had learned from history about men of principle and thus they wisely formed a secular state with freedom of religion. The American experiment was the first in the world. At that time, many countries (especially their primary "mother" country - England) were still in the ancient Old Testament mode of merging politics and religion, or at least having a state-approved religion.

There was a prior historical event that the Founding Fathers possibly considered. In 1521 Martin Luther, based only on faith, and some logical reasoning, refused to submit to the strength of the governing Roman Catholic authorities with their autocratic religious control (religion by force, and without choice). This suggested that Lutheranism (or any other creed) could do the same in the future. So then the rational thought came that a secular government, by allowing any religion, would avoid both internal and external conflicts, such as the Crusades, Inquisition etc. Thus the Constitution, the bed rock of the U.S. government was established and allowed for no favoritism in religion, only a secular choice of whatever the individual wished.

Wendy Kaminer, *Free Inquiry Magazine* Oct/Nov 2005. She superbly defines in succinct words that "Secular does not mean without religion. Secularism is a democratic system of government that accommodates religious beliefs, without endorsing or enforcing, - gives me and everyone else the opportunity to muddle as we may." "Secularism puts freedom of conscience first; it values religious liberty over popular notions of religious truth." Could it be said better?

Kurtz, Editor of *Free Inquiry Magazine* , Oct/Nov 2005 "Benjamin Franklin and Thomas Jefferson knew - that to be modern, a nation must be secular and dedicated to the pursuit of happiness through science and technology."

This point is so important, herewith another quotation - Thomas Jefferson said in *The Great Quotations,* "If we value individual liberty more highly than secularism, then the only kind of secularism that deserves support is one that supports and *protects both liberty of belief and liberty of disbelief equally.*" So my opinion is allowed, approved, and respected!

When the term "secularism" was applied to government it indicated neutrality towards all religions and the appropriate phrase "separation of church and state" that soon developed. In 1879, again in 1947, and in later rulings, the Supreme Court has confirmed secularism is what was intended by our founding fathers.

Ed Doerr- *Free Inquiry Magazine* Oct/Nov 2005- "The treaty with Tripoli, approved by the Senate and signed by President John Adams in 1797 declares that "The government of the United States of America is in no sense founded on the Christian religion." Though that comment may come as a surprise to those who think the U.S. was founded as a Christian nation, his comment illustrates, that in the opinion of President Adams, of the U.S. legislature, and of the U.S. Supreme Court that the secular principle of the U.S. constitution dominated, and that, even if as was reality at that time, most of the members of the congress and senate were Christians, nevertheless the nation was not founded as such.

The Tribune, 2006, "Todays political climate is enlivened by the Conservative Right clamoring for their views to be legislated. One of their early heroes Senator Barry Goldwater said, "I get even more angry as a legislator, who must endure the threats of every religious group who thinks it has a God-granted right to control my vote on every roll call in the Senate. I am warning them today, that I will fight them every step of the way if they try to dictate their moral convictions to all Americans in the name of conservatism." He left a profound statement for the contemporary "Tea Party" to consider.

Those non-conformist free-thinkers of the 1700s, made certain that the Constitution contained no reference to God, and spoke of, "We, The People" as the supreme authority. However, *apparent* religious faith remained important, and the old Bruton church in Williamsburg contains (Episcopal) family-seats for each of the first presidents. That veneer of presidential religiosity became an almost-*de facto* requirement over the succeeding 238 years. Preservation of the "religious voting base" of the President has made it politically mandatory to be overtly religiously-observant. But a challenge to the secular constitution comes in the form of religious schools (taxed or not), faith-based legislation, and particularly any presidential, or congressional, proselytizing.

The humanitarian non-religious nature of the Golden Rule qualifies it as secular. In my opinion there needs to be articulate, enthusiastic education in the superb concept of the secular Constitution, and emphasized on the higher plane of rational thought. Susan Jacoby, in the *Nation* magazine, April 19th 2004 says it clearly, "To reclaim their proper place in the public square, secular humanists must reclaim the language of passion and emotion from the religiously correct."

Conscience

Einstein comments in *The Great Quotations,* "Never do anything against conscience, even if the state demands it." I think, what our conscience says to us depends upon what has been said to it. It depends mostly on the teaching received as a child.

Dr. Brock Chisholm-Director General of the World Health Organization, Nov 17th 1963, *Los Angeles Times* headline: "Rigidity of conscience declared destructive." "Whereas men traditionally think of conscience as an unchanging absolute, it isn't. In fact, it must be amenable to continual alteration if man is to adjust to rapid change and survive." Dr. Chisholm categorizes the extreme right wing as composed of persons "who can't change because they use as a standard of authority their own consciences *accidentally acquired while still children.*" Dr. Chisholm did not ignore the left wing, but said only that the more extreme, "tend towards rebellion."

William Morley Punshon, English clergyman 1824 -1881 quoted in *The Arizona Republic,* "Cowardice asks, is it safe? Expediency asks, is it political? Vanity asks, is it popular? Conscience asks, is it right?"

Immanuel Kant in *The Story of Philosophy* says, "Now the most astounding reality in all our experience is precisely our moral sense, our inescapable feeling in the face of temptation, that this or that is wrong. We may yield; but the feeling is there nevertheless." He makes clear that he thinks that everyone's moral sense will tell him real right and wrong. I disagree. Conscience varies. The conscience is primarily formed, I think, by parental or societal influence. Mixed with geopolitical ideology, it assisted the growth of Nazism and Fascism in the 1930s when Heinrich Himmler (showing a perverted theological fear?) stated that, "-some Supreme Being is behind nature and I insist that members of the (Nazi) SS must believe in God." Religion by force! I wonder what was on his conscience when he prominently participated in the Wannsee Conference of 1942, which planned the Final Solution to exterminate the Jews. I think his conscience adjusted to what he believed. That is close to what is meant by the term brain-washing, which is an external attempt to modifyconscience.

In *The Story of Philosophy*, philosopher Voltaire is quoted: "Conscience is not the voice of God, but the fear of the police; it is the deposit left in us, from the stream of prohibitions poured over the growing soul by parents and teachers and press."

In 1948, General Omar Bradley made a very convincing point when he stated in *The Great Quotations*, "The world has achieved brilliance without conscience. Ours is a world of nuclear giants and ethical infants." He was of the age to have seen the lowest ethics levels ever achieved - the Holocaust. Then there was our Bible-quoting, ethics-pretending President George W. Bush, who, with his cohorts, planned, initiated and managed the unnecessary, immoral Iraq War, ravaging Iraq and its people, wasting thousands of Iraqi lives and young American military lives, while putting it on a still-owed Chinese credit card. I would think that his conscience, today, should be agonizing.

There is what I think of as a generally-accepted national conscience, probably, in our case, Judaism-Christian based. Ideally, that should be a morality based conscience. Our personal conscience, accepts that national conscience, by osmosis, or a "group-think." If our national majority thinks so, then some think it must beright!

In the 1960s there were many with immovable consciences such as the several Americans and numerous Buddhists who, facing painful deaths to demonstrate their conviction, burned themselves to death in protest against the Vietnam War. A five-lined newspaper insert in *The Tribune,* Nov 27th 2006. (Paraphrased). Nov 3rd 2006, Malachi Ritscher, set up a video camera; doused him-self with gasoline, and burned him-self to death near a Chicago downtown off ramp, to protest the Iraq War." Was it the only supreme demonstration against the Iraq War? Are our consciences less acute recently?

Faith, Doubt, Trust and Prayer

Many believers, trust in God, or in the Bible, and appear to be totally without any reservation. To them their belief has brought an element of complete, unreserved faith in their religion. However, we need a refinement of the word faith.

Corliss Lamont, Editor of *The Philosophy of Humanism,* "Faith is not something you have or don't have. But something that ebbs and flows in your life and soul. Doubt isn't the opposite of faith. It is an element *of* faith. Where there is absolute certainty there can be no room for faith." In other words, where there is absolute certainty there is no reason, or necessity, for faith. *Faith is only needed when you have doubt.* So if someone says, as I have heard so many times, "I have absolute faith --" they should be saying "I have absolute certainty," if, indeed, that is what they are thinking.

Julian Huxley, in his book, *Knowledge, Morality and Destiny*wrote, "Certainty derived from science, is different from certainty derived from faith. It (faith-based certainty), cannot be shaken by argument." He says again: "Faith is a state of relative certainty but which also includes relative uncertainty."

In *The Great Quotations,* John Stuart Mill referred to faith-based certainty as, "the deep slumber of fixed opinion." Some might say that I also have a "fixed opinion". Indeed, I do. Only my fixed opinion is that opinions should *not* be permanently fixed. It is not faith-based. In other words, I'm not of the opinion I've got the only answer, or that my present opinion, will be my final opinion. This is-where-I-am-at-now. Ronald S. Hendel, Professor- University California, discusses a contemporary example of a closed (faith-based certainty) mind in *Biblical Archaeology Review Magazine*, July/Aug 2012, "As John Calvin stated 'The testimony of the Spirit is more excellent than all reason.'" Referring to a derogatory comment by Alvin Plantinga about critical Bible scholarship Hendel says, "Plantinga is an evangelical Calvinist, speaking for those for whom the Bible is inerrant, and thus immune from reasoned inquiry. He holds that, 'Scripture is inerrant; the Lord makes no mistakes; what he proposes for our belief is what we should believe.'" As described by Hendel, Plantinga might be the believing-individual, who, I think, could, through a psychological-physical reaction, genuinely experience faith healing. In other words, a miracle. I relate these quotes, to illustrate the arrogant certitude of fundamentalism.

Immanuel Kant in *The Story of Philosophy* is quoted as saying, "Again miracles cannot prove a religion, for we can never quite rely on the testimony which supports them; and prayer is useless if it aims at a suspension of the natural laws that hold for all experience."

I don't believe in miracles per se, but acknowledge that the future may produce definitive evidence that there are psychological forces at work which can produce the desired result. I believe that prayer can be of deep emotional help to those who earnestly pray - and emotionally and physically helpful for those who are being prayed for - if they know it. This could be described as pure prayer person to person. I have seen, up close, the mental tranquility that prayer has brought to those who are fervently doing the praying. I appreciate, and have vicariously enjoyed, the warm security that suffuses the devout believer who is comforted by prayer. I would never dissuade any one from that level of belief. I do not crave it, and am content without it.

I have also seen the strength of prayer with one another or in groups; when reinforced by a religious setting such as church or cathedral setting, appropriate pipe organ music, impressive liturgy, moving eloquence and all the other priestly aids such as ornate vestments, incense, and candles. For the psychologically needy, it can be overwhelmingly helpful.

I think this is similar, but not equivalent, to the Serenity Prayer. To be effective, one must have that gut-level, visceral, feeling of religious compliance. Serenity is secured by seeking and then performing some action of change, "God help me to have the courage to change what I can change, have the serenity to accept that which I cannot change, and the wisdom to know the difference." I think it is also similar to something I have experienced in my own life, and something which probably happens to everyone. When you strive to arrive at a decision regarding a major problem - something crucial; you have sleepless nights worrying, planning and courage-building; you arrive at a decision and make it; you may not know the result for many months, but you have serenity, cease worrying and sleep contentedly. Because I do not pray for help in that situation, I think of the result as non-religious, and only psychological.

I have been appropriately placed several times in my life, to have been vicariously moved by the intensity of emotional conversion of a sinner into a, usually evangelical, religious order. Attributed to as the 'Holy Spirit' by the preachers, that emotional "high" cannot be frozen at that level, and, later there are the inevitable relapses, maybe as soon as the following Monday morning. It is impressively transfixing, but has no connection to the Golden Rule. It is not the part of religion that I admire. However, it maybe the part of religion most remembered by many who experienced it.

To the believer, religion can be of greatest help in times of personal crisis and pain. That is when prayer can be of great help to the believer. Theodore Dreiser-American author comments in *The Great Quotations*, "If I was to personally define religion I would say that it is a bandage that man has invented to protect a soul made bloody by circumstance." This is especially true in these days of senseless violence such as current school-shootings, international terrorism, etc.

Children and Religion

Herbert Spencer, Philosopher in the *Story of Philosophy* tells a child, "God made the world" and the child's unanswerable query comes back, "Who made God?"

Obviously, for the devout believer, the teaching of religion is a major part of the upbringing of their children. It is normal, natural, and fulfilling to have your offspring develop in the way you think is appropriate. But it is the "belief system," where caution is needed. I have previously referred to the freedom of thought that my parents employed. Conversations were never contentious; were occasionally argumentative; and never confrontational. As a child among adults, the free flow of ideas and opinion was great, and the idea emerged subtly that there was no monolithic point of view. The child was left with the understanding that there were at least two ideas, and maybe more. The clear message to the child was to think it through and then choose what he/she believed.

The minds of little children have been referred to as, "empty slates" in early life. From my memory of hear-say, I once heard that a deliberately stated policy of the Roman Catholic Church was that, "maintain the teaching of the child until 10 years of age, and the child would remain a Roman Catholic the rest of their lives." No doubt that was Bible-initiated, but applies to all belief systems learned as a child.

Proverbs 22:6 *The Bible,* "Train up a child in the way he should go, even when he is old he will not depart from it."

The Bible gave another view. Corinthians -13:11, "When I was a child, I used to speak as a child, think as a child, reason as a child; when I became a man, I did away with childish things."

This is the point where I think parents have frequently gone astray. The Bible was written by the scribes in a simple direct way for a simple, unsophisticated people. Traditionally, good-intentioned parents opt to continue "the faith of their fathers," and that means that the simple mystical fables and childhood beliefs maybe continued, as though they were truths, into adulthood.

Homer Jack, Editor, of *Religion and Peace* agrees, "Most mainline religions continue their beliefs as though they were little children." I see no reason for the child like stories that we still inculcate into our children without teaching them to question and think at the same time.

Richard Dawkins, *The God Delusion,* "If children were taught to question and think through their beliefs it is a good bet there would be no suicide bombers." He continues, "I thank my parents for taking the view that children should be taught not what to think, but how to think." I am also grateful to my parents for exactly the same reason.

George Santayana, American philosopher- *The Great Quotations,* "What religion a man shall have is a historical accident (usually parent-instilled), quite as much as what language he shall speak."

There is room for thought here because, as a parent, you are the instiller of your own conscience into your child! Think! What a responsibility! I would suggest using only the Golden Rule as your guide. Santayana uses the realistic word, "accidentally" because you are, "accidentally" born to your parents, not the parents next door. Not having yet arrived at self-decision making, your children will reflect your religion. But, as parents, we should not leave the Golden Rule to accident. Alva Edison, U.S. inventor, in *The Great Quotations,* "I do not believe that any type of religion should ever be introduced into the public schools of the United States." However, I insist, teach the Golden Rule as a philosophical non-religious class.

This becomes still more important when one thinks of the generation-to-generation continuation of any belief. I also feel so very grateful that my parents had the policy of freedom of thought, and required no compulsion of belief, and so did not instill into me the life-long burden of unreasoning dogma. In some countries religion is a state- dominated belief system. However, in the Western world countries we are fortunate to live where there is freedom of religion and thought. But guidance by suggestion and example in the Golden Rule is necessary. It is wrong to let a child drift into many mainline religions, where it is assumed a virtue to be satisfied without understanding; and consequently learn to believe that their liturgy and rote is, in their reality- view, religion! The result is that religion is often viewed as shallow in nature.

Margaret Mead in *This I believe* writes very clearly what is the logical over-all conclusion, "I believe that human nature is neither intrinsically good, nor intrinsically evil, but individuals are born with different combinations of innate potentialities, and that it will depend upon how they are reared - to trust and love and experiment and create, *or* to fear, and hate and conform - what kind of human being they become." We have a momentous responsibility in the raising of our children.

Religious Wars

The Bible, Deuteronomy, 20:16, "Only in the cities of these peoples that the Lord your God is giving you as an inheritance, you shall not leave alive anything that breathes." When one carries into battle with him such an unlimited seal of approval of his Almighty God, then one feels invincible, and can feel free to fight with any means in His Holy Name. It is a Holy Invitation to fight with scorched-earth zeal. It parallels todays example of ISIS (ISIL) cruelty against what they view as infidels.

Early histories recorded that people believed their own religion to be the only true religion (little change today), and that all others were a threat. (Fear again!) So religious intolerance came early and Old Testament "history" records many battles of religious origin. The Crusades exceeded all others in savagery. There have been wars over many things but history records the cruel ferocity that appears to accompany religious wars as being more intense than other wars.

President George Washington accurately commented in *The Great Quotations* that, "Of all the animosities which have existed among mankind, those which are caused by a difference in sentiments in religion, appear to be the most inveterate (habitual) and distressing, and ought most to be deprecated."

E. H. Lecky- Historian, *The Great Quotations,* "There is no wild beast so ferocious, as Christians, who differ concerning their faith."

George Sarton, American historian agreed in *The Great Quotations*, saying, "The most malicious kind of hatred is that which is built upon a theological foundation." All war is cruel! However, a divinely-permitted warrior who believes he has a God-given right to destroy another human being is known to exhibit an uncontrolled ferocity. Abandonment to God's approval; His protection; His cause; His service; justifies wanton brutality. Again, the recent (2014) beheadings by the devout ISIS soldiers clearly depict that fact. Washington, Sarton and Lecky were right.

The Golden Rule--Morality

Robert Millikan-American physicist-is quoted in *The Great Quotations* "Three ideas stand out above all others in the influence they have exerted, and are destined to exert, upon the development of the human race: the idea of the Golden Rule, the idea of natural law, and the idea of age-long growth or evolution."

Morality must be founded, not on theology, but on sociology; unchanging revelation or dogma must not determine the good. In my view, the morality of an individual is mainly determined by his use of the Golden Rule. In essence the Golden Rule is the basis for morality. The negative Ten Commandments are entirely, "Thou shall not" commandments, which have been replaced by the positive "ThoughShall" of The Golden Rule. *The Golden Rule* is a philosophical and moral concept, which is a component, but usually *not a mandatory, ritualistic component,* of religion.

The presence of the Golden Rule is so simple, logical, and rewarding that it is easy to think of it, *not* as a part of religion at all. However, it *is* a ubiquitous tenet in most religions; is a central theme of this commentary; and I have isolated over thirty unique ways in which humans have expressed this concept; but, as I do not wish to lose the impatient reader, I shall share only a few distinctive ones.

THE GOLDEN RULE--MORALITY

1. Emerson Hughes Lalonde, in his book *And Thy Neighbor as Thyself,* Quote "In 1790, the declaration of faith in the Universalist-Unitarian Church said: "We believe in the obligation of the moral law." "If we believe in brotherly love, there is no disagreement, can do us any harm." In other words, "the basis of fellowship and union was seen not to be in credo, but in the spirit of love and good will, as the rule of life." In 1949, Clinton Lee Scott in *Religion can make Sense* states that the Unitarian Church teaches that, "The Golden Rule in application, is the capacity to understand the feelings of another, to imagine oneself in his place, and to act in accordance with this imagination." This places the mind in sole control of Golden Rule usage, and is simply and sensitively stated. I think it is nearest to the feeling of "empathy."
2. Buddhism, in *The Great Quotations,* taught his students, "Hurt not others in ways that you yourself would find hurtful."
3. Mother Theresa, quoted St Francis of Assisi, "Lord give me a channel of Thy Peace, that where there is despair I will bring hope, that where there are shadows I may bring light, that where there is sadness, joy." Mother Theresa was a glowing, world-wide example of a life infused with the Golden Rule.
4. Islam - In his book *Muhammad,* Muhammad Assad (author) wrote, "The prophet says 'No one may call himself Faithful who eats his fill while his neighbor remains hungry.'"
5. Aristotle, (Circa 350 BC*), The Story of Philosophy,* "We should behave to our friends as we would wish our friends to behave to us."
6. Alfred Adler - Austrian psychoanalyst (1870—1937) - *The Arizona Republic,* This one, is my favorite version. "There is a law that man should love his neighbor as himself. In a few hundred years it should be as natural to man as breathing or the upright gait; but if he does not learn it he must perish." It

gives me confirmation that there was, and is, someone else out there who is optimistic enough in the human race to believe that it can learn and benefit from the teaching and maximum use of the Golden Rule.

7. Friedrich Nietzsch,1880, *The Story of Philosophy,* "- by Jesus; with him every man was of equal worth, and had equal rights; out of his doctrine came democracy, - socialism." The Golden Rule in Action.

In a **home** where pejorative terms for ethnic groups were never used, one word innocently used in our family in my growing years has made me aware of how imperceptibly one can adopt the usage of a word that maybe distasteful to others. Living near to an Indian reservation, the intermarriage of Indians and the general populace was frequent. The unnecessary word used for their children was *half-breed.* In our home, 80 years ago, it was only used informatively, and never derogatorily. But words develop, or change, and now the words native or Metis (half French and half native) have developed in, at least, Western Canada. I now view, as part of Golden Rule behavior, never to say the word half-breed. No matter how casual or unintended, ethnic slang may be insulting to those for whom it is used. Used with hateful conviction, it is psychologically cruel.

The ideal goal should be to always express approval, appreciation, affection and love for others. And it is important to do it with loving conviction. It will return love a hundred-fold. If that could be transmitted into a national movement or a political party, with that purpose in mind, it would be a winner. It would be part of the Golden Rule education of which I spoke earlier.

Morality: The Golden Rule in Action

Disregarding the negative comments I have made about the entrenched dogma and traditional empty rote of the mainline religions, there is an enormous amount of good that the mainline churches perform. They all have humanitarian programs to take care of the local poor and many support international philanthropic organizations. The average person has a visceral need to help those in need, and that desire, is often reinforced by church programs. An immense amount of the welfare needs of the poor of the nations is thus addressed. They, reliably provide a moral compass for the societal conundrums of their times. Their general aim is directed towards the betterment of all people. They create a cooperative, rewarding group experience. They universally teach the Golden Rule though, in my opinion, often with inadequate emphasis. But, their basic intent is to do Good.

I do not ascribe to the harsh, legalistic approach to separation of church and state by those who would meticulously try to take Christ out of Christmas; enforce a policy of allowing no public prayers and complain about every minor infraction of the law mandating separation of church and state. These are fringe factors in the admirable policy of separation of church and state. The slow progress of progressive change is underway. Mainline churches are routinely recording declining membership. Patience will suffice. These incidentals will eventually disappear.

From ancient times all regions have had their annual, usually religious, festivals. In the 1930s my father's Thanksgiving service, held in the Westmoor country school, was brightened by a drought-limited display of the vegetables and sheaves of grain that neighbors brought to demonstrate their thanks for a harvest however, limited. My child's heart was warmed by the mutual camaraderie, and the generous exchanges of produce. That warmth continued through the Christmas season and I see very good reasons for observing those fulfilling religious traditions. For some, these traditions are central to religious belief. For others they are peripheral. Either way they bring our families together, and provide happy occasions. Encourage them.

The LA Times, Sept 5th 1993, "Meeting of the world religions, leads to an ethical document calling on people to live by a rule that respects all life, individuality and diversity so that every person is treated humanely." A wonderful statement urging a minister, pastor or priest to care for the psychological and physical needs of the people of their community, is real religion.

The Arizona Republic quoting Benito Juarez, Mexican Statesman, 1806-72, "Among individuals, as among nations, peace is the respect of others' rights."

While my wife Olga and I were in Raymore, Saskatchewan, Canada in 2010, we saw the following wonderful social commentary on the wall of the Roman Catholic Church:

Catholic Social Thought:

Action on the behalf of justice and participation in the transformation of the world fully appear to us as a constitutive dimension of the preaching of the Gospel. (Synod on justice in the world, 1974).

- Economic and political decisions must be based on human dignity.
- The primacy of persons over things and of human labor over capital.
- Equality of man and woman.

- Preferential option for the poor.
- Right to life and defense of the human person.
- Constitution must be based on the rights and responsibilities of each human person and nation.
- Promote the good of all because we are responsible for all.
- Right of government to intervene for common and individual good.
- The market economy must be governed by justice and oriented to the common good.
- Common good is attained through cooperation and mutual assistance.
- Rich nations are called to sacrifice income and power for common good.
- Live simply so that others may live.
- Development must respect nature and the common good; human dominion over the Earth is not absolute.
- Everyone has a right to good water and food, the fruits of God's creation.
- Riches and freedom create a special obligation.
- Aid less-developed countries without thought of domination.
- All nations have equal dignity and right to self- development.
- Every human person and nation is interdependent.
- All individuals and nations should share in development.
- Development is a means to peace.
- Right to work and the dignity of work.
- Right of workers to assemble, to unionize, and to a just wage.
- Workers are part owners of the enterprise in which they invest labor.
- Resources are not for arms, but for the alleviation of human misery.
- Disarm, simplify lifestyles, and eliminate waste in rich nations.
- Christian duty calls for participation in public life.
- Infuse man's culture with a Christian spirit.
- Accept responsibility for one's share in injustice and for

conversion.

- Sinful structures exist and must be removed.
- Racial justice is integral to our faith commitment.
- Challenging injustice is an integral part of evangelization. To reference complete texts: www.scarboromissions.ca

From my point of view that is a perfect humanitarian statement. *The Golden Rule* appears in every sentence. This statement illustrates how the social conscience of mainline religions can be harnessed in the pursuit of, in their own words, "justice and the transformation of the world." This statement evokes Alfred Adler's futuristic Golden Rule in religious action and social policy. This statement also evokes the promise of the deep-in-the-future cooperation of all religions and humanists in the evolution of a better future world. This statement also helps to move my opinionated presentation to reality. I wonder if that progressive religious statement is because the church is located in, what was once (I think still is) one of the most progressively political regions in the Western world (see upcoming comments on politics). I hope not! I wish to see it as a world-wide Roman Catholic policy leading to universal global adoption. Meantime it gladdens my heart to have a major supporter of my social affairs opinion, and to see it presented in such a public way. Comments by Pope Francisco I appear to have been identical to the above encyclical. My heart is gladdened.

I think that our Golden Rule dealings with others should include upfront trust of others, until of course proved otherwise. Your trust in others is usually appreciated and reciprocated. Rarely, have I had someone take advantage of me. I have no regrets. Robert Hillyer, American author, poet and professor, agrees by his philosophical comment from *This I believe,* "I believe in the good intentions of others, and I trust people instinctively. My trust has often been betrayed in petty ways, and, once or twice, gravely. I cannot stop trusting people as suspicion is contrary to my nature. Nor would I because the numbers of people who have justified my trust are ten to one to those who have abused it."

In my stripped-down Golden Rule religion there is, as I view it, - a *sin*. It is the guilt trip that one has when one knows that he/she has not lived-up to the gold standard of Golden-Rule performance. I clearly remember, even fairly minor things, from many years ago, for which I still bear a guilty conscience. Conscientiously lived, this then becomes your burden of memory, and in the case of a sensitively remembered major remembrance of guilt, as a *Golden Rule sin,* it can then become your personal Hell.

Some may wonder if I fear death. I do not fear death and it is seldom in my mind, and never to dwell. Not believing in the "here-after", or any essential requirements to enter, what I view as a non-existent heaven, has freed my mind from that concern. I am happy and unworried. However, I do have on my wall a framed comment which reads, "Every day above ground is a good one." I agree with Editor Carroll Binder who, in *This I Believe,* said, "I love life but I am not worried about death." In fact, I find myself agreeing with that dubious authority Timothy O'Leary, (notorious, heroin-justifying, professor) quoted in the LA Times, who said, "I am looking forward to the fascinating experience which is dying. You've got to approach your dying the way you live your life - with curiosity, with hope, with fascination, and with courage."

As a compassionate liberal, my vote for any candidate for legislative office would depend, *NOT* upon the rigid religious concerns of the religious candidate but upon the candidate's promises, and, or, past support of Golden Rule issues such as education, health, social welfare, war, peace and freedom.

I have been married three times in my life. By "playing it cool" I have survived the religious wishes of my three spouses (Episcopalian, Baptist and Roman Catholic). Knowing the psychological, soothing effect that church attendance brings to the devout believer, I have tried to maintain my spouse's love of her religion. I have readily attended church with them; and have attentively listened to seventy years of homilies and associated dogma. I have never been a member of any of those churches, but I know that I have had more contented spouses, and a more tranquil home-life. Also, I know that I will not later bear the stressful psychological "sin" of having disregarded the Golden Rule in my relationship with them.

You could say, correctly, that religion should have formed a more important role when I was considering marriage in the first place; that a couple united on what they believe could have achieved so much more if they both believed in - whatever; that I was too acquiescent with my religious wives, and my friends; and that I should have taken a more influential or leadership role in making my own beliefs clear.

Yes, indeed! I plead guilty. However, I wished to respect the state of the other person's belief, and not preach my own. Maybe I was wrong, but to me, that exemplified my belief and simultaneously emphasized their freedom of belief. They each came to our marriage as adults with mature religious beliefs. I also came with a mature point of view. I would never have tried to convert their religious beliefs to my own individual point of view. My private and public life has been lived with others of differing views. I have never proselytized others. It is a missing quality in my personality that I have always been aware of - lack of assertiveness in presenting my point of view. That is why I was concerned enough to write the chapter titled *Do I have a* Conscience?

On all levels of society, the Golden Rule is fulfilled when one does their maximum to help those who are needy. Because she gave her maximum, Jesus referred to the poor woman who gave a 'mite' to the church as giving more than others. The mite represents the absolute minimum in coinage, presently similar to a penny. Everyone deserves appreciation for their gift. But when the very rich are generous, as in the case of Bill and Melinda Gates, it deserves comment.

USA Today, Dec 2nd 2015- "Mark Zuckerberg and his wife, Dr. Priscilla Chan, billionaires (currently worth about $45 billion), to celebrate the birth of a baby girl, plan to give away 99% of Face Book shares 'through a new initiative to advance human potential and promote equality for all children in the next generation'." That is the automatic personal Golden Rule response, which I have advocated.

Familial Golden Rule

Illustration of the usage of the Golden Rule is described clearly in this description of my father from *The Touchwood Times* newspaper, Punnichy, Saskatchewan, Canada, dated July 1st 1943:

"It is the good fortune usually for every district to have at least one outstanding personality - one to whom the neighbors can go for help and advice in time of trouble, sickness or adversity in any form. Such a one was Mr. James Meakes the news of whose death on Thursday of last week stunned with grief the people of the entire community." "To those who had known him for many years his loss would be deeply felt, for his kindly help had been experienced by many and in every part of the community, where he was so widely known, sorrow would be felt at his passing." "Seldom indeed does any individual command the respect and the admiration of everybody with whom he is acquainted, but of Mr. Meakes it can be truthfully said that he had no enemies. One came away from even a casual visit with him feeling uplifted and encouraged, and with a brighter outlook on life, feeling more determined than ever to overcome any and every obstacle. He will be sadly missed by all --." The independent observation of my father's consistent adherence to living the Golden Rule is made very clear by the writer. It is a great example of service-to-others on a small stage - his neighborhood. It is an adult demonstration of the childhood hymn, "Brighten the corner where you are." Our lives maybe lived in the most mundane circumstances but our lives can be of incremental significance to our friends, families, and to the next generations, merged of course, by equal genetic and cultural influences from each added spouse. It does not make us less responsible for our own actions, just more aware of past influences.

I, and my four older brothers, probably fitted into that mundane category. It is only that Harry through his religious integrity, and Frank through his political integrity, were probably better able to attain a greater level of Golden Rule dissemination than the rest of us did. Disregarding the gene input of the spouses it is tempting to trace my father's shining example to subsequent generations. This observation maybe simplistically true but with merging strands how can one measure?

My niece Lavona, grand-daughter of my father and daughter of my brother Jamie and Lucabelle, born 1939, graduated as a registered nurse in 1960, and that same year, married Mowat Edgar (Ed) Mc-Ilwraith (1936-2005). She spent her entire working life in a Premie (Premature birth) hospital ward. In addition to raising four children of their own, they performed the worthy task of fostering about 14 children. Then they adopted Jill at her age of about 6 months. With the diagnosis of Fetal Alcoholic Syndrome Disease (FASD) which brings the certainty of retardation, *they already knew* they were entering a generation-long period of frustration and anguish. What else, but an innate Golden Rule drive to help the helpless, would have them rescue Jill? Ed and Lavona possessed the resolute courage to strive to overcome those obstacles to success; struggle with the inadequate assistance of a malfunctioning foster agency; attend the FASD organization's informative meetings; frustratingly struggle with Jill's continual under-performance; her imprecise levels of communication and understanding; and suffer the anguish of knowing that success is neither perfection or normalcy - but only the best that is possible. Now about 30 years of age, Jill has many problems, but is functioning in a married setting within the framework of her ability, and is "showing signs of further maturation." My admiration for Ed and Lavona is boundless. What a tremendous act of dedicated, frustrating sacrifice to one of the neediest of individuals!

Their daughter, Naomi, also inherited their dedication to helping others, and also their determination, when faced with the "long haul." Retracing an historic trade route in the summer of 1989 she, and five other University of Alberta students, took an exhausting, but adventurous, three-month canoe trip along the North Saskatchewan River from the Canadian Rockies to Thunder Bay, Ontario, Canada. That was a trip of extraordinary exertion; paddling long hours; undergoing mosquito laden back-waters; carrying all canoes and supplies over numerous portages; and sleeping on the ground for more than a month. That alone, demonstrates Naomi's determination. That was not enough! In her early thirties, she raised funds for a camp for disadvantaged children in Edson, Alberta by riding a bicycle, by herself, across Canada, from the Pacific Ocean to the Atlantic Ocean. Can you imagine the endless mesmerizing miles of farmland and prairie; rocks and trees; the daily concern for "tonight's lodging"; navigating the incessant traffic in cities; slogging through the inevitable winds and storms; and the cramp-inducing climb on those high mountain passes. What a demonstration of grit, and of deeply implanted Golden Rule behavior! I was so proud of her!

Naomi then used that same determination to survive without a car; work part time at minimum wage; pay her own way; and in 2007, graduate with her Master's degree in Literature. But there is a Golden Rule motive at work here too. Through her grandmother, my Metis sister-in-law Lucabelle, Naomi is also of part native ("Indian") descent. Naomi's well-founded, deeply-held, accurate conviction is that 150 years of Anglo domination of the native Indian culture and religion, in both the USA and Canada, has sentenced the reservation natives to loss of their native language; to inferior schooling; to major unemployment; to inadequate medical and social attention; to worship the oppressor's alien religion; and to an aimless and hopeless existence from which very few can ever escape.

The dignity of the natives and their culture would receive a major stimulus if ever their language was re-established. I am reminded of how Israel could have accepted one of their occupier's languages (Roman, Arabic, Turkish, and English) as their nation's official language. But long before it reached its 1948 status as a nation, it was deeply influenced by Elizar Ben Yehuda, (1858-1922), an individual who single- handedly sparked a movement to restore the use of the "dead" Hebrew language to Israel. It is now used exclusively in official government and social affairs, schools, newspapers and home. It was resurrected from literal oblivion, and Hebrew now identifies Israel, as the land of those who speak it. It played a major role in the psychological restoration of Israel, and because it has been in official and universal Israeli use, it is inspiring Israelis in their unique authentic peoplehood.

Alice Phelps, Oglala Lakota College, in their booklet, *Awakening to Wisdom,* "Where my people speak the Lakota language, there is a sense of respect."

Naomi's thesis for her Master degree was, "A creative study of Nehiyawewin, the Plains Cree Language, and the reasons for its preservation." She has since co-authored *The Beginning of Print Culture in Athabasca country* (Lac La Biche, Alberta, Canada, a translation into English of a phonetic Cree alphabet, invented and printed, by Father Emile Grouard in 1883; authored *Kiyâm,* a book of mixed English and Cree language poetry, dedicated to the previously-mentioned Jill; and co-contributed to *Telling Truths - Storying Motherhood.* The latter has a glowingly eloquent tribute to her mother Lavona, and her thirty years of unsung, selfless dedication to a predestined incompleteness of result in the raising of Jill. She is currently under contract to the City of Edmonton, Alberta, Canada to write a book regarding Fetal Alcoholic Syndrome.

Naomi's life-long Golden Rule effort is to raise the dignity and standing of the Cree people, aiming first at getting the language on paper. I admire her focus of purpose and the resolute perseverance with which she is already achieving growing public awareness of the

150-year-old, historical, miscarriage of social justice. Illustrating the existing problem, as I observed in July 2013, a 55-year-old Muskowecan (Cree Indian) Reservation resident could not answer Naomi when she spoke to him in the Cree language. "The Mission never taught us," he said. How does one deal with those non-Cree roots, firmly established in every native brain? I hope I am wrong, but she appears to be faced with the same situation as were her parents, when they accepted Jill's less-than-perfect result.

Charlene, sister of Naomi, and her husband Dave Sorkin, while on vacation in Cambodia, about eight years ago, found and "adopted" an extremely needy school and orphanage. They visit the school annually, bringing school supplies, gifts, financial support, (including 4 tons of rice this year of 2014), and personally delivered unrestrained love from Edmonton, Alberta, Canada. What a wonderful Golden Rule gesture! You might say that that action is not financially possible by most of us. But even if we were able to, how many of us have the Golden Rule so deeply imbedded in our beings to do the same? I freely say, that I, for one, would probably not have done so. They have my great admiration! Just what the world needs! They have, as a close friend, *Phymean Noun,* founder of Peoples Improvement Organization, and winner of the *2015 Nobel Children Prize* presented by the Queen of Norway.

I am so very proud of my son, Michael Glenn Meakes, and my grand-daughter, Charity Joy Meakes. They appear to be on their own this-is-where-I-am-at-now life journeys, with very strong Golden Rule principles showing up in their lives.

Michael currently works as director of IT, for Living Classrooms,a non-profit, charitable organization in the Baltimore, Maryland harbor. Its object is to provide education and training for the under-privileged youth of society. He could be earning twice his current salary, working for a for-profit company. In observance of the Golden Rule, and in an undiluted gesture of good will, he recently, deliberately and generously, relinquished his interest in a family property to a much greater degree than was considered necessary or appropriate.

In the book *Religion Can Make Sense,* Clinton Lee Scott recalls, "A minister describing the great 1928 stock market collapse said that many at a large bank legally saved their fortunes and "urged my friend to do likewise. But he chose to surrender everything he possessed toward reimbursing the depositors of his bank. Fellow businessmen said he was a fool. Perhaps this was not success in business, but it was success in religion which is more important." Mike's gesture was also a Golden Rule success in inter-personal relationship. I admire him!

Will Durant in *The Story of Philosophy* quotes Immanuel Kant, "The only thing unqualifiedly good in this world is good will - the will to follow the moral law, regardless of profit or loss for ourselves." Mike has demonstrated the attitude of unrestrainedly helping others all of his life. He might argue about this, but I view him as a "religious" man in the best sense of the word. I am so very proud of him. Still another major intellect reminds me of Mike. In *The Great Quotations,* Benjamin Disraeli, British prime minister, comments, "It is more virtuous to act ethically without hoping for a reward in the afterlife, than with such a hope in mind."

Granddaughter, Charity J. Meakes, has simply exuded unrestrained good will all of her life. Through KIVA, and similar organizations, she has helped people in all parts of the world loaning money for home development or to start or expand private mini-enterprises. Using her own money, she has placed over 2,000 small loans to individuals or small groups in over 80 countries. Loving others, one at a time! The present and the future of these needy people will be immensely brightened. Another example is her support for *Women's Learning Partnership* (for Rights, Development and Peace). www.learningpartnership.org, Once again a future oriented concept. What a wonderful example to others!

Three quotations that remind me of her were made by Mother Theresa and taken from *Great Quotes from Great People,* "Do not wait for leaders; do it alone, person-to-person." Again, "If you can't feed a hundred people, then feed just one." And again, "In this life we cannot do great things, we can only do small things with great love." Howard

Zinn- *Peoples History of the United States* wrote, "We don't have to engage in grand heroic action to participate in the process of change. Small acts, when multiplied by millions of people can transform the world."

Charity's perpetually sunny personality is undoubtedly explained by President George Washington *in Great Quotes from Great Leaders,* "Happiness and moral duty are inseparably connected." Maintaining her happiness and her self-worth by good-works! Charity recently commented that she was going to defer moving from her apartment a few months as she didn't want to inflict stress on the landlord's family. Even landlords! I couldn't be more pleased, or wish for more.

Wonderfully appropriate of all of their actions, Albert Schweitzer, in his autobiography, *The Light Within Us,* commented, "It was, and still is, my conviction that the humanitarian work to be done in the world, should, for its accomplishment, call us as men, not as members of any particular nature or religious body." That comment is so wonderfully appropriate of all their actions. I am extremely proud of all of them. They are members of the "Golden Rule religion"! Schweitzer's "light within us" has shone from all of them!

As the inheritance line contains many other individuals, I will not claim, but only suggest, that my parent's Golden Rule teaching *may be* extending to at least the fourth generation. I have lived my entire adult years far from other family members, and if I knew, I would probably find others in my parent's extended family who have their own inspiring stories. I am sure that it may occur in all families, everywhere.

The Future of Religion

"Religion is not what is grasped by the brain, but is a heart-grasp." These insightful words came from Mohandas Gandhi, Hindu Nationalist Leader in *The Great Quotations.* He points clearly to the requisites of any true religion. "It must be satisfying and rewarding to the physical and psychological needs of every one."

A prophet I am not. An optimist I am. So I can only assume that religion will modify slowly to the wisdom of mankind. That would logically result in an increased understanding of the psychological reasons for the human need for theological belief. This, in turn, would lead to a diminishing role of theologically based religion. The inherent goodness of mankind would retain the residual basis for religion - the Golden Rule, with a natural increase in humanitarian programs. That is what religion is all about - minus the dogma. I was enormously encouraged by the progressiveness of the Raymore Roman Catholic social statement. Thinking optimistically, I think this process will take a century or two, or more.

Jawaharlal Nehru Prime Minister of India, 1936, in *The Great Quotations* says it plainly, "I want nothing to do with any religion concerned with keeping the masses satisfied to live in hunger, filth and ignorance. I want nothing to do with any order, religion, or otherwise, which does not teach people that they are capable of becoming a true man, master of his fate and captain of his soul. To attain this, I would put priests to work, also, and turn the temples into schools."

Eleanor Roosevelt in 1952, in *This I believe,* speaks so eloquently of what I feel, that I need to quote her more fully. "I think I was fortunate because I grew up in a family where there was a deep religious feeling. I don't think it was spoken of a great deal. It was more or less taken for granted that everyone held certain beliefs and needed certain reinforcements of their own strength and that that came through your belief in God and your knowledge of prayer. But as I grew older I questioned a great many things that I knew very well my grandmother, who had brought me up, had taken for granted. And I think that I might have been a very difficult person to live with if it hadn't been for the fact that my husband (President FDR) once said it didn't do any harm to learn these things, so why not let your children learn them? When they grow up they will think things out for themselves. And that gave me the feeling that perhaps that's what we all must do - think out for ourselves what we could believe and how we could live by it. And so I came to the conclusion that you had to use this life to develop the very best that you could develop." She then questions whether there is a future life and says that it doesn't really matter, "because whatever the futureheld you'd have to face it, just as whatever life holds you have to face it in the same way." Her final thought was that whatever we did, "to do it as well as we possibly could. ". Wonderful words!

Immanuel Kant is quoted in *The Story of Philosophy,* "Churches and dogma have value only in so far as they assist the moral development of the human race. Where mere credo or ceremonies usurp priority over moral excellence as a test of religion, religion has disappeared. The real church is a community of people, however, scattered and divided, who are united by their devotion to the common moral law."

Martin Luther King, *Where do we go from here?* Future religionists of any color would all do well to consider MLK's apt comment, "There are still too many Negro churches that are so absorbed in the future good "over-yonder," that they condition their members to adjust to the present evils "over here." In my view this applies to many mainline, (any color) churches. Martin Luther King also wrote, "I suggested that only a dry-as-dust religion (would) extol the glories of Heaven while ignoring the social conditions that cause men an earthly hell." That is why the Unitarian Church's concept of concern for the 'here and now' appealed to me.

The social thought of the Roman Catholic Church in Raymore, Saskatchewan, Canada made evident to me that regardless of the archaic ritualism and theological gibberish, mainline religions can still be socially progressive which appeals to me as a Golden Rule religionist. *As the whole law is fulfilled in the statement, 'you shall love thy neighbor as thyself' (Galatians 5:14), SO, taken literally, this could be Biblical permission that the Golden Rule can be a valid religion without rituals and dogma.* This is the Moral Code at its simplest and to the degree that formal mainline religions practice this concept, I approve and am contented with them.

Arnold Toynbee in *The Story of Philosophy* expounds, "Man cannot exist without fatherhood of mankind (God) or an orthodoxy or fixed pattern of fundamental belief."

Toynbee is joined in this view by Robert Hutchins and Einstein, and I think I understand their opinion that the unfocussed populace would need a central, driving, inspiring, devotion-necessary focus, to work for, and to follow. However, in his phrase, an "orthodoxy or fixed pattern of fundamental belief," why not consider a body of progressive thought which would probably become refined and more focused over the coming millennia? That core-focus would become a sort of polished, improved beacon in the search for the fulfillment of a better world of the Brotherhood of Man. This open-ended concept would allow us to, with free minds, search, surmise, question, and to continue our, this-is-where-we-are-at-now sojourn. I think maybe I may have dabbled too deeply in this philosophical morass!

Some wonderful warm Golden Rule comments follow, the first by Jackie Robinson the first black major league baseball player, who had suffered greatly from the injustices of black segregation in *This I believe*, "I believe in the human race - I believe in the warm heart - I believe in man's integrity - I believe in the goodness of a free society. And I believe that society can remain good only so long as we are willing to fight for it, - and to fight against any imperfection that may exist." This from someone who had suffered much at the hands of the bigotry of the time! What a kind, intelligent, forgiving guy!

Steve Zabilski, Executive Director of St Vincent de Paul. *The Arizona Republic*-Nov 19-2012, "400 years ago St Vincent de Paul dedicated his life to serving others. He lives in us, in each of us, and our actions strengthen those individual threads that bind us together. And through this we all come together to discover a special blessing like no other. The more one does for others, the greater one's abundance. Beginning today, let us commit ourselves to a bold vision. Today let us become the society of zero excuses. The society, that never gives up on people. The society of love. Indeed, is this not our destiny? Is this not what we are created to do?" An organizational Heart of Gold! Wonderfully, wonderfully stated!

From a placemat, in the *Pantry Restaurant,* in Penticton, BC, Canada in 1999:

> *The more you give, the more the more you get. The more you laugh the less you fret.*
> *The more you do unselfishly, the more you live abundantly.*
> *The more of everything you share, the more you'll always have to spare.*
> *The more you love, the more you'll find, that life is good and friends are kind.*
> *For only what we give away, enriches us from day to day.*

The future of religion is currently secure, though in my idealistic, distant future, I can see its' dogma dwindling under the impact of education, science, and philosophical inroads. That trend may be already underway. As long as it promotes the health, education, and social well-being of the world community, it will still have its place in society, and, I would be contented.

Tom Meacham, *Time* magazine, March 5th 2012, Titled Time to Compromise. "In 1908 the Unitarian William Howard Taft ran against the Evangelical William Jennings Bryan. Bryan supporters attacked Taft's faith; that year a Pentecostal newspaper wrote: "Think of the United States with a president who does not believe that Jesus Christ was the Son of God, but looks on the immaculate Savior as a low cunning imposter." Defending Taft, (President) Theodore Roosevelt said that the real test of a potential president was whether he was a good man, and the answer to that question was enough."

Tom Meacham, *Time* Magazine, August 16 2012, Titled, "Heaven can't wait." Meacham speaks eloquently of the heaven-on-earth concept. "Heaven thus becomes, for now, the reality one creates in the service of the poor, the sick, the enslaved, and the oppressed. It is not paradise in the sky but acts of selflessness and love that brings God's sacred space and grace to a broken world suffused with tragedy." Again wonderfully stated! My dream is of a world where these principles universally apply. The goal is a humanitarian one. I admire all the mainline religions which have a plan to achieve this Utopia. But PLEASE! Compassionate society only! The theological ritualistic, dogma-laden distractions are unnecessary!

Clinton Lee Scott, *Religion Can Make Sense.* Though written in 1949, it is still perfect for 2012 AD. "We need for our times a simplified religion. The old world theologies which dominate the religious thinking in America are not only confusing but they are quite unrelated to our Spiritual needs. So unreasonable is much that the churches teach, it is not expected that the people understand. What cannot be understood in any rational sense, we are told must be taken on faith. We need a religion that makes sense with the scientifically understood world that can live in the sane mind with reason. A second need is an understanding of religion, not as blind faith, but as a way of living. To remember that we are one family, and that we must learn to live together on this one planet, the home of us all, and this can be done only as we claim for ourselves that which we are willing to share

- this is to put into practice the gospel of Universalism in action."The Golden Rule!

As my where-I-am-at-now belief, seems to me to be closest to the belief system of the Humanist and/or Unitarian Church - the Universalist, all-inclusive concept, I will leave you with its guidelines.

But first Kurt Vonnegut, *Great Quotations from Great Leaders,* "I am a humanist, which means, in part, that I have tried to behave decently without any expectation of reward or punishment when I am dead."

Emerson Hughes Lalonde in *And thy Neighbor as Thyself,* "How does one become a Unitarian? Not by the required acceptance of dogmatic credo. To become a Unitarian, you should: 1 -feel within your heart and mind the love of freedom of thought and conscience; 2.-recognize the demand of the voice of reason, challenging you to examine the truths you would incorporate into the texture of your personal faith; 3.-affirm and promote the dignity of man; 4.-remain receptive to new knowledge and; 5.-uphold the ideals of democracy. It is your own mind and heart that will make you a Unitarian. "

Early U.S. Unitarians were: President Thomas Jefferson, President John Adams, President John Quincy Adams, George Bancroft, William Cullen Bryant, William Ellery Channing; Ralph Waldo Emerson, Supreme Court Justice Oliver Wendell Holmes, Henry W. Longfellow, James Russell Lowell, Horace Mann, Frances Parkman and President William Howard Taft.

I regret to say that though I agree with, and endorse, all I have described above, I have not been in any Unitarian Church for nearly 50 years. I thought I didn't need to be in a formal church, or need to perform any ritual, and was trying to elsewhere fulfill my concept of the Golden Rule. I have instead attended the traditional churches of my spouses. It could be said that I have failed in exposing myself to a Unitarian church environment in which to meet a "soul-mate" with compatible beliefs - which would, of course, be true. I guess I didn't think of religion as one of my priorities in marriage. Writing this, I have found myself more introspective, and realize that I should have.

PERSPECTIVE

As I said in my 1996 commentary, I have profound awe at the incredible immensity of the universe, the astonishing diversity of natural life, the marvelous complexity of their structures, their vibrant bodies, most especially our own. My 1938 question to my brother Harry still confounds me: If there is a wall at the end of space, then what is beyond the wall? Even with Albert Einstein's theory of circular space - what is outside the circle? There is so much that we will probably never know about this universe!

Albert Einstein in his writings in *Ideas & Opinions* comments, "I am satisfied with the mystery of the eternity of life and a glimpse of the existing world, together with the devoted striving to comprehend a portion, be it ever so tiny, of the Reason that manifests itself in nature."

My Religion

It should be clear from my previous comments what my personal religious principles are likely to be. Ideally I should have been active in full participation in a local church, or organization, in which I could contribute and achieve fulfillment. Due to real, or perceived, obstacles I was usually not active locally. That, I regret. My life would have been immensely enriched. Alternatively, my philanthropy has been home- based. I have, of course, tried to be a friendly, cooperative, helpful neighbor. Periodically, I have sent random contributions to those organizations in which I believed. These involve about 70 humanitarian organizations including American 'Indian' groups, refugees, international and American poor, the blind, Alzheimer's, etc. For many years, that has been *my religion.* It is important to first establish the integrity of the organization. Two websites to assist in doing this are: *thelifeyoucansave.org* and *givewell.org.*

The following nine organizations strive for worthy principles to improve the world of the future and in the process directly or indirectly, help the needy. I have removed them from the random list, and put them on a monthly, sustaining, contribution.

Tolerance. The Southern Poverty Law Center (SPLC), 400 Washington Avenue, Montgomery Alabama 36104. No others focus so relentlessly on discrimination, and on action against hate-based organizations.

Justice. The American Civil Liberties Union, (ACLU), PO Box 96265, Washington, DC 20077-7100. They impartially stand for constitutionally-based equality and justice for all. Their principles are so strong they sometimes make us uncomfortably question the stand that they take.

Religion. The American Humanist Association, 1777 T Street NW, Washington DC 20009-7125. They clearly state my moral beliefs, and moral beliefs are my religious beliefs. They are heavily oriented towards caring for the needy of the "here and now."

Public Integrity. The Center for Public Integrity, 910 17th Street, NW 7th Floor, Washington DC 20006. They are a very careful watchdog of integrity in journalism, politics and government.

Anti-war. American Friends Service Committee (AFSC), 1501 Cherry Street, Philadelphia, PA 19102-1403. Unequivocal, articulate and historical resistance to war.

Charity. United Nations Children's Fund (UNICEF), Dept. F, PO Box 27780, Newark, NJ 07101-7780. Trustworthy and reliable in their concern for the health, welfare and future of global children.

Global Education. United World College, PO Box 248, Montezuma, NM 87731-0248. They are an undisputed, seasoned leader in global education.

Global Movement. World Federalist Movement-Institute for Global Policy (WFM-IGF), Suite 1715, 708 3rd Avenue, New York, NY 10017. Having been over 50 years as a member, I view them as the leader in promotion of global federation.

Global Movement. Citizens for Global Solutions, 420 7th St SE, Washington D.C. 20003-2796. CGS is a 68-year-old organization, involved in major reforms to the United Nations at Hague Institute for Global Justice. If I were an American, I would support politically progressive entities or candidates, two of which are the following:

1. Senator Bernie Sanders, Democratic Socialist, PO Box 391, Burlington. VT 05402, running as a Democrat for the presidency.
2. Wellstone Action, Suite 170, 2446 University Ave W,St Paul, MN 55114. The progressive political heritage of Senator Paul (and Sheila) Wellstone killed in a plane accident in 2002, has been continued by their sons and an active staff, by creating and training candidates for a national progressive movement from local school boards to federal political offices. These are two entities that are attempting to make the changes about which I dream.

It is probable that the other worthy organizations that Icontribute to, will also be helped by the election of these progressive candidates. Your choice of organizations would probably differ in priorities from mine but all are worthy causes. Organizations, which work for the future, and which I feel fulfill my "religious" or philosophical beliefs, (most of which I have contributed to in the past few years), are the following:

Environmental Defense Fun
National Resources Defense Council
The Nature Conservancy
Defenders of Wildlife Greenpeace
The Wilderness Society
National Park Foundation
Union of Concerned Scientists
League of Conservation Voters

Common Cause
Progressives United
Democratic Socialists of America
Emily's List
Amnesty International
Human Rights Watch
Doctors Without Borders
The UN Refugee Agency (UNHCR)
The United Nations Foundation
Physicians for Social Responsibility (PSR)
Global Exchange
Peace Action, formerly, Sane Nuclear Policy
Alternatives to Militarism
War Resisters League
Citizen Soldier
RESIST
Center for Inquiry
The Interfaith Alliance
Kiva
FINCA
Heifer International

Also several specific charities and Indian charities that address today's humanitarian needs. These are my religion.

When I started this book, I could never have believed that I would ever find myself expounding on my "religious" beliefs. But this is an example of "where-I-am-at-now" thinking, and I now realize that, post-humously, I will be considered what in my life I was so desirous not to be - preachy! So be it!

Do I Have a Conscience?

This little digression is to inform the reader that my conscience has not always been sure it was right; and is even now demonstrating that it is also not unchangeable. The following conversation of "Old" and "New" is intended to show that perpetual, intracranial argument that probably many of us have. "Old" is intended to be an entity representing my thinking of previous years, while the words of New portray what has been in my head more recently. This is a method of conveying to you, that I am very aware of other points of view, and what might have happened had I reacted differently to my conscience of any given date.

Do I have a conscience? Yeah! I really do have a conscience. He is a new recruit and like a new broom he really wants to sweep clean. His current irritating message is typically pushy.

"Hi Dave: I'm NEW. HR (Human Relations) department fired OLD. Now his revealing files are *MINE!* He'd goofed enough! One of his bigger boo-boos was that he let you get away with *NOT* talking enough to friends, family, who-ever, - about those big things in life - your so-called religion, your unpopular politics, and about your fixation on the immorality of the Vietnam War. You maintained your cowardly 'loner' status because as the files record, you couldn't discuss this or that because you felt you shouldn't, because you were not a U.S.

citizen; that you couldn't discuss this or that because it would upset an opinionated spouse; that you couldn't discuss this or that because you would sound like a "know-it-all;" and your twisted view was that, as sins of omission, they wouldn't be as important as sins of commission-so keeping your mouth shut would keep your "sin-count" squeaky clean. But OLD never considered that these concerns would, in later life, become your long term views of your *Golden Rule sins of omission,* and so *now* you view them as equally bad! So now you have to live with the fact that, looking back, your record appears definitely deficient.

The files record that over 50 years ago, in 1962, you told that opinionated, domineering, inflexible Baptist pastor (HFC) that you thought all religions were "Bunk" and that they should just fade away leaving only humanitarian organizations. You know that I have no big problem with that. But why were you so uppity with him while you seldom really talked honestly with anyone else about those important things? And why could you write to all those important politicians about the immorality of the Vietnam War but seldom discuss the politics of it with others? You know what I think? J.K. Rowling nailed it in *Brilliant Thoughts* with the comment, "It takes a great deal of bravery to stand up to your enemies, but just as much to stand up to your friends." Dave, you just ain't the brave type!

You know, you sound like you think your opinion that you were a loner, served a sort of psychological need. But remember when you asked that psychiatrist Dr. "M" why you were psychologically comfortable in your office acting as "Dr. Know-it-all'," but was a reclusive mute at a party, and he said "It's obvious! You were the "expert" in your office, whereas you don't know a damn thing about social relationships. You should break out of your shell, say your piece, and mingle. You know something? He was 'right on.' If you had been a joiner of churches, school organizations, and many worthy business organizations it would have given you a fulfilling experience and a much better chance to practice your much-loved Golden rule! So instead you coasted along in your smug little existence, and, except for treating your patients, you were not living a complete, "life of service" to others. You failed to disseminate to others, what you *now* know was important. So now you're impelled to spend 4 years in writing this transparent clarification of what you should have been saying all along. You failed to exercise your ballyhooed Golden Rule when you had the opportunity!" Dr. M told you but, good!

Man! Are you ever hung up on your Golden Rule concept! You know it's been around for several millennia yet you talk about it like you invented it! The big difference is that they were doing it, and not just yakking about it! You gave up your 1997-98 mentoring of parentless boys! That was a wonderful opportunity! You could have gone on making time to do that. Remember how good you felt? Your new marriage brought "family obligations," you told them. Nuts! Why your lack of assertiveness? You never really had the guts to give an up-front opinion to others. You never even played square with your family! What a contrast with your Dad and your brothers! You never really talked to anybody about what mattered to you; what was really in your fat head. So nobody ain't ever listened to you because, you ain't ever talked. I guess I have to remind you again of those wise words of Mistahi Maskwa from *Kiyâm* "words ain't power if no one is listening. The silence will kill you." As your new conscience, I'm in a position to *know* that the silence is killing you. How could you keep it from me?

Somewhere in your unpublished manuscript *American Citizenship Reconsidered,* you hinted that coming to the United States in 1958, bringing your 36-year-old Canadian conscience with you, gave you such high-level integrity that you didn't feel free, with honesty, to sign the American oath of allegiance. Don't you think that bordered on baloney? The records show that OLD argued heavily to do as you did, but that he also presented another valid point of view. Put succinctly- if you had closed your eyes, held your nose, zipped your mouth, hunched your shoulders and swallowed hard - you could have signed the U.S. allegiance pledge, got the right to vote, and then went out and fought like hell for what you believed! You know you soothed Old by using your non-American-citizenship status so you wouldn't have to make those conspicuous overt statements about your beliefs. Instead, because you blended smoothly; you took the covert route regarding your non-citizen status. You kept mute!

President Woodrow Wilson in *The Great Quotations* was thinking of guys like you when he said, "Life does not consist of thinking, it consists of doing." Had you taken U.S. citizenship, your half century of doing-nothing wouldn't now be causing you sleepless nights, especially since this project became paramount! You know, Dave, your stupid lack of action, your abject loner-ism, and thus, your *apparent* lack of conviction in your causes - your silence - has now given me your ear. Remember that when you die no one will mess up your precious face, or force closure of your mouth. Those mocking hostile arguments, that you detested and avoided, will not be a problem. So mouth-off now!

You seem to love quotations so here is one from a very wise man in his book *Strength to Love,* Martin Luther King wrote, "Our lives begin to end the day we become silent about things that matter." Do you recognize yourself? Good! Then how about a couple more which apply to you now and *also* applied to you in those early years. Walt Disney in *Great Quotes from Great People* said, "Our heritage and ideals, our codes and standards - the things we live by and teach our children - are preserved or diminished by how freely we exchange ideas and feelings." Boy! Does that one ever nail you! Those missed opportunities to say your piece! But here's another: *Shakespeare* had Polonius tell his son Laertes, "First above all: to thine own self be true, and it must follow, as the night the day, though canst not be false to any man." Does it sound like you put on a false face Dave? You really didn't say what you *really* thought. Were you true to yourself? Nope!

In this account you have solved part of your problem by already getting "preachy" about your naïve "religion," so now you gotta do the same for politics. You know, Dave, you could shut my whiney mouth by remembering that "confession is good for the soul", which simply means, if you fess-up, I'll *have to* shut up. Oh yeah! A final comment: Your 54 years in the USA has left no mark, no life-statement and a wobbly life example. You were nearly worthless! You needn't have existed at all! If there is salvation for you now it is to unzip your mouth, not just about war-related politics, but about all things. So! Go for it! Signed, Your' prickly buddy - NEW."

You see what I mean? NEW has certainly perfected the put-down! I got along OK with OLD - but am I ever struggling to adjust toNEW. I guess I should have let him dominate Old a lifetime ago. He really is more overbearing and obnoxious than OLD. But I have tried to soothe him by telling him that *as his peace of mind and my peace of mind are synchronized, I will make him contented.*

PART THREE
POLITICAL OPINIONS

Contemporary Politics

Even though present day politics is not relevant to this writing effort, NEW now forces me to say a short "my-piece" about the 2012 U.S. Presidential election. I once owned a corporation (a mighty small one), so I know that it is considered by Internal Revenue to be a separate entity. But it is absurd that the U.S. Supreme Court allows a corporation to be considered as a separate entity for voting purposes and so to allow *UNKNOWN* immense interest groups to pour hundreds of million dollars to influence and finance elections. That is corporate money! That is buying election results! That *is NOT* the Golden Rule! The result will *NOT* be a vote by the people. The billions of dollars poured into the right wing political coffers by the Koch Brothers, and by others over on the left as well, are buying the elections! The Supreme Court should nullify it.

Anne-Marie O'Connor *LA Times* Aug 14th 2000, quoting Senator Russell D. Feingold, "We have devolved from a representative democracy to a corporate democracy. We do not have a system of one person, one vote. This is a system of one million dollars, one million votes." Feingold states the situation very clearly.

I despair at some people's reason for voting or not voting. For example:

1. He has the wrong religion.
2. He is the wrong color or sex. (Usually, it wasn't so delicately phrased).
3. He has the wrong stand on, whatever social issue *not* related to country management.
4. Neither are any good so who cares? I won't vote for either.
5. I know nothing about either so I won't vote for either.
6. Apathy. Apathy is mostly the end result of the first five points - added to lethargy and disconnectedness.
7. Distrust. The distrust of government has increased explosively since the lies of the Vietnam War and of Watergate.

To me, group-anger has become a new phenomenon. The political powers-that-be who stir the frustration-pot of the Tea Party appear to be the wizards of dissension. In the following segments of this discussion, you will find that I love cooperation. However, the current Tea Party movement is cooperative only within their own ranks. Thus they block legislative agreement. Ideology, distrust and anger stymie progress.

Over the years we all tend to grow more questioning of those in authority, so that when distrust creeps in it is not surprising. In *Demon-haunted World* Carl Sagan wrote that, "Thomas Jefferson believed that the habit of skepticism is an essential prerequisite for responsible citizenship." But it is distressing that the level of government distrust is prevalent at all levels. In my opinion, 95% of our elected officials honestly seek the best for their country. The remainder are the voices of contagious dissension.

James Carroll, in his book, *House of War: The Pentagon and the Disastrous Rise of American Power,* quotes George Schultz, Nixon Cabinet Minister, "Trust is the coin of the realm." Continuing the metaphor, the absence of that kind of coin, places the USA in "trust bankruptcy." A mammoth loss of trust occurred as the Vietnam War was found to be a wrong war. Added to that were the assassinations of President Jack

Kennedy, Presidential-Candidate Robert Kennedy, and Nobel laureate, Martin Luther King. Then the wrong Iraq War.

The dismally low numbers who turn out to vote at each election confirms the election of many mediocre candidates. President Thomas Jefferson spoke eloquently 235 years ago of the need for an "informed electorate," for the society to function efficiently. Think of those who you know, and I know that you will find that very few people study the issues, even superficially, and even then, many allow numbers 1 to 7 to influence their vote. So, as I see it, our electorate is not really an informed one. Will it ever be? How can the citizen with average education, who has the constraints of an average job and the usual home limitations, be expected to be able to study the issues of the day? What can one expect of the resulting government? It is so great to hear a political debate by well-informed individuals about the issues, versus a debate with those who can only derogatorily talk in negatives about the other party, or its members.

Quote: AARP Bulletin Aug Sept 2012, "President John Adams could just as easily been talking about today when he wrote in 1776 of his fears that the Continental Congress' decisions would be dictated by noise, not sense; by meanness, not greatness; by ignorance, not learning; by contracted hearts, not large souls." His conclusion is as appropriate today as it was then.

Benedict Spinoza 1670, said it well *in The Great Quotations,* "The fickle disposition of the multitude almost reduces those who have experience of it to despair; for it is governed solely by emotion, and not by reason." Wisdom 345 years ago! So Jefferson's, "informed electorate" stagnates, while the elections are won by the favorites of the "uninformed electorate"! There go the interests of the country!

John Kenneth Galbraith, Canadian-born American economist, quoted in *The Arizona Republic,* "The conventional view serves to protect us from the painful job of thinking." Or as "Unknown" said it, "To be avoided at all costs is the solace of opinion without the pain of thought." Again, at fault, is the lazy or uninformed electorate.

PERSPECTIVE

Even the informed can be corrupted as stated by Robert H. Jackson, U.S. Supreme Court Justice, *The Arizona Republic* 2012, "Men are more often bribed by their loyalties and ambitions than by money." Gloomy thoughts!

The Great Depression: "The Dirty Thirties"

I am now going to try to convey to you what I think is a more hopeful political system, one that is based mainly on cooperation; on the Golden Rule; consequently, less likely to be soiled by greed and self-interest; thus less distrusted; and thus more compassionate of all people's needs. For better understanding there must be some stage-setting history. Spanning the thirties, my age was 8 to 18 years.

The 1930s Great Depression was world-wide, and a disaster for everyone everywhere, but my home-region of Saskatchewan would have rated as one of the worst anywhere, especially in Canada. Pierre Berton wrote in *The Great Depression* (followed by several subsequent quotations), "In those stark days there was no sick leave, no pay for time off, no unemployment insurance, no hospital insurance, no crime compensation, and no federal old age pensions." In the USA or Canada there was no Social Security, no Medicare, no Medic-Aid, and no disability insurance. "In 1931, a third of the municipalities (about 35 miles by 35 miles in dimension) had suffered crop losses. Seventy-five percent were hopelessly in debt. Scores of municipalities, and one entire province (Saskatchewan), were too poor to shoulder the debt of relief (government assistance). The federal government squeezed the provinces (states), the provinces squeezed the municipalities, and the municipalities squeezed the people."

"In Saskatchewan, few could pay their taxes, which were years in arrears. Schools were closing because there was no money to buy coal to heat the rooms, (in our Westmoor country school, wood for the wood stove), or pay the teachers, or because the children had neither shoes nor clothes to wear to class." In our school many were barefoot in the spring and summer months. There are many pictures of barefoot "me." "It was the same with the doctors; those who stayed often worked for nothing and only those patients who were seriously ill sought medical help. It was no surprise when, after the depression ended, Saskatchewan was the first government on the North American Continent to establish universal medicine."

1936, "Saskatchewan was still the hardest hit. It had to cancel 75 million dollars in debt and taxes owed by the citizens."

1937, "Saskatchewan was still the hardest hit. In 1928 it had produced 321 million bushels of grain, in 1937, only 37 million bushels. *Two thirds* of the population was on relief. 290 of the 302 municipalities were bankrupt. Education suffered as municipalities reserves had fallen from 6 million to 1½ million. Half the cars were abandoned or turned into horse pulled "Bennett-buggies." Blamed for the depression, Bennett was Canada's Prime Minister (President). Half the telephones were taken out." At 8 to 18 years, I saw and heard of these events, but not knowing the 1920s were better, things didn't seem unusual. My parents showed worry and concern, but never gloom. I still retain a deeply ingrained attitude, coined by Anonymous, but acquired by many during the Great Depression, "Use it up, wear it out, make it do, or do without."

Edna Williams-Meakes wrote in her book *A Quest for Peace and Alternatives to War,* "- so that we received 19 cents for a bushel (for our wheat), the unemployment growing, the soup kitchens, theon-to-Ottawa trek (jobless march on the National Capital, in Ottawa), the freight train population (box-car riders), and the, "Bennett-buggy."

Only occasionally was I included to go to town (Lestock), and it was a big-deal to hear the trans-Canada freight train's warning whistle, signaling that it was speedily approaching town. I would run the two blocks to the tracks and frequently count those who were riding-the-rods, or the number of boxcars on the train. The rider numbers varied from none to twenty. In the small towns, and in the country, that type of worker found very little casual employment because potential employers avoided extra costs.

Note the similarity of events about 900 miles south of us, Robert Karolevitz in *Challenge-The South Dakota Story.* "As it was, commodity prices had dipped so low that farmers who had shipped hogs and cattle to market when they could no longer afford to feed them, did not receive enough in return to pay the trucker and the selling fees. With farmers having no money to spend, the depression spread quickly to the towns and cities too, and by the end of 1934 the number of South Dakotans on relief rolls reached 39% of the total population, the highest figure for any of the 48 states."

Similarly, *Saskatchewan History* publication, Volume 64, Number 1, 2012 records "The stock market crash and the 9-year drought plunged farm families into poverty for a decade. Year after year they would plant seeds, only to reap dust storms. The *annual* cash income for a Saskatchewan farmer went from $1,614 in 1928, to a mere *$66 in 1933*; by 1937 the annual income had crept up to $141. Farmers had little money to pay for their local teacher's salary. Annual salaries in rural areas for teachers with first class certificates *fell* from an average salary of $1,063 in 1928 to $461 in 1936. Some went as low as $360 a year. Because many farms were in, or near, bankruptcy, many salaries were underpaid, or paid by notes (IOUs)."

Robert F. Karolevitz in *Challenge-The South Dakota Story* quoted Mortimer Crane Brown:

We have no wheat, We have no oats,
We have no corn to feed our shoats (piglets).
We do not live, we only stay,
We are too poor to get away.

Saskatchewan's story was similar. It was always true that, though tempted, "you must not eat your seed corn." Your family could be starving and need to have the wheat (seed) ground into flour to survive, but you *must* save sufficient seed to plant next spring. One lived on in the nebulous hope of "Next Year," when rains would come and the depression would go. Then the next year was worse. When I lived in the Vancouver, BC area in the early 1950s, I met many, many families who had fled from the prairie-provinces during those terrible years.

Anne Marie Low, Country school teacher, in North Dakota, (south of the Saskatchewan border) kept a diary, in her book *Dust Bowl Diary*, "June 22nd 1936, Arrowhead Lake is getting very low. Jim Lake dried up weeks ago and dust is blowing out of it in clouds these days." In 1937 she said Arrowhead was completely dry. In our town of Lestock, on sports day, we played soft ball and ran races on dry *Lake Justine.*

Being in "parkland" (trees and open areas), grasshoppers, though a pest, were not near as bad as the bald prairies. Still, around small bushes and in the crops of grain they would come, in swarms.

Anne Marie Low continues, "August 1st 1936, July is gone and still no rain. This is the worst summer yet. The fields are nothing but grasshoppers and dried up Russian thistle. The hills are burned to nothing but rock and dry ground. There is one dust storm after another; it is the most disheartening situation I have seen yet. Livestock and humans are really suffering. I don't know how we keep going."

Ted Byfield in *Alberta and the Twentieth Century, Vol. 6,* quotes, "James Gray in his *Men Against the Desert* (Western Prairie Book),1967) "The grasshoppers would descend in a roaring whir, devour everything in sight and move on. A single flight was once trapped by a cold wind over Lake Winnipeg, fell into the water, and when blown toward land, covered the shoreline for twenty miles to the depth of an axe handle." The grasshopper infestation was a replication of the "locust invasion" of the Bible.

Alger Hiss in *Recollections of a Life,* "When (Franklin) Roosevelt assumed office, commerce and industry on any national scale had virtually stopped. Five thousand banks had failed, 38 states (there were only 48 states at that time) had closed *all* their banks. United Steel had laid-off its *entire,* full time work force. The New York Stock Exchange, the Kansas City Board of Trade and the Chicago Board of Trade were closed."

Hiss continues, In the U.S., "Unemployment was somewhere between 13 million and 17 million out of a total work force of probably less than 60 million. Additional millions on the farms were destitute, while unsold grain was piled in the open and the cotton carryover reached 13 million bales. State and municipal funds for relief never adequate were near exhaustion where they had not already run out months before." R.J. Samuelson, LA Times Oct 7th 1998, "Between 1929 and 1923, the output of the U.S. economy plunged 30%. Unemployment rose from 3% to 25%."

M.J. Coldwell (Canadian Political leader) in his book, *Left Turn Canada* wrote, "This was a time of drought, of grasshoppers, of crop failure, when people had no money, and poverty was extreme. In those years, vast accumulations of unsold and almost worthless grain filled the elevators and granaries on the farms. Price (sale price) of wheat fell to less than 20 cents a bushel at prairie points, eggs were traded at country stores for 2½ cents a dozen; horses, cattle, and hogs were almost worthless. Yet, in the cities, long lines of the unemployed sought relief. The man on the land *could not* dispose of (sell) his food stuffs, which the man in the city *couldn't buy.* This was a practical demonstration of the interdependence of farmer and worker."

When I joined the Canadian army in July 1940, I was sent, as reinforcement to a long-established unit, which was estimated to have about 94% permanent force members. Being under 18 years of age, my friends were mostly in their 20s and 30s. I soon heard their tales of frantic searches for work, food, medical care, shelter and their inability to care for their families. They saw joining the military as "being rescued." They joined the military to secure a free roof over their heads, free food, free medical care, and a job. Living on a self-contained farm I had had everything except money, for *which I had no need.* It was the first time that I became aware of the power of the military-dollar, though I know that I did not yet understand that it was taking a *great war to end the Great Depression.*

Cooperative Development

In our region, in the 1930s, cooperation was literally a neighborly requisite. The remoteness of the area; the limitation of communication, transportation, medical care - literally everything, made it necessary for one's survival, to cooperate with others. It was the utilization of the Golden Rule at its fundamental level.

In *Memories of Lestock* my Dad's early involvement in the cooperative movement is illustrated by a photo of his Jan 14th, 1918 receipt for $100 from the 'Canadian Cooperative Company' for his purchase of 5 shares.

My brother Frank, in 1980, wrote in *Emerald: Past in Prose, Poetry and Pictures,* "In the late 1930s and early 1940s we saw the beginning of our present cooperative store and our Credit Union. This philosophy of cooperation had been taught at our father's knee. He had been active in the organization of the old Coop elevator, later to become the Saskatchewan Wheat Pool." And a member of the United Grain Growers.

About 2006, my nephew, Manfred Meakes, loaned me the 4000 line (estimated) diary of his father (my brother) Harry for the depression year of 1936. I turned 14 years of age that year. About 2007 I wrote a short commentary about his diary and I made this comment about our brother Frank, "Jamie (oldest brother Jim or James), still worked on the Christie farm about 6 miles away. Because of having no car, and because of the slowness of horse-transportation, he was unable to routinely participate in the synchronization of effort happening at home. But the coordination of equipment, of horses, and the human efforts of Jon, Frank, Harry and Art (though he lived on an adjacent farm), was a challenge to be met every day. It was really a family cooperative."

The concept of neighborhood bees was a necessity. Groups of neighbors cooperated to build log buildings, thresh the annual crop, saw logs to firewood size, and to fight a building fire or grass or bush fire. "The cooperative community spirit, the mutual concern for one's neighbors, the free exchange and borrowing of equipment, the frequent bees, and the sharing of neighbor's burdens and joys, is abundantly clear in Harry's diary. That domestic and community co-operation, led to Frank's early membership and chairmanship of the Lestock Coop, later the Credit Union Board, the Wheat Pool Committee, and the Hospital Board. Then his membership in the political party - the CCF (Cooperative Commonwealth Federation) subsequently re-named the NDP (National Democratic Party). He was then elected the MLA (Member of the Legislative Assembly) for 16 years. He was Speaker of the House at one time. About 1962, his continued love of the Cooperative concept led to his appointment to the Cabinet, as Minister of the Cooperatives and Cooperative Development for the province of Saskatchewan. It was stated orally, that "he was the only cabinet-level minister of the Cooperative movement in the world." His gravestone carried the comment, 'He loved people'. Through the conduit of his political conviction, he carried our father's belief in the Golden Rule into government."

Farley Mowat, Canadian author, in his book *Eastern Passage,* describes the entire east-coast Canadian province of Prince Edward Island, in cooperative terms that sounded similar to my home community of Westmoor in the early 1900s. "The houses are small, simple, - but the people had not yet lost the need and the desire to work closely one with another on even terms. The people we met in stores,garages, and on the dusty streets of the little villages seemed to accept each other and us strangers as easily as if we were all relatives from the same family. They were not effusive, but they were sincerely interested in us and our problems and anxious to help solve them for us. I think maybe the whole damn island is one big neighborhood." That describes my 1930s neighborhood.

Autobiography of Henry O. Little, Sr. (Wikipedia) - Dr. Little was the area MD for the village of Wishart, Saskatchewan (near Westmoor), 1930 to 1936. He left there and practiced in New York City for the following 45 years, then wrote his book, and speaking of his time in Saskatchewan wrote, "I soon discovered that pioneer people are a different type of person. No matter what their race or religion they were just one big brotherhood and would do anything for each other. In all of the hundreds of times that farmers pulled my car out of the mud with their horses, or got me out of snowbanks in the winter,they would never accept a penny." He described how people, to help their neighbors, would not accept even gas money for their 115-mile trip to the hospital. He said: "It seemed that Canadians treat each other as if they were brothers and sisters. At least that is the way it was on the Round Plains." (A country school district that was adjacent to the town of Wishart.

The realization that several individual participants working together can be more efficacious then when working separately occurred to many early thinkers. In *The Story of Philosophy*, Plato, 427 -347 BC is quoted as saying, "In short, the perfect society would be that in which each class and each unit would be doing the work for which it's nature and aptitude best adapted it; in which no class or individual would interfere with others, but all would cooperate in difference to produce an efficient and harmonious whole. That would be a just state." That would be a very early concept of a cooperative society.

Seneca the Younger, 47 BC-65 AD (112 years old?), *The Great Quotations*, "We are members of one great body. Nature planted in us a mutual love, and fitted us for a social life. We must consider that we were born for the good of the whole."

Tim J. McGuire, Walter Cronkite School of Journalism, in *The Arizona Republic,* Feb 9th 2015. Telling how the U.S. had survived disease, depression and war, "- it was inherent in the souls of the people to embrace that special spirit called the common good, and that the interests of the whole would forever win out over individual, mean- spirited self-interest."

Charles S. Seeley 1960 *Modern Materialism,* "Only by cooperation can man solve his chief world problems. Eventually everyone will understand that cooperation is more advantageous than competition for the individual as well as for the group."

Julian Huxley 1957, wrote in *Knowledge, Morality and Destiny,* "The importance of this idea of participating; of cooperative partnership in a joint enterprise; as a necessary basis for UNESCO; as the concept inspiring the Colombo Plan, and the United Nations program of technical assistance ---."

Time Magazine Sept 30th 2013, U.S. President Barak Obama, "I've long believed that building networks of creative cooperation among governments; the private sector and the nonprofits is the key to overcome the challenges, both great and small, of our newly-independent world."

Common Cause, Political and humanitarian organization newsletter June 2013, "If you want to walk fast, walk alone; but if you want to walk far, walk together."

Remember that, like all other societies, 'this-is-where-the-concept- is-now' is what prevails. We are continually and routinely changing our laws etc. Very little remains unchanged. The above quotations go back over 2,000 years. The value of the cooperative concept remains the same. The steps to its fulfillment vary and are always being modified. The co-operative is simply a team effort. My *Webster's Dictionary* defines a 'cooperative' as being, "owned by people who share in its benefits." I think for a co-operative to function smoothly the Golden Rule must guide the co-op policy and work relationships. Great achievements become possible when people work together for a common cause. Another advantage of team work is my Dad's comment that," many hands make light work."

In the winter of 1945-46 I lived in the English city of Manchester where I routinely heard reference to the "CWS", the Consumers Wholesale Society. I recall that their coverage was very comprehensive, including many aspects of life such as food, clothes, utilities, burial spaces, and endless list of commercial items.

Colliers Encyclopedia 1955, "Originally, co-operation was a consumer's movement, started in 1844 by the Rochdale Pioneers (suburb of Manchester) in England, and the principles laid down still govern consumer's cooperation.

1. Sell goods to members at market price, in cash.
2. Distribute shares widely and pay only current interest rate.
3. Restore the 'savings' or profits of operation to members according to the amount of their purchases.
4. One vote for each member regardless of shares held or purchases made.

Colliers Encyclopedia 1955, "Very successful in England and Scandinavia. Their attainments demonstrate that cooperation is, actually, a form of business enterprise midway between Capitalism and Socialism." In 1947, "the International Co-operative Alliance, estimated from reliable figures, that one fourth of the world's families, were members of some type of consumer co-operative."

My home town, Lestock, Saskatchewan, Canada, founded its Coop store in 1938 and it still functions 75 years later. When one makes a purchase the usual question was "What is your number?" Now, I suppose, the usual plastic membership card. It operates very similarly to the original co-op concept of 160 years ago. From the book, *Memories of Lestock,* "It was a being-together force that welded friendships within the membership. There was a need for a neighbor in everyone's life." Many European immigrants had prior knowledge of the advantage given by the co-operative movement. "They were convinced that a true co-operative society was a better way of life; that men working together united, (sic) could not be beaten." As is usual, when private enterprise is threatened, local businesses were opposed. Their sales and profits could be expected to diminish. That opposition, probably, is the reason that in the United States, the realm of "rugged individualism," that, cooperatives have not usually thrived.

Harvey Mackay, *The Arizona Republic,* March 7th 2012 headline: "The power of "we" is central to teamwork." Mackay's Moral: "We" is a little word that sends a big message."

Death of Jean-Paul Sartre, Editorial in the LA Times April 17th 1980, Quoting Sartre, "Today, there are only two ways to speak of oneself, the third person singular or the first person plural. We must first know how to say "we" in order to say "I". True.

Time Magazine, June 2012. "Mrs. Eleanor Ostrum, the only women ever to win the Nobel prize in Economics, died June 2012. She was, at one time, presented with an "insoluble" conundrum about an area of land on which several families lived. The land varied considerably in quality, and the families planted crops that each thought would sell. However, this brought an over-supply or an under-supply of produce. Patterned after a similar situation in Switzerland a co-op was organized for the entire area, and everyone shared. In both locations this proved a very gratifying solution."

The Arizona Republic, Sept 19th 2012. "- the Alaskan Permanent Fund was established in 1976 after North Slope oil was discovered. Alaskans will get their dividend checks of $878 (down from $1,174 in 2011) from the state's oil savings account --." Not referred to as a coop, but "shared benefits" makes it cooperative in principle.

The last 15 years of his life (1928 to 1943 - the Great Depression), my Dad had the civil service job of Secretary-Treasurer of the rural municipality of Emerald, in the province of Saskatchewan, Canada. The job also included the distribution of 'relief' to the needy. Seeing the bankruptcy of businesses, towns, municipalities, school districts and individual neighbors, his political point of view, as related by my older brothers, moved leftward towards cooperative, progressive answers to the enveloping social problems.

The following short quotations each illustrates how team spirit works so effectively in organizations and in private enterprise. Private enterprise also understands this. In the cooperative movement there is that same team spirit feeling, plus the added incentive of knowing that what you are doing is going to benefit all of your fellow workers and yourself. In cooperative companies, all that participate get *their share of profit.*

The advantages of co-operation apply to business in general. Listen to a handful of business people extolling 'teamwork.' Vince Lombardi U.S. Sports coach, *Great Quotes from Great Leaders,* "Individual commitment *to* a group effort, that is what makes a team work, a company work, a society work, a civilization work." That is the magic of a cooperative 'team.' All effort is directed to cooperatively achieve results.

Sam Walton Founder of Walmart Stores *Great Quotes from Great Leaders,* "Individuals don't win. Teams do". Teams 'team up' to do a better job.

President Mandela South Africa *Great Quotes from Great Leaders* (Reverse of cooperation), "We can't afford to stand divided - If we stand together, victory of the liberation movement is assured." Cooperation with others, achieves success.

President Bill Clinton: Aug 31 2012 *CNN* interview, "Only by cooperation can these things be solved." Sept 4th 2012Another TV interview: "We are all in it together." "There is a need for constructive cooperation."

Some religions that actively include some of these principles in their core beliefs follow. Here are some examples.

Gloria Faizi, author *of The Baha'i Belief,* "The Baha'I, believe in a cooperative society of the future." "They will be able to pool their resources and work together instead of (each) going their own way."

"The individual is therefore expected not only to better himself in this life, but also to cooperate with his fellowmen in bringing about a better society." Personal responsibility helps all.

The Amish, Mennonites, Hutterites and Doukhobors work solidly together, when they live on communal farms. The 'kibbutz' formed the basic agricultural unit in the establishment of the state of Israel. They are cooperatives in organization.

Political Change

Prior to the 1930s Canada had only two political parties - the Conservatives (similar to the U.S. Republicans), and the Liberals, (similar to the U.S. Democrats). Because the Canadian prairie region, especially Saskatchewan, was affected more severely by the double-whammy of the drought and the depression than was the rest of Canada, it forced thoughtful, concerned, and desperate people to consider new and challenging ideas for a better system of government. The two-party system was inadequate because the two parties had the same inefficient answers to the disaster facing everyone in those terrible years.

When political, economic, and social problems deeply stress the people in all communities, and when they can't individually overcome those woes, it is natural that they would talk things over with neighbors, and try to get governmental solutions from higher authorities. When, after prolonged attempts, they find that those reasonable requests are not being addressed, the poorer people, who usually are most involved, and most aware, are therefore most likely to demand changes. This is what developed in many regions during the Great Depression and not the least in Saskatchewan. Many prominent people have said the same: Adlai Stevenson - Illinois governor, American U. N. Ambassador and presidential candidate wrote in his book *Putting First Things First,*

"In quiet places reason abounds - in quiet people there is vision and purpose - many things are revealed to the humble that are hidden from the great."

Emery Reyes wrote in his book, *The Anatomy of Peace,* "Plato said, 'Human beings never make laws; it is the accidents and catastrophes of all kinds happening in every conceivable way, that make the laws for us.' Great social and political structures and revolutionary ideasare usually born in times of crisis."

Arnold Toynbee-Historian, wrote in his book, *A Study of History,* "Great innovations never come from above, they come from below - from the much derided silent folk of the land - those who are less infected with academic prejudices than great celebrities are wont to be.

H. G. Wells wrote in his *Outline of History,* "Owen (Like Plato) looked to the common sense of men of any or every class to recognize the causal and faulty political, economic, and social structures and to make needed changes."

Thomas Hager in *Force of Nature* said, "A number of scientists in the 1930s to 1960s, adopted left wing politics because these were systems based on reason and rationality."

President Jack F. Kennedy in *Brilliant Thoughts* said, "Those who make peaceful revolution impossible will make violent revolution inevitable." President Kennedy's comment is illustrated by the fact that, Great Britain learned from the revolution of the United States colonies and when Canadian independence pressures increased in 1867 they allowed Canada independence, legally and peacefully, and that was soon followed by Australia and New Zealand. But, provoking rebellion, they waited until 1948 for India! Thanks to the nonviolent revolution of Gandhi, they never reached the violent revolution that had proved necessary in the United States.

Most appropriately, M.G. Coldwell in his book *Left Turn,Canada* wrote regarding this specific event, "It was in 1932, in the depths of the economic crisis, that the CCF was born. Canada's national income had fallen by half. The burdens as usual, fell hardest on the backs of the common people. Bread lines were forming in the cities. Western farmers were caught in the pincers of low returns for wheat; high 'freight rates' to ship the grain; high overhead costs for mortgage payments and monopoly price levels for farm implements. There was much social unrest throughout Canada. This might have produced no result more constructive than sporadic violence, or popular demands for phony money (a reference to the soon-to-be-described Social Credit Political Party). "The Liberals, Conservatives, and Communists failed to meet the challenge by making appropriate changes, and so those who were in the "spirit of political revolt" were guided into a radical economic program with a thoroughly democratic outlook." That was the CCF (Cooperative Commonwealth Federation) the Socialist Party revolutionary in spirit but in political inter-action, only by cooperative negotiation.

All of the above comments are reflected in Saskatchewan's crisis. Desperate people in Saskatchewan could have reacted violently, but didn't. But it was close! In the book *Alberta in the 20th Century* Fred Cleverey tells of how close, "The Communist attempt at its peak in the early Thirties would see hundreds of Alberta farmers marching behind the hammer and sickle flags of international Communism, strikes, riots, and skulls routinely cracked by police truncheons at Edmonton, Calgary, Drumheller, and a dozen other centers, and finally, a national march on Ottawa by the unemployed of the West that would be stopped dead at Regina (Saskatchewan) under a hail of gunfire from the Royal Canadian Mounted Police." The Communist movement was foiled but, next door in Saskatchewan, the Democratic Socialist movement was simmering to a successful boil.

With the entire world reeling from the Great Depression hopeful ideas were at a premium. New ideas are said to often begin in California and Wikipedia, Google and Yahoo describe how, about 1933, Frances Townsend MD, a Long Beach physician started the political "Townsend Movement," which planned on the federal government giving each citizen $150 a month, "which would result in 2 to 5 billion dollars a month being spent and then the depression would be over."

Over 2 million Americans were said to believe that God had "planted the divine thought" in Townsend, but the idea never succeeded.

In Alberta province, in Canada, in 1935, William Aberhart, a Son-Of-God evangelist, who may have copied the Townsend idea, founded the Social Credit Party planning to give everyone $25 per month. The Canadian federal government ruled the money plan unconstitutional, ('phony money') but the conservative-leaning party continued to function under the guidance of 'Bible Bill' until his 1942 death. The party exists today as a third political party.

Once again there was a California parallel to Canadian provincial activities. Yahoo describes it, and in his books *End Poverty in California* and *Candidate for Governor and how I got Licked,* Upton Sinclair documents it. As a journalist, Sinclair had previously run in the U.S. as a Socialist candidate but failed to be elected. He founded the ACLU (American Civil Liberties Union) about 1930. In 1934 he ran for governor in California on the Democratic ticket, campaigning on the slogan 'EPIC' (End Poverty in California). He won in the primary election with 279,000 votes but lost the general election. There was a general euphoria similar to the Townsend movement. My friend, Spencer Derby, living in South Pasadena, told me of his own enthusiasm, and of riding his bike from South Pasadena to Los Angeles so as to avoid blocked traffic near the huge Upton Sinclair political meetings. Sinclair offered a new way of life in which any normal man can find happiness and peace saying, "No matter how rich you may be, and how well satisfied with your world, you will be better off and a better man in a cooperative commonwealth."

Deceased U.S. Senator Paul Wellstone's slogan, "We all do better when we all do better." His organizational descendant, Wellstone Action, use that slogan today.

Democratic Socialism

In Canada, there was a similar story which had a different result. J.S. Woodsworth, a Methodist minister, demonstrated supreme integrity during his lifetime. His political persuasion, gravitated leftward, as documented by M.J. Coldwell in *Left Turn, Canada.* Prior to WWI, he had been involved in welfare work in Winnipeg, Manitoba. During WWI he questioned the church's emphasis on individual salvation without considering the social context in which the individual lived. He became Secretary of the Canadian Welfare League, and became a Socialist in 1914. He resigned from the church in 1918, being "morally opposed to the church being used as a vehicle for military recruitment." MJ Coldwell in *Left Turn Canada* wrote, "Woodsworth was an unflagging advocate for the worker, for the farmer, and the immigrant." In 1932 he founded the national political party, the CCF (Cooperative Commonwealth Federation), and as its first national leader he said, "I am convinced that we may develop here in Canada a distinctive type of Socialism. I refuse to follow slavishly the British model, the American model, or, the Russian model. We in Canada will solve our own problems along our own lines."

He died in 1942 and M. J. Coldwell became national leader. Democratic socialism (by the vote of the people) has often been lumped together with the dictatorial socialism of Communism.

Today, Oct 2012, there is a TV commercial speaking of (Hungarian) 'Socialism' pejoratively, as one unmodified word, as though all forms were the same as the Soviet variety. They are not. Hungarian Socialism may have been Communist but the U.S. media seldom clarifies the difference. This is misleading to an *uninformed* public. The Saskatchewan Communists were aware that "democratic" socialism was using their good points and abhorring their many highly offensive points, and that it was being done democratically. They recognized a real threat, and they fought back.

Coldwell continues, "Attempts to confuse it (CCF) with the Communist party failed, and the Communists fought it at every election and vilified it in every publication. Its difference from themataterialistic and atheistic socialism condemned by the Catholic Church became clear as its principles were better understood, and as it brought into its ranks men and women of unquestionable sincerity and repute. It drew considerable support from the Protestant churches, which saw in its programs nothing but the application of Christian principles to the economic sphere."

"The clergy had recognized that the basic tenet of democratic socialism was to work cooperatively together for the maximum good of all, so, they invited themselves in as candidates. In the 1935 elections there were 12 Protestant ministers running as CCF candidates."

Due to the monolithic view of, "Socialism" by the U.S. media,the reporters, editors, and others who work in the media, often appear to be unaware of the differences between Democratic Socialism and dictatorial Soviet-style Socialism. Contrasted with the freedoms of democratic socialism, the differences to Soviet socialism were stark. Briefly stated, Soviet socialism resulted in dictatorship; religious suppression; private property confiscation; elimination of the opposition (by murder if necessary); the loss of many freedoms, and a single-choice vote. Democratic Socialism viewed these qualities with anathema and incorporated only democratic principles.

Saskatchewan History Magazine, Vol. 65-Number 2 2013 Article heading: "The Socialist imprint on Saskatchewan politics." "Not long before the 1944 CCF's breakthrough, however, the (Roman Catholic) church expressed concern for (the status of) social welfare; declared support for the cooperative movement - Saskatchewan had the continent's most vibrant and told the faithful to 'vote for any party save (except) the Communists'."

M.J. Coldwell in *Left Turn Canada,* "As for the Liberal and Conservative parties, the CCF did not mince words. We consider that both of the old parties in Canada are the instruments of big business interests, and cannot serve as the agents of social reconstruction and that, whatever the distances between them, they are bound to carry on government in accordance with the dictates of the big business interests who finance them." "With these guiding principles before it, the CCF has avoided the monetary fallacies of Social Credit, the extremes of Communism, and the petty reformism which brightens at election time the programs of the status quo parties (Liberals and Conservatives)." In today's U.S. business climate, Coldwell's opinion takes on a harsh sound. But listen to the bluntness of President Abraham Lincoln in 1837, quoted in *The Wit and the Wisdom of Abraham Lincoln,* "These capitalists generally act harmoniously, and in concert, to fleece the people." That is blunt! But, I think, not true for all Capitalists, in either those days or now.

But equally as blunt, Pope Francis 1st, *The Arizona Republic,* Sept 13th 2015, "Uncontrolled Capitalism will devour everything which stands in the way of increased profits, and promote the idolatry of money."

Seventy-five years after Coldwell's comment, it still applies to the Liberal and Conservative parties of Canada, and the Republican and Democratic parties of the United States. Government by any of these parties is intensively lobbied and greatly influenced by many of the business leaders, financiers, corporations, and cross-over legislators (former legislators, now corporate negotiators). These opportunists have the political acumen, and the financial motives, to gravitate to the company that will pay them the most for their "inside" knowledge of governmental protocol, and their door-opening relationships with their former congressional buddies. Those buddies are of the, "who-you-previously-knew" variety. Many would fail to have the "moral compass" to work for progressive (Golden Rule) measures for *ALL* people. Self interest, and corporate interest dominates, not communal-interest!

In my opinion, the United States tends to honor entrepreneurs and thus has a bit more competitive and capitalistic society than Canada. Canada, also, has an abundance of successful entrepreneurs, but also tends to have more progressive and cooperative programs. In general, I think that Canadians do not view the government as the enemy as many Americans do. As a solo-practitioner, in both Canada and the USA, almost all my life, I would also qualify as an entrepreneur. At hospital staff meetings in the Torrance-Redondo Beach, California area, when Medicare was first introduced in the 1960s, there was considerable physician resistance, but in general, in my private and professional political circles, I heard little of the angry, distrusting anti-government rhetoric of the "Tea Party," and others, of today.

Though a substantial segment of the United States population is involved in the stock market, private capital tends to be highly concentrated, and in few hands. There is the formation of larger units of production at the expense of the smaller ones. For example, automobile manufacturing companies are concentrated in a small handful of companies. Thanks partly to "mergers" and "acquisitions" this is also true of department stores, banks, grocery stores etc. And those companies are getting bigger, and fewer! Laws governing monopolies have failed to be effective.

Near my office in North Vancouver in 1950, an elderly couple, Mr. and Mrs. Thomas, (who lived above their small grocery store), commented that the small 'independents' ('Moms and Pops,' like their own store), would soon disappear as the growing chain stores bought them out, and that they would in turn be bought out by bigger ones. To them it was obvious. They were right. The acquiring companies just became larger and larger. That was a hint of a coming corporation-dominated society.

Corliss Lamont in *The Philosophy of Humanism,* 1949 expounds upon *A Humanist Manifesto.* The 14th *rule* is, "The Humanists are firmly convinced that existing acquisitive and profit-motivated society has shown itself to be inadequate and that a radical change in methods, controls, and motives must be instituted. A socialized and cooperative economic order must be established, to the end that the equitable distribution of the means of life be possible. The goal of humanism is a free and universal society in which people voluntarily and intelligently co-operate for the common good. Humanists demand a shared life in a shared world."

Derek L. Phillips builds a case for the Golden Rule in *Toward a Just Order 1986,* "What is also necessary is that everyone have adequate food, clothing, housing, medical care, security and protection - an adequate level of education and income--. Provision of the basic necessities cannot be left up to the voluntary activity of various individuals, and groups, since private charity is unlikely to assume full and adequate benefits for all who may require them. Only the state has the ability to assure that these basic good or benefits are securely provided as needed, that they are equitably and impartially distributed to those who need them, and that the taxes providing them are equitably collected from those who have the required economic resources. - First, such state- provided benefits and services as free and comprehensive medical care, quality education, and decent housing ought to be made available to all persons. Second, the government ought to provide income security in the form of a social minimum generous enough to assure that all people will be able to obtain an adequate level of certain goods (i.e. food and clothing)."

It took a greatly respected man of unlimited integrity and intelligence to give an admiring defense of Socialism in a very opinionated, business-oriented society. That "greatest intellectual genius of the century," was Albert Einstein who provided a description of socialism in his 1949 analysis in *Ideas and Opinion,* Why Socialism? Paraphrased, he commented that, "Socialism is directed toward a *social-ethical* end, not a profit end. The ends themselves are conceived by personalities with lofty, ethical ideals. Science can only supply the means by which to obtain the ends." Even sixty years ago Einstein deplored the monopolistic growth of major corporations. Einstein continues, "The result of these developments is an oligarchy (government by a few) of private capital, the enormous power of which cannot effectively be checked even by democratically organized political society. This is true because members of the legislative bodies are selected by political parties, which are largely financed or otherwise influenced by private capitalists who, for all practical purposes, separate the electorate from the legislature." Today, in 2014, think of the power of money ("corporate" money) in politics. To make it worse, the Supreme Court now rules that IRS (Internal Revenue Service) may consider a corporation as equal to a person for money-raising for elections! What happened to the logical financial controls on the "buying" of an election? What is the advantage of "one voter one vote"? Einstein would be furious!

LA Times, Jan 9th 1997 "The 95th Congress in 1977 had 222 lawyers and 118 from business (the business community)." Every election changes these numbers but legislators consist largely of lawyers and businessmen, most of who lean towards the financial functioning of the community. The welfare of the needy of a community is not a topic of primary concern. The importance of business needs come first.

Einstein continues: "The interests of the underprivileged section of the population are minimally represented. Private capitalists inevitably control, directly or indirectly, the main sources of information (press, radio, education)." Today it includes television, internet, and social media, and this power of controlling the sources of information, is a powerful force in influencing public opinion, elections, schools, universities, and government at every level. Einstein continues, "It is thus extremely difficult, and indeed in most cases quite impossible, for the individual *citizen* to come to objective conclusions, and to make intelligent use of political rights." Those words describe the "informed electorate," of which President Jefferson spoke.

One has to KNOW by uninfluenced factual reports, the circumstances of any event, to be able to arrive at a logical, reasoned opinion. One has to recognize the biases of each source to be able to judge, and consequently to pick and choose. For example, the bias of left-wing opinion in the NBC news versus the bias in the right-wing view of Fox News. Thank common sense for more independent C-Span, National Public Radio and TV. Also, I think, for a more neutral CNN who consistently presents panels of four, with pro and con opinions. Whether right or left, I do appreciate FACT-filled explanations or discussions.

Never-the-less it is difficult for a concerned individual to achieve membership in President Jefferson's "informed electorate." Since Einstein wrote that opinion about 65 years ago, the improvement for the poor, and under-educated, has minimally improved. Our informed electorate rates only spotty improvement. Interest groups still try to influence citizen-groups and, in turn, the legislators, which is OK, but that influence needs to be balanced in opinion input, and free of any financial incentives or coercion. The health of the viable, just, democratic society of the future depends on the presence of that informed, and unbiased, electorate.

Einstein continues: "Production is carried on for profit, not for use. There is no provision that all those able and willing to work will always be in a position to find employment; an "army of the unemployed" almost always exists. The worker is constantly in fear of losing his job. Technological progress frequently results in more unemployment."

"The profit motive, in conjunction with competition among capitalists, is responsible for instability in the accumulation and utilization of capital which leads to severe depressions." Yet we cannot reverse scientific progress. Just watch the documentary of the manufacturing process of an automobile block, and then consider how many jobs no longer exist, to achieve the same purpose. We can't go back! Sound familiar? Think this through.

Einstein continues, "Unlimited competition leads to a huge waste of labor, and to that crippling of the social consciousness of individuals which I mentioned before."

"This crippling of individuals I consider the worst evil of capitalism. Our whole educational system suffers from this evil. An exaggerated competitive attitude is inculcated into the student, who is trained to worship acquisitive success as a preparation for his future career." Now, in the early 21st Century, it is so refreshing and encouraging to hear of young men and women who are intending to dedicate their lives to some cooperative Golden Rule application of their learning, to those that are in need; or to the progressive advancement of the world. When there is societal planning to remedy the social needs of all of the people of the world, and thoughtful analysis and planning to achieve those needs, then we will have achieved the primary objective.

Einstein concludes "I am convinced there is only one way to eliminate these grave evils, namely through the establishment of a socialist economy, accompanied by an educational system which would be oriented towards social goals." My Golden Rule dream! Einstein continues, "In such an economy, the means of production are owned by society itself and are utilized in a planned fashion. A planned economy, which adjusts production to the needs of the community, would distribute the work to be done among all those able to work and would guarantee a livelihood to every man, woman, and child. The education of the individual, in addition to promoting his own innate abilities, would attempt to develop in himself a sense of responsibility for his fellowmen in place of the glorification of power and success in our present society." That is the pure Golden Rule at work. That is why I count myself as a Democratic Socialist! Thank the 20th century's stellar intellectual for his candid analysis.

Nevertheless, it is necessary to remember that a planned economy does *NOT* necessarily indicate *Democratic* socialism. A planned economy as such may be accompanied by the complete enslavement of the individual. Think of Communism. Einstein's summation is important and his final sentence raises a very valid question. *"How, is it possible, in view of the far-reaching centralization of political and economic power, to prevent bureaucracy from becoming all-powerful and arrogant? How can the rights of the individual be protected, and there-with be a democratic counterweight to the power of bureaucracy?"*

I think the conjunction of the Golden Rule and Democratic Socialism is the main answer to Einstein's question. Norman Thomas in *The Great Quotations,* said, "The alternative to the totalitarian state is the cooperative commonwealth." Note that Canada's Socialist party was called, *Cooperative Commonwealth Federation.*

That has been one of those reasonable, skeptical questions regarding Socialism, which must be addressed thoughtfully. I would suggest that the same social-goal education would provide an answer - The Golden Rule. If your plan promotes the treatment of all others as you yourself would wish to be treated, then you will have the individual's interest at heart. In a democratic election, those who form the government administration, choose an enthusiastic, caring staff, those who wish to see the plan function successfully. That was the natural distinction arrived at with Saskatchewan Socialism. I remember living in Vancouver, BC Canada from 1950 to 1955 when the Conservative and Liberal political parties, concerned about the threat of the rising CCF (Socialist) party, decided to form a coalition government to oppose the CCF. They won that election, but then found it necessary to yield to the public demand for a medical plan similar to that of Saskatchewan. The plan quickly developed malfunctions; had overly expensive growth problems; and inadequate desired results, all of which were attributed to the Coalition government not inherently believing in the concept, while the successful Saskatchewan plan was constructed by enthusiastic "believers"!

Many of us have suffered at the whim of an officious bureaucrat, which is a frequent complaint about 'government bureaucracy' in general. I can visualize that under Communist rule that would be a systemic problem. This can happen even in today's capitalist society. But that does not condemn all of them.

DEMOCRATIC SOCIALISM

Quotation from my (1945-6) post *WWII Memories.* While working in Manchester, England, in the British civil service, "I had been able to have a close-up look at one microcosm of what has frequently been called 'the world's most efficient civil service.' It seemed to me the basic element was that the employees there had a genuine, polite, respect and concern for the people whose problems they handled; and that the employees were, in turn, respected by the public who came in person to our complaint counter each day." It had only been a few months since Labor election, removing the Churchill Conservatives and installing the democratic socialist government under the leadership of Clement Atlee. I know that it was too soon for the "educational system which was oriented towards social goals" to yet show an effect. I think that the employees had been carefully taught civil service protocol; had been carefully chosen; and/or, that it reflected innate courteous British manners.

I am constantly amazed how a number of different personalities can comment on a given topic, and all note different aspects on which to comment. Like the three blind men who were asked to feel an elephant and describe it. The first felt a leg and said, "it is like a tree." The second felt the side and said, "It is like a wall." The third felt the trunk and said, "It is like a snake." Note the differing commentaries of the following notable authorities on the very important topic Socialism.

Paul Pearsall PhD, in his book *The Pleasure Prescription, wrote,* "Despite claims that competition is natural, it is collaboration and agreeable cooperation that leads to the healthiest and ultimately the happiest planet people and other earth inhabitants. Modern sociologists (1996) have found that the theory that competition is natural and inevitable is incorrect."

President Thomas Jefferson, quoted in *The Arizona Republic,* "The government is the strongest of which every man feels a part." Tell me! Do you feel you are a part of the government today? The great majority did feel part of that great experiment in Saskatchewan in those post WWII years.

Lincoln comments in *The Wit and Wisdom of Abraham Lincoln,* "I go for all sharing the privilege of government who assist in bearing its burdens." That is the philosophy of the cooperative society.

Pope Pius XI, May 15th 1931, *The Great Quotations,* "Socialism - is drifting toward truths which the Christian tradition has always supported. Indeed, it cannot be denied that its programs come close to the just demands of Christian reformers." "So one can at the same time be a sincere Catholic, and a true Socialist." The great concern of many of the religious community was dominated by the belief that it was said that the Socialists were antireligious? Not true! That was the dictatorial Communist point of view, not the Democratic Socialist point of view. I can remember my inflexibly-devout, Christian, brother-Harry being heard in the very public Saskatoon, Saskatchewan airport, extolling the wonderful attributes of the Socialist Saskatchewan government! Godless Communism? - Yes it is. Godless Socialism? - No! When one is unencumbered by religious or political constraints, it is easy to visualize an ideal society.

Leon Blum, French president, *The Great Quotations,* "The aim of socialism is to set up a universal society founded on equal justice for all men and equal peace for all nations." All men and all nations!

Clement Atlee, British Prime Minister, The Great Quotations, "often observed that British Socialism owed more to Christ than to Marx." Universal love!

Hugo Chavez wrote in 2012, in *Understanding the Venezuelan Revolution,* "Here one recovers the "we-are," where was previously a domineering individualism, and failed sense of the common goal." The central 'I' of the entrepreneur is diminished.

George Bernard Shaw, *The Great Quotations,* "There is only one kind of socialism, the democratic sort, by which I mean the organization of society for the benefit of the whole people." That is the key the "whole people."

Jean Jaures, French Socialist Leader, *The Great Quotations,* "There is only one sovereign method for the achievement of socialism - the winning of a loyal majority." It would not be democratic, without the majority consent of the public.

Daniel de Leon, American Socialist Leader, quoted in *The Great Quotations,* "Socialism is neither an aspiration of angels, nor a plot of devils. Socialism moves with its feet firmly planted on the ground, and its head not lost in the clouds; it takes science by the hand, asks her to lead, and goes whithersoever she points." Socialism is not a theology; is not anti-religious; is realistic; and is led by the scientific approach.

John Dewey, American educator, *The Great Quotations,* "We are all for some kind of socialism, call it by any, whatever, name we please." His use of the word "all" maybe inappropriate, but an alternative name for Socialism, "Democrat," worked in the primary election for Upton Sinclair in the California 1935 election.

Jawaharlal Nehru, President of India wrote in his book *India's Freedom,* "Surely to the great human goal of social and economic equality, to the ending of all exploitation of nation by nation and class by class, to national freedom within the framework of an international cooperative Socialist world federation." This was a dismal time - 1936! His dream is still unfulfilled! However, as has been said many times, "without a dream --nothing happens."

Nina Gourfinkel, quoted Maxim Gorky in *Gorky,* "I lacked something essential to a socialist love of mankind perhaps." It is appropriate that, "He Loved People" appears on the tombstone of my political-leader brother Frank.

Edward Bellamy, *Looking Backward,* Foreword written by Erich Fromm in 1960, "The aim of socialism was individuality, not conformity; liberation from economic bonds, not the making of material aims into the main concern of life." This confusion had been caused when Communistic socialism, in the middle 1800s, had discussed the "perfecting" of the human being thus making a sort of automaton without individuality. That was never the Democratic Socialist aim or result.

Martin Luther King 1967, Nobel Laureate, in his wonderful last book, *Where Do We Go From Here?* wrote, "In the days ahead we must not consider it unpatriotic to raise certain basic questions about our national character. We must begin by asking: Why are there 40 million poor people in a nation overflowing with such unbelievable affluence? Why has our nation placed itself in the position of being God's military agent on earth, and intervened recklessly in Vietnam and theDominican Republic?" Long before Kuwait, Grenada, Iraq and Afghanistan! King continues, "Why have we substituted the arrogant undertaking of policing the whole world for the high task of putting our own house in order? For its very survival's sake, America must re-examine old presuppositions and release itself from many things that have for centuries been held sacred. For the evils of racism, poverty, and militarism to die, a new set of values must be born. Our economy must become more person-centered than property and profit-centered. Our government must depend *more on moral power* than on its military power." This is the Socialist viewpoint! What wonderfully, powerful words! If they could only be prominently displayed, thoughtfully considered, and then effectively placed into action.

John Lewis, 1961, *Socialism and the Individual,* Think of his prescient comments so true over 50 years later. "The competitive individualism of the 1800s has developed into the monopoly capitalism of the 1900s. The United States is to be run in the future not by the legislatures but by big business." How clear was his analysis of the future! With armies of lobbyists, Big Business has exerted its influence on all legislation emerging from the U. S. Congress.

In 1944, I was home on leave at election time, and was given a ballot for my vote in my home constituency. The Great Depression, and Saskatchewan's mainline government failure of the 1930s was still fresh in my mind. Not knowing the candidates, I was reluctant to vote, but Mother urged me to do so. It seems so sexist and unjust now, but in her twenties, women were not allowed to vote in the USA, Canada or Great Britain, and so, having experienced that situation, she felt strongly about the duty of voting. I do not recall my vote, nor, for which party I voted. Mom still leaned towards the familiar status quo, which was the Liberal administration. Most of the other family members, I remember, said they voted for the infant party, - the CCF (Cooperative Commonwealth Federation). The result was that Saskatchewan elected the first Democratic Socialist government in North America. That election brought buoyant optimism to Saskatchewan's stressed citizens, after the drag of 16 years of drought, depression and war. The provincial party leader was Tommy Douglas, a former Baptist minister, who became the premier (U.S. equivalent is Governor) of the Saskatchewan government. One of the first actions of the Saskatchewan government was to create a one-payer hospital insurance plan for the province. The Golden Rule came first!

After 18 years of satisfactory results, in 1962, the CCF government of Saskatchewan installed another plan, this time including doctor's fees (medical visits) in the plan. Doctors were initially upset. My radiologist cousin, practicing in Saskatoon, Saskatchewan got in touch with me to see if my contacts at the Harbor General County Hospital in Torrance, California could help him to immigrate to the U.S, - which they couldn't. In 1962, my brother, Frank, was a CCF member of the government during its medical plan conversion, and a period of coolness between the two cousins developed. However, late in life, my cousin told my brothers that he had been very contented with his life and practice.

In the late 1990s, a Canadian Broadcasting Corporation national survey, voted for Tommy Douglas as "the greatest Canadian of all time," thought to be largely due to him being the primary architect and originator of the Saskatchewan one-payer medical plan. Kiefer Sutherland, the Hollywood actor, is his grandson.

Michael Moore, *Dude, Where's My Country?* "Eight in ten Americans believe that health insurance should be provided equally to everyone in the country."

Studs Terkel, *The Great Divide* 1988, "Dr. Quentin Young Medical Director of the Chicago Cook County Hospital, also director of the Health and Medicine Policy Research Group says we (the United

States) are the only country in the world, with the exception of the union of South Africa, that does not have a national health plan." Here is an imaginary, but plausible, conversation at a corporate HMO. "Doctor X, we love you here, but you are seeing only 4.2 patients an hour. We'd like you to see 7.2." Profit is more important than patient-health!

Since the above was written, we now have the Obama-Plan, which is *NOT* a one-payer plan, as previously envisioned by *Presidential Candidate* Barack Obama. Incessant, intense lobbying made certain that the insurance companies were included and their traditional "cut" of the medical-dollar paid to them. Premiums will, doubtless, still rise. I predict that fact will doom the plan to much less than maximum efficiency.

The Canadian plan and the European plans rely on the tax roll to supply the revenue. They appear to be more economical, and at the same time more efficient. They are, of course, heavily criticized by the ever-vigilant, dread-laden insurance industry. There is an array of additional features contained in Obama-Care, which will affect the final analysis. It will correct its problems; analyze any inefficiencies; and, if the insurance companies don't want too much more money, we will hope for a successful passing grade. After 40 years of humanitarian effort the compromise plan was the result of settling for what was politically possible.

LA Times extract, October 4th 1993, (Near the time of Hillary Clinton's health-care proposal). "Toronto Canadian physicians are not too different from their U.S. counterparts. Back in the 1960s when legislators began to put together the pieces of what would evolve into this country's broad, single-payer health insurance plan, doctors fought the reformers with all they had. The doctors lost the battle, of course, and today, most would say that is a good thing. Even though Canada's health plan is now under financial pressure, one survey after another has shown that most doctors are glad that the government took over the health insurance." "We Canadians have a different attitude," said Michael Taylor, author of a history of health insurance in Canada. "Your (U.S.) emphasis is on individualism, whereas here we have a sense of collective responsibility. Here the government may be seen as ineffective and inefficient, but it isn't considered the enemy."

The LA Times continues, "The 1962 Saskatchewan election (to include doctor's services) was (mainly) a referendum on health insurance - when the voters returned the social democrats (socialists) to power, the government saw its victory as a clear mandate to set up the state-run program." "It was to be financed with modest tax hikes and premiums."

The LA times continues, "Still Saskatchewan's new health insurance program did not pop up overnight. There was still a nasty fight with the doctors of the province. Through their professional society they voted not to practice once the program became law. As many doctors were paid on municipal payrolls, there was virtually no help from the private insurance industry," which, of course, is where the largest amount of money comes from to fight against the one-payer system in the United States. The LA Times continued, "And, on July 1st 1962, the doctors struck. The Canadian Medical Association backed them up. They called on the federal government to investigate the events in Saskatchewan, in hopes of keeping the one-payer movement from spreading. But the doctors lost in Saskatchewan and at the national level."

"At the national level, the Canadian Medical Association got the inquiry it wanted, but the investigating panel came to the conclusion that a Saskatchewan-style program of universal, government-funded coverage was cheaper than a system in which the government subsidized only the poor."

"The persuasive force of the finding, combined with widespread interests in the events in Saskatchewan led to the federal government's passage in 1966 of a bill creating Canada's single-payer program." Thus the Saskatchewan Medical Plan was adapted to the needs of the country as a whole and a federal medical plan instituted.

"All the same, the *Medical Post* recently surveyed Canadian doctors and found that nine out of ten believe that the Canadian system is better than the United States."

Now, in 2014, it is 48 years since Canada's one payer health program was legislated, (70 years since Saskatchewan's), and it has frequently undergone the usual, necessary process of refinement. There have been program changes, financing difficulties, especially at times of recession, but very few Canadians would change it.

In 1963, 19 years after the Saskatchewan one-payer (tax-supported) hospital insurance plan was put into effect, I took my seven-year- old son, Michael, to the emergency department of the (Saskatchewan) Regina General Hospital for treatment of a forehead and nose laceration. The ER charge (for an American foreigner), was five dollars - with free follow-up. For a Saskatchewan resident it would have been free - covered by the annual taxes.

In 1958, after 4 years in a convalescent hospital, my sister-in-law Alice died of Multiple Sclerosis, and my brother Art told me that telephone calls had been his only expense. Fifty-six years later, in 2014, I don't know details, but know that the Canada's medical plan remains efficient, popular and less expensive than that of the USA.

Quotation from my 1996 unpublished manuscript *Memoirs,* "In my opinion, systems of medical care that would eliminate the profit motive would provide a more trustworthy medical profession. This would also eliminate the for-pay care by the HMOs, PPOs, etc., because their plans are designed to deliver the lowest acceptable level of medical care; the least amount of medication; the shortest possible hospital stays; so that their bottom lines are kept bright. As I see it, those medical practitioners who love their work, and are not driven by the money to be made, would thrive, and patients would receive the compassionate care required. In that kind of system, I know that I could be comfortable." The doctors of course would be paid a salary, with appropriate bonuses, commensurate with their education, expertise, efficiency, compassion and innovation.

Is Socialism discredited as many pundits are fond of saying? On the basis of name approval, the answer is probably, "Yes." On the uninformed and distorted linkage to Communism, often referred to as the unmodified word "Socialism," - of course! But on the basis of Golden Rule achievement of "Democratic Socialism," the answer is "No." Successive United States administrations have tried desperately to obstruct the threat of Democratic Socialism in the Western Hemisphere, but have not been completely successful. Some of the socialistic programs in foreign countries have failed because they retained much of the Communist dictatorial tendencies, and appropriately the leaders have been deposed.

The Soviets described their system as simply "Socialism." The merit of the concept of Socialism was immediately denigrated when the Soviet system became a secretive closed society, a brutal police-state, a confiscatory dictatorship, and an imposed atheistic society. The centuries-long, czar-ruled, servitude of the Russian masses made them more compliant to Communist enslavement. None of these qualities are part of Golden Rule-guided Democratic Socialism. Consequently, Socialism has been abused by its users as well as by its critics.

Socialism was originally introduced into Germany in 1869 and continued its influence there until 1923 when Hitler, capitalizing on its past respect, and on post WWI discontent, abused it again by naming his party the National Socialist German Workers Party, shortened to National Socialism, and shortened again to "Nazi." Though Nazism was not socialistic, Hitler thus gained the unthinking support ofmany of the socialist community. However, it was a misnomer, and was anything but Socialism. This abuse was part of Hitler's propagandist Joseph Goebbels policy of the "Big Lie."

Today, in 2015, we have Democratic Socialist Bernie Sanders running as a presidential candidate in the current election. In the early 1900s Socialism was an electoral option in the U.S., Canada, and Great Britain. Eugene Debs, Socialist, ran for the U.S. presidency 5 times. Later, Presbyterian minister and Socialist, Norman Thomas, ran 6 times in U.S. presidential elections. Wikipedia/Yahoo says he tried to start a Farmer-Labor Party similar to the Canadian CCF party. He was involved in the NAACP (National Association of the Advancement of Colored People), the ACLU (American Civil Liberties Union), and CORE (Congress of Racial Equality). His biggest contribution came in his insistent, compassionate, eloquent advocacy of social programs. He urged passage of President Franklin Roosevelt's Social Security legislation, and was persuasively instrumental in his advocacy of President Johnson's Medicare and Medicaid legislation.

These programs were all denounced as "socialistic." Indeed, they were, and they are great examples of Democratic Socialism. The old saying applies here, "A rose by any other name, would smell just as sweet." These compassionate, popular programs were successfully inaugurated under another name. As is true of all programs, they need some adjustments over time, but they are people-oriented, and compassionate, and reflect the Golden Rule. As in the 1934 California election with Upton Sinclair, there is a future for Democratic Socialism under other names. *As long as the Golden Rule dominates the principles, and cooperation dominates the practices of a political system, then, under any name, I would be contented.*

There is a need, and always an abundance of room, for individualism. Fertile, imaginative minds frequently recognize that some things can be improved, or that a new product, or service is possible. In today's system, there can still be the opening for an entrepreneur. In a purely cooperative society, a bonus, National Award or some other form of recognition would be appropriate.

The Golden Rule usage in government policy is parallel to that in personal use. In essence, it is appreciating and being there for your neighbor the same as you would for yourself. Your "neighbor" might be your fellow citizen, another state or another country. The principles of Democratic socialism parallel this concept, a compassionate society that *first* thinks of the good and the welfare of all of its citizens. All the freedoms must be there. Freedom of speech, freedom of education, freedom of religion, and freedom to throw "the bums" (any political party) out, if desired. Free medical care for everyone, cooperatively paid for by taxes. If I remember it correctly, the 1944 Saskatchewan medical plan annual taxes were ten dollars for a single person and twenty-eight dollars for a family which, even in those days, was an unbelievably low figure. I know it had to be soon increased.

The basic human needs of potable water, clean air, protected earth and clean energy were community-owned and regulated. Other important services, such as telephones, garbage-removal, home and car insurance, hospitals, and the pharmaceutical industry were controlled and prices negotiated. Contrast that with the current for-profit system that prevails in Phoenix Arizona. The two local electricity companies are governed by an elective board of commissioners. An editorial in *The Arizona Republic* Newspaper April 10th 2015 speaks of the "millions" spent by the one electric utility to elect cooperative commissioners. "Commissioners can require the utility to disclose political spending. None has. They saw what happened to those who did." How much better a state operated, controlled, non-profit utility would function.

I am stressing the Golden Rule underlying cooperatives and socialism. However, in *The Great Quotations,* George Bernard Shaw used a different "take" making clear some other attributes. "It cannot be too thoroughly understood, Socialism is not a charity, nor loving kindness nor sympathy with the poor, nor popular philanthropy but the economist's hatred of waste and disorder; the aesthetes hatred of ugliness and dirt; the lawyer's hatred of injustice; the doctor's hatred of disease; and the saint's hatred of the seven deadly sins."

The preceding discussion about the cooperative movement, the resulting natural development of democratic socialism, the Saskatchewan and Canadian medical plans, all follow naturally from the application of the Golden Rule to the political and social needs of the people of Canada. Each country that has developed their socialized government has done so with their own individual modifications. They are all in their own developmental trek to what they see as improved government. I say this to point out that there are some better, or worse, programs in every country, under every system. But having trust in the wisdom, good will, and commonsense of people, I know, that in the long history of the world, the trend will be only towards improvement. How desperately we need that "informed and compassionate electorate!"

Now, in 2015, I am a member of the Democratic Socialists of America. Their address is DS of A, 75 Maiden Lane, Suite 505, New York, N.Y., 10038. They state that Susan Anthony, Albert Einstein, Martin Luther King, Walter Cronkite, and Ed Asner, the Hollywood actor, and many more were Socialists. A few statements by the organization follow.

Quoted from pamphlets issued by the Democratic Socialist of America - "We think that our present economic system places too much power in the hands of too few people. It means that this power must be challenged if humankind is truly to move forward. It means we want a world where ordinary men and women control their own destinies. It means shared values: justice and equality; peace and understanding; tolerance; and brotherhood and sisterhood."

"Our vision is rooted in the enduring values of democracy, equality, and community. We believe that men and women can, and should, bring institutions under democratic control and enjoy full participation in every sphere of life. Every day, many of this country's important decisions are made not in the legislatures but in corporate boardrooms. That must end."

"We also believe that everyone must have an opportunity to develop their abilities to the fullest and the right to share in the wealth they create. For starters, that means we must provide everyone the decent housing, health care, and education that this country can so easily afford."

"Finally we believe the common good represents more than the sum of hundreds of millions of individual interests. Only by working together can we preserve our precious environmental heritage. Only together can we maintain the vital spaces - parks, libraries, museums, meeting halls, stadiums, schools, - that make public life possible."

As you may remember, the Canadian Democratic Socialist Party was called the Cooperative Commonwealth Federation, (CCF) lat er changed to New Democratic Party (NDP). Cooperation was the driving force and the Golden Rule was a paramount principle. The Democratic Socialist party has never governed the federal Canadian government, only some provincial governments. Not having lived in Canada for 57 years I now know little of 2014 Canadian politics. A new party *The Saskatchewan Party* won the 2007 election removing the NDP from power. However, next door in Alberta, in May 2015, the NDP won the provincial election in what had been thought to be Canada's most conservative province. The NDP won 55 of the 87-member legislature.

Saskatchewan History Magazine Vol.65-#2 - 2013 - The article is authored by Nelson Wiseman, associate professor in the Department of Political Science at the University of Toronto. "The Socialist Imprint on Saskatchewan political thought" says that the Saskatchewan party "hesitates to undo social democracy's legacy," - "disavowed designs to privatize the provincial crown corporations and the health care system and it promises a non-confrontational, cooperative approach to organized labor." "- nearly six in ten (survey) respondents opposed privatizing any crown corporations (government corporations) and fully two thirds of them favored policies to narrow the gap between rich and the poor. More believed that "the best way to deal with major economic problems" was "more government intervention than believed it is best left to the private sector, and while many respondents agreed that unions "generally ask for too much," more agreed that "strong unions" are needed to protect employees working conditions and wages." "Saskatchewanians opinions are, strikingly, congruent with socialist hallmarks; favoring an active governmental role in reducing income disparities and in macroeconomic management." "Saskatchewan's socialist party has lost power but socialist ideas remain imprinted on the provincial political culture. Like a recessive gene, or an impulse in remission, the diminished NDP and its social democratic ethos may well resurface as the people's choice."

Nelson Wiseman continues, and makes clear that the provincial voters have strong socialist beliefs, because the wishes of the defeat ed party (the NDP) are, generally, still being utilized and respected. The name change serves as an example of what Upton Sinclair did in California in 1935 when he changed his designation from Socialist to

Democrat. The name is unimportant but the democratic, cooperative, progressive, Golden Rule principles are what it is all about.

I have used the Canadian experience as a framework on which to discuss my views about political theory. Here, in the U.S. I could be classified as a far-left-wing Democrat. My comments here have been primarily about what, I think, generally, a Golden Rule-centered, compassionate society would be like. But, my politician-brother Frank used to say that, "Politics is the art Possible." The "possible" is dependent on not only your own efforts, and your own persuasive abilities, but also on the cooperative awareness and cooperative inclinations of the public at that time.

I am well aware that of the list of adjectives that may be used to contest my point of view. There is an automatic, reflexive, apprehensive resistance from the ever-vigilant pro-profit media of the capitalistic, individual-centered society in which I live. But our U.S. and Canadian societies are similar blends of political thought, only Canada's is a bit more cooperative-receptive. This-is-where-we-are-at-now always applies to both. Change will come to both. Times do change. The needs of societies change too. Living a bit longer, my opinions might change also. But the bottom line is that I have a positive belief that wisdom will prevail and that a more Golden Rule dominated society lies in the future. And that the "Past" that I have told you about, really is prologue.

Carl Sagan comments in *Brilliant Thoughts,* "Imagination will often carry us to worlds that never were, but without, we go nowhere." Imagination is crucial!

The Gaia Principle

John Muir, Google, "When one tugs at a single thing in nature, he finds it attached to the rest of the world."

Gary Marcus LA Times Jan 4th 2004, "St Francis is said to have called all creatures, no matter how small, brother and sister because he knew they had the same source as himself." Doctor Albert Schweitzer believed the same.

Having written glowingly about how the cooperative movement has accomplished wonders in this world, I would be remiss, not to speak of the theory of the Gaia principle, which could be called "systemic global cooperation." The Gaia theory suggests that "the organic and inorganic components of planet Earth have evolved together as a *single,* living, self-regulating, system." Visualizing the earth, its inorganic components, and all of its organic life-forms (birds, insects, animals, fish, plant life and ourselves) as one viable, evolving, ever-changing unit - all dependent on each other's health and well-being - is both the definition of the Gaia hypothesis and a powerful argument for protecting and nourishing our environment. The concept of us as, "being one" with the earth is supported by how all organic matter returns to being soil when it dies. The rich mulch which develops from tree leaves; the dust that develops from the carcass of an animal; the intoning of my father when he officiated at a funeral: "Dust to Dust"; all illustrate how we are one-with-the-earth. If true, the interdependence of all living things would be the pinnacle of involuntary, organic cooperation.

LA Times, Sept 5th 1993, Headline: "*Meeting of World Religions Leads to Ethical Document* which, comes at a time when religious, scientific, political and environmental leaders are talking of a 'paradigm shift' toward the development of a "global consciousness" the realization that all things are connected.'"

Charles Cook "Your deepest roots are in nature. No matter, who you are, where you live, or what kind of life you lead, you remain irrevocably linked with the rest of creation." The Native Indians of North America appear to have instinctively arrived at that concept in much earlier times. 'Sacred Mother Earth' was given her due supplications and reverence.

There is interesting, documented, intra-species cooperation recorded in crows, ravens, dolphins, ant-colonies and bee-colonies and less dependent inter-species cooperation such as bee-pollination; bigger fish and their attendant sucker fish; the Venus Fly Trap, etc. These are examples of cooperation and/or inter-dependence in nature. But those inter-species relationships are on a functional or behavioral level only.

It is in the genome where the biological similarities of all nature reside. Gary Marcus, Author of *The Birth of the Mind* in the LA Times Jan 4th 2004 headline: *'The Need for Cooperation is in the Genes."* Paraphrased: 'During the decades between DNA discovery and DNA sequencing, it was assumed that the apparently very complex human body, would presuppose a much more complex human genome. However, the surprise was immense when it was found how very similar the DNA in the human genome is to that of all living organisms. The DNA of a mouse is 80% identical to a human, and a chimpanzee is 98%. The most diverse of creatures have similar DNA templates."

In *Pleasure Prescription,* Paul Pearsall quotes Einstein, "A human being is part of the whole, called by us, "Universe." Our happiness depends on realizing that we cannot find joy alone and without bringing joy to others." In Hawaii, "Akahai" requires saying "I care deeply about how you feel and I will try to help you." Love requires us to make someone else feel good, and to feel very good when doing so. The universal Golden Rule.

Could it be that the salutary feeling one gets in helping others is felt so viscerally, because it is a deep, Gaia-related sensibility helping others helping "us" helping our Gaia-relationship - helping our "cooperative-whole"? Could it be that the Golden Rule is so important because it has a Gaia-related reason for existing? Consider that possibility. Even if only seen as theoretical fantasy, practical steps should be taken to approach the environment in a sensible, protective, ecologically-conscious manner.

The *Global Exchange* newsletter, fall/winter, 2011, "In 2008 Ecuador became the first country in the world to recognize Rights of Nature in its constitution, recognizing the right for ecosystems to flourish, regenerate and evolve. Between 2006 and 2011, "two dozen communities, including Pittsburgh, PA have passed laws that place the rights of residents and nature above corporate interests and as a result, have stopped harmful projects." In 2010, in Bolivia, "The World People's Summit on Climate Change and the Rights of Mother Earth," - proposed the Cochabamba Accords which have since been drafted and submitted by the Bolivian government as a, "Universal Declaration on the Rights of Mother Earth." Those were wise actions which immediately protected some of their natural resources from the inroads of money-oriented corporations. Our Western industrial nations would have massive resistance from the lumbering, mining and fishing interests who own or lease the world's limited natural resources. Gaia principle or not, the earth needs more protection.

I take seriously the supposition of the *possible reality* of the Gaia Principle. But a brief, imaginative diversion! In my 14-year-old son, Michael's selection of science fiction, I recall being enthralled by the fictional story of 'Elmer,' who was a member of a space ship's crew. Investigating an unknown planet, he was briefly separated from his colleagues; was sucked into an immense tubular plant; was physically and mentally and psychologically analyzed; was emitted unchanged except that he had no navel; sent on his routine way - while the planet carefully analyzed everything it had learned from Elmer's body, and his mind, and waited patiently for the next specimen to come along. Planetary Gaia! I don't think our planet has evolved to that level yet!

PART FOUR
MILITATY SERVICE, EDUCATION
1940 TO 1955

The Service: Canadian Army Medical Corps

Threshing grain; prior to new combine technology.

About Sept 1st 1939, while I was driving a team of horses and, "pitching" sheaves during threshing time, I vividly recall being told the radio news, and then telling Jon Tubeck, that Hitler's Nazis had just invaded his native Poland. Mild mannered Jon's only remembered previous bout of swearing occurred when, having just had a cow step on his foot, my brother Frank had heard him "teaching the cow some Polish." So Jon's rare, and precise explosion, is still vividly remembered: "Goddam son o' bitch! I cut 'em out (Hitler's) nuts!"

At that time, no-one knew that just three days earlier Hitler and Stalin had signed their mutual non-aggression treaty, (The "Hitler-Stalin Pact" or the "Nazi-Soviet Pact"). The pledge gave the eastern half of Poland to Russia in return for Russia not interfering with Hitler's planned invasion of Poland and Western Europe - which meant that Hitler would not have to leave large numbers of troops on the eastern front to guard *against* the Soviet. Until Hitler broke that treaty 22 months later he was free to consolidate his conquest of Western Europe. The static or "Phony" war, when no major action took place, lasted until early spring 1940, when Nazi forces invaded most of the rest of Western Europe.

In early July 1940, I went to the Canadian Air Force recruiting office in Regina Saskatchewan and my application to study as a pilot was immediately denied. I was less than 18 years of age and 10 ½ grades were *currently* insufficient to qualify for aircrew. *My WWII Memories,* "But around at the Army I was greeted with open arms. I was the classic example of the unthinking, immature 18-year-old recruit." Not a glimmer of my future concern for the immorality of war. The recruiting department chose my future and I blundered into the Medics, - a Golden Rule outfit, - not a "kill-em-all" unit. "I was warm, breathing, *and volunteering.* No written consent by your parents? No problem. No birth certificate? No problem. No high school? No problem. How about the medical examination? No problem. Missing basic training? No problem. Want to go overseas? No problem, just say you're two years older." On July 7th 1940 (saying I was born in 1920 instead of 1922) I was taken into the 250-man 10th Field Ambulance (10FA), a unit within the Royal Canadian Army Medical Corps. 10FA was attached to the South Saskatchewan Regiment (SSRs), and were in the 6th brigade of the 2nd Division of the Canadian Army.

Though I emphasized in the preface that this entire account is related to my anti-war stance, I do not think that relating the grueling training that is used to convert a clueless recruit into a competent soldier, is of any interest here. It has been described in books and movies very well. So the rest of this paragraph covers the first five months in the military. Without basic training we were sent as reinforcements to the 10FA at the Dundurn Military Barracks near Saskatoon, Saskatchewan for intensive training in First Aid, gas warfare, physical training, parade ground drill, and many route marches, all of it just *continued* training for the 10FA soldiers already there. As Canada strictly abided by the Geneva Convention International ruling that Medics could not carry guns, I did not ever receive rifle training. About Oct 1st, we were moved by train, about 2000 miles east, to the horse stables in the Toronto, Ontario fairgrounds.

From there we were moved by train to Halifax, Nova Scotia, on Dec 18th 1940 and embarked on the *S.S. Pennland* destined for Gourock, Scotland disembarkation. Our 10th Field Ambulance unit went on board with the South Saskatchewan Regiment (SSRs) but were directed to the bottom deck.

Thirty-five years later, in 1975, secret records were released telling of a brilliant British radar specialist, Jack Nissenthal, who was attached to the SSRs during the 1942, "Dieppe Raid." A book named *Green Beach* was then authored by James Leasor, about Nissenthal, and the SSRs, including their (our) crossing on the S.S. Pennland. Quote- "Following more than a year of training in Canada, the South Saskatchewan Regiment had sailed for England, December 1940, aboard a filthy ship that put into Halifax, Nova Scotia, carrying internees to the West Indies. The Dutch Captain admitted he could not control his supernumerary crew, who were renegades, and he warned the SSRs Commanding Officer, that if the ship were torpedoed, these men would seize the life boats and leave the troops to go down with the ship. So the Colonel detailed one hundred SSRs to keep watch day and night on A deck with rifles and Bren guns at the ready - just in case. Rarely had a ship ferried troops so far, under such conditions." We had only been told that it was a Dutch ship, captured by the Germans, recaptured by the British, crewed by the Dutch and had just unloaded German POWs in the West Indies.

My *Memoirs:* "We were on D deck, four decks down from the top deck - and from any whiff of fresh air! We had our hammocks hanging closely together and directly over our dining-tables. The benches and tables were bolted to the floor. There were ridges at table edge to stop dishes sliding off the table in rough weather and they were badly needed. The tables might be named 24-hour tables, because there was nowhere else for us to go to on board. We had to spend our entire time at the table except for boat drill etc. We were never without the pervasive odor of those who were sea sick and who didn't make it up to the A deck latrines. Naturally, I also had my share of sea sickness. It didn't help to wake up to our lurching hammocks and to a breakfast of English kippers (fried Herrings)."

"For each meal, a 'detail' of us had to go up to, and along, 'A' deck and down to 'C' deck to the kitchen. There we picked up large 'dixies' (containers) of our food, tea or coffee which we then carried up to, and along 'A' deck and back down to our quarters on 'D' deck. On the open part of 'A' deck, on the rougher days, water would slosh around our ankles. The sour odor back on 'D' deck didn't help our meals to be more appetizing.

It was said that our CO (Commanding Officer) Colonel Leach had to give his consent for our unit to be inserted below the SSRs in such a limited space. A similar account (from an unremembered source) of the Europe-bound U.S. troops on the Queen Mary in 1945, "- the blacks were stowed down in the depths of the ship near the engine room, as far as possible from the fresh air of the deck, in a bizarre reminder of the slave voyages of old." That was also us!

"We were initially a convoy of 4 ships, and two destroyers as escort. In a couple of days, they left, and then we had a battleship named the Revenge (built in 1913), which also left us after a couple of days. Finally, we were just two defenseless ships." Peter Kemp in his book *Decision at Sea: The Convoy Escorts,* states that "there were 217 ships sunk by the

Germans, in the Atlantic, in the four months of July through October 1940. Churchill in his *Memoirs of the Second World War* stated that in November 1940 one Atlantic convoy of 34 had 20 ships sunk by the Germans. So only a month later, our final defenseless convoy of only two ships was certainly at risk." We were lucky!

Peter Kemp in another of his books *Convoy Drama in Arctic Waters* told of the 37 ships, in Convoy PQ17, that had assembled in Iceland with accompanying protective naval vessels, in July 1942 of which 26 were destroyed by the Germans. "The stores and equipment lost with PQ.17 amounted to 430 tanks, 210 crated aircraft, 3,350 vehicles and 99,316 tons of general cargo. One hundred and fifty-three seamen lost their lives." This event was made much more severe because the Germans had just launched their annual summer offensive in the Southern front in Russia, in which, for the cost of 5 airplanes they "completely destroyed the Russian defenses." We had been lucky!

My *Memoirs,* "Our crossing was said to be the roughest yet --"The mountainous waves were estimated at over 40 feet at times, and the horizon would disappear even looking from the top deck. Some of the "deck-gear" and superficial deck structures were smashed - or washed away by the waves. There was a sheath of ice on the prow and the railings. At that time radar was not perfected and of course the ship was totally blacked-out at night. "

In 2005, Margaret Gaskins authored a book, published in the U.K.-entitled *Blitz, The Story of December 29th 1940.* She writes about the ship *Capetown Castle* which was a member of our convoy of four. There are some minor variations but there was a professional perspective providing the information from the Capetown Castle. My Saskatchewan neighborhood friend, Johnnie Hunt, was on the Capetown Castle. The comments regarding the convoy were, the same, or similar, so most could be made from our ship.

Gaskin Quotation, "A whole new batch of Canadians had only just arrived. Canada's newly appointed Historical Officer, Major J. G. Stacey, was among the 1400 troops who left Nova Scotia aboard the 27,000 ton RMMV, Capetown Castle, just before Christmas. And his account of his crossing showed something of the Battle of the Atlantic that had been waged, day in, ever since the war started. For there had been no Phony War at sea: 112 lives were lost when the Athenia wastorpedoed on the first day of the war; by December 1940 Allied shipping losses totaled 4,500,000 tons with a corresponding large death toll."

"A mail boat designed for the South African run, the Capetown Castle was not as well heated as it might have been for the north Atlantic in December. But she was comfortable and fast. Or would have been were it not for two other troop ships and the Dutch cargo ship she sailed with. By traveling in packs, unarmed and lightly armed, ships secured a naval escort; the price they had to pay was that of traveling at the speed of the slowest ship." That was probably us on the Pennland.

"Two destroyers had escorted them on their first day, an older battleship (Revenge) for a further four, leaving them half way across the Atlantic. Six destroyers two Canadian, two British, one French, and one Polish - were steaming out to bring them in, but somehow the rendezvous was missed and the destroyers hunted in vain for three days, while the convoy negotiated the Western Approaches alone and at just thirteen knots." In the 2005 book, I found out why we were just 2 (or lonely ships.)

"There were regular boat drills and, from reveille on the 20th of December, all ranks slept fully dressed and carried life belts; that afternoon the Capetown Castle's Lewis machine guns practiced firing and from the 22nd they were manned through daylight hours. Rifle parties were allotted positions. The next afternoon the ships began to zigzag - a standard evasion technique - which tended to scatter the convoy for long periods. At dusk, the Capetown Castle was given Admiralty permission to leave the convoy and 'proceed at best speed.' And on Christmas eve, flying kites to deter low flying attack, the ship received a cheery wave from a passing Royal Canadian Air Force flying-boat and Major Stacey saw his first British naval vessels on this side of the Atlantic."

"Christmas Eve was fairly thoroughly celebrated by all ranks that night and on Christmas morning the Capetown Castle started up the

Clyde (River). As it passed the great shipyards, where 'an incredible amount of naval construction was in progress,' the troops swapped good wishes with people on the banks and on other vessels. "Perhaps the warmest single greeting was from a colored crew of a Liverpool freighter." By nine thirty on Christmas night Major Stacey was on a train bound for London. Though, he never learned the fate of the slow Dutch freighter." As our ship was Dutch, that was probably us, substituting as a troop ship! We were still at sea, obviously not as fast as the Capetown Castle, dragging in the next morning. I have no photos of either the Pennland or the Capetown Castle, only photos from the Pennland. We took the train to Aldershot Military Barracks not far from London.

My *World War II Memories* "Three nights after our arrival - on Dec 29th 1940, London had its worst air raid of the entire war. The two following books were inspired by the events of that one night. David Johnson in his book *The London Blitz* - quote: "Hitler and Goering wanted revenge for the air raids against Berlin. And when the waves of Heinkel 111 and Junker 88 dropped their loads of incendiaries on London, hundreds were killed and injured, and architecture that had stood for centuries was irrevocably destroyed."

In Margaret Gaskin's 416-page book *Blitz-The night of 29th of December, 1940* she writes that, "the Luftwaffe planned a massive and multi-phased raid" - on the "Square Mile" as downtown London was known. "The intention was to start a firestorm of such proportions that it would level London's greatest monuments." From our London suburb we could hear the bombing; a full 75 degrees of the horizon was alight with fires; there was a steady drone of loaded planes, and (in the dark) we watched a nearby plane going down, maybe friend, maybe foe? It was another early awareness of war.

My first weekend leave, in January 1941, I went to visit Steve and Ruth Noble, former Saskatchewan neighbors, then working on a farm at Ovingdean, Sussex, which was on the south coast. I went with 50- year old Steve to his volunteer, evening duty at the Home Guard. The futility of the British defense to a Nazi invasion was evident as all their rifles were red-banded, condemned, WWI vintage. In April 1941, I went with 75-year old George Behrend, on his volunteer, Liverpool, (incendiary bomb) fire-watching duty. On a later leave, I went with 60-year old Tom Dunham in Marlow, west of London, on his volunteer, night time, airplane plotting duty. Many older civilians were doing similar volunteering service, including keeping the public away from the impressive-appearing, covered *wooden* anti-aircraft guns in London parks, thus fooling Nazi intelligence that they were real.

1941 inspection of troops by King George VI.

Many think of WWII as only D-Day and what followed. But five years of bloody war preceded D-Day. When I arrived in Great Britain in Dec 1940 the entire European continent had been over-run by the Nazis; the Nazi allies were Italy and the (not-yet-Nazi-invaded) *Soviet Union;* the neutral nations (who tended to support Germany), were Switzerland, Sweden, Spain, Portugal, and Eire (Ireland). The "view" from Great Britain was bleak indeed. Winston Churchill called it, "a gray time in a gray age." Michael Burleigh in *Moral Combat* stated that, "the aerial activity took place over three English counties - Kent, Sussex and Surrey. Time was at a premium as it took a German fighter only six minutes to cross the Channel." In my three years there, I was stationed in Sussex or Surrey the entire time, and so living in that six-minute stretch I saw a great deal of aerial activity, and much bombing and destruction.

My very limited private's income ($1.30 a day - half of which was "retained" in Canada until after the war) still allowed me extensive travel. Trains and busses remained cheap and regardless of gas shortage and bombing, they were reasonably reliable. In my three years there I qualified for about three months leave (One week every three months - and one 2-day weekend every month). Not smoking, minimally drinking, and, occasionally a little poker, made it possible for me to always go somewhere on leave.

Edinburgh Scotland
1942

Although I stayed at "service clubs" for a shilling (24 cents) or two shillings a night, I was also fortunate to have stayed at private homes in Aberdeen, Dundee, Edinburgh, Glasgow, Liverpool, Manchester, Leeds, Hull, Brighton, and London and some farm homes in Sussex,

Surrey, Kent and Buckinghamshire. For two years some of us at 10FA were paid 1 shilling daily (24 cents) above our army wage to help local farmers with their harvest. Thus I saw the British with their burdensome restrictions; their precise rations of plain food; their blackouts; and most of all, shared in their agony of family loss due to bombing or military service; their concern about "no worthwhile future"; their terror at every air raid alarm - was it "just" an air raid or was it a Nazi invasion? The British government had, a continuous revolving plan, whereby children were sent to non-target, quieter country homes, or to Commonwealth countries such as Australia, Canada or New Zealand. The psychological effects on children, by conditions of war, were being regularly discussed in the papers or on radio.

Now, in 2012, the future must be abjectly dim for people in the ravaged countries of Libya, Syria, Ruanda, Somalia, and Sudan. Their children will lack, what the British kids had: the hope, the social adaptability, the technological help, and the organized, unified government response that was needed. Todays' end result will be a thousand-fold worse breeding ground for hopeless terrorists.

My *Memoirs* continues "The black-outs were total. There were only tiny dots or slivers of light anywhere. You frequently ran into people in the dark and also found yourself apologizing when brushing against lamp posts, etc. Traveling the train at night meant that you had to contend with extremely faint interior lighting or even no lights at all." "In London, the deep subways (the "Tube") were semi-lighted and large numbers of people used them as bomb shelters; trying to sleep on the concrete floors; leaving just a pathway for people boarding the trains; and, depending on train schedules, even sleeping on the tracks." "There were seven-foot sand bag barriers in front of public buildings; tape cross-hatching on most windows; concrete and barb wire barriers on near-coast roads and hills; very few private cars; very plain and restricted restaurant food; never milk by the glass; fish-and-chip fast food but no hamburgers; the weekly ration of the British civilians was 1 ounce of butter and one egg."

The continual devastation by bombing was everywhere, some cities worse than others. In April 1941 I took my first 1 week leave and went to Liverpool to see Mrs. Keats-Behrend - a friend of my parents who they knew only by mail. My *Memoirs,* "March to May of 1941 was referred to by Winston Churchill as the "period of the tour of the ports," by the Luftwaffe, which of course included Liverpool. The German bombing was at its peak in April 1941, and some of the windows in the Behrend house (where I was on leave) where broken and had been boarded up, - the blast having been from a landmine (a parachuted bomb). Churchill stated that in Liverpool, in that period alone, there were 3,000 killed, 76,000 made homeless and 69 of the 144 shipping berths put out of action. I saw blocks and blocks of nothing but piles of bricks, fragments of walls, glass etc. That, of course, was true of other cities." I especially remember the devastation in Liverpool, London, Manchester, Brighton, Eastbourne, Leeds and Hull.

My *Memoirs:* "But there were some days that were memorable. One was June 21st 1941, when Germany invaded the Soviet Union, thus unilaterally breaking the German-Soviet Pact and thus putting the Soviets back on our side. The rest of 1941 the monstrous battles in Russia raged, until Dec 6th 1941 when the Nazis had reached the suburbs of Moscow. But the Soviets were desperately fighting for their Capitol and that was the closest the Nazis ever got to capturing Moscow. The next day was the attack on Pearl Harbor by the Japanese, and then the USA entered the war "on our side."

The Dieppe Raid: August 19th 1942

Though my participation was minimal, I was involved in the *Debacle at Dieppe* (my unpublished manuscript), so I will focus on it a little more intensively. The initial account covers what was known about the operation from 1942 to about 1974-5; the next 1972 portion will tell how the 30-year release of records brought secret information;and then about 2012 a 70-year release of ultra-secret records.

During the summer of 1942 there had been continuous military losses by the Allies in every theater of war, the Soviets had already lost millions of soldiers and civilians and were demanding a second front by the Allies. Rodric Brathwaite in *Moscow 1941* stated that the "Russian human losses between June 22nd 1941 and October 31st, 1941 were 2,952,000", By August 1942 their losses were probably 5 million. Having entered the war 8 months earlier the Americans were impatiently urging the British to consider a second front soon and to conduct more of their daring Commando raids on enemy coasts.

"Michael Brian Loring Villa in his book *Unauthorized Action* described the ill-fated Dieppe Raid. "One of the most memorable events in WWII took place on August 19th 1942, when the largest amphibious force in modern history, made its way across the English

Channel towards the occupied French port of Dieppe. The result a few hours later was a disaster. That 3,300 Canadian officers and soldiers should wait for 2½ years for combat, and then be killed, wounded or captured in a single morning is one of the great tragedies of the Second World War. It was the biggest raid and the largest air battle of WWII, - was the most tragic, and in ratio to participating forces, the most costly, allied offensive of the war."

Ross Munro in *Eyewitness to History* wrote, "We bumped on the beach and down went the ramp and out poured the first infantrymen. They plunged into about two feet of water and machine gun bullets laced into them. Bodies piled up on the ramp. Some staggered to the beach and fell. Bullets were splattering into the boat itself, wounding and killing our men." A little later he said "It was brutal and terrible and shocked you almost into insensibility to see the piles of dead and feel the hopelessness of the attack at this point."

Robert Prouse, *Ticket to Hell via Dieppe.* Prouse tried to swim to an LCT but "it received a direct hit from a bomb --. All around me arms, legs and bits of what had been brave men flew into the air. In the lulls between explosions I could hear the screams of the badly wounded. The sea was no longer green but an angry red, stained by the blood of the dead and dying. Bodies floated over the surface and, as the tide swelled higher, they washed against me in the ebb and flow." Prouse spent over 2 ½ years in German prisons.

Terrence Robertson in *The Shame and the Glory* recorded that, "five hospitals worked ceaselessly for five days and nights, the nurses in 6 hour shifts, the doctors non-stop. In the operating theater in one hospital four tables and eight doctors were ceaselessly occupied with surgery for forty hours. Another hospital admitted 401 patients in 12 hours, among them 80 surgical cases --."

My Medical Corps Memoirs, "This is being written in 1992, and mercifully 50 years have blurred the numbing, gory memories of the slaughter that were evident on those returning ships. It could be a factor that fading memories are why old men start the wars, while the young men do the fighting."

My unpublished manuscript *Debacle at Dieppe* recorded my impressions as we removed the wounded from the assault vessel Glengyle, and from the destroyer, Fernie. "The non-wounded left the ships first. Details are blurred in my ancient memory although there are some scenes that are very clear. We took the badly wounded off the ships to our ambulances. The dead were left where they were to be removed later. And the dead were in every corner on both the top and lower decks. The hand rails, and in many places the floor, were bloody and slippery or sticky, most of all the steps to the lower decks."

"There was a machine gun on the top deck of the Glengyle that was near the gang plank, and it had a dead gunner sprawled beneath it. But he had one arm stretched sideways over the path to the gang plank. Carrying our loaded stretchers, we walked over that arm every time we passed - but priorities were on the living, and with our hands loaded, no-one took time to remove the hand from being crunched. It was a vivid, stark memory of an unimportant miniscule incident, but the brutal indignity of that moment has always led my memories of that God-forsaken event."

It was with personal interest that I read in *The Arizona Republic,* Dec 30 2012, that Major General John Cantwell suffered PTSD, and had resigned from the Australian army because of his memories of a single incident in the Iraq war. Quote: "John Cantwell could see the ridges and calluses of the skin, and the pile of desert sand that had swallowed the rest of the Iraqi soldier. The troops that Cantwell was fighting along-side in the Gulf War had used bulldozing tanks to bury the man alive. This hand was so jarringly human, amid the cold mechanics of bombs and anonymous enemies." My small similar memory springs to my mind first, but luckily didn't result in PTSD.

My account continues. "Among the wounded, the curses, groans, and prayers were anguishing." In *Winning the Radar War* by Jack Nissenthal, he recalled, the "sickly smell of blood." Similarly, I recall the smell of blood, urine and vomit. My account continues. "Death in war is particularly grotesque. Death comes suddenly, so there is no sign of serenity or tranquility in dying, - only the imprints of agony; signs of frantic and spasmodic movements of abject terror; stark grimaces of pain in those last moments of violence. No reason for anyone to wonder what happened. The obscenity of violently inflicted death was etched on the faces of all." - "We worked all night moving the wounded to local hospitals, schools, halls, etc. When the ships were empty, we then started taking the less-wounded, or already-treated, to hospitals and treatment centers in cities and towns much further inland." This continued for three days.

My comments continue, "The atrocious waste of young lives, waste of expensive military equipment for what seemed like nebulous objectives and results, seem to be obvious to a reasonable, but militarily unstudied mind." The percentage of casualties for the total force was 59.5 %.

Churchill and Eisenhower later credited the Dieppe Raid for providing invaluable lessons for the later invasion of Europe. Admiral Louis Mountbatten, the raid commander said, "For every one who died at Dieppe, twelve lived on D-Day."

As I write this it is (2013), now more than 70 years since that day. The errors and final conclusion are probed more deeply in my unpublished manuscript Debacle at Dieppe. John Terraine in *The Life and Times of Lord Mountbatten* who commanded the Dieppe Raid wrote, "…that it:

- taught us the need for heavy fire support;
- taught us the need for better pilotage of the invasion armada;
- taught us about beach obstacles and how to overcome them;
- taught us the problems about the follow-up over the beaches;
- confirmed the need for headquarters ships, from which to control the battle."

These are all tactical lessons and were probably of value in D-Day, but useless in today's wars. Medical analysts found that wounds happened in legs more frequently, followed by head wounds etc. One major strategic lesson was learned: To capture an important port prior to 1942 it had been thought necessary to attack frontally (direct from the sea). But the slaughter on the Dieppe beaches stimulated the invention of Mulberry, the floating docks which, in 1944, were towed to French D-Day landing sites, thus allowing a landing to take place anywhere. So on D-Day, landings avoided the heavily guarded ports and landed instead at remote beaches. These are all *battle* lessons. In his *Memoirs of the Second World War* Winston Churchill wrote, "Dieppe occupies a place of its own in the story of the war, and the grim casualty figures must not class it as a failure. It was a costly but not unfruitful reconnaissance in force. Tactically it was a mine of experience. It shed revealing light on many shortcomings in our outlook." Churchill continues, "Strategically the raid served to make the Germans more conscious of danger along the whole coast of Occupied France. This helped to hold troops and resources in the West, which did something to help Russia. Honor to the brave who fell. Their sacrifice was not in vain."

What maybe the definitive book on the Dieppe Raid, *Dieppe - Tragedy to Triumph* written by Brigadier General Denis Whitaker (an infantry captain in the Dieppe Raid), was published 50 years after the event, in 1992. He was the only 4th brigade officer alive, unwounded, and uncaptured, to have returned from the raid. After 50 years of careful research of all records and of newly-released documents, he wrote his book. He evidently had wrestled psychologically with the "worth- whileness" of the raid in the manner that I had, only, of course, with infinitely greater reasons and superior and informed insight. His final words in the introduction are "With this book we demonstrate that there can, finally, be acceptance of the reality of Dieppe as an important element in the Allied Grand Strategy. That makes the losses just a little easier to bear for those of us who were there." His book appears to have brought answers to a multitude of questions.

All sources agree that Jubilee was an effective message to convince the Germans that it would be necessary to protect the West Coast by withdrawing military forces from the Russian front. Obviously that was pleasing to Stalin. The Dieppe Raid was also an answer to Stalin's demand for an immediate Second Front, but illustrated by its bloody failure that it was not currently possible for an immediate front. The same bloody failure also indicated to a restive American public, and American military authorities, that they were being very premature in their current demands of the British to mount a Second Front. It was also an inadequate explanation for an anguishing Canadian public.

These lessons and results were immediately obvious to the military analysts in 1942. However, as related above, the raid was considered only in battle terms, not secret intelligence terms which was kept secret for over 30 years. William Stevenson wrote the book, *A Man Called Intrepid* in 1976. Intrepid was the code name for Sir William Stephenson, (no relation to the author) chief of *British Security Coordination* (intelligence operations). Author Stevenson described a secret Camp X in an old farmhouse, east of Toronto and on the north shore of Lake Ontario. It was conceived, established, and directed by Stephenson, and became a subsequent headquarters for British, American and Canadian intelligence operations. Camp X taught commando tactics and intelligence techniques. Camp X is described in detail in *Inside Camp X* 1999, authored by Lynn-Philip Hodgson. Agents taught in this way were then sent *within*, but not as an integral part of military operations etc. Bringing a new view of the apparently "failed" raid, author Stevenson described how utilizing cover provided by the Dieppe Raid, made it the "most ambitious secret intelligence operation." He stated that "sixteen special operations were mounted in (within) the Dieppe Raid." Under cover of the operation, secret agents were inserted into Europe as saboteurs. One agent brought information to the intelligence chiefs that the Germans were working on atomic warheads. These operatives worked singly or in small compact units, and without the knowledge of the commanding officer under whom he served. The least number of people that know what spies are doing, the better.

My first awareness of the released intelligence came from a LA Times report on March 10th 1975 which dramatically described an eleven-man South Saskatchewan Regiment platoon (nine died during the raid) detailed to accompany Jack Nissenthal, a young British scientist who was delegated to go only to the radar tower above the Pourville suburb of Dieppe, to search for clues determining the level of German awareness of new advances in radar. The platoon was directed to protect Nissenthall but to kill him if he was being taken prisoner. What he knew was too valuable to fall into Nazi hands. None of the nine knew *why* they were protecting Nissenthal. They would not have understood. As Nissenthal wrote in his *Winning the Radar War*, radar was so unknown at that time that, "no-one would have believed that it was possible to monitor a plane 90 miles away." He related in his book how he marked his report "Failed" for the regiment commander, but sent his "Successful" report to his *intelligence* superiors. When the records were released 32 years later, Admiral Mountbatten, the raid commander, stated that he was totally unaware of the operation.

Stevenson said in *A Man Called Intrepid,* "Jubilee seemed planned to fail." He also said, "This was the strangest of invasions - one that was never intended to succeed." Again, "It was essential that the Germans should believe that Jubilee had failed." As viewed by the Nazis, (and the involved Allies), Jubilee had failed. They were not aware of how much intelligence that was gained. Winston Churchill later told parliament that "the general aim of Jubilee was to "deceive the enemy." Admiral Lord Louis Mountbatten, who had commanded the raid, "disclosed thirty-two years later that "Dieppe" was one of the most vital operations of the whole Second World War - it was the "Great Deception"." By then, even he knew what he did not know in 1942. That is why it is called "*Secret Intelligence.*" But, 2012 brought more surprises!

Seventy years after the raid, there was a release of more ultra-secret intelligence. In a CD named *Dieppe Uncovered,* military historian Dr. David O'Keefe says that even including the 1970s secret records release, he and most other historians, had never felt comfortable with any, or all, of the reasons for mounting the pre-doomed Dieppe Raid in the first place. The pre-raid deliberations had predicted a casualty rate as high as 50%. (It was 59.4%) What would justify a raid that was predicted to have a 50% casualty rate? None of the above listed reasons seemed adequate. Could there have been something else that only a tiny few in the upper echelon of planning knew?

In the *Dieppe Uncovered* CD, using the 70-year release of more secret documents, Dr. O'Keefe, by patient detective work, traced what was probably the most significant of the 16 ultra-secret operations conducted within the Dieppe Raid, but still without the knowledge of Commandeer Mountbatten or the regimental commanding officers.

The famous Enigma code had earlier been solved by the British, but in March 1942, the British Intelligence found they could no longer solve Enigma information. The Nazis had changed from a 3-rotor to a 4-rotor Enigma. The Commando platoon under the command of famous Commando Captain "Red" Ryder, was to locate and raid the Dieppe Nazi Naval HQ in the Moderne Hotel in the inner Dieppe Harbor and take any information they could, expecting that it would certainly include the 4-rotor Enigma. They were to take what they found to the intelligence commander of their intelligence operation, who was Commander Ian Fleming (called 17F), the author of the subsequent James Bond series, who was waiting on board the Fernie destroyer (from which we removed the wounded later that night). The platoon was on board a small vessel named the Locust, which was depending on the opening of the primary harbor channel by the Royal Regiment. Military objectives are often missed by small failures of plans. A very early morning English Channel encounter with German ships had made the Royal's Dieppe frontal landing 17 minutes late, which allowed the Germans abundant warning. They poured their relentless fire on the Royals; the channel could not be opened; the Locust never got into the harbor and the 4-rotor Enigma objective was not achieved. It was six more months before the 4-rotor Enigma was solved.

The urgency of the Dieppe Raid is now clear. The lives, ships, and supplies lost during that six-month period might have been avoided if the 3-rotor Enigma project had been a success. The shockingly high Dieppe Raid casualty rate was probably still dwarfed by the six-month loss in lives and equipment that continued to occur. The advance knowledge that the casualty rate could exceed 50% was acceptable to the intelligence planners, considering the potential valuable prize. Only a tiny fragment of the original participants are still alive to be cheered by that knowledge. Assuming the youngest participants were 18 years old in 1942, (I was 20) the 70-year release of secret documents would have come in their eighty-eighth year. Now, in 2015, they would be 91 years of age.

It has frequently been said that "though an unreasonably high" landing force price was paid in mostly Canadian deaths, that it was of inestimable value to the D-Day Allied invasion forces two years later." We now know that those valiant lives were expended in the reasonable prospect of a proportionately higher saving of Allied lives and equipment.

The comment has been made that there is no such thing as a "good" war but that WWII was a "necessary" war. These seventy-year secret intelligence revelations have modified my perception of the Dieppe Raid, but I would not change the ending to my *Debacle at Dieppe* (which did not include the 2012 intelligence), where I said that thinking of it that way, the "forgotten debacle at Dieppe now has a slightly more tolerable face for me to remember."

Transfer to the Canadian Air Force: Air Crew

On August 1st 1943, my three years of seeking an opportunity, and attempting, by examination and testing, to transfer to the Canadian Air-force to take pilot training, paid off! My *Memoirs:* "My Commanding Officer commented, "that he couldn't figure out why, in the middle of a war, that Second Division HQ would approve the transfer of a soldier with three years of experience in medical care, to anywhere else, let alone to the Air-force and back to Canada to train as a pilot." He was right!" It seemed like a screw-ball decision, when you consider the money to be spent on my transportation back to Canada; the money to be spent on training for aircrew; by then the war might be over, and it almost was; was I worth it? But at that time, no questions muddied my dazzling future! I was at my psychologically, exuberant peak when I left the Canadian army behind, and began my unescorted solo trip to fulfill my dream to become a pilot. It was pure, unalloyed adventure! Over three years of the army's military control and discipline lay behind me. The air-force's similar version was to come. On Sept 29th, 1943, on a limited 24-hour pass, I left my buddies, and headed to London.

Reporting to the Canadian Army Headquarters in London on Sept 30th 1943, I received a speedy discharge coupled with a very stern warning to not think of myself as a civilian, but as on leave from the Royal Canadian Air Force, to whom I *must* report the next day! Nevertheless, that night I rented a room somewhere, and tried, in vain, to enjoy my civilian status. On October 1st 1943 I reported to the Royal Canadian Air-force Headquarters in London, England; lowered my army age to my correct age of 21; was officially taken into the Air-force; sent to a repatriation-depot near Liverpool; met my future wife Joan "*Doe*"; on October 30th 1943 took passage on "a ship so fast it didn't need a protective escort" - the S.S. Andes to New York; took a train to RCAF HQ in Ottawa, Canada; travelled by train on a one-month leave with family; on Dec 8th 1943, enrolled at #3 Manning depot, Edmonton, Alberta; was transferred to the # 2 Initial Training School, Regina, Saskatchewan: graduating from there April 1944; and that was where I was when I received the hugely disappointing news that the Commonwealth aircrew training program had produced a glut of pilots and was training no more. It was a frustrating, conclusively-final, closure on my 4 years of attempting to get pilot training.

However, they needed navigator-bombardiers (called "Observers" in the British Air-force), a combining of two skills, thus, on some planes requiring one less aircrew. However, this was to involve bombing! My later war-resister level of conscience had not yet kicked in. I gave minimal thought about my future task of bombing remote, faceless people from a distant changing location in the sky. In any case, it was mooted, that our targets would be submarines!

The author, commissioned as pilot officer, Royal Canadian Air Force.

I was sent to #6 Bombing and Gunnery School, Belleville, Ontario, where, I was taught aerial bombing and ground and turret machine gunnery. Then to #10 Air Observer School at Chatham, New Brunswick, where the subjects were meteorology, Morse Code, log keeping, aircraft and ship recognition, aerial photography, and navigation using sextant, logarithms, and "wind speed and direction." Radar would have been a natural for this course, but as a new, and as yet unreliable technology, the other basics were emphasized. I graduated with a commission, "Pilot Officer" (2nd Lieutenant) on Nov 3rd 1944. In January 1945 I was sent for a "refresher" at #6 Bombing and Gunnery, Belleville, Ontario and then sent to 2 AirNavigation School in Charlottetown, Prince Edward Island, and later to #1 General Reconnaissance School, at Summerside, Prince Edward Island, Canada. The courses there were mainly ocean patrols, searching for submarines (no "collateral damage" in bombing submarines only enemy-combatants). It was during this last posting that I found myself in the Air-force hospital with an infection, on the day that President Franklin Delano Roosevelt died. Antibiotics were not yet in general use, or were not yet available, and I was on the old regimen of: "Incise, drain, moist compresses, topical antiseptic and bed rest."

Harry Meakes: Conscientious Objector

For the first time, while in the military, my bombing and gunnery classes were going to teach me in the taking of someone else's life. I do not remember any misgivings entering my mind. I was now a potential gung-ho warrior. Nothing in my studies spoke of compassion or empathy for the enemy. They were war studies! Conscientious Objectors have occurred in all wars, and, as a sub-topic of war, needs some discussion. I never, at any time, considered conscientious objector status, because, at no time while I was in the service did I have the remotest scrap of thought about the immorality of what I might be going to do. Any serious thoughts I might have had regarding any moral concern over my current air crew career was still deep in the future. But my brother, Harry's quiet, decisive, moral example was already awaiting my consideration.

Harry (Henry) born 1911; died 2004. He joined the Church of Christ in 1937. I, and my other brothers, may have also inherited some of Harry's qualities, but the collection he possessed, made him distinctively different from any of us. He was painstakingly precise, scrupulously conscientious, morally focused, and he possessed honor-bound integrity. He was absolutely, the most kind and tender of men.

And, he was innately humble. There was never a braggart moment in his life. That was a deep personality trait, and therefore he didn't have to be aware of the Bible admonition - Proverbs 27:2: "Let another praise you, and not your own mouth; a stranger, and not your own lips." It was just part of Harry. Harry was an out-of-range challenge to his youngest brother - me. Harry was meticulous in all things. His focused attention was at its maximum when measuring anything, an example comment being, "It's 1/64th of an inch wrong! - I have to make another." He measured himself; measured his conscience; and practiced his religion, in the same manner. His conscientious objector decision was inevitable. His careful consideration of any course of action was a challenge to me. In 1940, failing his aimed-for standard of perfection, and not having his religiously focused analysis of belief - I had just thoughtlessly, "signed-up" in the military service. Quote from my eulogy at his funeral: "In the early 1940s (age plus 30 and single), he resisted military admission due to his religious beliefs about the taking of human life. His show of courage was impressive." My *WWII Memories*, "The military convened a panel of religious authorities to interview him. His demonstration of integrity was clear and he was classified as a conscientious objector and was not required to join the military. However, he was required to leave his home farm, and for a year or more, work on a dairy farm providing Saskatoon with milk. Meantime, blithely and blindly, I had joined the army in middle 1940. Experiencing the bloody results of war, including the ill-fated Dieppe Raid in 1942, had brought me to understand Harry's compassion and conviction. Harry was many years ahead of me as a war resister and I am proud of his stand." Through the conduit of his religious conviction he carried our father's Golden Rule precept to its logical conclusion.

It takes a great deal of courage to act counter to your peers, or the prevailing public opinion. Conscientious objection to war, though misunderstood and rejected by a large segment of society, is reluctantly accepted by the military and honored by the laws of our Western nations. We can all be grateful that we live in societies that allow freedom of conscience. Just imagine how Harry would have felt if he had been conscripted to serve in the infantry and to use a gun to kill others! My similarly-minded, gentle friend, Spencer Derby of South Pasadena, California, humorously related how, in conscripted infantry training, he used to shoot at the next soldier's target, so that his lousy marksman record would make certain he would be sent to the medics.

Albert Einstein succinctly states his admonition in "Never do anything against conscience, even if the state demands it."

Colonel John Lilburne, *The Great Quotations.* In 1635, conscientious objection was being asserted, but required the penalty of imprisonment. Three prisoners in the Tower of London - Colonel John Lilburne, Master Thomas Price, and Master Richard Overton stated, "We do not empower them to impress or constrain any person to serve in war by sea or land every man's conscience being (sic) (needing?) to be satisfied in the justice of the cause whereto he hazards his own life and may destroy another." Their opposition to military enlistment is clear. Men of courage 380 years ago!

Winston Churchill, Nov 9th 1940, (excerpt from Yahoo), said in his eulogy of Neville Chamberlain, a man with whom he had vociferously disagreed, "The only guide to a man is his conscience. The only shield to his memory is the rectitude and sincerity of his actions. If you act with perfect sincerity and with the very best of ideals, and however, the fates may play, (the shield will always) allow you to march in the ranks of honor." His tribute to Neville Chamberlain was clear. He credited Chamberlain's conscience for what Churchill believed was a disastrously conceived British foreign policy towards Hitler. He credited Chamberlain's strength of conscience, for which he should be forgiven, for the error in judgment. No one doubted his sincerity or loyalty.

The collective, fundamental, institutional objection to service in the military is demonstrated by Donald B. Kraybill in his *Puzzles of Amish Life* where he wrote, "The Amish are conscientious objectors who will not serve in the military because of their religious beliefs. In WWII and after, many Amish youth received farm deferments while others participated in some forms of alternate public service. Certainly this is freeloading. How could freedom be protected if everyone did the same? Rather than speculate about hypothetical military outcomes, the Amish believe they must be obedient to the teaching of the Bible, the way of Jesus and their consciences, regardless of the consequences. In their own way they have contributed to a peaceful world order by creating a society where violence is prohibited; where patience, not force, is the norm; and where confession, not retaliation is esteemed. Such a community does not contribute directly to national defense. It is, instead, a powerful reminder that there are other ways of structuring human behavior. In the long run such examples may contribute as much, if not more, to national security and threats to use nuclear weapons." Descriptive words! It is not surprising that Harry commented to me how much he respected the Amish.

About 1944, under pressure by the Canadian government to force the military conscription of the youth of the Doukobors, (a Canadian Amish-like religious group), the women of the group performed passive protest by *en masse* removing their clothes in public. The mounted policemen, with great difficulty, sought to have them redress.

Albert Einstein in *Ideas and Opinions* makes it clear, "That is to say, the state should be our servant, and not we its slaves. The state transgresses this commandment when it compels us by force to engage in military and war service, the more so since the object of this slavish service is to kill people belonging to other countries and interfere with their freedom of development."

Einstein continues, "What you must fight for is liberation from universal military service." "Only if we succeed in abolishing compulsory military service will it be possible to educate the youth in the spirit of reconciliation, joy in life, and love toward all living creatures. I believe that a refusal on conscientious grounds to serve in the army when called up, if carried out by 50,000 men at the same moment, would be irresistible. The individual can accomplish little here, - (we cannot) wish to see the best among us devoted to destruction at the hands of the machinery behind which stand the three great powers: stupidity, fear and greed." My conscience forces me to fully quotehim, in his wisdom!

During my Canadian army service in 1940-43 there were two suicides of which I was aware - one caused by a love triangle and the other one involved money and a Captain "paymaster." In my son Michael's 1970s service in the American marines there was at least one suicide when a young man could not "take it." It would be interesting to compare the suicide numbers in the U.S. army of today with other countries. *The Arizona Republic,* Jan 15 2013, "Suicides in the U.S. military surged to a record 349 last year, far exceeding combat deaths in Afghanistan." I would assume that in the military records there is a compilation of the various reasons for each of the suicides. I feel certain that many of them felt trapped in the brutality of unjust wars such as the Iraq War.

Mexican General Ismael Ramos Ortega, had a personal conversation with me on March 23rd 2003, the 2nd day of the Iraq War. There were reports of world-wide protests. Speaking with passion he said, (Paraphrase), "Until the protestors make their points long enough and loud enough, that young men are influenced to just fold their arms and refuse to go, we will have stupid wars like this war. Only when the world association (the U.N.) is honored in its decisions by all, including the strongest nations, will peace then be possible." Similar to the words of Einstein, and, spoken spontaneously by a seasoned, WWII American-attached general! I was deeply moved by his words.

My Air Force Colleagues

By June 1944 it had been 3 years since the Soviet Union had become our ally, and the reports of the horrendous loss of life and property, on our behalf, on the Soviet front, had brought a great deal of good will for Russia who, at great cost, was keeping the Nazis busy rather than freeing them to invade Great Britain or elsewhere. During the drought and Great Depression, the Communist Party had gained some temporary strength in all the Western nations.

While I was studying for aircrew in 1943-4 Charlie B was the only one other student in our class from Saskatchewan. We were the only two with prior military experience. He had served in an air force security force on Spider Island in coastal British Columbia, and I had been overseas for 3 years. I was about 22 years of age and he was about 24. He freely told us (all of his classmates) that he had been a member of the Communist Party in the late 1930s. He was occasionally kidded in fun about his Uncle Joe (Stalin). As a city dweller, Charlie had been exposed to the abysmal depths of the Great Depression in a way that I had never experienced. Living on a family farm, I had worked without pay for my family's mutual survival. I did not have to look for rare jobs like a city dweller would. I had adequate food, a roof over my head, a bed, and no rent to pay. The permanent force members of my army unit had been estimated to be about 94% depression escapees, all looking for looking for those same things.

Brother Jamie, and his wife Lucabelle, were living in Regina at that time and I took Charlie to their house for dinner. He showed me the "Koffee Kup Kafé", where he and his Regina Communist friends used to meet. Charlie and I made our 3-day train trips to, and from, Saskatchewan on our east coast leaves. On the "Dead-reckoning Trainer" simulator (nick-named the "Cheeser"), Charlie was, optionally, my co-pilot ten times out of 18 times. We shared and paired, wherever we could.

Charlie was certain that his recorded status as a Communist would make his graduation as an officer very unlikely. But he graduated with officer status and his final grades were higher than mine. About Jan 10th, 1945, we were sent to the Regina Discharge Center to be released. Quote my *Memoirs,* "Charlie and I considered the possibility of transferring to the army while, at the same time, retaining our commissions - possibly to the Pacific Theater of War (7 months pre-atomic bomb), so we ran around the track every day to try to keep in shape. On the last day before our expected discharge, a staff officer asked anyone who was a navigator-bombardier to step out. Charlie and I were the only two so we were retained in the service and sent back to eastern Canada for further training."

At that time the Soviet Union was our ally against Nazism. He was my closest friend. My close relationship with a patriotic Communist added to my instinctive hope for a cooperative world in the future. In the compressed 4 years when it was "OK" to be friends with a Communist, I had experienced my own microcosm of wartime good will with a member of a generally disliked ideology. We had spent much time together. I remember no conversations about his ideology. He was quiet, courteous, amiable, and a focused student. I will never know at what stage in his evolution (this-is-where I-am-at-now) my Communist friend Charlie was, then, or later. I never saw Charlie after discharge in 1945.

After a couple of years of advance planning the (April 25th to June 26th, 1945) San Francisco founding meeting of the United Nations took place. A friend of mine, Don Peterson a former teacher, had occasionally talked with me about the developing United Nations. He should get the credit for providing the spark for my later intense interest in the United Nations. In May, or early June, 1945 we were all given 1 month of leave. Don invited me to come with him from PEI on the east coast, first to Toronto (on our free leave voucher). There we would seek to take a free (Air-force to Air-force courtesy - when available) flight on a "Sky-Master" to San Francisco, visit the on-going U.N. meetings, then hitch hike our way north to Vancouver and back to PEI. I think a bit over-optimistically planned. My potential first enlightenment-opportunity had arrived. I was still too one-track minded to take it. I went with Charlie to Saskatchewan - saw my widowed mother and I never saw Don again, and so don't know if he did as planned.

Illusion: 1945

July 24th, 1945 - As an officer, I was not discharged - but effectively the same quote, "Retirement on the completion of a term of voluntary service in an emergency and transferred to Class 'E' of the General Section of the Reserve." That day was the High Point! This was the beginning of a magical time! This was hyper-euphoria! The evil in the world had been destroyed! The forces of malignant conquest had been eliminated! The high echelon of the enemy hierarchy was destined for the Nuremberg trials court of justice! Along with multitudes of other servicemen I was released from my 5 years of restrictive servitude! It was glorious! The massive flow of WWII money spent on war *would now* go for the progressive needs of education, health care, and the social needs of all! Hadn't I just seen the appetizer in last year's Saskatchewan one-payer universal hospital insurance plan? The newly-forming United Nations was a hope-filled promise of control in the incipient stages, of all future wars! One was finally able to think of the future - about education, romance and family! The icing on the cake was that, shortly before discharge, I had learned that the Canadian Department of Veteran's Affairs would grant financial help to veterans for time served in the military! An unexpected and wonderful surprise! That is not why we had volunteered, but I know that there was no complaint from any of us. Only grateful, enthusiastic, optimism! The money could be used for land purchase, business establishment, or for education. I chose education. The only way was UP!

Why am I concentrating on how *everything was right with the world?* Because this buoyant exhilarating, psychological plateau was really a delusion. We were really, *all back in the Real World!* From that plateau, the only real way was not UP, but DOWN! From thisplateau, the trickle of events, both public and private, led relentlessly to my ultimate psychological *disillusionment.*

Listen to Edward W. Morton Jr. (Purple Heart) - seriously wounded in the United States Forces in France in 1944. Author of *Worshipping the Myths of World War II 2006,* His chapter, An Opportunity Lost: "For a few moments after it ended, World War II was remembered as it really was, before its myths clouded its harsh reality. Only a few of us, still alive, (2006) remember those brief, magical times when the world and its nations resonated with the hope for a better and more peaceful world. For a short time so many of us lived and dreamed that hope. We had seen a world destroyed. Some of us had killed, some of us had been wounded; all of us had lost friends. We had helped smash towns and cities, watched homes looted, known of rapes, descended to the animal in vicious firefights, liberated whole nations from the bootheels of Nazi conquerors and the brutal Japanese, smelled the horror of concentration camps."

Morton continues, "Out of that charnel house we had come home. Alive! I have no real words for the joy to be alive at that moment in history so long ago: the war was over and we had escaped death. The sky glowed bluer than it ever had before, leaves sheened with the colors of spring and summer, and even cold water became champagne. Women shimmered with a special beauty, their bodies, their warm faces, their breasts, their thighs all a promise and a delight. There was "nothing like a dame." Life, just plain life, was sweet."

Morton continues, "And from that life burst hope. The world must change, be purified. The pain and the suffering we had experienced would have its justification in the birth of a new world. I cannot emphasize strongly enough these emotions of hope that swept over us when we returned. And it was not just for me that the world shone with a special beauty. For a few short months the whole world lived in the belief that people might grow up and that the destruction of humanity and its environment, natural and man-made, would cease. It could not be otherwise. Enemies would become friends. The pain we had experienced and seen would unleash a new social order, a world free of war and built around peace. There would no longer be such disparity in incomes. The poor would be lifted, the weak empowered, the sick given health. People would, at last, after millennia, learn to live together, share their advantages."

Morton continues, "The formative convention of the United Nations in April 1945 in San Francisco began the first step toward that new world. This is what my generation had fought for. Our Fathers had failed the world by betraying the League of Nations after World War I. Our generation would not be so stupid. Our international organization would work. We had paid for it with blood." His words are forcefully pungent. They are forged in that crucible of war, suffering, hope, and later disillusionment. I think that one can write so movingly, only when the experience has come first hand, He wrote eloquently for all of us!

Adlai Stevenson - His sober words of disillusionment at the 20th anniversary of the United Nations, June 26th nineteen sixty-five, from *The Wit and Wisdom of Adlai Stevenson,* "In the bright glow of 1945 too many looked to the United Nations for the full and final answer to world peace. And in retrospect that day may seem to have opened with the hint of a false dawn."

William Stephenson wrote in the preface of *A Man Called Intrepid,* "Yet the incipient United Nations promised a commitment to comity and reason "We looked with yearning upon a planet in the springtime of safe coexistence."

Ludwig Bourne in *Brilliant Thoughts* says "Losing an illusion makes you wiser than finding a truth." He tries to cover the aching emptiness of disillusion by making us think that we have somehow gained in wisdom. Probably, but nevertheless it hurts.

PERSPECTIVE

Anne Sophie Swetchine, Russian-French author-1782-1857, *The Arizona Republic* - "In youth we feel richer for each new illusion; in mature years, richer for everyone we lose." *This* lost illusion? We felt much less rich, just, more wise!

Sentimental Journey by Horse-Boat

Education was on the horizon, but romance summoned me first. In October 1943, two weeks before leaving the Liverpool England repatriation depot to return to Canada for aircrew training, I had met Joan "Doe." Would you believe that, the only reason I was in a pub (bar) was because I was mourning the supposed rejection of a previous (and my first) heart-throb, a Scottish girl-friend? I was at my most vulnerable! This is true! Documents and careful calculation has confirmed, that in *less than 2 weeks* of limited exposure, I stupidly decided that I wished to spend the rest of my life with Joan! Talk about being naïve! At age 21, 3 years of adult hormonal-overload, coupled with 3 years of rigid hormonal-control, had left me with hormonal-distorted judgment.

I was in love with the concept of love, and retrospectively, *not* with Joan Doe. I had no clue! Then, even more blindly, two months later, by Xmas 1943, I sent her, by trans-Atlantic mail, an engagement ring! In my Meakes/Butcher culture a *promise* had been made! After two years of romance - only by mail - *I MUST* now (August 1945) fulfill my promise. That would require an immediate trip to Great Britain! And that, of course, *was no way to conduct a romance!* My life had been invaded by a war-fostered romance. Retrospectively, it is abundantly clear that I had not yet had the experience, or developed the mature insight to cancel out. Ten years later, in this account, I will cover the end of that romance!

August 1945 to April 1946 was intended to be only a personal foot-note in this account. Why would the depressing account of my failure at marriage be of interest to anyone? Because, the foundering of this war marriage, had common characteristics with the thousands of other wartime marriages, that had also failed their promise. Because failed wartime marriages were a constant by-product of war, and were equally as war-related as many military actions were! Because, as I emphasized in the preface, this account is all about war! This marriage was, too. Even more so the later divorce.

Still more war-related reasons to speak of my trip: the war in the Pacific still had not ended; I had been discharged about three weeks before; I was on a trip to make a foreign war-time girl-friend into a Canadian war-bride; the ship was making the trip to provide horse meat to a war-starved Netherlands; the Europe I was entering was a seething cauldron of political intrigue through which former Nazis were trying to escape; the trip itself, recorded the after-effects of war and, it was also an eight-month delay in starting postwar educational plans. All war-related! This unconventional, almost-free journey may prove to be a diversion from the serious topics which impelled me to write *Perspective* in the first place.

There was still another reason for relating the details of that voyage. It appears that cattle-boats, or horse-boats, were below commentary-level and that there was little reason to speak about, or record, them. They would be lumped together under Merchant Marine war-time trips, or wartime losses. My 2014 internet research seems to give only definitions of the term, and little more. I have never heard cattle-boats, or horse-boats, being mentioned in the past 70 years. Nor have I heard of anyone else who has experienced such a crossing. Could this be one of the only diary-supported accounts of a cattle-boat or horse boat crossing?

SENTIMENTAL JOURNEY BY HORSE-BOAT

Everything occurring in later-1945 was still war-related! So was this planned trip! Disregarding that there were many successful wartime romances, my hormone-driven, juvenile approach to marriage, was destined to fail! The entire, immature, well-intentioned, romantic, but stupid, affair was tainted by being war-fostered, war-distorted and war delayed. I should add that the impatient two-year (adult) celibate-wait, followed by the major travel-endeavor; made the trip irresistibly desirable, and the marriage plan inevitably fulfilled. Do you really think: that after all the planning for the trip; that after its built-in suspense and difficulty of execution; that before I got to the altar; that I would then have the foresight and the courage to then say about the marriage - "No!?" I don't think so either. Or would she? No. Even more to the point, I *now* know that it was not even necessary! Engagement be-damned! I should have cancelled out long before the trip! Without a war to distort it, this romance would probably have taken its natural course, and in due course, I am certain, would have petered-out. Everybody's questioning of life's delivery of deemed unhappy events, brings the same ubiquitous question: "What if --? You fill it in!

While still in the air-force, and on the east coast, someone had told me that there were such things as "cattle boats" which, during wartime, were taking meat to Great Britain, on which you could sign up, and "work your way over." On my previous trip to Regina, Saskatchewan to get my discharge, I had already taken a short, complementary side trip on a PBY Catalina flying boat to Halifax, Nova Scotia, only to find out that a cattle boat trip could only be made from Montreal. The window of time given to me to appear in Regina for discharge, forced me, about July 20th 1945, to pass right by Montreal on the train, leaving my questions to be answered later.

From the 24th of July 1945, until Aug 18th 1945, I visited Mom, in Saskatoon; helped my brother Frank, driving a tractor and harrowing, and, using horses, to mow and rake hay. On August 6th, and 9th, the U.S. dropped the atomic bombs on Hiroshima and Nagasaki.

Brother Frank had pulled some strings by arranging with Ed Johnson, the local Co-op cattle buyer, for me to be overseer of two box car loads of cattle from Lestock, Saskatchewan to Winnipeg, Manitoba. My responsibilities on the trip would be minimal. At all stops I would look through the spaces in the lattice-like box car walls, to check if there were any injuries to the cattle, or if one had laid down and couldn't get up. There was to be free train fare, no food, and I could sleep in the caboose each night. Ed Johnson would try to secure further free passage beyond Winnipeg to Toronto. Detailing the first three days will demonstrate the uncertainties of the trip.

Aug 18th 1945- My brother Frank, noting that I didn't have a camera, suggested that instead I should keep a diary. Being my first diary, I detailed much irrelevant un-interesting details, which I will exclude. I will, however, include enough to illustrate the difficulties of the trip. My diary, named *Sentimental Journey* has helped my diminishing memory. The very popular current song's first verse was:

Going to take a sentimental journey,
Going to set my mind at ease,
Going to take a sentimental journey
To renew old memories.

The words were factually true.

My friend, Joe Lazar, secured my pass for me from the Lestock CNR (Canadian National Railway) agent. I waved Good Bye to Joe and to my brother Frank. The planned promise of pleasant, uneventful, ease of travel faded in the first minute! It was Saturday, late morning, and the train crew wanted to start their weekend by getting off work early; so they left Lestock just before the scheduled time, so that while I was waving Good-Bye to Frank, I found myself waving Good Bye to Jake Griffin as well. That was because Jake was just arriving with his horse-drawn dray loaded with 40 bags of flour, for shipment. His loud cussing emphasized that he had missed the train by seconds. My diary comments "Jake Griffin mad, train crew glad." The Conductor (foreman in charge of train and crew), seeing that I knew Jake, linked me to Jake's descriptive invective and lets me know that I was off to a tainted start. It didn't help that, at a little later stop at Fenwood Saskatchewan, another free-loader like me, named Bill Timkiev, got on the train with another box car full of cattle. I wondered if I would then have competition for the Winnipeg to Toronto portion of my trip!

The train arrived in Melville, Saskatchewan at 4.30 PM, and, as this was a *divisional point,* I had to change train crews and caboose. My next connecting train was not due to arrive until 5:00 AM (12½ hours later) so Bill and I shared a three-dollar room at the King George Hotel and I got up at 4:00 AM. I then found out the train wasn't going to leave until 9:30 AM four and a half hours later.

As the train moved out at 9.30 the next Conductor demanded a copy of my contract, which came as a surprise, as I didn't know it was needed, and guessed that Ed Johnson hadn't given it to me. My diary relates that he "uses words of contempt," which was my awkward way of saying that he was swearing at me, and "he says I would be put off at the next stop" and "that the Lestock Station Agent 'pass' was 'nothing!' "Ed Johnson later tells me that he was, "the toughest conductor on the line." However, the next stop is Rivers, Manitoba, another crew change and there, the next Conductor neither speaks about it, nor even asks for a pass; the train arrives at Winnipeg at 10 PM Sunday evening August 19th and Bill and I share a room at the Corona Hotel.

"As I am supposed to meet Ed Johnson, I check his room at the Seymour Hotel. He's not there. On Monday, I get nowhere; "walk over acres" of the St Boniface stock yards; repeatedly try his hotel and his stock yards office; finally connect with him on Tuesday 10 AM." I was greatly relieved because it was 36 hours after my arrival. He was handling some cattle from Staples, who was from Punnichy; who had OK'd Ed taking the cattle to Toronto; and then OK'd me when Ed said he would send me in his place. So Ed now had me hooked up with five car loads of cattle. I never saw Bill Timkiev again. I was given my old contract and issued a new contract which stated I was a bona fide member of the Canadian Livestock Coop Ltd, which - I wasn't.

On Wednesday August 22nd the train passed into the scenic north shore of Lake Superior. Having travelled the same route, at least 8 times from 1940 to 1945 when in the military, I wrote briefly, "This country is wild and beautiful. On the "flier" (military train) it wasn't as noticeable as you travel so much faster. However, on this caboose, you can thrust your head out in the fresh air and enjoy it all to your utmost." One could also ride on the small back veranda and steps of the caboose. Being less frequently used by the crew, the look-out was available to me also. There, one had to step up to a small secure platform, so your head was in the little lookout tower, and then one can see in every direction. I added "I am entranced by the deep, azure blue of those beautiful lakes nestling cozily amongst the rocks. I could watch the country go by endlessly." In 1997 I drove through this same area, and once again noted the unusually deep blue of Lake Superior and its bays. In Hornepayne Ontario, all the cattle were let off for about 4 hours; for a close check by me; for food and water; a little exercise; and then, reloaded.

Quote from my diary, "Struck another (Conductor) lemon. Thank Heaven that I have a contract to partially pacify him with. He accuses me of "just having a ride." Trouble is, I don't want to allow myself too much back-talk as the truth hurts. He says I can't use any of the bunks. The switchman promptly rolls down his bunk and tells me to use his. I hope that makes him boil!" I arrived in Toronto two days later, on Friday, Aug 24th at 10 PM.

It had been an interesting trip; there were few motels in 1945, so it might be noted that only hotels were mentioned; it had taken 6 ½ days from Lestock to Toronto; staying with the cattle when side-tracked during crew changes; never arriving at a station platform only remote areas of the railroad station; trying to placate irate conductors; checking the cattle at each stop; checking all the cattle off, and on again, at Hornepayne, Ontario; there were five boxcars of cattle, totaling 176 cattle on the Winnipeg to Toronto portion of the trip; there had been 11 different freight train crews, and cabooses, between Lestock and Toronto; and there had been a couple of days of viewing the scenic north shore of Lake Superior.

At 10 PM on the 24th, I walked "for three quarters of an hour to find a hotel which turned out to be only a half block in the other direction! It was named the Westmoreland. I had a bath of course, and Wow! Does that ever feel good! Soak until 12.30!" On Sunday Aug 26th, I watched a Chinese Victory Parade celebrating the still-developing defeat of Japan." It was a little premature as it would be seven more days before General MacArthur and the Japanese signed the peace agreement. In my diary, I get enthusiastic about the parade, "Very good! Much forethought, splendid planning, magnificent costumes, tremendous expense, and many Chinese have gone to make this parade a smashing success. It is rumored that $10,000 dollars had been spent on it!" As I now remember the parade, I am inclined to think that even in 1945 dollars, even with enthusiastic volunteers, it was probably more expensive than that. At that time, in my eyes, a dollar had a lot of value! And it did! However, seventy years of inflation have occurred since. On the evening of the 26th, I took a train to Montreal. Quote from my diary, "I stayed in two different hotels (the Alberta Hotel and the Victoria Hotel), the first two nights, the second of which was $1.50 a night."

My diary, I probably thought it was going to be easy, but it wasn't. There was no telephone book listing for "cattle boat!" Preconceived ideas are often misleading and I think I had it figured that someone would immediately tell me where I could sign up for a cattle-boat. The phone book was no help. No one knew! So, on the morning of Monday August 27th 1945, I took off optimistically, girded with a Montreal Street map and a rested pair of feet. Someone at each of these locations sent me on to the next place. In rotation they were; The Merchant Seaman's Club which sent me to see Mr. McMaster at The National Seaman's Union, 484 McGill St; who said they could do nothing, but to go to the ship La Fourchet at Shed 14 on the docks; where I was told that La Fourchet had sailed 3 days earlier; but I am told to go to the National Seaman's Pool; which send me to the John Stores Shop on St Antoine St (no number); in the general area where the shop should be I try the Red Cross. They don't know, but they helpfully phone the Montreal Service institute, who say that John Stores has been out of business since about a year before the war; they suggest the National Seaman's Pool again, so, I returned there and this time am told to try the docks area, because, regarding cattle boats, the shipping office "will know." As usual, they don't. They say to go to Mr. Munro at Walker's Hardware on St James St "near McGill St." He is away until morning. On Tuesday morning, Aug 28th, I find him in and he says he cannot help, but told me to go to the Stock yards, and finally that is the right place, and even the timing was right.

My diary: There is a big mob of about 50 guys or more, all waiting for Mr. Sylvester, who will be back at 10 AM. I found out from the other guys that I have to have passport, photographs, exit permit, Seaman's Certificate, and a National Selective Service Release none of which I have. However, I wait. I also find out that it is to be a horse- boat, not a cattle-boat. The diary continues, At 10.15 Mr. Sylvester comes and takes about five men into his office. About ten minutes later he takes five more, and tells the rest of us, "Nothing until Thursday morning." Everyone jabbers in French and tries to push in. He closes the door emphatically and puts one of his henchmen on the other side holding it. I decide I have to see him. I push on the door, stick in my foot, and start to talk. I tell him (the henchman) that mine is a special problem. He says "OK. Stand over there." An hour later he (Mr. Sylvester) gets time for me and asks me what I want. So I explain how all my papers etc. are back in Saskatchewan; but that I have my Discharge Certificate; that growing up with horses I have lots of experience with them; that I have crossed the ocean twice before; etc. He says "OK" and puts my name down on his list. I am to be, probably, on one of two ships about ten days from now, one going to Rotterdam and one to Le Havre. Things are becoming complicated. How am I going to get from the Continent to England? Wait and see, I guess.

My diary reads: The full impact of the political turmoil taking place in Europe was starting to impact my thinking! Simplistically, I had been thinking that the ship was probably going to Great Britain, and that as a member of the British Commonwealth, my papers would be easily processed. But it was going to be ten days so in the afternoon, with the help of the YMCA, I moved to share in a suite with two other guys, one of which was an 18-year veteran of the French air-force, named Dan Forget. The suite was owned by Mademoiselle Brisset Des Nos, 1455 Rue Drummond, Suite 618, Montreal. My diary doesn't say, but I expect it was more comfortable and that, probably, I saved money because of that move. I stayed there 15 days.

I had met MacGuire (Mac) at the sign-up by Mr. Sylvester. He was fiftyish in age; reminded me of the Hollywood actor Victor McLagen; was pleasant in personality; and as time passed, I realized he was an alcoholic. He wanted to work one day at a time so I accompanied him to the Canadian National Railways, shipping companies, Canadian Packers, three different hotels, the Stockyards, the Bus Depot and the Old Brewery Mission, but neither of us got work.

In the next few days I got the Selective Service Clearance Certificate at 205 La Gauchatier St; a set of fingerprints, and an ID card at Commission D'Assurance Chomage' at Apt 118, 275 Notre Dame St; two more sets of fingerprints and an Identity Card in the Canadian Merchant Marine at Capt. Gray's office. I was being urged to get a passport and it took five addresses before I found the passport application at (like now), the post-office. Now I wasted more time trying to find a sponsor - a professional who "had known me for at least two years."

My diary reads: The first try was a lawyer, Mr. Mason, at the Dept. of Veterans Affairs. He said "No! I haven't known you for two years. No-one else will sign either." But Mac, who seemed to know all the angles, assured me that we could find somebody local. The next trial was, "Honest Harry" a pawn broker, a Justice of the Peace, and a friend of Mac. However, Harry said 'No', because his applications only, 'bounce back from Ottawa', Canada's capitol. I guess his reputation, in Ottawa indicated that he didn't live up to his moniker of 'Honest Harry'. Mac's friends hadn't been much help, but now he had another, Gasper, whose nephew worked as a secretary to Mayor Houde of Montreal. We found Gasper, and his nephew, at the Silver Dollar Tavern at 10.30

AM. The nephew said Mayor Houde would have been delighted to sign but it was clear that I had been in the service for the past two years, and that everyone who knew Mayor Camille Houde, (especially in Ottawa) knew that he had been in jail for more than 2 years. The Canadian government had put him in jail for counselling the French-speaking youth of Quebec to refuse military induction in late WWII.

However, Gasper's friend, a reporter called Flannigan, recommended the correct answer. Following his advice, I sent a wire to my longtime family friend, Mr. Jack Matley, the Post Master in Punnichy, Saskatchewan, who sent a return telegram declaring his long-time acquaintance with me.

Now, how do you get quick action on a passport? Move on the problem early! I hadn't done that! I had not learned to prioritize! Very clearly I should have solved my valid sponsor problem first. Instead I hadn't focused. I had wasted time going to several movies; seeking unnecessary one-day jobs with Mac; visiting with old army friend Johnny Linkutis; taking a tour of Montreal, climbing Mount Royal on foot; and according to my diary "wandering" everywhere! It was now Sept $6^{th,}$ nine days since I signed up with Mr. Sylvester. I must now go to Ottawa and attempt to speed the processing of my passport! On Thursday evening, Sept 6th, the 10 PM Ottawa train pulled out as I approached! So instead of starting my day in Ottawa at 9 AM on Friday Sept 7th, I arrived on the morning train at 11.40 AM! Fortunately, I found the Department of External Affairs quickly, and they said they could have it ready by 5PM! Can you imagine a passport being produced in 5 hours today! Well, it wasn't then either, but they promised it would be in the mail in the morning. It arrived on Monday Sept. 10th two days before boarding the ship! Little did I know how desperately I would need it in Rotterdam.

For the trivia-minded, in the 22 days from August 20th to September 11th, I had gone to 11 movies, all by myself. They were: Salome, Where she Danced, Twice Blessed, Dorian Gray, The Valley of Decision, Eve Knew her Apples, Three Caballeros, Song to

Remember, Barbary Coast, Conflict, Incendiary Blonde and Out of this World. I saw no more movies during the rest of the trip.

My diary reads, On Sept 12th I took a taxi, taking my luggage to the ship. It was a 5240 ton, American Liberty Ship, named The Mexican. We will be taking about 670 horses from Montreal to Rotterdam. We were told that the horse population of Holland in 1939 was thought to be about 50,000, and by 1945 it was less than 5,000. The Nazis had commandeered replacement for their military horses, and the rest were eaten by the starving Dutch population. Rodric Braithwaite states in his 2006 book Moscow 1941 that, "the German army in 1941, was almost as dependent on horses as Napoleon's army (1812), and took much longer to get there (Moscow)." Four years later, the German Army now gone, we were bringing replacement horses for Dutch farm use, but primarily for horse-meat for the starving Dutch population.

My diary reads: There are two full decks of horses and the top deck has a hundred or more on it. The bottom deck is filled with bags of bran, of oats, and baled hay. There are 40 in our horse crew and three foremen, two cooks, two guards and Dr. MacDonald, a veterinary. Our first taste of work is lifting about 150 pails and iron U-shaped hooks out of one hold and setting them up (on a breast-level bar) in front of the horses. There will be a pail placed in each U-shaped hook, and then filled with water from a hose. Later the water is removed and then hay, and/or a bran mix, put in the pail. We feel plenty warm. Work until 5 Pm, supper, then back to move some bales of hay, by block and tackle, from the hold to horses on the top deck. Our primary job for the entire trip will be to feed and water the horses; occasionally mix bran and oats (2 to 1), probably when Dr. MacDonald requires it; using hoses, and wash away the horse manure into the ocean. I meet Dave Miller, who is part of our four-man crew who are responsible for an 87-horse section of horses, on the second deck.

My diary reads: Sept 13th 12 Noon, We are towed to midstream by two tugs; the purser oversees the weekly opening of the duty-free canteen. A carton of 200 cigarettes cost 70 cents, so a package was 7 cents each. Packages are sealed with sticker printed, SEA STORES For consumption outside the U. S. Penalty for fraudulent re-landing or sale in the U.S. Our gang appear to be a pretty fair bunch of guys. Meals are good. At free time in the afternoon, we watch the scenery we are passing. In the late afternoon I estimated that the St. Lawrence River, at that point, was 8 to 10 miles wide.

Horses, in general, are affable and cooperative to handle. However, we had an exception. I never mentioned her in the diary but she is firmly in my memory. The first day or two out, she got our attention. She was a medium sized black mare and she either inherited a terrible temper, or she had a terrible child hood. She persistently kicked or tried to bite everything that was close. She would try to bite whoever was feeding her, and did the same for the horse on each side. She could arch her neck around the stall and had bitten the shoulders of horses on each side of her. So we arranged to place her, where there was an empty stall on each side.

Sept 16th: Each day so far, has been primarily doing our work. We've been travelling for three days and we are still seeing occasional land. This general area was where, just in the past year, I was training as a navigator in the air-force, so I have spent the last three days, speculating about what land I have been seeing. My guesses all seem to be wrong! So mocking myself in the diary I wrote, I'm starting to acknowledge that I am actually lost! Anyway, we are sailing east which is what is wanted. Starting to wonder where the skipper took his Navigation course, though! We had our first burial at sea tonight. One of the horses had to be shot. Sprained my ankle today and the purser bound it up for me. It hasn't stopped work though. I have become quite battered and bruised through various knocks. The purser, Ray Rose, certainly seems to be a jack-of-all-trades. He looks after the canteen, looks after valuables, does all first aid treatment, and pays you at the end of the trip. I wonder what else he does.

I am starting to wonder about our horse crew. I don't trust some of them. A couple of them have openly confessed to being thieves. One told about the night before he came on board, when the police were at his front door talking to his wife, while he was escaping through the back door. He was exulting that, 'They wouldn't be able to knock on the door here!' The other described how he was able to steal truck tires off an air-force base, chisel identification names or numbers off the tires, and sell them!

Sept 17th: The sea is quite rough. The horses have quite a time keeping their feet. We have to go down every hour or so and help some up. It means quite a bit of work. By supper time the sea is running very heavily and when standing on the top deck, many waves come over away above eye level, but only the odd one, breaks over the deck as the ship rides well over them. Some of the horses are beginning to get their sea-legs and accustom themselves to the roll of the ship. Quite a few of the guys have been sick today. But so far, I've been fortunate and have felt good. I was never sea-sick on the trip.

Sept 18th: Up at 5 AM the same time as usual, and work the whole day hauling up baled hay. The sea is rougher than ever. The storm has followed us for two days. However, we are sailing with it and we may get there sooner? The horses all seemed to have learned how to maintain their feet. It was interesting, and impressive to see that when the ship rolled from side to side, the heads and tails of all horses facing sideways would disappear into, or emerge from, their stalls. And the horses in the length-wise stalls would all lean left, and then, all lean right. That of course was complicated by the big waves which the ship rode straight over, so that the ship would go up and down in a forward direction. Then the sideways facing ones leaned to the left or right, and the length-facing ones, leaned forward or backward.

Sept 19th: I helped toss another dead horse over board today. There are only a few grey horses on board but both horses that have died and another that is very sick were grey. I wonder? Dr. Mac Donald said he didn't know why. He said that the dying horses had a 'form of seasickness without the vomiting,' an easy answer I suspected, prepared for a bothersome questioner. Every dead horse represented a loss to the company, so I know that he was stressed. They had lifeboat-drill today, which I wondered about because it was at the peak of the storm, not at an early point in the St. Lawrence River quietly preparing for the coming trip. I had a shower, do a bit of sewing, read until 9 PM and then to bed. I had learned early in life, and in the army, to patch up my clothes. My diary continues, This is some gang of guys I'm with. Nobody can speak a civil word to anyone else. Tip Neil, the foreman, gets and gives more hard words than anyone else. Sure can't handle the guys successfully. There would be an out and out mutiny if we had to be under him much longer.

Sept. 20th: Two more dead horses over the side, the grey, and one bay. The storm has subsided a bit but the waves are pretty hefty. However, the old ship doesn't feel like a cork, like it did yesterday. She is a 5240-ton boat but she was treated like a toy yesterday.

Sept 21th: Bags of excitement around here this morning. Down in the hold where I am working, there was a colt born last night. By dinnertime (lunch), everybody, including the (ship's) crew had come down to see it. However, there are three more dead ones going over the side today two bays and a black. I smashed my thumbnail today. I'll be going off this boat a wreck, if I don't go careful.

Sept 22nd: There were two more burials today, one grey, and one black. We change our watches today, for the last time.

Sept 23rd: I've never seen such a quarrelsome bunch as this gang! Individually, I get along with everyone OK, but there are bitter words flying every ten minutes between someone. No-one likes the foreman and no-one fails to let him know all about it. We have to keep everything locked up too. Someone is mighty light-fingered. I think the only thing stolen from me was a bar of soap. But I still wore my army era money-belt next to my skin.

Sept 24th: At 4 PM, a high cliff is seen to port. It is easily distinguishable as Beachy Head and confirmed about ten minutes later when we see Eastbourne. We've been seeing a lot of freighters today. We passed Dover about 8.30 having picked up a channel-pilot a little earlier." My geographic recognition was much more comfortable there, than it had been in the St Lawrence River, because in the years 1940 to 1943, I had been stationed near this coastal stretch.

Sept 25th: Because of a very high wind the ship remained anchored in one spot all day.

Sept 26th: There have been ten horses die during our trip, four of them grey. The last one to die was in the English Channel, and overboard burial was rejected in place of local disposal in Rotterdam Harbor. No sight of land in the morning, but at about 5PM we approach the mouth of the Lower Rhine River, where the river enters the English Channel. Rotterdam Harbor is about 20 miles east, up the river. During that cluttered 20 miles there were many, partly sunken vessels, remnants of World War II. The voyage had taken 13 days from Montreal to Rotterdam. My next 7 months would give me another up-close look at the ravages of World War II.

We arrive and dock about 7 PM. Within an hour and a half, the stevedores and longshoremen have begun to unload the horses. They have huge electrically- driven cranes which run on rails. The horses are led into a cage, which then is hoisted off the ship to the dock below. The moment the gang plank was attached, many people swarmed on board wanting to buy tobacco, chocolate, gum, candies, clothes, nylons, and especially cigarettes." The S.S. Mexican was part of the United States Merchant Marine, and on the way over we had access to the canteen. The items in the canteen had been very cheap. My Diary continues "The 7-cent pack was being sold for 2 ½ to 4 guilders ($1.05 to $1.68) in American exchange! Not smoking, I sold just one pack, saving my cigarettes, and the nylons I brought, for future gifts. "There are cops all over the place with their natty uniforms and jaunty air." I described them that way because I recall the uniform as trimly fit, and the hat was brimless and sort of box-like, and, I think, the color was blue.

The policemen do just as much dealing as everyone else. One cop traded a Zeis-Ikon (sic) camera for 3 cartons of cigarettes ($2.10) and a $1.25 package of tobacco. Baker, one of the cooks, said he could resell the camera in London for about $24.00. About 1 in every 15 stevedores, wear wooden shoes, and I tried a pair on and was astonished how comfortable they were. The Dutch government has just recently issued a new set of bills so we have to learn the difference between the old and new in a hurry, as the old is unacceptable now. The new rate of exchange was 42 cents per guilder.

Sept 27th: Getting up at 5 AM to feed the remaining horses, I found 3 boys (about 11 years old) sleeping in a pile of hay in our hold." They did not appear afraid, but said they were hungry. Dave Miller commented that wherever he had been stationed in Holland that the children seemed to speak English to a fair degree, "We had them stay there until after our breakfast, when we brought them some of our food. Our cooks subsequently provided food for them on the other days we remained in port.

Rotterdam was a barely functioning city. There was devastation everywhere. There were just acres of bricks, portions of buildings. We couldn't find any cafes, any food shops or grocery stores only a Seaman's Club (a previous Nazi officer club) which only served rolls and sodas. None of us had ration cards which were necessary to purchase food. I was told later that there had been a big article in the paper today about "the 40 Canadian cowboys", who had brought a ship load of horses from Canada. I did get a different, small clipping later.

A quote from my *Memoirs*, "A historical note: On May 15th 1940 the Nazis had surrounded Rotterdam; the Dutch government had fallen; the Queen had left to live in Ottawa, Canada through the war; there was no remaining Dutch army or air-force; and the airport had fallen to the Nazis. As previously agreed with the Germans, surrender of Rotterdam would, when they were ready, take place by putting up surrender flares. This, the Dutch did, and then waited for the German army to move in. Instead, at 12 noon, 30 German planes took off from the captured airport, and forming evenly spaced distances apart, at 4500 feet elevation, they methodically flew over the center of Rotterdam, carefully spacing their bombs in grid arrangement for maximum devastation. The shuttling planes with new loads continued for 2½ hours, with no opposing Dutch planes or artillery. The end result was almost 25,000 men, women, and children, killed. (Producer, Frank Capra's U.S. film, Why We Fight, said 30,000). There were over 26,000 buildings destroyed including the City Hall, train station, major churches, hospitals etc. The object was said to be to frighten Paris and London, so that they would surrender quickly when their turn came. Paris's time was to come very soon."

The compact harbor area seemed in good condition, but just beyond it, the 1940 destruction was overwhelming. As I had seen in London, Liverpool and other British cities, there were block and blocks of nothing but bricks.

The fall of 1945, was the "peak-alert" time to watch for Nazis escaping from Europe, so the red tape was complex, suspenseful and uncertain. We were told that the SS Mexican would be leaving on Saturday 29th at noon. So our time would be very limited to arrange our discharge. After feeding the remaining horses on the morning of Thursday Sept 27' the eight of us who wished to sign off and go to England, got shore-passes from the purser, and then fanned out, trying to find out how to get there.

A Canadian Army officer, still stationed in Holland, met his brother Jerry Horran with a station wagon, and invited me to go along. We went first to a transit house for British troops, who sent us to the British Consulate. That is where our dire situation was spelled out! We were Canadians, on an American ship, in Holland, under contract to the Dutch Government, trying to get to Great Britain, and we had no discharge from the ship! Four countries that were all about to give us problems. They said that the "bottom line reason for the great caution by the authorities was that, there were "abundant reports" of SS troops and other German officials escaping from Europe in any way possible. So there were maximum efforts being made to refuse anyone who did not have clear, clean documentation. The British Consulate said that, "There is absolutely no transportation from Rotterdam to Great Britain, so there was no use trying anymore." Their words were supremely discouraging but, we felt, not necessarily final. From there we went to the American Consulate who told us to "try the British Consulate," from where we had just come! No progress there!

Back at the ship we had the sympathy of the skipper, Captain Grundy, who told us he would issue us discharges only when we had the written guarantees of passage to Great Britain, and a visa issued by the British Consulate. Meantime, some of our other members had tried transportation companies, and some of the small vessels that travel The English Channel. They had all said "Yes, but only if you have the consent of the British Consul." No progress there either! So our first day had got us nowhere.

Sept 28th: We had to wait awhile to be paid our wages ($50.00) and, of course, there were no discharge papers. I teamed up with Dave Miller, who had served in the Canadian services in Holland so much of what we were able to do was thanks to Dave being able to speak Dutch. Bear in mind that everywhere we went from here on, we walked. Fortunately, downtown Rotterdam was fairly compact.

Dave Miller and I went to an Information Office, who referred us to the U.S.W.S.A. (United States Wartime Shipping Administration) office. They had already heard about us and knew that the British Consul had definitely said "no" to all of us, and "will not let us enter England." However, a Captain Schumalt said he was going to the British Consulate later in the day, and would try to intercede for us. However, he later said that he could not go until Saturday. That would only leave us a couple of hours before the Mexican left, so we were resigned to probably not making connections in time. However, on returning to the Mexican we found that it would not be leaving until Tuesday morning at 5 A.M. Though it is a weekend, it is more time!

September 29th: On return from the British Consulate, Captain Schumalt informed us that the British Consul had decided to only help those who had passports and were born in Britain, which reduced our group to five from eight. He had also said that "Canadians were out, passports or not." No British Commonwealth love there! All offices were closed for the weekend, but Dave Miller and I phoned the Canadian Consulate in The Hague (the Capitol), and were able to make an appointment for the two of us at 10.30 AM Monday.

My *Memoirs*: Friday, Saturday and Sunday evenings the five of us had endless discussions on how to solve our problem. One of the objects of our hopeful discussion was the contract that we had all signed in Montreal. Quote: An agreement between the Undersigned and Donald Munro and Sons acting for, and on behalf of the Economic, Financial & Shipping Mission of the Kingdom of the Netherlands.

I, the undersigned, agree to sign on the S.S. Mexican as alivestock attendant at a wage of $50.00 U.S. funds, for the voyage Montreal to Rotterdam or other port designated on or about September 13th 1945. Should I be discharged from the ship on arrival at Rotterdam or other port designated to await another vessel for repatriation, I agree to accept a sum of $4.00 per diem, U.S. funds, for board and subsistence, plus $2.00 per diem for personal expenses. Should I not be available to sign on the repatriation vessel when required, this allotment is to cease immediately. I also agree that I will receive a further sum of $25.00 U.S. funds for the return trip. All payment of wages shall be subject to approval of the master of the vessel. Decision by the master of the vessel shall be considered mutual consent for discharge at the port of arrival. Donald Munro & Sons Ltd. Per ______________

The last sentence continued to give us hope, because we were at least getting sympathy from Captain Grundy. But he had emphasized to us that we had to have British consul approval and guarantee of passage. And most importantly, we appeared to have zero influence, or even sympathy, from the British Consulate. Another hopeful factor was that our Canadian passport stated, "British subject by birth" although the British Consul was ignoring that!

My *Memoirs*: Monday morning Oct 1st 1945, was our last chance. Dave Miller and I caught the 9.10 AM train from Rotterdam, arriving in The Hague at 9.35 and looked up the Canadian Consulate which was in the Des Indies Hotel, on one of Holland's famous canals. Mr. H.J. Feaver, who was the First Secretary at the Embassy, sympathized and said that he couldn't understand why the British Consul wouldn't consider us. So, on our behalf, he phoned the British Embassy and was told that it would take 2 months to check our papers and passports. Mr. Feaver said that someone at the British Embassy had said, "Don't quote me, but if I was those guys I'd just go down to the first British ship on the docks, and as the papers sound to be in order, just climb aboard." We explained that our group had already tried that, and that the skippers of the vessels all said, "OK but only if a British visa, etc. was also presented. Anyway, he gave us a letter on Canadian Legation letter head which stated:

> TO WHOM IT MAY CONCERN: This is to certify that I have examined Canadian Passport No. 404262, issued at Ottawa on Sept 8th 1945 to David Meakes, Esq. This passport is valid for travel to the United Kingdom. Signed; H.J. Feaver, First Secretary.

So once again, nothing concrete! Our time was rapidly diminishing! With low spirits we returned to Rotterdam and the ship at about 1.30 PM. We were immediately told that Captain Grundy had got "something going" and to get down to the American Consulate quickly. On arrival, the American Consulate sent us to Captain Schumalt back at USWSA. He sent us to the Dutch Ministry of Shipping, to obtain a letter guaranteeing passage. We got the letter and then returned to USWSA, who added a letter of OK, all of which we took back to the American Consulate. We found Captain Grundy there, and (without British Consul approval) he signed our discharges - from the U.S. Coast Guard (Certificate #3021684), of which, of course, we had not been members. Somewhere in their fine print the Coast Guard evidently stated that on discharge you must be paid your wages. We had been paid the previous Friday. So to keep it legal we were all paid one cent each.

UNITED STATES COAST GUARD
Certificate of Discharge

Serial No. G 302168

DAVID MEAKES

Canada — 44762

Horse Attendant

September 11, 1945

Montreal, Canada

October 1, 1945

Rotterdam.

MEXICAN

203,971 — Steam

Foreign

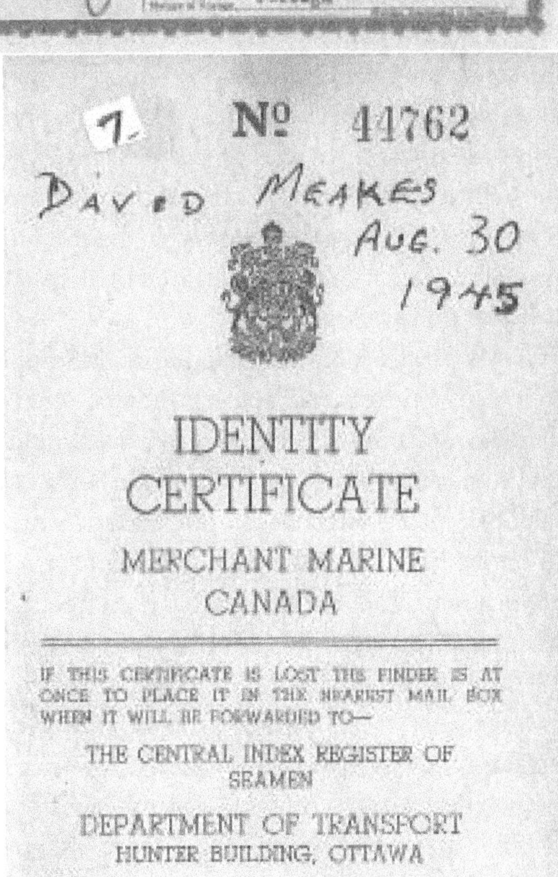

7.

Nº 44762

DAVID MEAKES
AUG. 30
1945

IDENTITY
CERTIFICATE

MERCHANT MARINE
CANADA

IF THIS CERTIFICATE IS LOST THE FINDER IS AT ONCE TO PLACE IT IN THE NEAREST MAIL BOX WHEN IT WILL BE FORWARDED TO—

THE CENTRAL INDEX REGISTER OF SEAMEN

DEPARTMENT OF TRANSPORT
HUNTER BUILDING, OTTAWA

4500
9-44

31 days in limbo. Was I in the Canadian Merchant Marines or the U.S. Coast Guard... or neither?

With elation we returned to the Netherlands's Shipping Company which was at the Dutch Ministry of Shipping, to get our actual tickets. There, we were told that we could not get our tickets, "because the consent of the American Consulate and the discharge papers are insufficient. We still require the consent of the stubborn British Consulate! It sounded like we still had the main hurdle and were back at the beginning! So us BIG FIVE were told, in effect, "Look, we don't have anything to do with Canadians, so if you want to go, then, just go." I think they were just tired of us! After all, the British Consul should still be responsible as to who enters Great Britain, whether we had a major argument with them, or not. We certainly had a growing dislike of their officialdom. I do not state in my diary, or recall, if any letter was provided to us, stating their new position. Without a further letter the revised British Consulate statement would not have satisfied those little British vessels around the port. However, the Netherlands Shipping Company, who wished to make a little profit, knew, and that was all that mattered. So without final British Consul approval, we were on our way!

My *Memoirs*: Now the Netherlands Shipping Company was ready to issue the tickets - except that they said that the weekly boat leaving Tuesday morning was full and that we would have to wait a week to go. Sometimes being a loud-mouth helps. And at this time Baker's talent shone brightly. He became our strident, demanding spokesman. What he basically said was "Look! We have a contract with the Dutch government and we have a letter at the American Embassy from your superior the Dutch Ministry of Shipping, which guarantees our passage to Great Britain. So if you can't provide us with immediate passage, then it will be up to you to provide us with lodging and food until next week - because there is not anyone who can provide us with ration cards to obtain food otherwise." It worked! The officials huddled and then suggested that we could go on the ferry tomorrow, on Tuesday - if we were willing to sleep on the top deck in the open. We all five agreed. For $26.30 U.S. funds (Six English pounds or $4.20 in Dutch guilders) we got our one-way tickets. Sweet success!!

My *Memoirs:* It was about 5.30 PM when we all returned to the ship for supper. As the ship was leaving so early in the morning, Dave Miller and I decided that we would get off of the Mexican tonight. Sleeping-in would have been disastrous. We took some food for tomorrow's brunch; took our bags and went to a police station on the docks, where they consented to let us leave them in their police office over-night. They recommended a hotel but we found it full. On trying another police station, one of the policemen, Mr. Greutens, took a break and took us to his home. He had to return to work, so Dave and I went to the United Nations Seaman's Club."

The United Nations Seaman's Club had been our evening rendezvous over the weekend. It had been a German Officers Club during the long Nazi occupation; was consequently furnished comfortably; less Spartan than many servicemen's clubs; could not serve meals, wine, beer or liquor; but carried rolls, sugarless black coffee, and an unidentifiable soda mix without ice, and they had a small pleasant band. From a newspaper article of the previous week, and from our clothing, the band had recognized our group fairly easily, calling us cowboys. [I wore a black leather zipper jacket with narrow red piping, and a Stetson fedora (not a cowboy hat), with much broader brim than wartime European hats]. "The leaving of the *Mexican* was mentioned, and thanks were given to Canada for sending the horses that were so badly needed. Then the band played "South of the Border" and "Mexicali Rose."

My Diary: Dave and I returned to Mr. and Mrs. Greutens at about 11:30 PM, we had black coffee, and conversation about the German occupation, but only in Dutch; we slept on the floor; in the morning a breakfast of coffee, bread and jam; later in the morning Dave and I picked up our bags from the Mexican; returned to the Greutens to leave them some money and cigarettes; and went to Mae West Café to eat our sandwiches; 'and have a glass of lemonade, which when we got it, turns out to be grape, orange or something else.' We hear all about our crew from the restaurant manager. It confirms our suspicions of some of them. I did not record any of the complaints about our crew. We regathered with our Big Five on the "Batavia II." The ferry left Rotterdam at 6 PM and we were given 2 bully-beef sandwiches for our evening meal. We slept on deck. The ferry docked at Gravesend, U.K. at 8.45 AM; 14¾ hours from Rotterdam. Took the 2:15 train from London's Euston station and arrived in Manchester at 7:30 PM.

You can understand that the British Consul was detested by our *"Big Five."* He had made himself clear by saying that he wouldn't consider Canadians, with or without passports. Yet it appeared very simple to us that he was wrong. In my passport it stated that my "National Status" was "British subject by birth." Simplistically, that appeared all that was necessary for him to consider us. The official representative of the King (or of the "British Commonwealth") in Canada is the Governor General. He has no authority in Canadian affairs. But on the inside cover of the passport a clear appeal to anybody considering our plight, was printed this flowery statement by the Englishman who was then Canada's Governor General. "We, (he and the King) Alexander, Earl of Athlone, Knight of the Most Noble Order of the Garter Etc., Governor General and Commander in Chief of Canada. Request in the name of His Britannic Majesty, all those who it may concern to allow the bearer to pass freely without let or hindrance and to afford him or her every assistance or protection of which he or she may stand in need." At that time, in our view, he had no basis on which to exclude consideration of our needs.

However, now, 70 years later, it has long been very clear that Sept 1945 was a peak time for some of the most heinous of Nazis to flee from Europe to avoid capture, and to avoid the Nuremberg Trials. Germany had very few port cities, and port cities such as Rotterdam, would be the most likely location for escape. Two of those prominent people who did so, were Adolf Eichman, and Dr. Josef Mengele. I can easily imagine the pressure that European consulates were all feeling. No-one wanted it to happen on "their watch." Anything that hinted at less than perfect documentation was avoided. Within the framework of the "Big Picture," our minor personal needs were easily sacrificed to security. Maybe I would feel differently if we hadn't succeeded, but, I have long ago forgiven the nameless, faceless British Consul!

My *Memoirs*: It had been 46 days since I had left Lestock; had got paid $50.01 for the Atlantic crossing, and had spent about the same amount for the two fares from Toronto to Montreal, and from Rotterdam to Gravesend (London), Great Britain. I had 13 differing descriptive designations along the way: I had been designated as a caretaker on my Lestock to Winnipeg railroad cattle shipment; thanks to Ed Johnson I had then been declared a "bonafide" member of the Canadian Livestock Co Ltd', so that I could then be designated as "stock attendant" on the Winnipeg to Toronto railroad cattle shipment; was referred to as a livestock attendant on the Netherlands (Donald Munro) contract; as #SR/179428 on my identity card of Commission D'Assurance-Chomage; referred to as a horse attendant on the Canadian Dept. of Agriculture Exit Permit; and also as a horse attendant on the American Coast Guard discharge certificate; as a horse-tender on my Rotterdam Shore pass; as a student on my Canadian passport; as a seaman on my Merchant Marine ID card; as a Quebec youth in the Montreal newspaper; as a cowboy in one Rotterdam newspaper and at the United Nations Seaman's Club in Rotterdam; as David Meakes Esquire at the Canadian Legation in The Hague; and, (I think) as a "Man aan Boord Zijn" in the other Rotterdam newspaper. With a little foresight, - and the usual hindsight - I should have taken a camera. I did retain the diary and about 15 related documents.

To give final credits: I had reached my destination with a lot of Golden Rule assistance from some very helpful people, nine of whom were strangers to me. . The main ones were: Brother-Frank, Joe Lazar, cattle buyer Ed Johnson, drifter MacGuire, Mr. Sylvester, Reporter Flannigan, old friend Jack Matley, Captain Schumalt, Captain Grundy, Dave Miller, mouthy Baker, and Mr. and Mrs. Greutens.

England

On November 24th,1945, Joan 'Doe' and I got married at St Peters Anglican Church in Blackley, a suburb of Manchester, England. While in Great Britain, October 3rd 1945 to April 16th 1946, I had two jobs. The first month-long job, acquired 3 days after arrival, was as a checker at a freight terminal, ("goods depot") and except for the bald tires on the lorries (trucks), and the threadbare clothes and "clogs" (wooden shoes, hinged at the arch), which many people wore, I do not recall any war related items of interest on that job. I do remember being offered high prices for my leather jacket which was keeping me warm in a cold, unheated, freight terminal. I never considered it.

My second job was a British government, 4½ month, civil service job where I worked for the "Price Regulation Committee," part of the Board of Trade. It was a still-existing, wartime attempt to stop excessive profits in the capitalist business society. My wage was better than my first job and I was paid $17.28 for a 40-hour week. My father-in-law was a lorry driver for the London, Midland, and Scottish Railroad; he had severe untreated asthma; which, aggravated by the permanent "Manchester Mist" (industrial smog), led to his mid-50s death four years later. My *WWII Memories:* It was a terrible winter for the British public (and all of Europe). The war had only been over 5 or 6 months. The country had not been occupied, but its families, farms and cities were all devastated. Abba Eban (future Israeli Ambassador), in his book *Personal Witness,* wrote of London in 1946, his remarks being equally applicable, or more so, to Manchester. "London was weary and drab, its people underfed and ill dressed, during a winter of unparalleled severity. Food was not only scarce; the very procedures for obtaining it required an exhausting effort that was marked by the poverty of result. With shortage of fuel, English houses were colder than English houses had been throughout history. The hulks of shattered buildings------.

My *WWII Memories*: Some essentials were returning to the stores etc. but no luxuries were available. There was a very careful distribution of the first, post-war shipment of bananas so that only children would get them. The Ministry of Health (Department of Health) published food saving suggestions, including their advice to, "Put your butter, margarine, jam, jelly, etc. onto your bread, not onto the plate first." The widow in the house adjacent to the Doe house burned some of her furniture to keep warm. There were line-ups of people two blocks long to fill their sacks with "brickettes" of "coke" for their fireplaces. "Coke" was a flammable by-product of coal, which would glow, produce considerable heat, but which, in my memory, had minimal flame. There was no bath in the Doe home, so every couple of days, Joan and I went to the local bath house for a shower. The charge was one shilling and six pence (about 36 cents at the "then" rate of exchange).

No-one Joan knew had a car, and there was still no petrol (gas) in any case. So we, and everyone else, used buses, trams, trains, and feet. Food and clothes were still rationed, were in limited supply, and of poor quality. The "poor food" led to a painful hemorrhage of my gums, and when I went to the doctor in early 1946, it was diagnosed as Vitamin-C deficiency (the "scurvy" of ancient sailors). There had been no fruit and very limited vegetables in our diet. When I was put on Vitamin C tablets, it cleared up in a few days. One unusual pub (bar) was The "Shambles," appropriately named, as it was the only usable portion that remained of a building in a totally flattened 3-block area in downtown Manchester."

While in Manchester, my Air Force friend Don Peterson's influence surfaced, when I purchased a small book explaining the details of the 6 month-old United Nations. I also purchased *Left Turn, Canada,* now a part of this account's bibliography. In Feb 1946, there was a hint of the Cold War to come, when Churchill gave his Fulton, Missouri speech speaking in foreboding terms, speaking of the of the "descent of an Iron Curtain (Communism) over eastern Europe." Though he had just lost the British election, he would always be someone to whom everyone listened.

Unlike most returning Canadian war veterans I was now a civilian, so we paid full fare for me and my war bride trip to Canada. On April 16th 1946, we took the French ocean liner, the *Ile De France,* to Halifax, Nova Scotia and then travelled by train from there to Saskatoon, Saskatchewan, Canada. I recall only one memory on that ocean trip.

My *Memoirs*: At that time Great Britain had very strict monetary controls and regulations. There was a precise allowance on the amount of British money that could be officially transferred out of the country, in our case to Canada. The amount to be transferred was already recorded on an official form, and all the extra money could not, at that time, be changed into foreign currency. With an unknown higher limitation, one could carry surplus, unchanged British cash. We had already been allowed our maximum limit. However, the first night on the Ile de France, while I slept soundly, Joan was able to get consent from the purser's office and she exchanged about another 50 pounds ($242.00) to Canadian currency. In the morning she was ecstatic, saying she had accentuated the "suffering war bride" persona to the purser. As convincing as that was, I wished I could have seen her accomplish it.

Education: April 1946 to December 1949

At the CVTS (Canadian Veteran's Training School) in Saskatoon, with an accelerated course, I was able to complete my remaining half of Grade 11 and my Grade 12 by December of 1946. There was no graduation ceremony just a certificate. During my time in Saskatoon I received a visit from my Air-force fellow graduate, Bob Spinks. He was attending University of British Columbia and he gave a lecture at the University of Saskatchewan on the political concept of "Technocracy." Webster's Dictionary defines Technocracy simplistically as "Government by scientists and engineers." I remember two of their ideas. 1. The use of "energy certificates" instead of money (a unit of energy was named an "erg"). 2. Cooperative, planned, continental energy control. For example, Canada, USA, Mexico, and the other Latin American countries would have a unified energy control so that continental resources were used efficiently, economically, equitably and cooperatively without water disputes. It was a thinking-outside-the-box, thought-provoking concept, and a tribute to both free thinking universities. It could be a step towards the needed cooperative world society of the world in the future.

Jawaharlal Nehru wrote in his book *India's Freedom,* "In America a great stir was caused by the Technocrats, a group of engineers who want to do away with money itself and to substitute for it a unit of energy, an "erg." How many of us can conceive of a world without money and with an invisible erg as a measure of value? And yet this is soberly and earnestly advocated, not by wild agitators, but by well-known economists and engineers."

At Saskatoon CVTS, I had a professor named Mr. Elliot. He was a WWI Canadian veteran; had fought in the Canadian segment of the, 1918 Allied "White Army" against the Bolsheviks in Northern Russia in 1918; married a Chinese lady and lived in China much of the 1920s-30s. He provided a foreboding commentary on the one-year-old United Nations saying that, "it would prove little better than the toothless League of Nations." His two complaints were:

1. That the U.N. "Peacekeepers" were not "preventers." Recruited from member countries, they were to be used primarily as buffers between already hostile countries, such as Israel and Lebanon. The arrogance of those who wield power had not been curbed because of the League of Nations. *Disillusionment!*
2. That the Security Council (the executive body) was permanently constituted by only the strong members of World War II, the USA, Great Britain, France, Russia and China. They were given the veto over any action. By now, 2012, the number of the Security Council has been increased to eight, out of the 193-member organization. But the veto power remains only with the original five members. Any one of those five members, if their countries interests are at stake, can deter the wishes of the other 192 countries. The current issue, as I am writing this in the summer of 2012, is the failure to take any decisive world action to stop the carnage in Syria. Both Russia and China have used their vetoes to avoid action. Mr. Elliot is still right - 67 years later. *Disillusionment!*

EDUCATION: APRIL 1946 TO DECEMBER 1949

The Illinois Department of Education accepted my Saskatchewan Grade 12 certificate as the equivalent of 1 year of college in Illinois, satisfying entrance requirements at the Chicago College of Chiropody (Podiatry), and I was able to sign up at the last accelerated post-war class for veterans, intended to allow veterans to start making-up their lost years of civilian life at an earliest possible date. Time off from study and clinic would be 1 week in the summer and 1 week at Xmas/New Year. Working a 20-hour-a-week spare time job in addition to studies left minimal spare time.

Though I received major financial help from the Canadian Department of Veterans Affairs, I still found it necessary to work, and recorded income every week of my years there. My jobs were grocery store clerk, shoe salesman, and night superintendent at the Iron Fireman Stoker and Oil Burner Company.

I shall skip description of my irrelevant studies in Chicago but here are some of the political events of those three years: The Truman Doctrine (Hold the Soviets were they are); the Nuremberg Wartime Trials; the Soviet Czechoslovakia coup; the Krupp Trial; the Marshall Plan (to help Europe {and deter Communism}); the formation of UNAC (Un-American Activities Committee); France was at war in Vietnam; and Howard Hughes flew his Spruce Goose. At my evening work I retrieved a copy of the famous, now valuable, Chicago Tribune's headline blunder, "Dewey Beats Truman" newspaper from a trash can - only to have it settle into a fist-full of pulp, about seven years later, in my Mom's flooded Saskatoon Saskatchewan basement.

During WWII it had seemed to me that, because of the great international popularity of FDR (President Franklin Delano Roosevelt), that no-one in his home country could not also love him. Though it was over 2 years since his death, I soon heard about the Republican dislike of him. But, while in Great Britain in the earlier winter of 1945- 46, I had also heard similar criticism of universally respected Winston Churchill, who had lost the 1945 British election just before my horse- boat arrival. The old modified adage: "A prophet is not respected in his own country." In Canada, our bland, play-it-safe

William Lyon McKenzie King, Canada's Liberal Prime Minister, was still in power.

In early 1947 a traveling salesman came to our Chicago apartment and coaxed me into buying my first history of WWII, entitled *The Complete History of World War II.* This book has 1000 pages of text plus many pages of pictures. It is the official U.S. Armed Services Memorial edition. There are one page letters of dedication by President Roosevelt (who died 2 years before its publication), General Eisenhower, and the Chiefs of Staff of all the Services and some government departments. It was a U.S. Federal Government authorized and approved nation al literary effort. It should have been authentic, and above reproach. Maybe just a little jingoism, here and there, because, after all, look who thought they were solely responsible for winning the war!

However, it said of the Canadian Dieppe Raid, quote: "The Dieppe raid proved conclusively that the Allies were mastering that intangible and elusive key to every great military victory "perfect synchronization." As a Canadian, I would have loved to believe it, but in reality it was the reverse. Quote my unpublished manuscript, *Debacle at Dieppe,* "The Dieppe Raid was a major, chaotic, disorganized, military blunder." I am glad that book came first. That analysis was pure high- grade hype, including many other errors. It was clear that that portion was not written by a reputable historian but instead by a space-filling writer. The Random House Dictionary defines "hack" as, "A writer who exploits his or her ability primarily for money." The writer ofthat analysis qualified as a hack, for sure.

Edward W. Wood Jr. author of *Worshipping the Myths of World War II* wrote, "By believing the myths of world war II as the truth of war we have but created another monstrosity, resembling our failure in Vietnam, another war that will not only cripple those who fight it, harm our armed forces, erode our reputation throughout the world, and, this time, turn much of the world against us." From the day of the disaster, it was clear that The Dieppe Raid was a disaster. I would have to hope that the rest of the book was more reliable.

Perceptively phrased, Ambrose Pierce comments in *Brilliant Thoughts* "God alone knows the future, but only a historian can alter the past." The "Big Lie," in this account, caused me to be much more wary of future war histories. The U.S. history writers included Canada, as one of the Allies, in the flood of patriotic, valorous verbiage regarding Dieppe. However, it failed truthful analysis when it came to speaking of the efficiency of the operation. Maybe it was too soon for informed analysis. The, as-yet, unanalyzed battles of WWII, were being commented upon, by the victors of the war.

On graduation with the degree of Doctor of Surgical Chiropody (changed in 1957 to Doctor of Podiatric Medicine), in December 1949, Joan and I traveled by the Zephyr, Chicago to Minneapolis, our first non-steam train ride; visited brother Jamie and Lucabelle in Winnipeg; visited brothers Harry, Art and Frank at Lestock, Saskatchewan; visited Mom in Saskatoon, Saskatchewan; went by train to Vancouver, British Columbia; wrote my provincial examinations (state board); got a security guard job; initially practiced part time with Dr. Stan Gillis in downtown Vancouver. Then I used *all* of my savings, and taking a bank loan, I hired a carpenter, and concentrated on a month-long period of construction of my North Vancouver office; opening the office in June 1950; and continued to work evenings as a security guard, part time postal worker, and in occasional construction.

As the Korean War started on June 25th 1950, I was snowed-under with concern for life survival and practice survival. I had only a cursory impression of the politics in the developing Korean War, but I did experience that first, major, post-UN-formation feeling of disillusionment at the United Nations failure! James Forrestal, U.S. Secretary of Defense said that the "United States could expect 40 to 45 years of military confrontation." I wondered then, and again at Soviet collapse time in 1990, how anybody could be so prescient. My time in North Vancouver extended from January 1950 to April 1955.

Marital Disillusionment; Mexico; Toronto and Why California?

Helen Rowland, 18751950, American writer quoted in Thought of the Day, *The Arizona Republic*, "Falling in love consists merely in uncorking the imagination and bottling the common sense." Aptly phrased!

By June 1953, we had been in North Vancouver 3 ½ years. I was realizing I was in a slow-growing profession. I later realized that I was a lousy networker. My podiatry practice was barely surviving; I continued to work as a security guard. To my knowledge, credit cards had not yet been invented which was a real blessing! I couldn't conceive of borrowing more money from the bank. Using a card table, a hot plate and a couple of cots, we initially used a 250 square foot space behind the office in which to live, then an apartment, and by 1952-53, the main floor of a small furnished house. We forced ourselves to live within our income.

Though I was desperate, Joan still refused to get a job. She had always wanted me by her side all the time possible, and she was by then, more demanding. Her bizarre, paranoid, jealous, suspicious behavior had become violent, breaking things and attacking me. On patients' inquiries, I twice used the same excuse, saying that the deep gouges in my face were because of, "our neighbor's German Shepherd."

She was jealous of the time demands of my office, and of any females I might have as patients.

Through a wonderful, free, community agency called the Family Welfare Bureau, directed by a social worker named Mrs. Chown, we got the personal counseling help that we both needed. They arranged for psychiatric counseling. The psychiatrists said that Joan was severely schizophrenic; the condition was life-long; that "maybe" five years of twice-weekly psychiatric analysis office-visits could help, but not cure; and that there was no medication that would be of any appreciable help. I later found out that, about then, in the mid-fifties, the first tranquilizer, Miltown, was being developed. In the meantime, she had frustrated a succession of three lawyers saying she wanted no divorce only a "life-long" exorbitant separation agreement. Because of her unreasonableness two lawyers refused her as a client. Our 8 years of post war effort was in major uncertainty.

Near this time an optimistic life-line was thrown to me by a friend, Dr. EC. He had an office in South Vancouver, and we figured that we could start a partnership in a central Vancouver city office, and ultimately close our two peripheral offices. We established a formal partnership in the spring of 1953. We first started a tiny test office, shared with an optometrist in a village named Whalley, about 30 miles southeast of Vancouver. It failed, so we closed it in May 1953.

By early 1953, Joan had become increasingly jealously upset, over Dr. EC. I use the term jealousy, because, though it was for our financial improvement, she was very envious of the time needed to try to improve my mediocre practice. In June 1953, I moved out of our rented house, and into my office, and for the next 18 months I lived in my 48-square foot #2 treatment room, still paying her maintenance.

In August 1953, Dr. EC and I, opened a ground-level office at 531 Seymour St in downtown Vancouver and failed again, closing it August 1954, still owing the last two years of our 3-year lease. This was partially resolved by a next-door business partially taking over our lease, but leaving us still owing $1560. On Dec 31st, 1954 we ended our partnership. The terms were - Dr. EC would take over my North

Vancouver practice, it's equipment, it's patients and its outstanding original loan; he would assume all debts related to our Vancouver office including the debt we had assumed to get out of the lease, - and in return I would get *only my freedom.* Though, I would have neither money nor property,it was most welcome.

In Feb 1954, widow Marguerite (Peggy) McLaughlin (nee Young), had come to our Vancouver office for foot care. By late 1954, Peggy and my relationship had advanced to a point that we started considering a mutual future. At that time there were no divorces in my family, and divorce was considered a "cop-out," a failure, a religious sin, and a disgrace. At that time Canada had a divorce law that was the same as New York State, and similar to many other state's laws, - divorce only for adultery. Her "cold" nature made it clear she would never be adulterous, and she died unmarried in 1989. She would find herself jealously contented if I committed adultery - as that would validate her demand for life-long financial support. I would not cooperate.

Planning, for a normal life in Canada was no longer an option. Nevada was known as having the most liberal divorce laws in probably the world, but my attorney found that the USA and Canada had a mutual agreement which stated that if a married individual of either country wished to move to the other country, that it would require the written consent of the spouse. Joan was decisively away ahead of me. Seven months earlier, she had her lawyer put in the U.S. immigration file a signed letter saying, "Don't let Dave go to the U.S." As there was always news about the Hollywood movie stars going to Tijuana for a "quickie" divorce, or a weekend divorce, I decided to go and see the Mexican consul in Vancouver BC, and to inquire from him about immigrating permanently to Mexico. We decided that, wherever we went, we would get a divorce and re-marriage in that country, and then live there, thus making our lives secure. The Mexican consul courteously advised going to Mexico first to see if we liked it. I think it was through him that we got in touch with Senor Arturo Trevino, an El Paso, Texas attorney who would arrange divorces over the border in Juarez, Mexico. Later, fearing bigamy charges, I retained a series of documents and letters which detail our efforts, culminating in our Mexican divorce on April 22nd 1955. My comments on that event from my *Memoirs* follow:

Peggy's faith in me must have been at peak level! Only with monumental faith could she have done the following: Quit her job and give up her comfortable apartment to take up *with an ageing and bankrupt fiancée with no credit card who*

- *had a 10-year record of failure in marriage*
- *had a five-year record of 3 failed Podiatry practices*
- *couldn't get a divorce in either Canada or the USA*
- *only expected to get a divorce in the foreign land of Mexico*
- *only said that he then intended to marry her*
- *had now cut off his return to his B.C. practice*
- *had not eliminated her foot problem*
- *couldn't dance, while she could*
- *didn't own a car*
- *had no idea if he would ever practice his profession again*
- *didn't know where it would be if he did practice*
- *didn't even have any worthwhile, "back-up" skills, if he couldn't practice*
- *therefore, didn't know what he was doing*
- *owned nothing but the clothes he was wearing*
- *was using her limited money to take a meandering bus trip to Mexico where neither of us had ever been before and neither could speak Spanish*
- *had not had a shower for almost 2 years*

This final comment was because there was no shower in the 48 square foot space in which I lived during that time. There was also no gym or YMCA in North Vancouver so I "sponge-bathed."

If the past was prologue, then I should not have been considered a good prospect. By Peggy's willingness to leave Vancouver with me, under those circumstances, she was bringing me hope in a very uncertain and obscure future.

Mexico -1955

Joan had finally gone to work in our 22 months apart, and by her first demanding forwarded letter, we later found that she was leaving Vancouver to return to England at about the same time that we were leaving for Mexico. Peggy and I went by bus from Vancouver B.C. to El Paso, Texas; got my official divorce in Juarez, Mexico; were married in the Recorder's Office in Juarez, Mexico on April 29th 1955; both divorce and marriage authenticated in United States at the El Paso Consular Office); proceeded by bus to Mexico City; met and were greatly helped by Americans Aurelio (Ray) and Muryl (Mu) Medina, and by Tony and Donna Vega; lived very economically, while we avidly sought permanent residence, Mexican citizenship and employment; moved with the Medinas and Vegas to their rented chicken ranch in Texcoco, Mexico; still continued our efforts; through Austrian attorney Dr. Oswaldo Scholl, successfully found how to secure Mexican permanent residence visas. However, we gave up because our language had improved only minimally; the realization that in Mexico the Podiatry profession existed only as a Dr. Scholl's commercial operation; and that our (Peggy's) limited money was running out. We saved just enough of our money to buy non-stop bus tickets from Mexico City to Trenton, Ontario in Canada at, or about, the beginning of July 1955. But we were enticed by Ray and Mu (the Medinas) to first go with them, on a much-needed, 4-day, very hot, very humid, off-season, exceedingly-interesting, unbelievably-economical, spectacular, suspenseful, romantically-remembered, humor-laden, car-trip vacation, in beautiful, entrancing, exotic (especially then), pre-famous, Acapulco; and we continued to fall in love with Mexico.

Toronto, and Why California?

We stayed July and August 1955 with my new in laws, Arnott and Maud Young; I wrote the provincial state board exam; attempted a transitory practice with Dr. DC in Kingston, Ontario; now-pregnant Peggy and I moved to Toronto in October; got a job selling shoes; later started a tiny practice in East Toronto; and worked in the office of my colleague Dr. Ed Morgan. By then, our initial plans to save money, study Spanish, and return to Mexico were fading. With the Korean War in the recent past, a pro-return to Mexico entry in my *Memoirs* reads: *Mexico less likely to enter a war.* Our son Michael Glenn Meakes was born July 6th 1956.

Early in 1958, a 3-week long series of disturbing phone-calls came, in which someone waited on the line for us to hang-up. Our paranoia over an uncertain divorce, and a possible bigamous law-suit arose. I went to a highly rated Toronto divorce attorney, Nathan R. Cappe. His comments were: "You permanently left North Vancouver BC, your place of domicile - Good! You got nothing for your North Vancouver practice - Good! So you don't own anything Good! You tried to live in the country of your divorce and marriage - Good! Your intent was - Good! But I cannot tell you if your Mexican divorce and marriage are acceptable here. That could only be established in a court case."

It was clear that we would probably never feel psychologically comfortable living in Toronto! Joan, from her Great Britain perch, remained a threat, as her letters to Dr. EC back in Vancouver, were confirming. So once again we considered emigrating to the U.S. By then, 3 ½ years after our previously failed attempt to go to the U.S. that previous BC barrier to U.S. entry was not mentioned. We held our breaths. There were no problems getting our green-cards. We now had a paid-up second hand 1956 Chevrolet station wagon, a pre-need set of Colliers Encyclopedia for 2-year old Mike, about 1800 dollars, and everything we owned was all in a paid-up 4x4x4 box-trailer. At ages almost 36 years of age for me and almost 39 for Peggy, there would be a major effort to make no mistakes this time!

We were not having failing love for Canada and its future opportunities, or for an increasing love of the U.S. and its wonderful history of freedom - because Canada had a 100-year history of similarly equal freedom. We thought that California, because of the Hollywood-

Mexican divorce connection, might be more tolerant of our Mexican divorce. California, though it had a reputation as having a very tough state board exam - was a better state in which to practice. Why? For the sake of curious family members here is another diversion starting 15 years earlier, with my army days.

Quote my *Memoirs* in England, "May 22nd 1943, I was sent to Maida Barracks, Canadian Military Headquarters, Aldershot to take Course 1934, Serial # - 12. This was a 28-day course on foot-care for soldiers. I placed first in the examinations for the 2nd Division, and official and unofficial compliments helped make it such a pleasant experience, that it had an influence on what to do when the war was over, and consequently it also had a direct influence on the rest of my life." Having read about my growing years, it will be easy to realize that there were minimal role models for me to look at and say, "I want to do that."

Abraham Lincoln was quoted in *The Wit and Wisdom of Abraham Lincoln,* "There was absolutely nothing to excite ambition for education. Of course when I came of age I did not know much." His assessment of his home opportunities was the same as my own. My entire home region, of Saskatchewan was drought/depression blighted. In 1935 the MD was paid only by salary, and was getting $12.33 per day for being available 24 hours a day for 365 days a year ($4,500 dollars per year). See *Autobiography of Henry O. Little, Sr.* on the internet. There was no occupational counseling at my 1946 veteran's high school.

My inexperienced, farm-impregnated mind seemed to see only that one very bright spot of foot care accomplishment. The three military teachers on that army course had all been very up-beat on the profession. My lack of awareness of Chiropody (Podiatry) in my rural Saskatchewan region, only meant that I would find the profession more prevalent in larger cities, which, of course was correct, but, that still did not tell me, that as a profession, it was rare in all of Canada. I visited the 3 Saskatoon chiropodists, who were all well established and all contented with their profession. Too late, as I was graduating from Grade 12, my literature professor recommended that I "consider" Journalism. However, I was, at that time, already accepted at the

Chicago College of Chiropody. With my own personal experience overview as my emotional guide, I found myself in the *C.C.C.* - Chicago College of Chiropody - because there was no Canadian Chiropody college. To an analytical mind that should have raised the question, 'Why? That hint passed me by.

Why was there no college in Canada? I had found out in B.C., and now, in 1958, I found out in Ontario, that Chiropody/Podiatry was an unknown entity to the average Canadian citizen. If you had a foot problem you went to your MD. Realizing we were competition the MD-dominated state/provincial medical boards, discouraged Podiatry laws, licenses etc.; and they also greatly resisted any increased scope of Podiatric practice. For example, we were not allowed to practice many things that we were taught in our medical training. This was also true in many of the U.S. states.

During my years in Chicago, I had spent 100% of my study on the medical aspects of our profession, but I had never received any training about the business aspects of a private healing profession; my inability to advertise (no profession could at that time); my view of a medical practice as not being a business; and my diffident demeanor all spelled probable failure. I knew nothing about negotiation with landlords; office location; leases; the importance of networking etc.

I had committed my World War II educational credits on a 4-year course of study and work, and 8 years of unproductive practice in what I finally understood was a medically-limited profession; a legally-restricted profession; a generally unknown profession; and, primarily, - an American profession. My Dad's still-true maxim of "an education is easy to carry and goes with you wherever you go," only meant that my choice of education had not been a wise one. The only long term good answer to make use of my educational asset was to go where it could be used.

I now realized that opportunities for success should be greater in the U.S. The British had a generally recognized, but technician-level profession dominated by the medical profession. I now knew that Mexico had an abysmal Scholl's-controlled business called *Especialistas de Los Pies*, again medically controlled. Not having a Podiatry college in

Canada was an indication that Podiatry didn't have a firm legal status in Canada. Thus insurance companies, governmental medical agencies were not constrained to honor any requests for payments for service, etc. Both the U.S. and Canadian professions had one year earlier, in 1957, changed their official name from Chiropody to Podiatry. That only meant more current confusion. The official view was that it would take 30 years or more for the new name to become firmly known. By either name very few of the American public knew what a podiatrist was. Fifty-eight years later, in 2015, many don't know, even now. But in Canada the profession was even less known or recognized. There were variables in both Canadian provinces and American states. I had landed into Ontario, the most populous but the most MD-controlled, Podiatry-restricted province in Canada. California was known as a leader in advanced Podiatry legislation and practice in the U.S. - and in many other ways. "Green pastures" beckoned!

In the 18 years since I had left home I had acquired some experience in every-day living in 4 countries, each of which had its own appeal and reasons for consideration. But I had already lived in the U.S. for 3 years (all of 1947 to 1949) and had 8 years of Canadian Podiatry practice experience. So now that we were able to enter the U.S. and take the California State Board exams, the Mexican divorce problem should have lesser significance. I would not have believed that 57 years later I would not be a U.S. citizen. Nor that my 85-page treatise, called *American Citizenship Reconsidered* would be in the University of California in Santa Barbara. That was far from the plan. A year later, in Los Angeles, when changing my occupation from construction worker to taxi-driver, I signed a *Certificate of Intent* to become an American citizen. That was our intent. I came to the U.S. with some reservations but only about their foreign policy. Those doubts were soon found to be true resulting in this commentary, 57-plus years later!

PART FIVE

War

War I abhor, yet how sweet
The sound along the marching street
Of drum and fife, and I forget
Wet eyes of widows, and forget
Broken old mothers, and the whole
Dark butchery without a soul.
Richard Le Gallienne. *The Great Quotations.*

General Douglas MacArthur, *The Great Quotations,* "I know war as few other men now living know it, and nothing to me is more revolting. I have long advocated its complete abolition, as its very destructiveness on both friend and foe has rendered it useless as a method of settling international disputes."

The topic of war and peace is too immense, and thus this task is too daunting, for any-one of my limited skills to fully fathom, discuss or write about, *unless* they are obsessed. I guess I'm obsessed. My obsession probably began when, as a medic, I was necessarily deeply involved in, "processing" the revolting stream of broken, bleeding, and dead bodies in the aftermath of the 1942 Dieppe raid in WWII. Abhorrent as that was, later history led directly to the sad realization that an excessive number of lives were paid for the gains attained. That raid was said to have served to make war more efficient, and so D-Day more successful.

Maybe true - for that war. But the passing years bring continuous change. Strategies may be similar, but advanced technologies dictate that the tactics of WWII are mostly obsolete. The lessons learned on the Dieppe raid are of minimal practical value today. So, using new technologies we design, train, and fight, on and on, - on and on, - and on and on - *ad infinitum* - The war industries will see to that.

War, and the fear of war, is universal. In all countries, war has been a cursed affliction and a despairing topic for thousands of years. But these melancholic pages are still predicated on hope. The preface made clear that this account was intended to be about causes and prevention of war, and not about battles etc. However, I will attempt a short at-random review to re-enforce why we are discussing the causes of war.

In *Eyewitness to History*, William Howard Russell, a Crimean War survivor of the Battle of Balaclava and the Light Brigade, Oct 25th 1854, wrote of the six-hour battle in which 409 0ut of 607 British cavalrymen were killed. Note in his writing the resigned acceptance of the result, and the patriotic appeal to valor, courage and daring. "In the exhibition of the most brilliant valor, of the most excess of courage, and of a daring which would have reflected luster on the best days of chivalry can afford full consolation for the disaster of today, we can have no reason to regret the melancholy loss which we sustained in contest with a savage and barbarian enemy. *"We can have no reason to regret!"* What passive resignation to a two-third mortality rate! The eight-hour battle and the disastrous figure of over 3,000 casualties of the WWII Dieppe Raid, was a 59% casualty rate (including wounded and prisoners). I wonder what the casualty rate was for the British in the Crimean War and what the mortality rate was for the "savage and barbarian enemy," the Russians?

Howard Zinn related in *The Peoples History*, "World War I. In the first battle of the Marne, the British and the French succeeded in blocking the German advance on Paris. Each side had 500,000 casualties." Later: "The British and French moved forward a few miles and lost 600,000 men." - "One day the British launched an attack with 800 men, twenty fours later, there were 84 left. Back home British newspapers told nothing of the slaughter." The government policywas evidently not to anger the home front. And it appears that they had the cooperation of a compliant press. Erich Maria Remarque, in his great novel *All Quiet on the Western Front,* used that similar absence of news of front-line carnage in the German newspapers, for the title of his book.

Howard Zinn continues, "In July 1916 British General Douglas Haig ordered eleven divisions of English soldiers to climb out of their trenches and move towards the German lines" --"twenty thousand were killed and 40,000 wounded."

WW1 log of J.S. Woods in *Saskatchewan History,* Vol.66 #2, Fall issue of 2014; "More than 10,000 Canadians were killed on Vimy Ridge (WWI) but it was considered a glorious victory."

James Carroll in *House of War*: "U.S. mythmakers neglect the burden other nations carried as well as their role in military history.

U.S. *military* deaths in WWII were approximately 292,000, British Commonwealth 344,000, France 200,000, the Soviet Union over 11,000,000. Civilian deaths in WWII, U.S. zero to miniscule, Poland 6 million, Great Britain 60,000, Holland 190,000, France 400,000, and the Soviet Union over 20 million."

William Manchester in *The Last Lion,* "Since 1914 (to Nov. 1918), Britain had lost 908,371 dead, 2,090,212 wounded, and 191,652 missing. Victory had indeed been bought so dear as to be indistinguishable from defeat." "Between 1914 and 1918 Britain's generals slaughtered the most idealistic generation of young leaders in the history of England, and all to no purpose. Never in the history of human conflict have so many suffered so much to gratify the pride of a few. And this was clear to some men at the time." "Siegfried Sasoon, a decorated war hero of the trenches, threw his medals away and wrote, "Pray God that you will never know/the hell where youth and laughter go."

"How long," D. H. Lawrence wrote in *Seven Pillars of Wisdom,* "will the nations continue to empty the future?" The disastrous high percentage of deaths between 1914 and 1918 virtually demolished the young generation of British servicemen. This was then followed by the similar destruction of the next young British generation between 1939 and 1945 in WWII. This ruination of the most promising generations of young men is credited with being the prime factor in the diminished status of Great Britain, and its much reduced international influence in the last half of the twentieth century.

In his book, *The Peoples History,* Howard Zinn speaks about his time as a U.S. air force gunner, when he was sent on a test mission shortly before VE Day to *test* newly-invented napalm, on a German occupied French village. A test Mission, on people! By the Korean War napalm was in general use. Zinn continues, "A BBC journalist described the result, 'In front of us a curious figure was standing, a little crouched, legs straddled, arms held out from his sides. He had no eyes, and the whole of his body, nearly all of which was visible through tatters of burnt rags, was covered with a hard black crust speckled with yellow pus --. He had to stand because he was no longer covered with a skin, but with a crust-like crackling which broke easily.' I thought of the hundreds of villages reduced to ash which I personally had seen and realized the casualty list which must be mounting up along the Korean front."

Carroll: "The Soviet air-force lost 1200 air-planes on the first morning of the German invasion - June 22nd 1941."

James Carroll in *House of War,* "Russian losses between June 22nd 1941 & October 31st 1941 (4-months) were 2,952,000." This period followed Hitler's breaking of the Nazi-Soviet Pact when he released his ruthless, professional army on the fleeing Russian army. The Russians were handicapped by Stalin's purge of the experienced upper ranks of officers (colonels and generals) a few years earlier. Pity the sacrificed, unskilled, Russian soldier with inferior equipment and very limited poor food. The horror of war!

Carroll continues, "By one measure the number of people involved the Battle of Moscow was the greatest battle in WWII and therefore the greatest battle in history. More than seven million officers and men from both sides took part. The Battle of Moscow swirled over a territory the size of France. The Soviet Union lost more people in one battle, 926,000 soldiers killed to say nothing of the wounded, than the British lost in WWI. Their casualties in this one battle were greater than the combined casualties of the British and the Americans in the whole of WWII."

Carroll continues to describe the bravery, tenacity and desperation of the out-gunned Russians. "The Russians went on fighting not only when fighting had become pointless, but even when it had become physically impossible. Encircled, out-numbered, disorganized, often without commanders, without ammunition, without fuel, medical supplies, or food, they were cut down or surrendered only when they had nothing to fight with."

Benjamin Schwarz, LA Times, June 22nd 2000: "The main scene of the Nazi's defeat wasn't Normandy or anywhere else Americans fought, but rather the Eastern Front, where the conflict was the most terrible war fought in history. - Americans should recall that about 88% of all German casualties fell in the war with Russia."

Michael Burleigh relates in *Moral Combat,* "Eugene Sledge, an American marine described how another marine used a large combat knife to take out the gold tooth of a wounded still-alive Japanese soldier. Another marine shot him in the head to end his agony. This was said to have been related to finding a dead marine whose head was decapitated and his hands cut off at the wrist - his head was posed on his chest - while his penis had been cut off and stuffed in his mouth." War-produced hatred!

Burleigh continues, "Four out of five German soldiers killed in WWII died on the Eastern front, but they killed many times their numbers of Red Army troops. He states "that Poland was subject to the most brutal regime (German occupation) in occupied Europe, which in the course of the war murdered three million Christian Poles as well as 90% of the country's Jews."

The U.S. has much to feel guilty about also. *The Tribune* (Phoenix) headline April 14th 2007, "The (U.S.) official order to shoot *civilians* escaping from North Korea in the Korean War." LA Times, May 6th 2001, "- the My Lai massacre in the Vietnam War; and the Abu Ghraib prison scandal of the Iraq War, though said to be aberrations, are nevertheless stains on the American military services. All countries probably experience these anecdotes in the 'fog of war.'"

Sheehan in *A Bright Shining Lie,* (Paraphrased), "Platoon leader, Wm. Calley, Jr. was found responsible for 337 deaths in My Lai, Vietnam and personally guilty of twenty two of those deaths, including children; was sentenced to life in prison at hard labor; President Nixon intervened and Calley was confined to house-arrest for just 3 years." Reversal, not compromise!

Martin Luther King, 1967, wrote in *Where Do We Go from Here,* "When I see our country today intervening in what is basically a civil war, mutilating hundreds of thousands of Vietnamese children with napalm, burning villages and rice fields at random, painting the valleys of that small Asian country red with human blood, leaving broken bodies in countless ditches and sending home half-men, mutilated mentally and physically, while refusing to negotiate, all in the name of peace, I tremble for our world."

Sheehan in *A Bright Shining Lie,* "By 1966, Vietnam civilians (men, women and children), were dying at the rate of 25,000 yearly, and there were 2 million refugees.

Did you ever hear of the "Laos War?" No, I didn't either. It was included under the name of the Vietnam War. The Ho Chi Minh Trail to supply South Vietnam from North Vietnam passed partly through Laos. Aug 2015, The National Geographic, T. D. Allman, "The U. S. dropped more than 2 million tons of bombs on Laos, (from 1964 to 1973), during the Vietnam War. That's equal to a planeload every eight minutes for 9 years. In total 270 million bomblets, ("bombies") and 4 million big bombs were dropped. The weight of the bombs dropped worked out to be as much as a ton per person (in Laos).

Allman continues, "Periodically during the (Vietnam) War, Washington announced a "bombing halt," but the munitions conveyor belt stretching from the stock pile in the U.S., 8,000 miles across the Pacific, could not be switched on and off. Bombs that did not fall in Vietnam were redirected to Laos. It was the world's first supply-driven war the pent-up munitions constantly generating a demand for their use. The mass production of airborne death had no quality control. Possibly 80 million of the 'bombies' didn't explode on impact and are still considered alive. Up to 10% of the big bombs also failed to explode."

As Stephen Wilkes the photographer said, "I hope this piece opens American eyes to the tragedy of the war and that, as a nation, we begin accepting our responsibility to do more." T.D. Allman, "The U.S. spent $13.3 million a day conducting the air war over Laos. In *2014* it spent $12 million clearing unexploded ordinance from the war." That was our unnamed, secret Laos War! We weren't even at war with Laos! The United Nations would have found major reason for U.N. forces to intervene against the aggressor the USA! But remember, the U.S. possesses the right to use its U.N. veto.

Before the Iraq War, but regarding the 1991 Gulf War, Professor Robert Jensen in the LA Times May 22nd 2000, described the U.S. dropping of 88,000 tons of bombs on Iraq killing large numbers of "targeted and untargeted" civilians, both war crimes under the Geneva Convention. But don't think of "bombs" as just the conventional blowthem-up-and-kill-them variety. He continues "Remember the brutality of U.S. weapons. We used napalm to incinerate entrenched Iraqi soldiers. We dropped fuel-air explosives, ghastly weapons often called near-nukes, because of their destructive capacity through fire, asphyxiation and concussion. We dropped cluster bombs that use razor-sharp fragments to shred people. To penetrate tanks, we used depleted-uranium shells, the long-term health effects of which are unknown. Widely accepted notions of proportionality and protection of civilians go out the window with such weapons."

I have a book named *War Against War-* authored by Ernst Friedrich (born 1894), published in 1924 by Zweitausendeins, Postlach, D-6000, Frankfurt am Main 61, Germany; republished by the Red Comet Press, Seattle in 1987. Friedrich was a life-long ardent pacifist;

was imprisoned in 1917 for anti-militarism by the (German) Weimar government; was released in 1918; established the Anti-War Museum in Berlin in 1924; wrote his book in 1924; his museum was closed by the Nazis in 1933; fled to Belgium where he opened a second museum; where, upon the Nazi invasion in 1940 his museum was again closed; "Disrupted by two world wars, Ernst Friedrich remained passionately dedicated to calling all nations to peace; died in 1967; his book reprinted in 1987, with introduction by Douglas Kellner.

Quoting Kellner "In the documents assembled in the opening pages Friedrich suggests that children's toys, schooling, the church, and other agents of socialization prepare them psychologically for warfare. Throughout the book he attempts to document how these institutions, groups and practices are allied with big business, the state, and the military in the manufacture of both the machinery and the mentality of modern warfare."

Friedrich's text is succinct, pungent and portrays revolting German militarism... as he intended. The pictures document the atrocities, brutalities and horror of the First World War. He intersperses the pictures with patriotic slogans, the incongruities of distorted faces with missing jaws, cavernous wounds, missing limbs, ditches filled with the dead, a picture of smiling, handsome "Papa"' and then a picture of his remains, "two days later."

The opening entry to his book as follows: "To Human Beings in All Lands - I, whom am falsely called "German," instead of just simply "man." I call out to the icy regions of the north. I call out to Africa, and to America, to Asia and to Europe."

"To all regions that have ears to hear. I call out but two words and these are: *Man and Love.*" "And even as the Australian weeps when he encounters pain, and laughs and makes merry when joy and happiness are granted him, even so dost thou weep, my brother Eskimo, and so, O African and O Chinese, weepest thou too, and so do I."

"And, as we all, all human beings equally feel joy and pain, let us fight unitedly against the common monstrous enemy, War." *War against War* is unforgettable.

These pages about the brutalities of war were inserted here to remind us what this study is designed to understand. It is our enemy WAR. The knowledge necessary for achieving success in our anti-war movement is essential. It is essential that we view war as the monster that it is. The physical agony of war wounds, the psychological agony of loss of loved ones, the disruption of life plans, the blinding tears of mothers, the depletion of our world's natural resources and of our nation's (and every nation's) financial resources. The elimination of these depends upon our success.

Commentary on War

President (General) Eisenhower said it very emphatically in *The Great Quotations,* "I hate war as only a soldier who has lived it can, only as one who has seen its brutality, its futility, and its stupidity."

Because I am reticent by nature, and remote by residence, probably only a few of my family and friends have been aware of my past, and present, concern about world peace. World Peace is an esoteric and nebulous concept that does not easily intrude into casual conversations. *War is a malignant horror that has been prayed about in all the world's religions and languages. But prayer is of such an ethereal nature that one is led to believe that it is only God who can, or will, achieve world peace. So having prayed over it, one is inclined to go on hisway thinking he has done his share and God will do the rest! One feels contentment in having appealed to the ultimate authority to do something about it. But in reality the only effect is that one then makes no other action towards world peace. The only results of the prayer are that the one who prays feels better, but it lessens further action towards peace. That is the reverse to what was intended.*

My father used to comment "God helpeth him who helpeth himself." In the Quaker's "*Friends Journal*" Dec 2011 Anne-Marie Witzberg commented, "God has no hands on earth but ours." It takes action to achieve results. Small initial efforts have often achieved major accomplishments, but, more often without strength, tend to go nowhere. So how do we get more strength? How could anyone feel anything but impotent when considering *how to make the world pay attention? Who would possibly listen? For me, my ingrained sense of cooperation surfaced. There is strength in numbers! So my natural conclusion over fifty years ago was to join war resistant organizations.* Probably my first was The United World Federalists, now called World Federalist Movement - Institute for Global Policy. (See listed organizations at the end of this book).

How do you choose an organization that you feel represents your point of view? If you have studied who the Founders were, the Vision, the Policy, the Strategy, the past Accomplishments and the future Goals, and you are then contented, then you may have arrived at your primary support group, and remember again that it is cooperative support. It is conscience-satisfying and fulfilling to know that you are being cooperatively-effective in placing some effort and money towards future world peace.

My antipathy to war in general will doubtless make it sound that most causes are bad. I think most are! A great number of knowledgeable people have spoken about war, some of which follow. The hoped- for effectiveness of this book should rest not just on my opinions, but also on the varied opinions of those wise people.

Pope Pius XIII about 1890. *The Great Quotations,* "Nothing is more important than to war on war."

General Napoleon Bonaparte quoted in *The Great Quotations,* "War is the business of barbarians."

General William Tecumseh Sherman, famed for his unrelenting, aggressive, "scorched-earth" Civil War "March to the Sea" through the State of Georgia, is quoted in *The Great Quotations,* "You cannot qualify war in harsher terms than I will. War is cruelty, and you cannot refine it."

General Robert E. Lee, *The Great Quotations,* "It is well that war is so terrible - we would grow too fond of it."

President (General) George Washington, The Great Quotations "My fervent wish is to see this plague of mankind, war, banished from the earth."

President J.F. Kennedy, *The Arizona Republic,* "Mankind must put an end to war, or war will put an end to mankind."

Erich Maria Remarque writes in his classic *All Quiet on the Western Front,* "We must prepare systematically an uprising against war."

Martin Luther King- wrote in *Where, do We go From Here,* "The greatest purveyor of violence in the world today is my own nation." The United States arms sales comprise three quarters of the world's sales.

Adlai Stevenson-American Statesman, Presidential Candidate - *The Wit and Wisdom of Adlai Stevenson,* wrote, "We doubt whether any nation has so absolute a grip on absolute truth that it is entitled to impose its idea of what is right on others."

T. E. Lawrence (Lawrence of Arabia) wrote in his book *The Seven Pillars of Wisdom,* "Life was so deliberately private, that no circumstances could justify one man laying violent hands on another." This was a testimonial by a military hero on the futility of war. Lawrence emphasized that wars of nationalism or of religion, are both irrational.

In *House of War: The Pentagon and the Disastrous Rise of American Power,* James Carroll writes, "How briefly on earth we are. Too briefly, I insist, not to find another way to live than by killing." The son of Lieutenant General Joseph Carroll, he writes of the Pentagon in which he literally grew up, bringing an understanding how immoral wars develop.

Norman Cousins in *A Thought for Today* says that regardless of one's wealth, "If no answer is found to war, all men will die poor." Cousins added that this world can't "have guns and butter." How many schools, hospitals, teachers, nurses etc. would one 132-million-dollar F-135 airplane buy?

John Milton, English poet, *The Great Quotations,* "For what can war but endless war still breed?" The infamous account of the generations of hatred and violence between the Hatfields and the McCoys of Tennessee is a localized example of the international tensions between Russia and the United States. War begets hatred - which begets more war, which begets more hatred, etc. Russia and the West have been at it for 150 years. Many other examples of dual, long-lasting inter-nation feuds exist.

In the last generation there has occurred what I view as a sanitizing of war. The threat of death to an enlisting serviceman is far more unlikely than it used to be. However, the impact of death is not lessened. Families grieve as much as ever. It is statistically clear. One hundred and sixteen thousand Americans died on the battlefield in America's 2 year-long World War I; four hundred and five thousand Americans died in the 4-year long U.S. involvement in WWII; 54,000 Americans in the 3-year Korean War; 57,000 in the 7-year Vietnam War. Now, about three thousand-plus have occurred in each of the 9-year Iraq war and the 12 year-long Afghanistan war. The Canadian Dieppe Raid on the French coast in 1942 produced over 3,000 casualties in 8 hours.

The military geniuses have reduced our nation's personnel risk, lowering the body-count of our military forces to record low levels. Remote, but highly accurate bomb targeting; robot surveillance and bombing by drone; surveillance from space stations; refined intelligence and espionage; and a current reluctance to "put American boots on the ground." all of which account for lower death counts - of U.S. personnel. Now, would you believe, the military scientists are working on military robots!

Human Rights Watch newsletter Jan 10th 2013 "Military-industrial researchers are working this minute to develop fully autonomous weapons or "killer robots" with the ability to select their own target and decide on their own when to kill them." How will they explain or account for their actions? How would a killer robot interpret a soldier who was surrendering or one too wounded to be a threat?" How would the human quality of compassion be instilled into a robot? Success in war! But it would be a failure in humanitarianism.

Think of the enemy's body-count! They are our fellow-humans! It is notable how former enemies frequently become good friends. Now, more than ever before, using that detached impersonal description "collateral damage," civilian men, women and children are dying. Where is our compassion? Don't leave the problem to the conscience of the military. It is *OUR* problem. But we must speak up to our governments and to the military. The July 2014, one-month war between Israel and the Palestinians with approximate Israeli deaths of 48 and Palestinian deaths of 1800, are a test of the morality of the participants, especially those in top-level war management.

LA Times May 28th 1975. Headline: "Annapolis grapples with morality of war." "The U.S. naval Academy is teaching midshipmen a course which grapples with the morality of warfare." However, little of the discussion centered on the Golden Rule, or on being humane in war. Except one news interview where an American soldier in Vietnam was asked his viewpoint and he replied" It stinks! They're scared of us because we kill 'em and take everything they've got." Vice Admiral W.P. Mack, course superintendent, made a strong point that the Military, at some level, was responsible for the false body counts in Vietnam. At every level, the soldier wished to sound successful.

Another changing factor, at least for the American services, is the level of enticement used by the military recruiters. Seventy-five years ago my choice was limited. Once they had refused me for aircrew, the army recruiting office chose to not even send me to basic training, but instead, as reinforcement of an existing unit. Now, the recruiter (who comes to you if desired) negotiates with the recruit (and parents!) over what military occupation the recruit will have and what their reward will be on discharge. Large bonuses are paid to military personnel who sign-up for another tour of duty. It sounds like patriotism is tinged by, "what am I going to get out of it?" Beyond medical pensions I do not know what happened following WWI. In WWII, (in my home region) patriotism and escaping the Great Depression were the primary reasons to have enlisted. I was unaware that I would have any "Brownie- points" until over 4 years into my WWII military service. I just felt grateful acceptance.

Emery Reyes in *War and Peace,* "Superficially it looks as though wars have been waged for a great variety of reasons. The struggle for food and mere survival, feuds, quarrels, religious fanaticism, rival commercial interests, antagonistic social ideals, the race for colonies, economic competition, and many other forces, have exploded in fatal and devastating wars." Let's review some of the causes of war.

Causes of War: Fear and Insecurity

Seneca The Younger, 2,000 years ago, *The Great Quotations,* "Worse than war, is the fear of war." The fear that engenders our insecurity is probably the most deep-seated of all the causes of war. As such, it needs abundant thought. In the early depression years, President Franklin D. Roosevelt, famously agreed with Seneca saying," All we have to fear is fear itself."

In the rural society in which I developed, we and our imperfect neighbors were, nevertheless, trusted. The need for the security of door-locks was minimal. Most homes had doors that could not even be locked, our home included. That fundamental trust was a tiny step toward our co-operative society, and toward the concept of world- brotherhood. That statement is consistent with my page-one statement, "I contend that our security lies not in our strength of arms, but, in the long term, when our neighbors (other nations) trust us as we trust them (love will follow) and only then will we have genuine security." The Golden Rule! Trust your neighbor as you wish to be trusted. It is logical, and therefore essential, that the reasons for distrust be removed. Suspicion, anger and invective must go. Personal security can only come with a benevolent society, adequate housing, adequate food, necessary medical care, and education to the level of aptitude and ability - for ALL. What an example that would be! There would be minimal reason for fear.

The American Friends Service Committee Newsletter, March 25th 2013, "As Pentagon bloat takes more and more of our resources, the nation's true security needs - health care, affordable housing, environmental protection - are being squeezed to a breaking point. We need a better budget for the true security of our nation. This year, the Pentagon has more than $653 billion of our tax dollars in their proposed budget. If we took just 10% of that money, we could pay for:

- 960,000 school teachers.
- 935,000 police officers.
- Medical care for 8.3 million veterans.
- Head start programs for 8.6 million children.

Insecurity-based war would fade away if the Golden Rule was used in international affairs. Simplistic? Naïve? Wishful thinking? Impossible? Who said, "The possible is for today. The impossible will take a little longer?"

National Public Radio April 2nd 2013, reported, "A language analysis" performing a sort of "emotional archaeology" of words used between 1945 and 2000 AD. They found that fear definitely lessened in use after about 1990 which, of course, synchronizes with the perceived end of the Cold War. Insecurity! Two names associated with thatstudy were Baker and Bentley.

The Atlantic magazine, Spring 2013, John J. Mearscheime, Political Science Professor, University of Chicago, "The leader of one great power in this anarchic jungle of a world can never know what the leaders of a rival great power are thinking. Fear is dominant. This is the tragic essence of international politics."

Fear is a marvelous tool to promote war. Michael Moore in *Dude, Where's My Country? says,* "Fear is so basic, and yet so easy to manipulate that it has become both our best friend and our worst enemy. And when it is used as a weapon against us, it has the ability to destroy much of what we have come to love about life in the U. S. A."

Edna Williams Meakes, *A Quest for Peace and Alternatives to War* "Jan 12 & 13th' 1991, Canadian Peace Congress, "Imagine what could be done with 10 per cent of the world's arms budget. This would amount to $100,000,000,000 per year!" "The hospitals in less developed nations, the sustainable development alternatives to rain forest destruction it could foster, the schools it could build, the jobs it could create. Imagine the amount growing every year as the arms budgets are cut further every year. Imagine the stability this funding would bring to fragile programs of development and environmental salvation around the world. Imagine the reduced climate of fear that such an action would have on rival states in all regions of the world. Neighbors would have less and less reason to fear neighbor *(Golden Rule).* Peace may even break out where it is needed most, in the poorest regions of the world. Such a campaign would benefit everyone except arms manufacturers and those who prepare for war. There is, however, a real need to plan conversion to a peace economy, and this must be part of such a program. This appeal to cut the military budgets of the world is one part solidarity, one part peace work, one part economic sense, and one part respect for the earth. It is applicable to all nations and serves the needs of all peoples. We hope that you join us in making this a reality." Edna Williams-Meakes spoke very eloquently to the Canadian Peace Congress.

Emery Reyes wrote in his book in 1945, *The Anatomy of Peace,* "At the end of the Second World War, we are seeing American forces assuming islands and other bases thousands of miles away from the American mainland, for reasons of security."

Scare everyone sufficiently and the money will flow for military appropriations and MIPUGU will smile.

W.W.Comfort in *The Quaker way of Life* 1920 said that armaments were against Quaker principles. "They impoverish the people. They tempt men to evil and they breed suspicion and fear and the tragic consequences thereof. They are therefore, not legitimate weapons in the Christian armory nor are they sources of security. You cannot foster harmony by the apparatus of discord, nor create good will by the equipment of hate. But it is by the harmony of good will that human security can be obtained. Armaments aim at a security in isolation; but such would at best be utterly precarious, and as a matter of fact, illusory. The only true safety is the safety of *ALL."* In myopinion, this 95-year old viewpoint could not be said better. Include, or exclude, the word Christianity and the truth of every word would remain the same. Michael Moore, *Dude, Where's My Country:* "Wow! War without end! If you get the people to believe this, they'll let you do anything as long as it is in the name of protecting them. This is Bush's version of the old Mafia protection racket. There is someone out there who is going to mess you up." - "And to maintain the endless war, they need endless fear, a fear that can be only extended indefinitely by taking away our basic rights."

Robert Robb in *The Arizona Republic,* Aug 29 2012: "The United States, did not purchase $1.4 trillion worth of additional security from the wars in Afghanistan and Iraq. U.S. efforts to ramrod democratic transformation became a cropper and were quickly abandoned."

In the Iraq War, confirmed deaths of over 3,000 American military and over 200,000 Iraq military and civilians occurred, because we were made afraid about lies about WMDs. Paul Kurtz, Editor of *Free Inquiry Magazine,* Aug/Sept 2005, asks, "Where is the moral outrage? In Iraq the United States engaged in precisely the sort of behavior we condemn in our adversaries. Our leaders leapt to the ultimate human rights violation 'presumptive warfare' for reasons that were either simply untrue, or worse, known to be untrue. Today, America stands discredited among nations, an aggressor, its moral authority shattered."

Past failures of American diplomacy has brought the nation to the point, that I must grant that for the immediate foreseeable future, the United States is forced to maintain a national defensive military force, and to maintain protective measures of our citizenry. This however, *MUST* be ratcheted down! Now, (2013) the current (Obama) U.S.

administration is doing that. Remember, it must be recognized that, to other nations, those "protective measures" may only mean that we are making ourselves secure under our protective umbrella so that we may go ahead covertly with more aggressive measures. *What is security for us is threatening to them.*

Fear, legitimate or not, provides the impulse to the Administration to prepare for war. President James Monroe, *The Great Quotations,* "Preparation for war is a constant stimulus to suspicion and ill will."

British Prime Minister William R. Gladstone, *The Great Quotations,* wrote, "We have no adequate idea of the predisposing power, which an immense series of preparation for war has in actually begetting war."

United Nations President, Trygve Lie, *Oxford History of the American People* said, "Wars occur because people prepare for conflict, rather than for peace." If you have an army you're much more likely to use it. The future aim (reality not utopian) is to "wind-down" the need for a security force and increase the good will (Golden Rule) relationship with all other nations.

Norman Thomas, American Socialist, said in *The Great Quotations,* "The very existence of armaments and great armies psychologically accustoms us to accept the philosophy of militarism. They inevitably increase fear and hate in the world."

Martin Luther King, wrote in his book *Strength to Love,* "We say that war is a consequence of hate, but close scrutiny reveals this sequence: first fear, then hate, then war, and finally, deeper hatred. If we assume that mankind has a right to survive, (security), then we must find an alternative to war and destruction. In our day of space vehicles and guided ballistic missiles the choice is either nonviolence or nonexistence."

Albert Einstein wrote in his book *Ideas and Opinions,* "The real ailment seems to me to lie in the attitude which was created by the World War (II) and which dominates all our actions; namely, the belief that we must in peacetime so organize our whole life and work so that in the event of war we would be sure of victory. This attitude gives rise to the belief that one's freedom and indeed, one's existence is threatened by powerful enemies." Insecurity! Because our opponents will perceive our *security enhancements* it *as a prelude to war it means increased insecurity*. Einstein continues, "It must--lead to war and to far reaching destruction. It finds expression in the budget of the United States. Only if we overcome this obsession can we really turn our attention in a reasonable way to the real political problem, which is: How can we contribute to make the life of man on this diminishing earth more secure and more tolerable?" What wonderful words, written 65 years ago! If only our "power-elite," with these words in mind, instead of just bemoaning the obstacles, would study the relationship of the history of the past century to the financial, political, and social chaos that exists today, I have to believe that the world would benefit tremendously. In the long run, though, I know the world's human intelligence will prevail.

Religion, Nationalism, Patriotism and War

The Bible-Exodus 15:3, "The Lord is a Man of War. The Lord is his Name."

James Carroll states, "Beware the House of War when understood as the House of God." He is speaking of the American penchant to view the Pentagon as a patriotic, pseudo-religious protector of the 'American way of life.'

All three of the categories comprising the above heading, may be responsible for building a prejudicial opinion regarding an individual or group, thus leading to opinionated behavior. The headline in the LA Times April 30th 1989 said it all, "IN THE SEARCH FOR WORLD PEACE, IT'S THE STERIOTYPES THAT FIRST MUST GO." Thomas J. Osborne, history professor at Rancho Santiago College (California) related that, as a director on the national board of the *Beyond War Foundation,* he was in Moscow, meeting with Plekhanov who was a leading voice in the Soviet Union on perestroika, glasnost and human rights." Plekhanov was active in the Russian, political, Gorbachev transformation. Paraphrasing: "Osborne related how, as a middle-aged, church-going, American family man from Conservative Orange County, California, he found himself feeling unpatriotic at being there. He was talking to a 'bunch of Communists.' He realized, it was the prejudices he had carried around since he was a child in the McCarthy era of the 1950s." He said, "Significantly, I came to see that my old Cold War stereotypes and prejudices needed to allow for change."

Religious belief is a generally respected attribute in everyone. Patriotism is a much admired and respected quality, and is obviously an important element in the mind of a soldier. But these are two qualities that have been harnessed by the unscrupulous in support of war and of preparation for war. Think carefully! This is where the definitions of patriotism and nationalism are similar. However, there appears to be one defining difference: "my nation, right or wrong" is patriotic, but defines the nationalist. The 1965 patriotic, nationalistic bumper sticker that read "My country Love it or leave it" was quickly answered by the patriotic, progressive sticker, "My country - Love it and repair it." Both political views claimed they were patriotic. The nationalist tends to see only what he views as his country's ideals, not its actions. A patriotic realist, deplores his country's bad behavior and applauds the good behavior, and says, "let's' fix it."

Echoes of my 1965 Unitarian church pastor, Rev Al Hendricksen, who said, "In this Vietnam War, we judge ourselves by our ideals and judge others by their actions." Seldom the reverse!

Paul Kurtz continues, "Where is the will to submit that we, as a nation, have done wrong? Where is the moral outrage? America has become an Imperial Empire in which chauvinistic patriotism tends to dominate. The United States spends as much on arms as the rest of the countries of the world combined."

There are of course mercenaries (soldiers-of-fortune), who fight only for money and may sign up with any country. Patriotism would not be expected to be so much of a factor when one is working for "the buck", rather than for one's country. This category may, or may not, include all the sub-contracted support services so important in the recent Iraq war.

The Tribune July 5th 2007, "Contractors outnumber Iraq GIs. Privatization of war effort raises fresh questions." There appears to be a message in those figures. What has developed is that the military recruitment services have not been able to use patriotism to get recruits to sign-up for transport, engineering projects and support services, as in most earlier wars. So they have subcontracted those services and *bought* some of those services, by exorbitant salaries. And they also have *bought* the military personnel.

The Tribune (Phoenix) April 12th 2007, Headline "Bonuses soar for re-enlistees. Military struggles to keep soldiers, Marines for war."

The Tribune (Phoenix), Sept 2nd 2007, "Unable to get sufficient army recruits to fight in two wars, the Pentagon offered $20,000.00 to new recruits to sign up. This included college tuition assistance and medical and dental care." By Oct 11th 2008 the Tribune reported that the Pentagon was considering discontinuing new recruit bonuses but, "the Army and Marines (still) aggressively encourage troops to re-enlist for a bonus of as much as $40,000."

USA Today, July 31st 2015, "The Army paid **o**ut $117 million in bonuses and educational incentives in 2014." About 2008, I remember overhearing a handsome recruiter in an immaculate, perfectly-fitted uniform; sporting impressive medals; negotiating with a potential recruit and his parents, over what "brownie points," the enlistee would receive. To me, this does not rise to the level of pure patriotism. Today, there is a fairly safe opportunist, 'patriotic', military choice.

The blind patriotism of nationalism can lead to wars of *noblesse oblige* where the aggressor believes he is fulfilling a noble impulse and, as in the case of the Iraq War, save us from WMDs, while bringing "democracy" to the enemy nation.

When religion is included (or merged) with patriotism a potential recruit can become highly motivated to enlist. And it would be probable that he/she would become a more intensely focused soldier in his/ her devotion to military "obligations." This combination of religion and patriotism can then be catch-phrased to hate the enemy and (as in the Cold war) *save* us from "Godless Communism." To an idealistic youth the dual appeal can be overpowering. The Department of Defense (renamed from the Department of War) need only use a few inflaming words such as: atrocities, brutalities, torture, rape and the military ranks will grow. The Christian Crusades, The Irish Catholic/Protestant conflict, India's Moslem/Hindu conflict, and our current Judeo-Christian-Islamic tensions are all examples. It is revealing to note that in WWI and WWII the German/Italian God, was the same God as the Allied God, so, though God was invoked to support the goal of each side, it seems obvious that religion was not the primary cause of the war, nor was it going to "win" the war for either side.

When monotheism came to the Jews, to the Christians, to the Moslems and others, a perceived allegiance to any other religion became a concern. That concern, could easily be perceived as a threat, and consequently, as a potential cause of war. The simple statement, "I am a Christian" emphasizes that the speaker is not a Buddhist, a Jew, or Muslim etc. This line of difference may be perceived as a line of disagreement, or even contention. It is at this point that children need to be taught how similar we are as people, not emphasize our differences. This is the time to emphasize that all religious beliefs are to be equally respected. We should not fear other religions. The fundamentalists in all religions are the ones who tend to feel insecure, fear the differences of other religions, and perceive them as a threat. The 'brotherhood of man' should involve no fear.

Most religious people have that innate desire that their beliefs become a global religion for the world. But humans are too individualistic, and the world's theologies too compartmentalized, for theological unity. For the gut-driven, religious, fundamentalist these differences can become very real. These theological radicals of the world are found in all religions and create wars. As of this date, the Islamic fundamentalists, ISIS, are our global concern. However, we have had our own previous national horrors in the garb of the Ku Klux Klan, extremist Jim Jones and the poisoning of over 800 of his religious adherents.

James Hillman, in *A Terrible Love of War* writes, "- the age old question how do wars begin? They begin in the shrill voice in the heart of the people, the press, and the leaders who perceive "enemies" (see; fear, and War and Paranoia) and push for a fight. The deceptive rush and a rush of deceptions promote each other, so that we are deluded by feelings of urgency and cover ourselves with the hypocrisy of noble proclamations."

Hillman continues, "The people can always be brought to the bidding of the leaders," said Reich Marshal Hermann Goering at his trial at Nuremberg. "This is easy. All you have to do is tell them they are being attacked, and denounce the pacifists for lack of patriotism and exposing the country to danger. It works in every country." The voice of a highly qualified and seasoned expert!

Using Mark Twain's words, Hillman illustrates how Twain would have nailed the hawks of today, "- next the statesman will invent cheap lies putting the blame on the nation that is attacked (think; President G. W. Bush/Hussein/Iraq) and every man will be glad of those conscious soothing falsities (WMDs), and will diligently study them, and refuse to examine any refutation of them, and thus he will, by and by, convince himself that the war is just, and will thank God for the better sleep he enjoys after this process of grotesque self-deception."

To soothe our conscience, thank God that President George W. Bush assured us that there were WMD's to justify America's invasive war! There were none. I wonder if God still approved. I guess that God could approve someone else's invasion of us! Because we have those same WMDs in the thousands!

Uniforms radiate romanticism and Patriotism. To idealistic youth male or female what could be better! Hillman comments, "Soldiers felt proud to wear specific uniforms, which advertised their prowess." Any uniform does it, but think especially of the Green Berets, American Rangers and Commandos. To others the visual appeal of a trim uniform suggests honor, respect of patriotism, and enhanced virile manhood. To the guy wearing the uniform it exudes the implied glow of the attributes listed above, plus the excitement of adventure, the pride in the unit, the camaraderie of fellow soldiers, and of course the attraction of females to the guy in uniform. A military uniform transfers the immature teenage boy into the masculine world of the seasoned military professional.

I remember! In WWII the Canadian army uniform was intended to be highly functional; was drab, simple and plain; but nevertheless it spoke for me, and it identified me as a volunteer for the country and as a patriot. The Canadian wartime military never approved "dress" uniforms, which are usually attractively designed to emphasize the virile, militarism of youth. The Canadian military policy was to authorize very few medals. There were none for marksmanship, general efficiency; but mainly for time and region served and for bravery. Consequently, very few Canadian soldiers were bright with decorations. When the Americans arrived in England in 1942, many already sported several medals causing the apocryphal British soldier to exclaim, "Blimey! The whole ruddy American Army is made up of heroes."

To further lubricate the path to war, only the collaborative stew of supportive psychological factors is needed such as patriotism, pride, religion, paranoia, insecurity and hate and, oh yes, the arms merchant's greed! Relentlessly pursued by the fit, persuasive, recruiter flawlessly attired in an enhancing uniform, with a splash of colorful medals; approved by the clergy; urged by the military traditionalists; exhibited by a proud family; what is a young, idealistic, patriotic youth likely to do? You're right! He signs up and war continues to thrive.

Author James Hillman in *A Terrible Love of War* goes into great detail regarding how the pageantry of war is a method of impressing both the observer and the wearer with all the braid, ribbons and polish, precision drills and martial appearance. In 1918 strutting General George Patton wrote to his wife, "Now - I am a regular Beau Brummel. I wear silk khaki shirts made to order, khaki socks also made to order. I change my boots at least once during the day and my belts are wonders to see they are so shiny and polished. I have the leather on my knees blancoed (recolored) every time I ride and my spurs polished with silver polish. In fact, I am a wonder to behold." "This aesthetic excess serves merely to embellish war by dressing it up, to mask its ugliness."

James Hillman - *A Terrible Love of War*, "So when war clouds gather, religious belief electrifies the air. When our belief is in the republic, and our republic is declared endangered, we rally around the flag for which it stands. Whatever the object of belief the flag, the nation, the president or the god - a martial energy mobilizes. Decisions are quick, dissent more difficult. Doubt, which impedes action and questions certitude, becomes traitorous, an enemy to be silenced."

Richard Dawkins, *The God Delusion.* Dawkins quotes Spanish film director Luis Bunuel, "God and Country are an unbeatable team; they break all records for oppression and blood-shed. Recruiting officers rely heavily on their victim's sense of patriotic duty." Dawkins writes, "People despise conscientious objectors, even those of the enemy country because patriotism was held to be an obsolete virtue. It is hard to get more absolute than the, "My country - Right or wrong!" of the professional, patriotic soldier, for the slogan commits you to kill whomever the politicians of some future date might choose to call enemies."

E.J. Montini in *The Arizona Republic* Headline, "Waging war for my Bible class, just one option." "How about an elective class for Arizona high school students called, 'The Warmonger's Bible'? Legislation proposed by Rep. Terry Proud would permit, "school districts and charter schools to offer a high school elective course pertaining to how the Bible has influenced Western culture." What better way to get kids interested in the 'concepts of the history and literature' of the Old and New Testament eras, as House Bill 2563 requires, than pointing out how political leaders through history have used the Bible as a propaganda tool for war? It could happen. After the attacks of 9/11, for example, President George W. Bush spooked our European allies by invoking a, "crusade" reference. He said, "This is a new kind of evil, and the American people are beginning to understand. This crusade, this war on terrorism, is going to take a while."

GQ magazine reported years later that the covers of top-secret intelligence briefings that Defense Secretary Donald Rumsfeld gave to Bush each day, featured Bible verses superimposed over military pictures. For instance, over an image of a tank, was a quote from Ephesians 6:13, "Therefore put on the full armor of God, so that when the day of evil comes, you may be able to stand your ground, and after you have done everything, to stand." "References to the Bible have been used byleaders on all sides of just about every war fought by what Proud calls the, "Western culture."

"Throughout history, religions have used the Bible to regulate behavior of--people--as in don't kill anyone and don't take their land or property--while nations have used the Bible to justify behavior - as in kill people and take their land and property." Montini goes on to say that, if such a class evolved, that it could range from Bush's crusade remark to the real crusades, "in which warriors from the Middle Ages were urged on by biblical verses, like Jeremiah 48:10, 'Cursed is he who does the work of the Lord with slackness and cursed is he who keeps back his sword from bloodshed'."

James Hillman writes in *A Terrible Love of War,* "In the trenches in World War I, French, German, Russian, Italian, English, Scottish, Irish, Austrian, Serbian, Canadian, and American to name but a few engaged in killing each other, invoked the name of one, and the same, god. Northern and Southern armies of the war, between the States, killed each other calling on the same one god. The god of Israel and Palestine and the god of Iraq is this same one god, and is also the very one invited to the White House prayer breakfasts."

Larry Dorsey, *Healing Words,* "Most recently in the Persian Gulf War, Americans prayed to God for aid in defeating Iraq, while Iraqis were simultaneously beseeching Allah to exterminate the Western infidels. What's a God to do?"

Albert Einstein, Physicist, writes in *Ideas and Opinions,* "They say further, and truly, that the greatest obstacle to international order is that monstrously exaggerated spirit of Nationalism, which also goes by the fair-sounding, but misused, name of Patriotism."

Michael Burleigh writes in his book *Moral Combat,* "Like the Italian Fascists and the Japanese militarists, the German National Socialists regarded war as a release from what they called the, "lingering war of peace." They would have agreed with the great Prussian historian Heinrich Von Treitrchke, who claimed that "war was morally sublime." It was "where the enthusiastic hurrahs of patriotic boys were transformed into the steely determination of men."

Sydney J. Harris, *LA Times,* August 1960, "If we love our deity in the wrong way, as an exclusive property, we soon begin to hate those who do not share those devotions. This is why religious wars have been the most prolonged in history. The same is true of patriotism, which has become the modern religion. True patriotism loves its country and wishes the best for it; but for every one person who has the right kind of love, there are a hundred who love it - for vanity, for greed, for display and for all the material rewards it may offer."

Goethe, quoted in *The Great Quotations,* "There is something peculiar about national hatred. You will always find it most extreme and violent on the lowest levels of culture."

Edward Young, English poet 1750 AD, said in *The Great Quotations,* "To murder thousands takes a specious name, War's glorious art, and gives immortal fame." Immortal fame! Patriotism! Nationalistic fervor! The great distinction is between killing one, or, as in the military, legally killing many. Truthfully, speaking from personal experience, I think, when I volunteered in 1940, I probably was still open to that thoughtless, immature, patriotism.

Spencer Kimball, Mormon Church President, quoted in *Time* Magazine, Oct 8th, 2012, "We become anti-enemy, instead of pro-Kingdom of God. We train a man in the art of war, and then call him a patriot, perverting the Savior's teaching, "Love thy enemy."

Charles Elliot Norton, Harvard professor, humanitarian, eloquently quoted in *The Great Quotations,* "So confused are men by false teaching in regard to national honor and the duty of the citizen that it is easy to fall into the error of holding a declaration of war, however, brought about, as a sacred decision of the National Will and to fancy that a call to arm from the Administration, has the force of a call from the lips of the country, of the America to whom all her sons are ready to pay the full measure of devotion." That is the point where I and my brother Harry diverged. I think I blindly viewed WWII as a patriotic responsibility, not as a duty. Is that semantics? I cannot recall my specific thought process. Harry's thought processes were clear.

James Hillman writes in *A Terrible Love of War,* "Besides, we certainly do not like its good, preferring to imagine the God who justifies American wars in particular, as a "Prince of Peace," baptizing all horrors of war in the name of peace; we go to war "to end all wars" and, our twenty first century battalions go abroad "waging peace."

Albert Einstein-Physicist-humanitarian writes in *Ideas and Opinions* of a time of compulsion of military service, but deplores the same chauvinistic inculcation. "The present high development of nationalism everywhere, is in my opinion, intimately connected with the institution of compulsory military service, or, to call it by its sweeter name, national armies. A state which demands, (or requests), military service of its inhabitants, is compelled to cultivate in them a nationalistic spirit, *thereby laying the psychological foundation for their military usefulness.* In its schools it must idolize, alongside with religion, its instrument of brutal force, in the eyes of the youth."

Trevor Powell, *Saskatchewan History* Magazine #2, 2012, (Regarding WWI, 1914-1918), "It was from the pulpit, however, that Anglican clergy made their greatest contribution to the war effort; namely that of recruitment. Rev. E. C. Earp, Grace Church, Regina, Saskatchewan, taking as his topic, "Why should I enlist?" and his text, "Be strong, Show Thyself a man," Earp said it was "the duty of all to enlist and fight for the holiest things entrusted to us," and hoped, "that as a result of his sermon, an atmosphere would be created which would make it uncomfortable for those in the community who were shirking their real duty." Then came those motivating words, "tortured women of Belgium," "mutilated children," and "the graves of helpless men shot as hostages."

However, what if the perpetrators are on our side? *The Toledo Blade,* "won the Pulitzer Prize for investigative reporting for its series, "Buried Secrets, Brutal Truths," about a long list of atrocities committed by a U.S. Army platoon operating in Vietnam in the central Highlands in 1967, The 4-year long army investigation, revealed 18 soldiers and the commander, Major James Hawkins, were at fault but, "no onewas charged."

Colman McCarthy, *LA Times,* Feb 5th 1991. He headlines his article, "Asking God to bless war is blasphemy." He describes the religious support for The Gulf War. Billy Graham spent the first night of the war in the White House blessing, "the saturation bombing in an unctuous sermon." Cardinal John Law of Boston, said that it was right to "defend the cause of justice with arms," and (then there was) the adulation of the almost "divinely inspired," President George Herbert Bush, by the National Association of Religious Broadcasters. The religious approval of a beginning war is mandatory!

Michael Gallagher, *LA Times,* Oct 27th 1996. His article is headed "The Chaplain as an Instrument of War." He speaks of the unseemly naming of the destroyer '*Laboon,*' "that brings terror and death," after Father John Laboon, a chaplain at a 1961 American naval base. He describes a survey by Father Zahn of WWII Royal Air Force chaplains who interviewed British air crew who, "due to the strategy of area bombing were in effect committing mass murder every day by attacking civilians directly and intentionally. This was forbidden by the "just war doctrine" long preached by the church." Yet the "major concern" had been that the airmen resist the sexual temptations near the base, and, "if they had to die, would die in a state of grace. It's OK to roast women and children and babes in the womb, boys, but keep your zipper up off duty." Gallagher asks, "How can a chaplain be free if the Pentagon pays his salary?" He suggests the salary should be paid by the "religious faith groups," and if the Pentagon complains we should be, "terribly concerned" about the Pentagon's plans for us.

James Hillman in *A Terrible Love of War,* "Western Christianity's god comes front and center, when war is in the air. War brings its god to life. In World War II this god was a co-pilot on bombing runs." In World War I, "Clergymen dressed Jesus in khaki and had him firing machine guns." The bishop of London, exhorted his Christian fellows to, "kill the good as well as the bad - kill the young men as well as the old - kill those who have shown kindness to our wounded as well as those fiends --." How could a man with a mission of morality say such things? Old Testament theology! No Golden Rule espoused by that ecclesiastical authority!

The previous references have been universal in nature but the following bigoted opinions are from the Nazi point of view: Adolf Hitler- *Mein Kampf*-There was a large number of Jews who were involved in the Marxist/Communist movement, which Hitler abhorred. Hitler's hatred of Jews appeared to be both political and religious based. In *Mein Kampf* he refers to the Jews as "mortal enemies of free folk state and national states" "Jewish world dictatorship" and to "the hissing of the Jewish world hydra."

In the preface of the 1939 American publication of *Mein Kampf* (16 years after the German publication), "These reflections are copied for the most part from the "Dearborn Independent," Mr. Henry Ford's magazine. Much of the anti-Semitic propaganda once disseminated by the journal is still current in Germany (1939)." Hitler found support of his prior hatred of Jews from the great industrialist, Henry Ford.

Michael Burleigh wrote in his book *Moral Combat,* "German General Hoth issued a decree referring to the Jews, "Their extermination is a dictate of self-preservation. Whichever soldier is critical of these measures, has no understanding of the earlier, decades-long, subversive and treasonable activities of this Jewish-Marxist element among our people." Hitler/Henry Ford influence at work!

Here is a little perspective on the anti-Islamic sentiment being voiced today (2012). (General) Sir John Glubb, wrote in his book, *Muhammad,* (His spelling of Mohammed), "After the death of Mohammed, Islam and Christianity became involved in mutual warfare for a thousand years. The causes of these wars were political. These long centuries of war between Muslim and Christian governments produced intense and fanatical hatreds, which gave rise in Europe to the most profound prejudices against Mohammed." "Far from Islam being the essential enemy of both Christianity and Judaism, it sprang from the same source of both Christianity and Judaism." The causes of these wars were said to be political but were pervasively, also religious. The undercurrent of anti-Moslem sentiment seems to have seeped through from times past. The radical fundamentalist religious factions on both sides intensify the distrusting relationship.

Paul Kurtz, *Free Inquiry* magazine, Oct/Nov 2005, "In our own day most people are rightly appalled by the lack of moral compunction displayed by Islamic suicide terrorists who bomb innocent civilians in the name of "jihad." But in retrospect, think of the bombing of the "open cities" in WWII by all sides - including the Allies - and America's unleashing of nuclear weapons that killed so many innocent civilians. Slaughter of this kind should offend the moral consciences of humankind. We should not forget these terrible, brutal bombings."

Michael Takiff in the *LA Times,* July 4th 2004, (16 months after start of Iraq War), "Our government doesn't track civilian deaths, but according to the independent organization Iraq Body Count, as many as 11,000 Iraqi civilians have died since we first struck Baghdad in March 2003. When we mourn the 3,000 innocent Americans murdered on 9/11, do any of us recognize that over three times that number of innocent Iraqi's have died since we have made war on their country?" - "We want to believe that it is the American way never to make war except on the side of the angels. But we trouble the angels with the killing and dying we have practiced in Iraq. Righteous intentions do not guarantee righteousness; justifications for war based in deceit and delusion are no justification at all."

Money, Power and War

In 1963, having been in the United States for five years, I was at the decision-point regarding citizenship. I had a "bucket full" of pre-Vietnam concerns. My *American Citizenship Reconsidered,* written in 1997 quotes my #7 concern for reconsidering U.S. citizenship as, "President Eisenhower's speech at the 1961 President Kennedy inauguration when he warned of the "military-industrial complex." In my view he could have included the unions, politicians, governments, and universities.

The arms-industries contracts for new, more sophisticated military hardware makes the *Military* happy, protected, effective and needed; the *Industry* (corporations) happy with their profits; the *Politicians* happy with their constituents "full-employment" votes; the *Unions* (workers) happy with their jobs; the *Government* happy with the taxes from company profits and workers' employment; and the *Universities* happy to be involved in research and teaching contracts. These segments of society lumped happily together, comprise the *Military-Industrial-Political-Union-Government-University complex. MIPUGU!* Contentment with the status quo comes to everyone involved with war, except those being killed, their families, and everyone with a moral hang-up on wars that may involve unnecessary killing. The ogre aptly named 'MIPUGU.'

Emery Reyes, 1945 *The Anatomy of Peace* wrote, "Modern science has made war a highly mechanized art which can be mastered only by the major industrial powers." Much more true 70 years later!

Those with the money! Big wages are paid to those with the knowhow. "This keeps the sixth leg of MIPUGU, the Universities who provide the know-how, happy. Research projects mean big money for the universities.

Carl Sagan in *Demon Haunted World* commented that "roughly half the scientists on earth work at least part time for the military."

Marcus Tullis Cicero, 60 BC Roman Statesman, *The Famous Quotations,* "The sinews of war are infinite money." In those times the 'arms' would be bows, arrows, swords, spears, clubs, and for security, shields and castle walls. All Secretaries of Defense call for more military spending. We are repeating ancient history over 2000 years later!

Bernard Baruch, American financier, in *The Famous Quotations,* "Take the profits out of war." "The sinews of war are five: men, money, materials, maintenance, and morale."

Will Durant in *The Story of Philosophy* wrote, "(Immanuel) Kant had before complained as apparently every generation must, that "our rulers have no money to spend on public education - because all their resources are already placed to the account of the next war, The nations will not really be civilized until all standing armies are abolished." He preceded my complaints by 300 years.

Think intently about the wise words of W.E.B. Dubois in 1915, quoted by Howard Zinn in his book *Peoples History of the United States.* In an early grasp of Eisenhower's military-industrial concept, and my MIPUGU, he recognized the combined interest that businesses and unions had in war promotion. "Dubois saw the ingenuity of capitalism in creating a safety valve for explosive class conflict." One hundred years ago he said. "It is no longer the merchant prince, or the aristocratic monopoly, or even the employing class that is exploiting the world: It is the nation, a new democratic nation, composed of united capital and labor." - "American capitalism needs international rivalry, and periodic war, to create an artificial community of interest between rich and poor--." In other words, profits for business and wages for labor. He saw how jobs, bring the employer and the employee together in their wish for war contracts.

Smedley Butler British poet 1835-1902, *The Great Quotations,* "War, like any other racket, pays high dividends to the very few, but what does it benefit the masses? The cost of operations (in lives) is always transferred to the people who do not profit."

Howard Zinn, *The Peoples History of the United States,* "When WWI started in Europe the United States was in a recession. But by 1915 war orders from the Allies stimulated the economy and by April 1917 two billion dollars-worth of goods had been sold to the (mostly European) Allies." As historian Hofstadter says, "America became bound up with the Allies in a fateful union of war and prosperity."

Albert Einstein, *Ideas and Opinions,* "One has to realize that the powerful industrial groups concerned in the manufacture of arms are doing their best in all countries to prevent the peaceful settlement of international disputes." "Is the current atomic arms race leading to another world war or a way to prevent war? A competitive armament is not a way to prevent war. Every step in that direction brings us nearer catastrophe. On the contrary, real peace cannot be reached without systematic disarmament on a supra-national scale. I repeat. Armament is no protection against war, but leads inevitably to war." Force begets opposing force. Incisive words!

Howard Zinn, *The Peoples History of the United States,* "Back in 1907, President Woodrow Wilson (using war-provoking language) said, "Concessions made by financiers must be safeguarded by ministers of state even if the sovereignty of unwilling nations be outraged in the process, the doors of the nations which are closed must be battered down. Our domestic markets no longer suffice and we need foreign markets." In 1919 he said "he supported the righteous conquest of foreign markets." These are harsh words from the acknowledged, primary founder of the League of Nations! It does not reflect the Golden Rule. Albert Einstein, *Ideas and Opinions,* 1934, "The armament industry, is indeed, one of the greatest dangers that beset mankind.

It is the hidden evil power behind the nationalism which rampant everywhere. As regards the munitions industry and the export of war material, the League of Nations has busied itself for years with efforts to get this loathsome traffic controlled - with what little results we all know. Last year (1933) I asked a well-known American diplomat why Japan was not forced by a commercial boycott to desist from her policy of force. (Japan had invaded China) "Our economic interests are too strong" was the answer. How can you help people who rest satisfied with a statement like that?"

Michael Burleigh in his book *Moral Combat* wrote, "British Prime Minister Neville Chamberlain referred to war as "hateful" and "damnable" when he spoke, reluctantly, of the need for rearmament, at the expense of the alleviation of suffering, - the opening of fresh institutions and recreations the care of the old, the development and minds of the young. All the amenities that a liberal civilization was capable of bestowing would be wasted on inert grey metal and brass casings, whose ultimate function was to kill and to maim." This came from a right wing British Conservative statesman in the late 1930s.

Martin Luther King in 1967, wrote in his book, *Where Do We Go From Here?,* "This business of war cannot be reconciled with wisdom, justice and love. A nation that continues year after year to spend more money on military defense than on programs of social uplift is approaching spiritual death."

Stanford Professor David M. Kennedy in the LA Times May 5th 1985 observed how World War II enriched and transformed the USA and, "radically reshaped its role in the world." "Almost in one stroke, the war swept away the blight of economic depression that had afflicted the United States for 12 stagnant years before Pearl Harbor. Booming war production and federal deficit spending brought the unemployment rate from 14% to close to 1%." MIPUGU was happy. That one paragraph presents the challenge to U.S. capitalism. The economy thrived but the social needs of the country where placed on the back- burner. The lesson learned, was that war produced a better economy. So how could the good times be extended? Make your potential enemy angry! Ponder the Cold War, to understand how fear and paranoia provided the ideal conditions for the necessity of keeping the arms industry busy. Little thought was directed to how to produce a healthy thriving economy in other ways than war.

"Historian Gabriel Kolko, after a study of American wartime policy *The Politics of War* concludes that," the American economic war aim was to save capitalism at home and abroad." In April 1944 a State Department official said, "As you know we've got to plan on enormously increased production in this country after the war, and the American domestic market can't absorb all that production indefinitely. There won't be any question about our needing greatly increased foreign markets."

Howard Zinn continues, "Bruce Catton in his book, *The War Lords of Washington,* described how the wealth of WWII war sales became more and more concentrated in fewer and fewer corporations." "The war rejuvenated American capitalism." "Charles E. Wilson, the president of GE Corporation, was so happy about the wartime situation that he suggested a "continuing alliance between business and the military for a permanent war economy." That is what happened!

Zinn continues, "Quietly, behind the headlines in battles and bombings, American diplomats and businessmen worked hard to make sure that when the war ended, American economic power would be second to none in the world. United States business would penetrate areas that up to this time were dominated by England." Political lobbying got Roosevelt to approve Lend Lease aid to the biggest oil producer, Saudi Arabia, which thus produced protection of the interests of the giant American corporation ARAMCO. You scratch my back, I'll scratch yours. That arrangement with Saudi Arabia still exists.

Zinn continues, "In 1944, Britain and the U.S. signed a pact on oil agreeing on "the principle of equal opportunity." This Open Door Policy allowed American businesses to compete everywhere, and was said to be "triumphant throughout the Middle East."

Scottsdale Tribune Oct 28th 2005 (Quoting LA Times), Headline. "Exxon Mobil sales soar to record (quarterly) $100.7 billion". Jerry Hirsch, "More than a billion dollars a day, $45 million an hour, almost $340 for every living American that's what Exxon Mobil Corp. reported in third quarter revenue Thursday." $402 billion yearly!

Zinn continues "Before the war was over, the administration was planning the outlines of the new international economic order, based on partnership between government and big business. The flow of dollars for the military interests of the nation would continue! The poet, Archibald MacLeish, then an Assistant Secretary of State, spoke critically of what he saw in the postwar world, "As things are now going, the peace we will make, the peace we seem to be making, will be a peace of oil, a peace of gold, a peace of shipping, a peace in brief without moral purpose or human interest."

Zinn continues, "The Soviet Union was recovering quickly. The Truman administration however, presented the Soviet Union as not just a rival but as an immediate threat. In a series of moves abroad and at home, it established a climate of fear - of hysteria about Communism - which would steeply escalate the military budget and stimulate the economy with war-related orders. The combination of policies would permit more aggressive actions abroad, and more repressive actions at home."

Zinn continues (1955), "It was an atmosphere in which the government would get massive support for a policy of rearmament. The system, so shaken in the 1930s, had learned that war production would bring stability and high profits. Truman's anti-Communism was attractive. The business publication *Steel* had said in November 1946 - even before the Truman Doctrine (Containment of Communism), that Truman's policies gave the firm assurance that maintaining and building our preparation for war will be big business in the United States for at least a considerable period ahead." The prediction turned out to be accurate.

Zinn continues, "President J. F. Kennedy increased military spending by 9 million dollars. By 1962, based on a series of invented scares about Soviet military build-up, a false bomber-gap and a false missilegap, the United States had overwhelmingly nuclear superiority. It had the equivalent in nuclear weapons, of 1500 Hiroshima-size atomic bombs, far more than enough to destroy every major city on earth - the equivalent, in fact, of ten tons of TNT for every man, woman, and child on earth. To deliver these bombs, the United States had more than 50 intercontinental ballistic missiles, 80 missiles on nuclear submarines, 90 missiles on stations overseas, 1700 bombers capable of reaching the Soviet Union, 100 fighters on aircraft carriers able to carry atomic weapons and 1,000 land-based supersonic fighters able to carry atomic bombs. Over-kill! The Soviet Union was obviously behind - it had between fifty and one hundred intercontinental ballistic missiles and fewer than 200 long range bombers."

Zinn continues, "But the U.S. budget kept mounting, the hysteria kept growing, the profits of corporations getting defense contracts multiplied, and wages moved ahead just enough to keep a substantial number of Americans dependent on war industries for their living. By 1970 the U.S. military budget was 80 billion dollars and the corporations involved in military production were making fortunes. Senator Paul Douglas' noted that six-sevenths of these contracts were not competitive - the government picks a company and draws up a contract in more or less secret. A senate report showed that 100 large defense contractors, who hold 67.4 per cent of the military contracts, employed more than two thousand former high ranking officers of the military." Secret contracts are a very poor business approach.

Martin Luther King *Where Do We go from Here?* 1967, "The Washington Post has calculated that we spend $332.000 for each enemy we kill. It challenges the imagination to contemplate what lives we could transform if we were to cease killing. The security we profess to seek in foreign activities we will lose in our decaying cities. The bombs in Vietnam explode at home; they destroy the hopes and possibilities for a decent America." MLK was descriptively and accurately prophetic. The hopeless desperation of the underprivileged areas of our cities was ripe for explosion. And, exploding into riots, it did. This waste of taxpayer money on war was to make that certain!

Jesse Unruh, Californian congressman, famously said, "Money is the mother's milk of politics." The words are even more apt when applied to war. Money is everything for the military. Money is the mother's milk of war! Those successful corporations (the arms-makers that win the contracts, and sell military equipment and supplies), are the envy of the industrial world and the dream of the lobbyist and of MIGUPU. In our money-oriented, money-necessary world, full employment brings contentment. When there is a consistent flow of Jesse's mother's milk, everyone is benefitted except those people being killed.

With the aid of the relentless lobbyists, the military corporations are delighted with the docile acquiescence of the politicians who approve the expenditures of taxpayer money at every lobbyist whim. They give no consideration to the great need of that money, for the educational, medical and social needs of the people and they are doubly delighted with the additional profits in the international arms sales, regardless of the cruel deaths of faceless citizens in questionable political causes in other countries. Full employment! Wonderful! This political and psychological detachment from morality, while achieving top jobs creation and obscene profits, is the war corporation's triumphant zenith. Money! Power!

League of Conservation Voters, 2012, "The five largest oil companies BP, Chevron, Conoco Phillips, Exxon-Mobil, and Royal Dutch Shell made a record $137 billion in profits in 2011, ranking them among the most profitable companies in the world. Big oil has used some of their tax subsidized profits to help build the most anti-environment House of Representatives in history and now they are determined to pack the Senate with pro-pollution, anti-EPA, pro Big-oil cronies."

L. A. Times June 14th 2004, "Pentagon officials have acknowledged that the decision, overruling the advice of an army lawyer, eventually resulted in the awarding of a $7-billion, no-bid contract to Haliburton for the post-War recovery of Iraq's oil sector --." Two days later the *LA Times* editorialized "The incentive for the company is strong. Costplus means Halliburton gets a set percentage above actual costs, so in general the more cost, the more Halliburton profits.

Robert Scheer *LA Times,* Aug 1st 2000, "From the vantage point of (Dick) Cheney the (Gulf) War was wonderful. It landed him a job in the oil business and a whopping $43 million windfall in salary and stock options, after only five years as head of Halliburton Co, a Texas-based oil services firm." Consider the obscenity of the contrived, immoral, Iraq War that President George W. Bush and his buddies planned and out-sourced to a legion of subcontractors, mostly without competitive bids, including Halliburton.

Earthwise, the newsletter of the *Union of Concerned Scientists,* fall 2014: "There is no bigger consumer of oil than the U.S. armed forces, which burn through more than 100 million barrels each year."

Associated Press, Sept 16th 2007, "Ex-Fed chairman Alan Greenspan said, 'I am saddened, that it is politically inconvenient to acknowledge what everyone knows: The Iraq War is largely about oil." The nation's financial wise man knew!

Look who invests! *Arizona Tribune,* Apr 4 2008, (The Associated Press): "Members of Congress have as much as $196 million collectively invested in companies doing business with the Dept. of Defense." They made millions off of the Iraq War. That is a conflict of interest!

Colonel David Hackworth (America's most decorated soldier 8 Purple Hearts, 9 Silver Stars, 8 Bronze Stars, 4 Legion of Merits and 4 Army Commendation medals) in his book *About Face,* Page 827 says, "This incestuous relationship between military and industry has got to stop." He was speaking of the 2nd career types who were the Colonels, Generals and other "Brass" who, leave the military and go to work for the defense contractors (or the government) in their second careers, using their in-service contacts and know-how to further the company's profits. He also speaks of the contractors who, "pay for campaign contributions in home states."

Parade Magazine Nov 27th 2005, Headline, "War planning pays off." "Former CIA director George Tenet negotiated a $4 million book deal. Paul Wolfowitz, No. 2 at the Pentagon, is now at the World Bank, with a $300,000 tax-free annual salary, with a mortgage allowance and golf club membership. Retired General Tommy Franks reportedly collected $5 million for his memoirs --." And it was only 2005 yet!

LA Times, Jan 10th 2002, Headline, "Arms Buildup is a Boon to firm run by Big Guns." The Carlyle Group is a "private equity company" that has shown returns of more than 34% through the last decade, particularly through timely defense and aerospace investments. On a single day last month Carlyle earned $237 million selling shares in United Defense Industries, the Army's fifth largest contractor." At least seven members of present and past U.S. administrations were leaders in the company including former *President George H. Bush." So when President (George W) Bush declared war on terrorism last September, few were better poised than Carlyle to know how and when to make money."*

At every turn there is the appearance of conflict of interest by political officials. The obscene amount of money necessary to maintain the military services, and fight the wars thought to be necessary, call for major discussion. The following quotations help to define and illustrate the problem of military spending.

The Tribune, March 31st 2007, President W. Bush had just asked Congress for $100 billion for the Iraq and Afghanistan Wars through the next 6 months. "Reporter Bartholomew of Scripps Howard News Service tried to put $100 billion into some kind of perspective. That amount, he found, translates into spending $5,500 every second, $331.73 for every person in the United States, - and it's all borrowed on Uncle Sam's credit card."

Physicians for Social Responsibility, March 5th 2013, There will be "More than $100 billion (spent) over the next ten years on new spending on America's Nuclear arsenal (total spending $700 billion), and a projected $5.8 trillion on the bloated military budget as a whole over the next decade. Over $24 billion last year alone on subsidies, tax breaks and other giveaways to dirty fossil fuel industries like Big Coal andthe oil giants."

Earthwise, Newsletter of the *Union of Concerned Scientists,* fall 2014: "There is no bigger consumer of oil than the U.S. armed forces, which burn through more than 100 million barrels each year."

American Friends Service Committee newsletter, 2009, "The total cost of the Iraq and Afghanistan Wars is now a trillion dollars. $765 billion dollars could provide the 15.3 million unemployed Americans with a job paying $50,000 for one year just three quarters of the total war bill. Our unemployment rate could be zero and we'd still have $235 billion left over to build schools, provide health insurance or office training." Health and education were on the back-burner!

That fact was forcibly brought home to me in 1968. A close family member, diagnosed as a paranoid schizophrenic had tried three times to commit suicide. Her pastor advised "pray for her"; her doctor refused a house call for psychiatric referral, saying he "hadn't seen her for 8 months;" the social workers refused saying, "they didn't have the power". The Long Beach (California) Health Clinic said they could do nothing because their, "limited money and personnel had been diverted to the needs of the Vietnam War." Fortunately, a compassionate psychiatrist rewarded my sobbing, embarrassing public telephone call (no cell phones) with 72 hours of diagnostic admission, which, on evaluation, validated priority admission. The needs of society are neglected in all wars.

A timeless 1990 cartoon. Now, the plane would be the F35 priced at $132.9 million. Cartoon by Paul Conrad, Los Angeles Times, P. B7, April 5, 1990. Reproduced with permission of the U.S Library of Congress.

Time Magazine, Apr 25th 2011 Headline, "How to Save a Trillion Dollars" "Do we really need 11 carrier strike groups for another 30 years when no other country has more than one? Can the U.S. re ally afford more than 500 bases at home and around the world? Do the Navy, Air Force and Marines really need $400 billion in new jet fighters when their fleets of F-15s, F16s and F-18s will give them vast air superiority for years to come? Does the Navy need 50 attack submarines when America's main enemy hides in caves? Does the army still need 80,000 troops in Europe 66 years after the defeat of Adolf Hitler? Partly as a consequence, we are an increasingly muscle-bound nation: we send $1 billion dollar destroyers, with crews of 300 each, to handle 5 Somali pirates in a fiberglass skiff." What a disproportionate use of force! That is the modern equivalent of "killing a mouse with an elephant gun!"

However, as Stephen Beschloss, said in *The Arizona Republic* Jan 22nd 2012, "proponents of a perpetual war economy need not worry." Those "responsibilities" appear to require the domineering power of the U.S. military! Beschloss continues, "By 2010, military spending rose to $698 billion, more than double its total of $302 billion a decade earlier. That is more than double the spending of China, France, the United Kingdom and Russia combined, and it surpasses the totals of the top 15 countries."

Beschloss states, "While the USA can easily assert its military superiority, our infrastructure is ranked 24th globally, primary education is 37th, science education is ranked 51st and life expectancy is 32nd, according to the 2011 World Economic Forum's Global Competitiveness Forum." Think! Terrible numbers! Yet we continue to assert that our nation is the 'best in the world.'

The quotations of Author Beschloss, state my conviction in clear words, "It is clear that it is the excessive drain of tax-payer dollars and of natural resources that have gone into the military in the past 60 years that has left the U.S. with an immense multi-trillion dollar deficit, excessive taxation, a degraded populace due to decreased social, medical, and educational programs; a much deteriorated infrastructure; a very distrusting electorate and a dismal foreboding future for our next generation."

The following are more of the myriad of senseless details that illustrate how militaristic our nation has become. Speaking only of American servicemen, the lives lost were: WWI 116,000 killed, WWII - 405,000, the Korean War - 54,000, and the Vietnam War - 58,000.

Oceans of family tears! We have put ourselves in the same financial bind that Napoleon Bonaparte did, when, to finance his wars, he sold the state of Louisiana to the United States for less than 3 cents an acre. Our vast, "limitless" resources are in reality - *limited* --, and will someday be depleted. We will be haunted by those national debts for generations to come. Today, June 2012, we are approaching national bankruptcy. Aiming to pay for WWI as it occurred, the U.S. tax on the wealthy was 77% and in WW2 was 91%. Recently, our right wing, won again. And we are relying on our next generation to pay off our Chinese credit card! We are bankrupting ourselves and also our future generations! We are clueless!

LA. Times, April 28th 2004, "Lockheed Martin Corp, the biggest U.S. military contractor, stated that their "Aeronautics profit climbed 42% to $206 million in the quarter, and will rise about 25% to as much as $860 million for the year --. As a result of the conflict in Iraq, Lockheed could see some additional demand from the U.S. army for the firm's multiple launch rocket system, or for intelligence, surveillance and reconnaissance gear."

Robert Robb, *The Arizona Republic,* Aug 29th 2012, "So far the wars in Afghanistan and Iraq have cost American taxpayers $1.4 trillion. The United States did not purchase $1.4 trillion worth of additional security from the wars in Iraq and Afghanistan. U.S. efforts to ramrod democratic transformation in the Middle East, came a cropper, and were quickly abandoned."

The invention of the drone industry of the last few years is described by John Horgan in the *National Geographic Society* March 2013, "The Pentagon armed the Predator and a larger unmanned surveillance plane, The Reaper, with missiles, so that their operators sitting in offices in places like Nevada or New York - could destroy, as well as spy on targets thousands of miles away. Aerospace firms churned out a host of smaller drones, with increasingly clever computer chips, and keen sensors cameras, but also instruments that measure airborne chemicals, pathogens, radioactive materials. The U.S. has deployed over 11,000 military drones."

The Arizona Republic, April 17th 2013. A news report describing the advantage to a state which gets the approval by the FAA for drone development, "- estimated 70,000 jobs, and $13 billion of economic impact from drone operations within the first three years." The futures of the children of our nation are being squandered in the military money pit!

Free Inquiry magazine 2005, "The United States spends as much on arms as the rest of the countries of the world combined." The preceding is an indication of the militaristic country that the U.S. has become.

The *American Friends Service Committee* Newsletter (Quakers), June 2012, "Who wins when our country goes to war? The defense contractors."

To this point we have been mainly discussing manufacture and sale to the U.S. military services. However, arms sales to other countries are even less morally defensible. Our nation's sales representative cannot claim fear, religion, nationalism, territory acquisition, rebellion or paranoia as *OUR* country's reason for the sale to someone else. However, he can use these same factors, as a sales pitch, for his prospective client country to consider. He is left with little more than profit as our country's primary motive. In addition, our sales have been to countries with repressive regimes where our guns have been used to shoot down innocent political protesters. Lawrence Kolb and Caroline in the *Boston Globe,* April 2005 wrote that "Between 2000 and 2003, our country sold $76 billion in arms to other countries, more than the rest of the world combined."

LA Times, March 29th 1997, "Abu Dhabi, UAE International Defense Exposition. Over 500 exhibitors from 42 countries (were represented). The instability six years after the Gulf War had the U.S. urging all countries to arm them-selves for protection." That is using fear to create their sales talk! The profits from those sales return to the "Because the U.S. manufacturers pocket the largest share of arms revenue, weapons programs are seen in some quarters as thinly disguised foreign aid *TO* the United States."

But, be sure to protect your sales. 4/6/1997, *LA Times,* "Defense Secretary Wm S. Cohen, warns Seoul (political friend and client, South Korea) not to buy Russian arms."

LA Times, Oct 8th 1997, Between 1993 and 1997, "the top arms dealers of the world were U.S. - $32 billion (46% of the total), UK

$18 billion, Russia $8 billion, France $5 billion and China $3 billion." Note that these 5 nations are the exclusive, permanent members of the UN Security Council. "The leading recipients were: Saudi Arabia 29 billion, Egypt 6 billion, Taiwan 4 billion, Kuwait 4 billion and South Korea 3 billion." The recipient list definitely adds 'food for thought.'

Highly respected, past President of Costa Rica, Oscar Arias, 1987 Nobel Peace Laureate, LA Times July 31st 1997 said, "As the world's foremost arms merchant, the United States has a responsibility to take the lead in curbing the arms trade. Since 1991 the United States has entered into more new agreements to sell arms than all the major arms suppliers combined. The five permanent members of the UN supply 85% of all the weapons delivered on the international market. In 1996 the U.S. government gave arms manufacturers $7 billion dollars in subsidies, to export their wares. In today's world where one billion people are illiterate, more than one billion lack access to potable water, and 1.3 billion earn less than a dollar a day, the arms trade simply perpetuates poverty. Our children need schools, not tanks; playgrounds not guns and health clinics not fighter jets."

Possibly, the most important statement in this book is the one that follows. I have saved to the last an account of *how a society can become militarized because it is dominated by the corporations that influence it.* We should study carefully how "IG", an immense arms supplier, developed into a monolithic militaristic corporation pushing Germany in its various martial ventures. Similarly involved, was the mammoth company, "the House of Krupp." *We should seek to control the influence of the similar, but more diverse, massive arms dealers, in the U.S. who also control our military.* How did Hitler and his brutal Nazi thugs finance a huge military successfully? First think of the warning words of President Eisenhower in 1961 and know that he was warning the United States of the corporate power of militarism in the affairs of our country. "In the councils of government we must guard against the acquisition of unwarranted influence by the military-industrial complex. The potential for the disastrous rise of misplaced power exists and will persist. We must never let the weight of this combination endanger our liberties or democratic process." Eisenhower, who had seen Auschwitz Concentration Camp up close, had to have had I. G. and Krupp, the worst examples of money-controlled war industries, leading in his mind. He started by forcing the local village residents to be escorted through the Auschwitz Concentration Camp, so that they would know there could not be a later denial of the atrocities committed there. The German people would come to understand that three generations of life-long *JOBS* for the loyal employees of IG and Krupp, were jobs causing destruction, and suffering and death to others.

In 1920, H. G. Wells had written in *The Outline of History,* "At the very core of all this evil that has burst at last in world disaster lies this Kruppism, this sordid, enormous trade in the instruments of death."

Peter Batty, *The House of Krupp,* "The First World War was indeed the first war of materials, the first industrialized slaughter on an international scale. Krupp's wide spread factories produced prodigious amounts of armaments in WWI, and did the same as Hitler rearmed in the 1930s.The avalanche of armaments from the nationwide Krupp factories was immense. The factories, especially at Essen, Germany were intensively bombed during WWII. The primary owner, Alfred Krupp, was tried as a war criminal at the Nuremberg trials, given 12 years imprisonment, but released in 2 ½ years, and by 1966, was "one of the richest men in the world. A recent (1966) valuation of his properties put them as being worth around 1500 million pounds. In 1966 currency, that would be probably four to five billion dollars."

Joseph Borkin writes in *The Crime and Punishment of I. G. Farben* (IG or IG Farbenindustrie), "Without IG's immense productive facilities, its far-reaching research, varied technical experience, and overall concentration of economic power, Germany would not have been in a position to start its aggressive war in 1939. IG truly was a mighty industrial colossus. So huge were its assets, admitted and concealed, so superior its technological know-how, and so formidable its array of patents, that it dominated the chemical business of the world. IG fortified this commercial leadership by constructing a maze of cartels whose members included such industrial giants as Kuhlmann of France, Imperial Chemical Industries of Great Britain (for whom, in 1943-45, as a "chemist's assistant", my future wife Joan "Doe" worked), Montacini of Italy, Aussiger Versein of Czechoslovakia, Boruta of Poland, Mitsui of Japan, and Standard Oil (New Jersey), Dupont, and Dow Chemicals of the United States." It is obvious from the forgoing that some war industries have become globally entrenched. IG diversified into other nations to bring profits to their home nation.

Borkin continues, "I.G. Farbenindustrie established one of their production plants on the grounds of Auschwitz concentration camp, so that the slave labor from the camp could be used to make the multitude of company products including ZYKLON B, the poison gas to be used in their own extermination. Twelve IG executives were found guilty at the Nuremberg Trials for which they served 1½ to 8 years."

Borkin continues, "- immediately after the defeat of Germany in 1945, IG's crucial role in making it possible for Hitler to wage the greatest war in history for over five and a half years, did not go unnoticed by the Allied leadership. Even before Germany officially surrendered, General Eisenhower ordered an investigation of IG's place in Germany's war effort. After a detailed analysis of every facet of IG's operations creation and production of synthetic oil and rubber to its international cartel agreements, the investigating team concluded that IG Farben was indispensable to the German war effort. Without it Hitler could not have embarked on the war or come so close to victory."

Eisenhower's specific recommendations were:

- Make IG plants available for reparations.
- Destroy IG plants used exclusively for war purposes.
- Break up IG's monopoly control by disposing ownership of the remaining plants.
- Terminate IG's interests in international cartels;
- Take over IG's research programs and facilities."

Borkin, "Due to legal agreements, showing Standard Oil and IG Farben as cooperating with each other, Judge Charles Clark volunteered a startling observation that Standard Oil could have been considered an alien national in view of its relationship with IG Farben, after the U. S. and Germany had become active enemies."

Borkin concludes, "Due to corporate camouflage and legal maneuvers, by 1955 the IG Farben company had been reduced to 3 of its component companies, Bayer (think Aspirin) being one of them. Their profits already outstripped those of their monolithic predecessor. The combined value of BASF, Bayer and Hoechst stock represented over 15% of the value of all of the West German stock exchange. In 1977 the three were among the thirty largest industrial companies in the world. Hoechst is the largest company in Germany and each of the three is larger than IG Farben was at its zenith." Follow the money!

Charles Higham in *Trading with the enemy* (in WWII) write, "Standard Oil of New Jersey shipped the Nazis precious oil through Switzerland, while Allied forces endured restriction of supplies, and shortages were widespread. Ford Motor Company trucks were built for Nazi troops with authorization from Ford directors in the United States. The chairman of ITT supplied much of Hitler's communication system. Throughout WWII the list of those who chose, "Business- As-Usual," even when the business was conducted with their country's enemy during a war - is as extensive as it is shocking."

Charles Higham in *Trading with the Enemy* (paraphrased). "A list of some of the American firms found to have been involved in business transactions with the Nazis during WWII: Ford Motor Company,

American Motors Company, General Motors Company, Standard Oil Company of New Jersey, Dow Chemical Corp, Dupont Chemical Co, IT&T (International Telephone and Telegraph Company), Chase National Bank."

George Santayana, *The Great Quotations* "Those who do not remember the past are condemned to repeat it." *WE ARE REPEATING IT!* Like Germany had, we have a long list of corporations, many immense, that exist only for feeding the voracious appetite of the military and its desires for ever-newer inventive technological miracles only to kill our fellow human beings. *No wonder this segment on war makes so little mention of the Golden Rule! The citizen, most-especially the American citizen, by feeding that militaristic appetite with their countries wealth, have deprived their children of reasonable and appropriate education; their citizenry of free, necessary health care; their society of its humanitarian social needs; and the nation of routine up-keep of its decaying infrastructure. America! World! Wake up!*

The United States economy could only survive the shock of a drastic cut in its defense, if some clear headed individuals of the country learn how to devote an equivalent increase to health, education, and housing, feeding the hungry millions of the backward areas or financing their reconstruction. That academic, economic conundrum became real for the armament industries when the unplanned-for collapse of the Soviet Union took place in 1990. Suddenly, the militarily-oriented economy of the Western nations was confronted with the specter of *No Enemy!* For them, an economic chaos existed in the 1990s! Re-tooling for peace? Or, as Lewis had said: "some other totally useless way?" No! Instead, the dissipation of the "peace-dividend" (education, health, social programs) became another of my painful disillusionments. Hail the terrorists!

The headline in the *LA Times,* July 15th 2004, describes a continuing abuse "Advocates of (Iraq) war now profit from Iraq's reconstruction." There is profit in destroying it, and again, when rebuilding it!

Jim Mann, *LA Times,* Sept 17th 2000, "In its attempt to eradicate drugs and drug-traffickers a limited rescue for some defense industries took place with the Colombia Plan in 2000. Lockheed Martin, United Technologies (Sikorsky), and Textron all benefitted in the planning and building of helicopters for Colombia."

But for the armament manufacturer's big emergency the terrorists came to the rescue. No wonder there were conspiracy theories about 9/11. Those faceless, ideology-driven souls, who needed no country borders, laid the climactic dream at the feet of the armament industries - a world-wide, unending atmosphere of insecurity which can only mean a permanent fear-driven war economy. Good times had returned! *The American Friends Service Committee* Newsletter, Sept 12 2012, speaking of the budget mess of that date with "sequester" cuts coming: "We cannot be silent at such an important time. Especially because our country wouldn't be in such a fiscal mess if it weren't for the billions spent on war and defense in the first place."

Orange County Register, June 2nd 2004, "Even by Washington standards, the $119.4 billion that President George W Bush and Congress have provided for the past two years of the war in Iraq is real money." Listing other suffering priorities in the budget the Register writes, "Or it could reduce the runaway federal deficit." That comment made at only 1 ¼ years into the nine-year Iraq War.

The American Friends Service Committee, September 7th 2012, "I believe we have a moral responsibility to remind every one of our leaders that one of the most effective ways they can spend federal money is on institutions that preserve and create new jobs. And pouring billions of dollars into the defense industry simply is not the way to do that. The fact is that moving military spending to health care or education will generate more than twice as many jobs. *For every 12 jobs created by military spending, we could create 29 jobs in education alone!* The cost of a single (just ONE) F-35 fighter plane (132.9 million dollars) - the Pentagon's costliest weapons program - could create health care for 11,760 people, and at the same time improve access to care for those who need it most. " PEOPLE! *WAKE UP!*

American Friends Service Committee, March 25th 2013, "Social programs have been hit hard. Now it's the Pentagon's turn. The

Pentagon budget has grown by 42% since 2000 - and that's without even counting the costly wars in Iraq and Afghanistan!"

Finally, listen to the current woes of a local economy, the east-of-Phoenix, (Mesa) Arizona community in which I live. *The Arizona Republic,* December 21st 2014. Headline, "EAST VALLEY WARY OF DEFENSE CUTS."

"Defense contracts awarded in Arizona fell by $1.7 billion from 2012 to 2013. It was felt from Scottsdale to Mesa to Chandler, where there is a concentration of defense-industry workers and employers, the largest being the Boeing Co. and Honeywell International. Military experts said that in the long run, defense dollars will remain 'critical to Arizona's economic future,' which is why state and private officials are focused on making sure the drops in spending do not continue." - "We're making sure our congressional delegation understands the importance of Arizona's contracts, said Garrick Taylor, senior vice president of government relations and communications at the Arizona Chamber of Commerce." - "Margaret Mullen, chief operating officer for the Science Foundation Arizona, believes that defense dollars are vital for Arizona due to the many military installations the state has. "In Arizona, defense spending is critical, she said, noting that the state has more than 1,200 aerospace and defense companies providing more than 150,000 jobs." *Our militarized nation is composed of thousands of similar local defense-dollars addicted communities.*

The Arizona Republic headline, Nov 2nd 2012, An award was given for, "championing the F-35 training center at Luke Air-force Base." *The Arizona Republic* April 15th 2014, "Each F-35 costs 131.9 million dollars! A Phoenix-area fleet of 144 planes is planned! The project is "7 years behind schedule and roughly 70% over budget." Jobs keep our local MIPUGO very contented.

Time magazine, about Feb 2014, headline: "The most *EXPENSIVE* weapon ever built." Included in the extensive F-35 article they state that the U.S. military is also buying "459 V-28 tilt rotors for $53 billion; three first class battleships (aircraft carriers), for $42 billion (the necessary planes extra); 30 Virginia class attack submarines for $93,000 billion; and $126 billion for missile defense." *Revolting!*

The Arizona Republic continued, "In an attempt to protect the future, the governor charged the science foundation in 2010 with developing a plan not to just sustain the industry, but to help it grow. The plan laid out 31 objectives to increase the military footprint in the state, including securing F-35 training missions for Luke Air Force Base in Glendale, and keeping the 612th Air Operations Center at Davis-Monthan Air Force Base in Tucson. Both of these goals were met. Retired General Thomas Browning, who co-authored the plan, said at least seven of the (31) objectives were met, and a number of others were (being) implemented." Our local defense industries and their lobbyists have succeeded. This local story is similar to a multitude of local stories in all of our 50 states, in our defense-contracts, addicted nation. It's called *JOBS!*

In a militaristic nation, the costs of the military establishment extend into retirement. *The Arizona Republic,* Jan 12 2014, "Top officers, make more in retirement than they do in uniform. For instance, a fourstar officer (general) with 40 years of experience would receive an (annual) pension of $237,144, according to the Pentagon." Medical care and pensions form a substantial (justifiable at some level) military cost. *Physicians for Social Responsibility* newsletter, March 5th 2013, "Pushed by special interests, Congress and state lawmakers are wasting our taxpayer dollars on things that put your family's health in grave danger: More than $100 billion over the next ten years on new spending on America's nuclear arsenal (total spending $700 billion), and a projected 5.8 trillion on the bloated military budget as a whole over the next decade."

This is a vivid illustration of the stresses involved in cutting back on military spending. Elections hinge on the major electoral concern, the current availability of jobs, which determines the viability and economic health of the community. Visualize the wrenching of the nation's economy if, or when, the defense industry is converted to a socially planned economy directed to the education, health and wellbeing of the nation and world. In time, it must, and will, happen, but only when the peoples of the world get desperate. It might have happened in 1990, when the collapse of the Soviet Union occurred, but the terrorists came to the rescue of the defense industry. In the profit driven world of today it is difficult to visualize conversion to a socially- oriented economy. However, the massive projects needed to establish a socially-progressive, global community bringing health, education and food to the smallest communities of the world should give the big companies incentive to convert from their war-driven economies. Failing that conversion, only a futuristic, cashless society, (eliminating the profits of war) as visualized by Technocracy, will free us from of the scourge of war.

Territory and War

Border disputes have notoriously produced small skirmishes, but territorial disagreements can produce major wars. Examples are the Mexican/American war of 1846, and the Canadian/American war of 1812, and the Israeli/Palestinian War of 1948. *USA Today,* Aug 6 2015, "The violence stems from claims to the land between Palestinian and Israeli settlers."

President (General) Ulysses S. Grant, *The Great Quotations,* "I do not think that there ever was a more wicked war than that waged by the United States in Mexico. I thought so at the time (1846) when I was a youngster, only I had not moral courage enough to resign --.It was the instance of a republic following the bad example of European monarchies, in not considering justice, in their desire to acquire additional territory."

German history provides another illustration. Germany, with a highly literate and tech-conscious populace, had flourished and grown during the Industrial Revolution of the late 1800s. Large manufacturing plants and an associated, growing work-force placed more pressure on the available land. German colonies in Africa were earlier envisioned as potential expansionist, over flow, safety-controls - however, the 1918 Versailles Treaty had eliminated German colony ownership. Hitler's design for war was highly influenced by a desire for more living space for Germans. "Lebensraum" (living space), Hitler called it. A Hitler-quote from *The Rise and Fall of the Third Reich* by William Shirer, "Germany must expand to the East - largely at the expense of Russia."

Dilemmas, similar to the Israeli situation above, occur in population-filled countries. About 1990, "Mr. Stoltzfus," described to me how, about 225 years earlier, his ancestors, on pioneering near Lancaster, Pennsylvania, had been allotted a specific amount of land. As families grew they built an adjacent house, and continued to live on the same land. The inevitable result was that, as the allotted space filled with people, land prices soared. By 1990, there was insufficient land for almost any growth. The younger Amish generation, though wishing to live locally, were being pressured by circumstances, to move elsewhere, or, (as the Amish had always done) coalesce into even more compact family groups.

Paranoia, Personalities, Politics and War

"He who strikes terror into others is, himself, in constant fear."
— Claudian.

The history of Julius Caesar would confirm, "Watch your back!"

Prior political and military alliances influence, and restrict, the ease of war-avoidance negotiations. Giving as a cause of WW I, "People being People," the *Edmonton Journal* announced on June 28th 2014, "Canadian historian Margaret MacMillan has published a major book, *The War That Ended Peace*, which presents a synthesis of many different factors: alliances and power politics, reckless diplomacy, ethnic nationalism and, most of all, the personal character and relationships of the almost uncountable number of historical figures who had a hand in the coming of war. Her work helps to highlight the fact that for all the great powerful forces that seemed to grind the world inexorably into the war in 1914, everything ultimately came down to the beliefs, prejudices, rivalries and schemes of a great array of personalities and people." The list is long but paranoia would also have been a trait of one or more of those personalities.

Paranoia is that primal, visceral, adrenaline-rush that allows us to escape the charging bull by clearing the 8-foot wall on the same day that, without the bull, you would struggle to climb over a 3-foot wall. It is that self-preserving, gut-driven reflex, beyond normal fear, that may have saved our ancestors from having a saber-toothed tiger administration. Nevertheless, focused paranoia, in an appropriate circumstance, is a logically protective and life-saving attribute.

However, there are a few unfortunate souls, called paranoiacs, who inappropriately look on "others," as threatening adversaries, which can aggravate their own lives as well as those with whom they come in contact. It seems appropriate to pose a few psychological queries at this point: Is trust inherent? Is it induced by parental attitudes? Does it come gradually during infantile development? Is it induced by life's experiences? Is there an appropriate level of trust and distrust of others? Would President Reagan's, "Trust, and verify," be that appropriate level? Or, should we start with unlimited trust?

U.S. Secretary of War, Henry Stimson in a 1945 recommendation to President Truman regarding Stalin, "The chief lesson I've learned in a long life is that the only way to make a man trustworthy is to trust him; and the surest way to make him untrustworthy is to distrust him, and show him your distrust."

Albert Einstein, Oct 1952, *Bulletin of the Atomic Scientists*: *"The real ailment it seems to me, to lie in the attitude which was created by the world war* (he was thinking WWII, we are thinking Cold War) *and which dominates all our actions, namely the* (paranoid) *belief that we must in peacetime so organize our whole life and works so that in the event of war we would be sure of victory. This attitude gives rise to the belief that one's freedom, and indeed one's existence are threatened by powerful enemies. It must lead to war and far-reaching destruction. It finds expression in the budget of the United States. Only if we overcome this obsession and we really turn our attention in a reasonable way to the real political problem, which is: How can we contribute to make the life of man on this diminishing earth more secure and more tolerable."*

These are important, germane words of 64 years ago. He was demanding The Golden Rule! A wonderful compassionate, wise voice in the wilderness! If he had only been listened to then! Over sixty years later we continue to be the same militaristic nation that he feared, always proclaiming we are peaceful, but just in case, we are preparing for the worst.

S. L. A. Morison wrote in *The Oxford History of the American People*, that in WWI. "On the excuse, or the belief, that the country was honeycombed with secret agents of the Kaiser, Congress passed the Espionage Act of 15th of June 1917, and the Sedition Act of 16th of May 1918, as extreme as any similar legislation in Europe. Fines were $10,000 and 20 years' imprisonment for interfering with the draft; encouraging disloyalty; uttering disloyal or abusive language about the government, country, flag or uniform; discouraging recruiting; discouraging sales of American government bonds. Socialist candidate Eugene Debs, and Socialist Congressman Victor L. Berger, were sentenced to long terms."

Morison continues, "It was a wonderful opportunity to bring patriotism to the aid of neighborhood feuds and personal grudges. German-Americans, who did as much to support the war as any group, suffered the most. Stay-at-home patriots indulged in an orgy of hate, which even extended to passing of state laws forbidding the teaching of German in schools or colleges, throwing German books out of public libraries, forbidding German or Austrian musicians to play in public or their music to be performed." That was similar to the imprisonment of Japanese-Americans in WWII. Normal concern for possible sabotage had morphed into paranoia. Currently ISIS has become our perceived nemesis.

The classic illustration of paranoia in the cause of war is in the study of the origins of the Cold War, and can be reviewed in the detailed, vivid, and easily-readable history of the same period appears in descriptive detail in *House of War: The Pentagon and the Disastrous Rise of American Power.*

The political systems of the Soviet and the west were founded on opposing principles and the fear of each other made the Cold War paranoia mutual. National paranoia in Russia developed because the country had been invaded 12 times by 7 different countries in a 300-year period; had been invaded in 1918 by the 'Western' countries to unsuccessfully attempt elimination of Communism; and had lost over 20 million citizens in WWII. *Josef Stalin's* personal paranoia probably came because he had been expelled from a seminary several times; as a young agitator had been sent to prison several times; by ruthless means ascended to leadership in the Soviet; and retained it in a similar manner.

In the United States one paranoiac, *James Forrestal,* as Secretary of the Navy and subsequently the first Secretary of the Department of Defense, was able to implant into American consciousness the paranoid outlook that the United States was the primary target of Communism, and that Communism was also a direct menace anywhere it gained influence in the world. He was able to influence political leaders to put through influential programs and legislation that led to permanent, fear-inducing, national military preparedness. *George Kennan,* a clerk in the U.S. Embassy in Moscow during the 1930s, sent an 8,000- word telegram to Forrestal describing the current Stalinist atrocities. This ignited Forrestal's concerns.

James Carrol in *House of War* relates "- despite it being a classified document, he circulated the text. He ordered hundreds of Navy officials to read it, and even pushed it on those over whom he lacked authority. Because of Forrestal, thousands in the Washington establishment read the telegram and took it seriously." "Forrestal did more to establish the ethos of National Security than any other person.

Beginning in 1945, he consistently exaggerated the dangers of the Soviet Union" and regularly overestimated the strength of the Soviets and underestimated American strength. His intense concern that some evil menace was out there for us to worry about, meant to any adversary, that we would not be afraid to attack them! So they must also prepare! Ergo: The arm's race! Were there other reasons? Of course! Check the portion on "money and power" for one. However, his paranoia pervaded the newly-minted Department of Defense, and the State Department. So the public reason given was always "defense." The Department of War, renamed the Department of Defense (DOD) in 1946, brought emphasis to the future rather than the present. The psychological perception of war by the U.S. public was being subtly reconditioned to prepare for future war, when there was no war.

Forrestal, in establishing fear in the United States, also established it in the Soviet Union. In establishing The National Security Act in 1947, he placed in American consciousness, that everyone else outside our borders should be suspected. National paranoia! That state of mind, fostered Soviet paranoia. And of course it fostered the arms race.

He had recruited his old friend, *Paul Nitze,* (from his stock market days in 1929) into the administration in 1940. Nitze "loved" and respected Forrestal and for the next 44 years Nitze, in several capacities, was able to extend forward Forrestal's paranoid outlook. The Cold War spawned the Korean War, Vietnam War, Gulf War and several other interventions and then resulted in the Iraq War the war of President George W Bush and his like-minded "neocon" buddies. Guess what? It was based on "Hussein is out to get us with his WMDs." There were none. Do not think that paranoia doesn't appear in the governance of our country and reach deeply into our taxpayer pockets.

Forrestal had groomed, and encouraged those personalities who most closely approximated his own. In a panic in 1949 he committed suicide, asserting someone was after him. The developing Cold War was past its formative stage and with congressional tactical help continued on auto-pilot. End of paraphrase.

Carroll states, "Paranoia, is defined as a psychiatric disorder, involving systematized delusion, usually of persecution. The Pentagon was the very heart of such systematization, with money, influence, promotion and prestige flowing to those who were most convincing in warning of threats. And if the threats were great enough it would not matter whether they were delusional or not, the bureaucratic jargon spoke of "worst case scenario" planning, and the new idea of national security demanded it, imagining weird scenarios was a requirement." National insecurity!

Carroll continues, (Following the Vietnam War), "The Pentagon would go on adding to its massive nuclear arsenal. As always, it did this, it said, to prevent the use of the massive nuclear arsenal. "Arms control," justified the next phase of the arms race that the spirit of Forrestal unleashed. Madness! Paranoia! The demonic! The nation was at the mercy of currents leading toward Niagara."

The Arizona Republic, March 7th 2013, "Nixon's Chief of Staff, Al Haig, asked Robert Bork, to become Nixon's chief defense council. While pondering Haig's offer, Bork sought the advice of a Yale colleague with whom he spoke, "in a dark semi-rural road" in suburban Virginia. It's an indication of the paranoia of the time that I really wanted to be someplace where it was impossible to be overheard." Bork was not alone. Paranoia was a distinctive facet of the mentality of President Nixon. It is not a coincidence that the clandestine conversations of, "Deep Throat" with journalist Bob Woodward, occurred around that same time.

The 9/11 opportunity was seized by President George W Bush and the Afghanistan War, and the previously-contemplated Iraq War were soon undertaken. Bill Moyers in *A World of Ideas* interview with Noam Chomsky, "We can decide the Russian invasion of Afghanistan, as what it was. But the American invasion of South Vietnam was (called) defense. Even when we were wiping the population out, even when we were blocking the political system and so on, it was always "defense." Paranoia nurtures war.

Mike McClellan, *The Arizona Republic,* January 30th 2013. "We must counteract political paranoiacs whenever possible. We are based, of course, on a healthy suspicion of government. That's entrenched in our Declaration of Independence and in our collective DNA. But as historian Richard Hofstader pointed out years ago, bubbling beneath that skepticism is the paranoid element. In his 1964 essay *The Paranoid Style in American Politics* Hofstader characterizes the element. 'I call it the paranoid style, simply because no other word adequately evokes the sense of heated exaggeration, suspiciousness and conspiratorial fantasy that I have in mind.' As he notes, both sides of the spectrum have indulged in this over the years."

McClellan, "However, the current tilt, though, comes from the right - And so those who obsess over internet conspiracy sites, who believe that any restriction on their pet freedom is the beginning of the end of our country, increasingly dominate our politics. So when gun control became an issue after Sandy Hook, the paranoid among us saw it as the first step in, "taking our guns." So their reaction was to buy more guns, before the government comes after them." *McClellan*'s comments tend to solidify opinions about subliminal American paranoia and relate primarily to national politics. However, in war, especially in the case of the Cold War, many lives are at stake. Paranoiacs assume, "the worst" and negotiations appear useless. But that is where loss of life can be avoided. Paranoia in the upper echelons of government is to be avoided. Examination of the past record of those aspiring to office should, in time, be automatic.

Rebellion and War

My son, Mike's, homepage: Benjamin Franklin, 1706-90, "Any society that would give up a little liberty to gain a little security, will deserve neither and lose both."

Martin Luther King wrote in *Why We Can't Wait,* "A social movement that only moves people, is merely a revolt. A movement that changes both people and institutions is a revolution."

Are there honorable and just reasons for taking up arms in rebellion? What would those reasons be? We probably instinctively know the primary ones such as persecution, tyranny and loss of freedom. Those factors may be caused by a single dictatorial leader or by a dictatorial government. When there is poverty, racism, oppression and abuse, it is to be expected that there will also be frustration, hopelessness and despair. Desperation drives desperate people to do desperate things. Revolt follows easily. But, as always, patient negotiation, reasonable peaceable appeals, legal appeals, non-violent protests, and the legality of the protest should precede military measures.

The United States and Mexico took up arms against their oppressors, and shed much blood to secure their freedom. Canada,

Australia and New Zealand succeeded in securing their independence from Great Britain, by negotiation. India succeeded by non-violent protests and negotiation, thanks to Mahatma Gandhi.

Today is August 23rd 2014, two weeks since the killing of a black 18-year-old male, by a white policeman in Ferguson, Missouri. Regardless of the pros and cons of the legitimacy of the shooting, the legitimacy of the uprising of protesting marches is very clear. In a city that has a 67% black population; only 3 blacks appear on a 53-person police force; 86% of police traffic stops for blacks versus 14% for whites, and police arrests are similarly disproportionate. The police force was greatly strengthened by free Pentagon military equipment including Humvees, gasmasks, automatic rifles and armored vehicles. Thus the police presence was highly militarized to the point of "overkill." That is not how a helpful police force should function. The black population of the region clearly did not have equivalent opportunities to the whites of the region.

I have placed this news item before the following commentaries on rebellions. Thus the reader will have an opportunity to decide if the commentaries, some ancient, and some contemporary, are appropriate for peaceable Ferguson protests.

President Thomas Jefferson, *The Great Quotations,* "Resistance to tyrants is obedience to God."

Samuel Elliot Morison observes in *Oxford History of the American People,*1963: "War can be abolished forever by providing clothing, food and housing, instead of bombers, destroyers and rockets."

Adlai Stevenson, 1950s, *Putting First Things First,* "A hungry man is not a free man." Stevenson also coined the term, "revolution of the rising tide of expectations." Television had only recently been invented, and had become ubiquitous in the previous ten years. Stevenson accurately realized that TV would spread quickly to other countries where people would see many things that they wanted, thus, "rising expectations." Those rising expectations also applied to the poor of the United States.

Congressman Henry Clay, 1818 in *The Great Quotations,* "An oppressed people are authorized whenever they can, to rise and break their fetters."

Clarence Darrow, American lawyer, 1920s *The Great Quotations,* "As long as the world shall last there will be wrongs, and if no man objected and no man rebelled, then wrongs would last forever."

Supreme Court Justice William O. Douglas, *The Great Quotations,* "The right to revolt is deep in our history." "All men recognize the right of revolution; that is the right to refuse allegiance to, and to resist, the government when its tyranny or its insufficiency are great and unendurable."

U.S. President Ulysses Grant, 1882-1885, *The Great Quotations:* "The right of revolution is an inherent one. When people are oppressed by their government, it is a natural right they enjoy, to relieve themselves of the oppression --."

Henry Steele Commager, American writer and historian, *The Great Quotations,* "We should not forget that our tradition is one of protest and revolt, and it is stultifying to celebrate the rebels of the past, while we silence the rebels of the present."

U.S. President Woodrow Wilson, 1856-1924, *The Great Quotations,* "We have forgotten the very principle of our origin if we have forgotten how to object, how to resist, how to agitate, how to pull down and to build up, even to the extent of revolutionary practice, if it is necessary to adjust matters." Without social revolution there can be no lasting peace.

Comment by Mahatma Gandhi on revolution, using his very effective technique of non-violence. Mahatma Gandhi, India freedom leader in *The Great Quotations,* "Disobedience to be "civil" must be sincere, respectful, restrained, never defiant, and it must have no illwill or hatred behind it."

U.S. President Franklin Delano Roosevelt, 1882-1945, quoted in *The Great Quotations,* "In the spring of 1933 we faced a crisis - we were against revolution. And, therefore, we waged revolution against those conditions which make revolution against the inequalities and resentments that breed them."

U. S. President John F. Kennedy, *Brilliant Thoughts,* "Those who make peaceful revolution impossible will make violent revolution inevitable."

LA Times May 28th 1975 Vice Admiral William P. Mack, in a comment about military dissent, said, "If you're going to live in this country from now on, you've got to find a way to preserve dissenters. Don't throw them out. Don't send them off to Vietnam - like we used to throw out colonels who disagreed with the system."

Martin Luther King. The lack of the usage of the Golden Rule was very clear following the Watts riots in South Los Angeles in 1965. In *Where Do We go from Here?* MLK said, "A riot is at the bottom the language of the unheard, it is the desperate, suicidal cry of one who is fed up with the powerlessness of his core existence that he asserts that he would rather be dead than ignored." These words also capture the frustration embodied in the Ferguson, Missouri protest in August 2014.

In internal rebellions and civil wars there are two primary humanitarian issues. First of course is the issue of the innocent lives being lost, on both sides of the rebellion. Most frequently the rebel side suffers more, simply because the offending ruler or government is better equipped, supplied and trained. The other factor is that the conflict may spread to other countries causing casualties elsewhere.

Children and War

The parental instinct of mankind is to love, protect and to teach our children our beliefs. Our patriotic and religious beliefs are expected to become theirs also. However, unless we first teach freedom of thought, our misconceptions, our hatreds and our prejudices will also become theirs. And the acceptance by the naturally gullible, unthinking youth will pass the "faith of our fathers" to yet another generation.

In the area and era in which I developed there were no movie theaters, television had not yet been invented, and there were very little visual war stimuli with which to impregnate a child's mind. Our most offensive weapon was every boy's ubiquitous sling-shot. I do not remember, though I would imagine, that in the cities there were the sounds of, "Pow! Pow!" shouted by running boys with wooden hand guns. In our area there were absolutely no known fireworks used in celebration, and so they had no attraction to me. With several guns in our home, (two functional) I was of course taught to safely shoot a rifle. Our rifles were used to kill steers and hogs, the meat used for domestic meat consumption. To augment our meager depression-era food supply, when it was available, wild game was also shot. That might be called the "passive level" of our militaristic hardware.

But now we have the flourishing, abhorrent market for participatory, military video games. They maintain combative behavior, dull sensitivity to violence, hone military skills, make great profits for the manufacturers and maintain the boy's skill and military interest until adulthood. That problem was still in an earlier phase when I wrote to a California legislator in 1967. Here is his reply:

From Assemblyman John L. Burton, California Legislature, March 10th 1967: "Dear Dr. Meakes: Thank you very much for your kind letter concerning my bill that would require the labeling of war toys as being harmful to children. I appreciate your kind words." He then appealed to me to contact other state representatives regarding his legislation approval.

General William Tecumseh Sherman, in *The Great Quotations,* "There is many a boy today who looks on war as all glory, but boys, it is all hell. You can hear this warning voice for centuries to come. I look on war with horror." He was the General responsible for the "scorched earth" march (demolishment of all crops, industrial equipment, buildings, and all opposition) on Atlanta, Georgia in the Civil War. If anyone could speak knowledgably about war, he could.

Grossman & Gaetano, *Stop Teaching our kids to Kill,* 1999, "By the time the typical American child reaches the age of 18 he or she has seen 200,000 dramatized acts of violence, and 40,000 dramatized murders. Half the videos that a typical seventh-grader plays are violent."

Ursula K. LeGuin, *Brilliant Thoughts*: "He grew up in a country run by politicians who sent the pilots to man the bombers to kill the babies to make the world safe for children to grow up in." Well said! The reference guide does not describe her identity, nor of whom she speaks - but her words are sufficient.

In 1957, The National Committee for a Sane Nuclear Policy (*SANE*) was established. (I joined). "In the U.S., a nation traumatized by McCarthy-driven Red-scare, the disarmament movement including Sane continued to be associated with Communism, a Soviet plot to defang the West from within. Even Dr. Spock, once he had become associated with Sane, would be regarded with suspicion by many who had depended on his child-rearing advice." Sane is now named, *The Peace Action Council.*

Howard Zinn 1980, *The Peoples History of the American People,* "Young and old were taught that anti-Communism was heroic.

Three million copies were sold of the book by Mickey Spillane published in 1951, *One Lonely Night,* in which the hero, Mike Hammer says: "I killed more people tonight than I have fingers on my hands. I shot them in cold blood and enjoyed every minute of it. They were Commies - red sons-of-bitches who should have died long ago." A comic-strip hero Captain America said, "Beware, commies, spies, traitors, and foreign agents! Captain America, with all loyal free men behind him, is looking for you --." And in the fifties, schoolchildren all over the country participated in air-raid drills in which a Soviet attack on America, was signified by sirens; the children had to crouch under their desks until it was "all clear."

Robert B. McLaren-Professor, *LA Times* 1999, "An American society that glorifies violence is fulfilling a prophecy of raising a generation of moral imbeciles."

Howard Zinn 1980 writes in *The Peoples History of the United States,* "The boundary between fantasy violence and reality violence, which is a clear line for most adults, can become very blurred for vulnerable children. Kids, steeped in the culture of violence, become desensitized to it, and more capable of committing it themselves." Glamorized and sanitized violence, made to appear as acceptable fun to do, by both good and bad individuals in movies and on TV, gives the wrong message.

Citizen Soldier newsletter, 2013, "As the carnage from gun massacres and what occurred at the Washington Navy Yard, regularly unfold on TV news, America stands humiliated before the world community --. It may be hard to believe, but we recently learned that the Pentagon has quietly operated a "gun familiarization" program for several years, that invites children as young as 8 years onto its combat training bases, to "test-fire" weapons. Local gun advocacy groups are encouraged to sponsor young Americans on visits to military bases throughout the United States. Thousands of teens were welcomed onto installations and introduced to lethal weapons last year." In this year of 2014, a child shooting an assault rifle accidentally killed her instructor.

Citizen Soldier continues - "The military, these days, use "simulators," which condition a soldier to shoot instantaneously, not at a bull's eye, but at a human figure when it pops up." Now, these simulators are in our homes and in our arcades - in the form of violent video games. The MACS (multipurpose Arcade combat simulator) is nothing more than Super Nintendo game." The Duke Nukem has, "scantily clad women" who are defenseless and bound, who plead "Kill me. Kill me." Then there is the House of the Dead, in which you blow away chunks of the bodies you fire at, and get clean kills only for head shots." "In June 1999, legislation proposed by Rep. Henry Hyde of Illinois was designed to restrict violent material from being made available to minors. The legislation was defeated by a two thirds majority, having been opposed by such a powerful industry." (in turn supported by the NRA - *National Rifle Association.)*

The Arizona Republic, Dec 12, 2011, "An Arizona Gun club has held another event allowing children and their families to pose for photos with Santa, while holding pistols and military-style rifles. - Families get to pose with Santa while cradling military-style assault weapons, in front of a Christmas tree and an $80,000 machine gun."

The Arizona Republic, 2012 Headline, *"Modern Warfare 3 game sales up."* "U.S. retail sales of video-game hardware, software and accessories in the important month of November rose 0.4 percent to $3 billion thanks to strong sales of Call of Duty Modern warfare 3. "We greatly need more Assemblyman Burtons and Congressman Hydes!

So, what can one do? Grossman and De Gaetano in *Stop Teaching our Kids to Kill,* outline a logical plan, "The FCC exists to serve us, not the industry. We can challenge the stations at the local level, by picking up the phone and voicing concerns about what we are seeing (or not seeing) on our hometown channels. Anyone with a computer and some friends (church group, PTA, Service organization), - can set up an E-mail group - to send letters of complaint *en masse,* voicing their joint concerns and demanding changes - to presidents and CEOs of entertainment companies --. At the same time, with the same key- stroke, a copy of this message could be sent to senators and representatives, at both state and federal levels."

In 1999 a bipartisan group of senators, "headed by former Education Secretary William J. Bennett, unveiled on the Web (www.media-appeal.org) a signed public appeal - calling on the entertainment industry to adopt a voluntary code of conduct to protect children and curb excessive violence and sex. No less than Jimmy Carter, Gerald R. Ford, Colin Powell, Norman Scwarzkopf, Mario Cuomo, Steve Allen, Naomi Judd, and many other politicians and entertainers signed the petition --." The entertainment industry is there to serve us. They have to maintain their licenses by satisfying the FCC. The entertainment industry will listen to mass complaints. I urge you to spearhead a group to do the same.

Guns and War

I grew up in the 1930s in rural North Western Canada, where guns were an integral regional necessity in every home. As related earlier we had 3 rifles, only one of which functioned and a 10 gage shot gun that was outlawed for sale but for which we could still purchase shells. By 1966 my four older brothers had left rural life and no longer owned guns. The guns had been used for four purposes:

1. - to add to our depression-limited income with the pelts of coyotes, weasels, rabbits, skunks, and an occasional badger;
2. - to add to our depression-lean diet with ducks, prairie chickens, partridges and a rare deer (rare because the number of deer were limited by the drying-up of water sources);
3. - to use in killing steers for beef and pigs for pork;
4. -for killing domestic animals in the cases of their serious injury. In our region there was no hunting for sport or for a trophy, and the depression limited our money for very little fun of target practice. No-one thought of purchasing a gun for protection. I was not aware of firearm registration at that time, though I do know that Canada did, at some time, develop a careful registration of guns.

Fortunately, Canada did not experience any of the growth-wars that dominated the USA. There was no military necessity for a war of independence from Great Britain, Canada negotiated hers in 1867. There was no civil war as regional differences were respectfully negotiated. There was limited Indian bloodshed in the 1700s and early 1800s but there was no Indian-war *per se,* as Canada's Indian policy, compared to the USA, was more humane, and less exploitive. Treaties were negotiated, and the Indian treaties were respected, which frequently U.S. Indian treaties were not. There were also none of the Wild-West- Shoot-Outs that occurred in the U.S. Guns were never deemed necessary, to protect self and family.

James Hillman, *A Terrible Love of War,* 2004, "Some historians have credited the War of Independence for American's love of guns. But Michael Bellesiles argues that it was not the Revolution against the Crown that put the gun into the hands of the people, but the Civil War and its millions of combatants. The armaments industry is so entrenched in the U.S. that its defense extends beyond the National Rifle Association, beyond the gun lobby, (beyond) Libertarians and into churches and academia. World-wide violence depends largely on our violence, for the United States is gunsmith to the world. While regulations more strictly govern the manufacture and distribution of weapons in most Western style nations, hand-guns are so easy to get in the United States that they are part of our shadowy export trade keeping alive terror in foreign lands. For example, in Northern Ireland."

"The wars we try to officially stop, by offering our good services are aided and abetted by the weapons business at home. For terrorists around the world, the United States is the Great Guns Bazaar. If violence in the United States depends upon its most efficient tool, which is the gun, and that gun is loaded with economic profit, patriotic 2nd Amendment memories, and religious idealizations - how in any god's name can gun control find its way through the American psyche?" Historical, traditional and visceral reasons, deeply bury gun reform.

Joe Secola, *The Arizona Republic,* July 5th 2013, Joe gives the sensible, reasoned solution to today's contentious issue, "I say the Second Amendment is woefully out of date and not applicable today. Some 230 years ago the Second Amendment may have had some validity, when muskets were the weapon of choice. The muskets of the "wellarmed militia," were pretty much evenly matched with the federal government's well-armed militias, and their muskets. The original threat of the (British) government take-over was still fresh in the minds of the Founding Fathers, so this amendment made sense at that time." Secola continues, "Today our "muskets" are up against the largest military in the world, larger than the next 15 largest militaries all together. Your government has tanks, jet fighters, rockets, long range missiles, hundreds of thousands of soldiers, drones and nuclear bombs. The "muskets" of today aren't going to be used to fight the government. So, using the Second Amendment argument hardly makes sense. I see only three uses for gun ownership today - sport (hunting, target shooting), personal protection (not from the government), and as an aid to committing crimes."

Secola continues, "I'm for responsible ownership of as many muskets as you feel you need for sport or protection." "Background criminal mental checks are a start. Calling people who say the Second Amendment doesn't apply today "musket-grabbers," demonizes and clouds the issue. No-one wants to put your gun "on a list." What I'm suggesting is that we change the laws based on making sure we minimize the ability for criminals to have possession yet, allow the personal and sport aspect of gun ownership to be logically addressed. What we need is cooler heads, a dose of common sense and less demonizing of the issue." Common sense!

E. J. Montini, *The Arizona Republic,* Dec 23rd 2014, Montini speaks of Christmas gun sales. "It begins on Black Friday (The day after Thanksgiving "shopping" day). Apparently, when Americans are filled with the Christmas spirit, with that sense of community and charity and commonality, with as the Bible says, peace on earth and goodwill toward men, they buy firearms. Lots, and lots, of firearms.

According to the FBI, the federal background check system set a record of 175,000 checks this Black Friday. That works out to roughly three (sales) per second. Imagine that! Although, it's not that difficult. It's who we are." Growing up in the rural backwoods culture that I did, a rifle could have been an appropriate Christmas gift. But here and now? I think not.

James Hillman, in *A Terrible Love of War,* writes, "The vicious passions aroused by discussions of gun control show how aggressively devoted much of today's citizenry is to keeping and staying armed.

"Congress may have camouflaged The Department of War, as it was called from the beginning of the Republic, by wrapping it in a security blanket called "Defense", but "Mars" remains as dominant as a god in U.S. culture as he was in the Roman republic." That mind-set of viewing guns as though they were sacred objects has brought about a paralysis of political action regarding the Second Amendment. The mistaken idea that gun-violence can be controlled by buying more guns is obviously erroneous. Both sides seek reduced gun violence. The solution lies logically in respectful, thoughtful, cooperative negotiations for a mutual agreement.

The Media and War

Eleanor Roosevelt, (Mrs. Franklin D. Roosevelt), in *This, I believe. wrote,* "Wars have frequently been declared - with the backing of the nations involved, because public opinion has been influenced through the press and though other mediums, either by the governments themselves or by certain powerful interests which desire war."

War may originate in the minds of passionate, committed, and well-meaning men. With religious or political zeal, it becomes easy for the media to get involved. It is especially easy, when powerful people, or interests, are promoting it. The classical "powerful man" syndrome was epitomized by William Randolph Hearst.

William Randolph Hearst, newspaper magnate, in *The Great Quotations* (to stimulate newspaper sales), wired a message to artist Frederick Remington who had just arrived in Cuba in 1897, "You furnish the pictures and I'll furnish the war." How blatant can one be? He clearly indicated that he could influence the administration. Most newspapers wish to be called patriotic and support the country when war clouds gather, so they also prove patriotically amenable (can be manipulated) to the controlled point of view of the administration. I found it particularly offensive in the Vietnam War, and more obviously with imbedded reporters, during the Iraq War.

Regardless of the complexities of the Spanish-American War of 1899, Samuel Eliot-Morison relates in *Oxford History of the American People* that President McKinley's "minister" in Madrid cabled that he could negotiate an agreement with Spain that would bring "autonomy, independence or even cession (of Cuba to the United States!)." "The Hearst Newspaper and Joseph Pulitzer exaggerated atrocities in their race for circulation. President McKinley gave in, and the war took place. But a year later, President McKinley, "confessed" saying, "But for the inflamed state of public opinion, and the fact that Congress could no longer be held in check, a peaceful solution might have been had." He might have been fully truthful and acknowledged his acquiescence to media influence. Spain was deeply humiliated and lost both Cuba and the Philippines.

Albert Einstein wrote in his book *Ideas and Opinions* in 1931, "And those who have an interest in keeping the machinery of war going are a very powerful body; they will stop at nothing to make public opinion subservient to their murderous ends."

Noam Chomsky, MIT professor, stated to Canadian *Mclean's Magazine*, March 22nd 1993, "Major newspapers and network broadcasts choose which topics are covered, frame issues in certain ways and ensure that dissenting viewpoints rarely receive space. They determine, they select, they restrict." "In American society the role of the mass media is overwhelmingly controlled by large corporations and is to manufacture the majority's consent for the continuing rule of the rich and the powerful." Chomsky refuses to forgive those who uncritically consume what the media produce. "People allow themselves to be deluded and manipulated by the system."

In *The Progressive* magazine, May 2004, Chomsky made a persuasive argument that the media in a free society is controlled "by wealthy men who have every reason not to want certain ideas expressed." They thus control what the public hears or reads, similar to a closed or restricted society.

The Associated Press, Jan 24th 2008, A study by two nonprofit organizations, Center for Public Integrity, and the Fund for Independence in Journalism, stated that "in the two years following the 2001 terrorist attacks, that President George W Bush and top administration officials, had given 935 false statements about the national security threat from Iraq." "The study concluded that the statements "were part of an orchestrated campaign that effectively galvanized public opinion, and, in the process led the nation to war." He was more blatant in lying to the media than other presidents, and those lies were screening an approach to an illegal and immoral war.

News is the mother's milk for the voracious appetite of the media, but savory morsels of minimal importance can sink a politician's career. Michigan governor George Romney, running for President, commented that the U.S. Defense Department in their briefings had "brainwashed" him. The term brainwashing (Webster "an external attempt to modify conscience and belief"), had been used derogatorily about prisoners who adapted the beliefs of their captor. But Governor Romney was simply ahead of others in recognizing that the information given him about the Vietnam War was vastly exaggerated, and in fact, was not true. The media portrayed him as weak-minded and his campaign standing plummeted. Another simple event sank the hopes of Senator Edmund Muskie in 1972, when, in a New Hampshire news conference, he shed some tears at a reference to his wife's serious health problem. The media portrayed him as "weak." The media can make or break a candidate using only trivia.

The mainstream media tends to support the political and patriotic position of the administration. However, each newspaper publisher, or any news media, should have a policy of truth in all news. But unless the newspaper has journalists with integrity reporting to them, the editors won't have accurate news on which to produce relevant editorials. The editors can manipulate the news by omitting, or including, parts of the news; omitting the views of the journalist; or make a story out of the associated trivia as happened at a personally-observed event that occurred in the middle 1960s in Los Angeles.

As a member of a former generation, Dr. Spock needs a short description. LA Times July 5th, 1972, Keith S. Felton reviewing a book *Biography of a Conservative Radical,* authored by Lynn Z. Bloom about Dr. Spock, refers to Dr. Spock as a "psychiatrically oriented pediatrician" and "a politician who speaks from the heart in opposition to the Indochina War." Felton said, "It is doubtful that a diaper was changed in this country since the 40s without a copy of Baby and Child Care (authored by Dr. Spock), no further than the pail" (before disposable diapers). "From baby doctor to peace worker, Spock will affect many generations to come. Through all his singular efforts, it is this gifted man's hope that no other pediatrician will help a mother agonize over her child's formula, only to stand by helplessly 20 years later as the same child goes off to kill or be killed in war."

David Meakes, unpublished manuscript, *American Citizenship Reconsidered,* "Also a major event at the Los Angeles Sports Arena, where the key-note speaker was Doctor Benjamin Spock, and at which a "police-estimated" crowd of 35,000 turned out. It was always clear, but especially at that event, that TV and the press, tended to ignore the message, and instead concentrate on the spectacle. TV coverage allowed the usual one 10 to 30-second, "sound-bite" of Doctor Spock, and zero coverage of the great majority of the crowd of beardless "squares" wearing business suits like me. Instead, the TV would avidly follow the half dozen or so who wore outlandish clothing, garish hair-does, long hair, and beards, and carried off-beat signs, when those things were associated with the "hippies." General W. C. Westmoreland, U.S. Army Chief of Staff, had a weird imitator, who wore an immense imitation of a general's hat, with toy guns, torpedoes, airplanes, etc. all over it, and was carrying a big sign saying, "General Waste-more-Land." The TV never missed him, but the serious anti-Vietnam War message never got through to the general public." Of course, it was the trivia that made the mornings headlines.

Michael N. Nagler, Classics professor, in the *LA Times,* Nov 25th 1990. With the approaching Gulf War in mind, Nagler comments that "You'll hear, see or read precious little, about the complex relationship of religious passion to politics in a modern Islamic state," or "whether we have explored every other option than war," but will instead be" informed of what the Administration would like you to believe.

Michael Moore 2002, *Dude, Where's My Country:* "The supposedly "liberal" media, joined forces with the White House (President George W. Bush) media field office at Fox News, to create a well-oiled pro-war propaganda offensive that was almost impossible to avoid. Payment for that co-operation by the media was to be unlimited access to the copious flow of patriotic news assured by allowing the "embedding" of selected reporters in selected units." For the administration's purpose it was brilliant. "Accompanied by round-the-clock patriotic, marchto-war music and flag-inspired graphics on the sorry-excuses-for-news channels, the images were relentless. Tearful farewells from proud families, as brave soldiers headed overseas; heroic American girls rescued by daring American guys; smart bombs doing their brilliantly destructive work; grateful Iraqis toppling the Saddam statue; a united America, standing by Our Resolute and Determined Leader. Then there was the footage beamed directly to us from the harsh Iraqi desert, where reporters "embedded" with the ground troops were given great leeway, without interference from the Pentagon (as we were supposed to believe). What was the result? There were lots of up-close and personal stories about the hardships and dangers faced by our military, and, virtually nothing examining why we had sent these fine young people into harm's way. And there was even less about what was happening to the people of Iraq." That illustrated the obsequious shallowness of our media and the secrecy of our military, during a national war.

Moore continued, "The American public was confused by the whole event. The widespread misconceptions were understandable. It was almost impossible to hear the perspective of anyone who questioned or opposed the Bush administration's rationale for rushing to war on American television. The media watchdog group FAIR studied the evening newscasts for the first 3 weeks of the War. The study examined the affiliations and views of more than 1600 sources that appeared on camera in stories about Iraq. The results were hardly a surprise. Viewers were 25 times more likely to see a pro-war U.S. source, than someone with an anti-war point of view."

"Of a total of 840 U.S. sources, who were current or former government or military officials, only four were identified as opposing the war." Those interviewed who opposed the war were "street opinions," short sound-bites, and rarely, a deeper sit-down interview.

Patt Morrison, *LA Times* Nov 11th 2003, Noting the excessive news about Jessica Lynch, the momentary U.S. heroine of the Iraq War, Morrison goes on to say that, "what you had not seen on TV, were the other 383 veterans who returned from the eight-month old Iraq War in flag-covered coffins, in March (2003), (because) as the Iraq War was about to start, a Pentagon order forbade news media from showing the nation, images of coffins arriving or departing at any bases, here or abroad." Prior wars had no such restriction. President Bush wanted minimal visual reminders of the human cost of his war. A picture is worth a thousand words.

Morrison continues, "The army recently (2003) signed a $470 million contract with Microsoft which is co-owner of MSNBC along with NBC. NBC is in turn owned by General Electric, one of the nation's largest defense contractors. GE military contracts run in the billions." Since Hearst, I would estimate that there has been over a century of the same behavior.

The conflict of interest is clear. Our news sources and our news conveyors should have totally independent management and ownership. News agencies should report all available news, but editorial opinion should be clearly separated from the sources. War news is too vital, in human lives, to be contaminated by money or power influences. To those who continued to analyze why the Iraq War took place, facts were difficult to ascertain. The media could not completely hide the nobid contract with Halliburton and with Bechtel, Raytheon, Lockheed Martin and others. Vice President Cheney had recently been CEO of Halliburton. Nor could they hide the frantic administration efforts to sign up "nation-volunteers" to validate the war, the result only being what Michael Moore called the, "coalition of the bribed, coerced and intimidated."

The inflated body counts of the Vietnam War were military-doctored information for the media. But they lacked the brazenness of the uncovered policy of the American military not to tell the truth in the case of Pat Tillman. After 9/11 Tillman refused a huge contract with the NFL's Arizona Cardinals, and instead joined the army and was killed by "friendly fire" in 2002.The Army told a manufactured, heroic story of his valor in death, for which he was awarded a posthumous Silver Medal. However, in a Tribune account on April 25th 2007, details were given before a Congressional inquiry that "a Ranger was ordered to hide the truth about the friendly fire. Even his family was denied the truth." The media is clearly the tool of those who conduct a war. It has been said that in all wars, truth is the first casualty. A fiercely independent media should be the pillar guarding truth and the interests of the people. The shattered family, were devastated enough by reality.

Tribune, June 6th 2008. From the LA Times, "The Senate Intelligence Committee rebuked President (George W) Bush and Vice President Dick Cheney for making prewar claims, not backed by available intelligence." The committee said "In making the case for war, the administration repeatedly presented intelligence as fact, when, in reality, it was unsubstantiated, contradicted, or even nonexistent. Sadly, the Bush administration led the nation into war under false pretenses." Media distributed truth, was a casualty at the highest level, trying to justify the war before it ever began!

Negotiation and War

"Never negotiate in fear, but never fear to negotiate."
— President John F. Kennedy

Dealing with rational, reasonable people it should be possible to talk-through differences and conflicting opinions, respectfully negotiate, and successfully arrive at understanding, mutually-approved compromises and agreements. The very concept of negotiation is that neither negotiator gets all that they want. One has to be able to relinquish something in order to get something else. Obviously negotiation with a suspicious, paranoid personality or group is much more difficult because they cannot so easily shed their distrust. Negotiations, agreements and treaties are viewed by them as untrustworthy. Three examples of types of negotiation hurdles are:

1. Reluctant Josef Stalin who had a deep-seated over-load of paranoia and suspicion to overcome.
2. Eager Adolph Hitler who would have agreed to negotiate - and sign anything- and then would have ignored the agreement.
3. Present-day, hereditary, paranoiac dictator, Kim Jung Un of North Korea, who does not appear to be available to

negotiate at all. Now, there are faceless inflexible groups, with elusive leadership, such as ISIS, who are also not available for negotiation. Complex and impossible challenges for negotiators!

The following three bad negotiated peace results vividly illustrate the comment by Tacticus Agricola *in The Great Quotations* is true, "A bad peace is worse than war." All international agreements should have the Golden Rule as its basis. If agreements are made on the basis of "doing for the other what you would want them to do for you," there should be minimal future resentment. And you would more likely get what you want from the agreement. But one-sided negotiations can lead to agreements that end in bad results. Three examples of seeds for the next war:

1. The WWI Versailles Peace Treaty was later recognized as being vengeful, punitive and too demanding of reparations (repayment of war-costs), by the Germans. The victorious Allies said that the treaty was appropriate, as Germany had started the war in the first place. Clay Thompson, Sept 14th 2014, in *The Arizona Republic* commented that Sir Eric Campbell-Geddes, Britain's First Lord of the Admiralty made the remark, 'We will squeeze the German lemon until the pips squeak,' and look where that got us." The treaty produced an angry, suffering, and resentful German populace, which provided an ideal psychological stew, in which Hitler's philosophy came to maturity and to his ascendancy to Third Reich leadership. The result was WWII. David Fromkin, named his book *A Peace to end all Peace,* probably after General Archibald Wavell's comment, "After 'The War to end War,' they seem to have been pretty successful in Paris, at making, A Peace to end all Peace." Winner-driven one-sided negotiations!
2. The 1922 British-imposed boundary agreement arrived

at in the Sykes-Picot Treaty, formed the new, artificial country of Kuwait, based on the Sabah family which had an ancient history of being ruled from Baghdad, capital of Iraq. In 1991, 68 years later, Saddam Husain thought he had a valid basis for his attempted reclamation of Kuwait as a province of Iraq, but which, instead, resulted in his Gulf War defeat. Retrospectively it became clear that protection of Kuwaiti and Saudi-Arabian oil, and of massive Kuwait and Saudi investments in U.S. corporations, were the main reasons for U.S. entrance into the war, and to maintain Kuwaiti autonomy for those reasons. It was stated by K. C. Associates on NPR, in 1991, that President Reagan's U.S. Ambassador, April Glaspie, (about 1988) had orally assured Saddam Husain that the U.S. "would not be involved," if Iraq invaded Kuwait. If that were true, then there must have been a revised understanding in the President George H Bush's White House, when he finally went to war (The Gulf War). Had the British not imposed historically inappropriate boundaries in 1922, there would have been no basis for the Gulf War. Winner-driven, one-sided negotiations.

3. The 1953 Korean War was a civil war between two parts of the same country. Had they been allowed to conduct their own affairs, the eventual outcome would have been one political entity. Negotiations, or their own civil war, would have settled their differences of opinion. However, the U.S. foreign affairs domino-effect policy (in which it was assumed adjacent regional countries would automatically become Communist), convinced the U.S. to get involved (as was also done in Vietnam). Had the U.S. remained out of the Korean War, there would be only one country; the American taxpayer would not have been stuck with paying to continually keep over 30,000 American troops there for the past 60 years; 54 thousand American military would still be alive; the three-generation Kim dynasty may not

> have occurred; and this morning's headlines (March 2013) would not have informed us of the threat of a nuclear-tipped ballistic missile threat by Kim Jung Un.

When it comes to avoiding war, absolutely every tiny opportunity for discussions must be pursued. Professional negotiators and diplomats have frequently achieved unexpected success where none was thought to be possible. From the historical record it appears that almost no attempts were made to search for a peace-making solution in those early Cold War years. The past bad behavior of Josef Stalin probably had a defeatist effect on any peace-making attempts by the U.S. But that should not have prevented attempts. Maybe Stalin would change. The Past is the Past.

During those early Cold War years there appeared to be impatience by American foreign policy analysts. There was lack of understanding that, "this too will pass;" that the threatening Communist system was itself in a process of change; that greater confidence in the American example of freedom would be copied by all. But the opportunity was not seized. The old adage: "Make a better mouse-trap and the world will beat a path to your door," coupled with the Golden Rule, would have produced a brilliant American example for the world to envy, or emulate. How wonderfully successful that Golden Rule philosophy would have been if we had not poured our taxpayer's billions of dollars of national treasure down Forrestal's national security pit! What a wonderful, healthy, well-educated, happy and contented country we could have been! Disillusionment!

Charles Elliot Norton, American educator, *The Great Quotations,* "But if a war be undertaken for the most righteous end, before the resources of peace have been tried and proved vain to secure it, that war has no defense, it is a national crime."

U.S. President (General) Ulysses Grant *Great Quotes from Great Leaders* "There never was a time, in my opinion, some way could not be found to prevent the drawing of the sword." Negotiations!

Two years into the Vietnam War an opportunity came. The International Control Commission consisted of United Nations members from Canada, India and Poland. Robert McNamara in *In Retrospect* said both Canada and Poland informed President Johnson of apparently positive Viet Cong feelers looking for peace talks in early 1966. However, President Johnson ignored the leads, one of them on the basis that they had used the term "talks" not "negotiations!" He was deathly afraid of appearing weak. By a year later we were losing 1,000 to 1,800 soldiers weekly! At least 40,000 American soldiers may have been saved. Tragic!

U.S. President Harry Truman, *Great Quotations from Great Leaders,* "It is understanding that gives us an ability to have peace; when we understand the other fellow's view-point, and he understands ours, then we can sit down and work out our differences." The perfect words! However, Truman failed to listen to the Golden Rule counsel of Secretary of War Henry Stimson in 1945, and so he failed to intensively try for negotiations with scary Stalin. President Truman is quoted as having said about 1946 that "unless the Soviet changed, negotiations were of no use." So no negotiated curb slowed the Cold War.

Golda Meir, Israeli president, *Great Quotes from Great Leaders,* "The only alternative to war is peace; the only road to peace is negotiation." Martin Luther King, in *Where Do We Go From Here? Said,* " - when I see the unwillingness of our government to create the atmosphere for a negotiated settlement of this awful conflict by halting bombings in the North and agreeing unequivocally to talk with the Vietcong - and all this in the name of peace - I tremble for our world."

Robert McNamara in his book, *In Retrospect,* writes about 1966, "Our - efforts to stimulate movement toward a negotiated settlement continued, but they were sporadic, amateurish, and ineffectual." He then relates a lead through Prime Minister Lester Pearson of Canada, relaying a message from North Vietnam's Premier Pham Van Dong that if we stopped the bombing, "for good and conditionally, we will talk." President Johnson dismissed the lead, and also another later genuine lead by the Polish representative to the International Control Commission, Januscz Lewandowski. Missed negotiations, while over a thousand American soldiers per month were dying.

Bill Moyers, 1989, *A World of Ideas.* Moyers question to Noam Chomsky, "What elementary truths are buried? Noam Chomsky, "The fact that we are standing in the way, and have stood in the way for years, of significant moves towards arms negotiations."

Adlai Stevenson, U.S. Democratic presidential candidate, *Putting First Things First,* "I will tell you now that I will never fear to negotiate in good faith with the Soviet Union, for to close the door to the conference room, is to open a door to war. Man's tragedy has all too often been, that he has grown weary in his search for an honorable alternative to war, and in desperate impatience has turned to violence." He never got the opportunity. He lost the election to ultra-popular General Eisenhower.

Nikita Khruschev, Soviet leader, *House of War,* "We believe that, however, acute the ideological differences between the two systems - the Socialist and Capitalist - we must solve questions in dispute among states, not by war, but by peaceful negotiation." Words like that tell why Khruschev, was considered more pliable, and an improvement over Joe Stalin. But they weren't enough of an inducement to get our "peace - loving" negotiators to follow-up.

Indira Gandhi, Prime Minister of India, commented in *Brilliant Thoughts,* "You cannot shake hands with a clenched fist." U.S. Senator Alan Simpson, 2012, *The Arizona Republic,* referring to the Tea Party," "Show me a guy who won't compromise, and I'll show you a guy with rocks for brains."

July 14th 2015. Prolonged, intensive negotiations have today led to President Obama announcing a 6-nation nuclear agreement with Iran. It has immediately been reviled by many congressional leaders, and by Israeli leader Benjamin Netanyahu. Negotiations do not lead to perfection because of the give-and-take needed to reach agreement. Considering the alternative dangerous status quo, it appears to be a reduction in war tension. The devil is in the details. Only time will confirm its worth.

Martin Luther King 1967 *Where do we go from Here?* "Therefore I suggest that the philosophy and strategy of nonviolence become immediately a subject for study and serious experimentation in every field of human conflict, by no means excluding the relations between nations." I wonder to what degree anyone has considered, studied, or tried this. It seems designed to lead toward negotiation and peace.

The League of Nations

Samuel Eliot Morison, *Oxford History of the American People,* President (General) Ulysses Grant said, "Nothing would afford me greater happiness than to know that, as I believe will be the case, at some future day, the nations of the earth will agree on some sort of congress which will take cognizance of international questions of difficulty and whose decision will be binding as the decisions of our Supreme Court are upon us. It is a dream of mine that some such solution may be." Unfortunately, the international "congresses" after World War I and II, disregarded the word binding and national interests have always trumped international interests.

Senator Alan Cranston, *The Killing of the Peace,* Quote by President Woodrow Wilson in 1916, "- some common force will be brought into existence which shall safeguard right as the first and most fundamental interest of all peoples and all governments, when coercion shall be summoned not to the service of political ambition or selfish hostility, but to the service of a common order, a common justice and a common peace."- "At a convention of the "League to Enforce Peace," a new and powerful movement was born for the creation of a world organization to keep the peace. Both, previous-Republican President Howard Taft and the then Democratic President, Woodrow Wilson, used wonderful words of support. "The idea of a world organization won wide and growing support in the United States in 1916 and 1917, and 96% of 700 business groups and 91 out of 97 leading newspapers (approved). The British and the French sent friendly messages." Cranston continues, "There must be, not a balance of power, but a community of power, not organized rivalries, but an organized common peace."

The world's first international attempt at developing such an organization was when the League of Nations was initiated by the participants in the Versailles Peace Treaty in Paris. Morison says in *Oxford History of the American People,* "The function of the League was to "promote individual cooperation and to achieve international peace and security." The League "became an *integral* part of the treaty." And that fact alone predestined its inadequacy because the U.S. Congress refused to approve the Versailles Treaty. The treaty, with its stringent German peace terms, was instrumental in establishing a foundation of discontent in Germany, resulting in the rise of Hitler and WWII. The apparent lack of quality of the international diplomats assembled, caused the Swedish chancellor to lament, "By how little wisdom is the world governed."

Nevertheless U.S. President Woodrow was given great credit for his idealistic leadership in the whole process. Carrying the treaty, he triumphantly returned to Washington, only to find a hostile congress awaiting him. Wilson tried three times, but Congress rejected approval of the treaty and with it the integral League of Nations. Thus during the 20s and 30s the U.S. was not represented in the League of Nations, and the League lost Woodrow Wilson, one of its most articulate founders and strongest proponents. He had a stroke soon after.

Senator Alan Cranston, *The Killing of the Peace,* "President Harry Truman, but speaking as a Senator about the League of Nations Nov 2nd 1943, said, "A small group of willful men kept us from assuming our world obligations in 1919-1920, and the same thing can happen again. I am just as sure as I can be, that this world war (WWII), is a result of the 1919-20 isolationist attitude, and I am equally sure that another and worse war will follow this one, unless the United Nations and their allies, and all other sovereign nations, decide to work together for peace as they are working for victory."

Morison observes in *Oxford History of the American People,* "We have come to assume that after WWI we went isolationist because we were tired, tired of war and tired of the world. We have come to conclude that the United States Senate, led by Senator Henry Cabot Lodge, was supported by a good part of the people of the land when it kept us out of the League of Nations and apart from the world. The fact is, isolationist sentiment was a product of the fight to prevent American participation in world affairs. It was not the cause of it. All surveys of opinion, in 1918 and 1919, showed that the American people wanted to join a world organization to preserve the peace. The idea was supported by most of the press, most of the pulpit, business, labor unions, war veterans, gold star mothers, and 76 out of 96 senators."

Albert Einstein had been a supporter of the creation of the League of Nations but became disillusioned. From his biography *Ideas and Opinions,* "A 1923 letter from Einstein regarding his resignation from the League of Nations Committee of Intellectual Cooperation in protest at the inadequacy of the League stated, "It is precisely because I desire to work with all my might for the establishment of an international arbitration and regulative authority superior to the state, and because I have this object so very much at heart, that I feel compelled to leave the Commission. Further the attitude of the Commission in the matter of combating the chauvinistic and militaristic tendencies of education in the various countries, has been so lukewarm that no serious efforts in this fundamentally important sphere can be hoped from it."

Einstein continued in 1932, "But the League is not much more than a meeting place and the Court of Arbitration has no means of enforcing its decisions. These institutions provide for no security for any country in case of an attack upon it --. Unless we can agree to limit the sovereignty of the individual state, by binding every one of them to take joint action against any country which openly or secretly resists a judgment of the Court of Arbitration, we shall never get out of a state of universal anarchy and terror." - "Mere agreements to limit armaments furnish no sort of security. Compulsory arbitration must be supported by an executive force, guaranteed by all participating countries, which is ready to proceed against the disturber of the peace with economic and military sanctions." As you read this think of the context of the 30s. This was long before the formation of the United Nations - and also before Einstein embraced world federation. He was practicing the "art of the possible." He was still only considering the "nuts and bolts" of his present day political realities. Once he experienced the disregard of treaties by Hitler, he realized that only world federation would solve the problem. Then his reference to treaties would cease. But he recommended one more during that year.

Einstein continues in 1934, "Only the absolute repudiation of all war can be of use here. The creation of an international court of Arbitration is not enough here. There must be treaties guaranteeing that decisions of this court shall be made effective by all the nations acting in concert. Without such a guarantee the nations will never have the courage to disarm seriously." "- The world is more than ever dependent on its moral strength today. The way to a joyful and happy existence is everywhere through renunciation and self-limitation." It appears Einstein did not arrive at the concept of a global government with no further need of treaties, until the 1950s.

During the WWI Versailles Treaty negotiations, the victors dominated. Negotiations succeeded, but the peace treaties failed, partly because the United States was not a member. As the U.S. found that it lacked international influence, brought by international organization membership, wiser heads realized that the isolationists had it wrong. So as the concept of a new international organization was developing in 1944-45 the U.S. made sure that they had a voice in its development. The Franklin Roosevelt administration lobbied hard and successfully, that the U.N. Headquarters would be built in the United States, placing it in New York City when they succeeded.

The United Nations

Albert Einstein, 1947 *Ideas and Opinions,* "The power of this (future) world government would be over all military matters, and there would be only one further power. That is to interfere in countries where a minority is persecuting a majority, and so is creating the kind of instability that leads to war. (Rebellion) There must be an end to the concept of non-intervention, for to end it, is part of keeping the peace." In the world of today, Syria is the country causing the most serious debate. No country wants to put their personnel or their money on-the-line, even for serious humanitarian reasons. There are strong voices in the U.S. to intervene. If, in 1945, the founders of the United Nations had originally faced up to this problem and had provided for a substantial U.N. military and avoided the political impasse by veto, *no individual country would now have to agonize over whether to intervene or not.* Regardless of the inadequacy of the United Nations, it is hopeful that there is now, at least, serious discussions about intervention. As I write this in 2012, the slowness of progress means that there is a daily death count, in Syria alone, of a hundred or more. Other countries currently needing stabilizing assistance are Bosnia, Somalia, Mali, Libya, Nigeria the Sudan and Egypt.

World Federalist Movement-Institute for Global Policy newsletter (WFM-IGP), April 16th 2013, "It is remarkable that the U.S.

government, such a fierce opponent of the ICC (UN) Coalition for the International Criminal Court program in its early years, is now a strong advocate for the Court's investigation in the DRC (Democratic Republic of the Congo). WFM-IGP has worked closely with the current administration and their cooperation with the Court has steadily improved." "Twenty years ago, the idea that the international community could intervene in the affairs of a sovereign state to protect its population, or that international law could end impunity for those who commit the worst crimes against humanity, were deemed impossible." Some things are encouraging! Having, over 50 years ago joined the United World Federalists (the above-mentioned WFM-IGP), and participated in their 1967 Los Angeles Convention, it is wonderful to see them still surviving and having influence on global policy.

Sir Peter Ustinov (President of WFM/IGP), in the World Federalist News, winter issue, 1997-1998, "The organization was created by visionary politicians in the wave of idealism which was the legal consequence of the most terrible and wasteful war in history."

Senator Alan Cranston, In *The Killing of the Peace* said, "When the vote on the approval of U.S. participation in the new U.N. took place, "so high were the hopes, so deep the dreams, that only two votes were cast in the U.S. Senate against the plan to save succeeding generations from the scourge of war." Remembering the League of Nations, 94 Senators (48 states) used their historical memory, and voted for the formation of the United Nations.

In 1946, when the UN was one-year-old, my history professor Mr. Elliott (paraphrasing), said, "The United Nations is not going to be any better than the League of Nations, because all they can do is to talk about problems, so it will only be a debating society. The same as the League, it has no military power to prevent war. The same as the League, the top executive (the Security Council) is composed only of the leaders of powerful countries of today (France, Great Britain, Russia, China, and the USA). The Security Council has to have a unanimous vote to act, and with the power of veto, any one member of the Security Council can vote against anything because of their national interest, and so rule out any action, and with it the wishes of the Security Council and the majority vote of the rest of the members of the world, in the General Assembly." He was right on both counts. By their veto power in the Security Council, and ostensibly because of their arms sales to the Syrian government, Russia and China are currently, in 2012 and 2013, preventing UN involvement in the tragic human disaster occurring in Syria. *The* Arizona *Republic* May 7th 2013, Headline, "Russia says it will sell missiles to Syria." In the early years of the UN, the Soviet Union said "Nyet" (No) using the veto more than any other nation. Now they said it again.

Sir Peter Ustinov, in the World Federalist News in 1997/1998, wrote, "The most habitual user of the veto today is the United States. When Boutros Boutros-Ghalis tenure for Secretarial Generalship was up for reappointment in the Security Council, all nations without exception supported his candidacy. The United States used its veto and the Secretary General was replaced by Kofi Annan without dissent. This was hardly an example of democratic practice." It was certainly arrogant. And being arrogant, only stores up antipathy and aversion by others.

The pretense, only effective with those who do not know, is that the UN is a world representative body. But the reality is that the effective veto of any one of those 5 nations (the ones that were powerful *in 1945*), is all that is necessary to thwart the desires of the other 192 countries that are members of the General Assembly. It cannot be a successful organization! This is my greatest of all post WWII disillusionments!

Inadequate performance of both the League of Nations, and the United Nations, have caused many of the American public to lose respect in the organization, and to relegate it to the back-burner level of daily awareness. In addition, it had a 15-year period in the 1980s-90s, when it was highly criticized for some excessive expenses and departmental mismanagement, which resulted in deferred annual dues payment by some countries, most notably the U.S. Because of the veto, and lack of militaristic policing power, as a war-preventing organization it has been only minimally successful during the 70 years since 1945. But as a humanitarian organization it has excelled. In my view the *inter*-national war-preventing part of the UN, needs to be replaced by a unified global organization.

Disillusionment! Many other urgent global problems demand attention NOW, such as: global warming, global population control, global energy policy, global resources control (forests, mining, water), global cultural preservation, global sharing of knowledge and global monetary policy an incomplete list. These world-wide issues need urgent consideration and our ailing organization the United Nations is, impotently, attempting to do so.

But the very nature of (*inter)*nationalism gets in the way of action. Executive decisions are arrived at because of the back-home national directives of the member governments, especially the Security Council members. National priorities, cultural differences, financing, communication-lags, all contribute to sluggish action or no action. Our own federal government is similar, with 50 different states, each with its own priority, interest and regional need. The qualities of cooperation, compromise, and good will (Golden Rule) seems to have recently failed us, leaving us with frustrating, futile legislative gridlock. That can also be true of the varied wishes of each international entity in the United Nations. With a unified global policy, but with regional priorities, it could be initially true of a future global administration. But that is part of an on-going process of perfecting the government that one already has. The bottom line of this commentary is that failure to address these present-day global problems, can introduce the seeds of the next war.

In 1945, there were 51 members; in 2013 there are now 193 members. In 1945 China was represented by the government of Chiang Kai Check, which fled to the island of Formosa, now called Taiwan. The Communist People's Republic of China assumed UN membership later. The UN functions as though it is a foreign nation within the USA, using even its own postal system, with attractive stamps.

The Departments within the UN are:

The General Assembly — Deliberations
The Security Council — Executive
The Economic and Social Council
Secretariat — Study, information, facilities
International Court of Justice — primary judicial organization. It is located in The Hague, The Netherlands.

There are six official languages utilized in the UN: English, Russian, Spanish, French, Chinese and Arabic.

Permanent UN agencies:

World Health Organization - (WHO)
World Food Program (WFO.)
World Children's Fund (UNICEF)

Organizations and Specialized Agencies of the United Nations:

Food and Agricultural Organization.
International Atomic Energy Agency.
International Civil Aviation Organization.
International Fund for Agricultural Development.
International Labor Organization.
International Maritime Organization.
International Monetary Fund.
International Telo-communications Union.
United Nations Educational, Scientific and Cultural organization.
United Industrial Development Organization.
World Tourism Organization. Universal Postal Union.
The World Bank. World Food Program.

World Intellectual Property Organization.
World Health Organization (WHO).
World Meteorological Organization.

The UN is financed from assessed and voluntary contributions from member states. The assessment is, "broadly based on the relative capacity of each country to pay; is measured by their own GNP; with adjustments for external debt and low per capita income." Currently, in 2013, the Secretary General (CEO), is Ban Ki Moon from South Korea.

The League of Nations, of course, failed to prevent WWII (1939-1945). The UN officially came into existence on the 24th of October, 1945 upon charter ratification by council members and a majority of the other 46 signatories. The UN headquarters building in Manhattan, New York was completed in 1952.

The United Nations, after approval by the Security Council, sends peacekeepers to regions where armed conflict has recently ceased, or paused, to enforce the terms of peace agreements and to discourage participants from renewing hostilities. Since the United Nations does not maintain its own military forces, peacekeeping forces are voluntarily provided by the member states (out of their own national budgets). Canada is the only country that has continually provided troops *every* year since the beginning. The forces, also called the 'Blue Helmets', who enforce UN accords, are awarded "international decorations," not military decorations. The peacekeeping force, as a whole, received the Nobel Prize in 1988.

The founders of the United Nations had envisaged that the organization would act to prevent conflicts between nations, and make future wars impossible, however, the outbreak of the Cold War made peacekeeping agreements extremely difficult, because of the division of the world into hostile groups. Following the end of the Cold War, there were renewed calls for the UN to become the agency for achieving world peace, as several conflicts continued to rage around the globe. Disagreements in the Security Council about military action, and military intervention, are seen as having failed to enforce Security Council resolutions, and consequently have not prevented regional conflicts etc. Wikipedia "Regulation of disarmament was included in the United Nations charter in 1945, and was envisioned as a way of limiting the use of human and economic resources for the creation of them. However, the advent of nuclear weapons came only weeks after the signing of the charter and immediately halted concepts of arms limitations and disarmament. The arms race picked up in intensity!" *Disillusionment!* Again!

The Arizona Republic, April 5th 2013, "The UN General Assembly overwhelmingly (154-3) approved the *first* UN treaty regulating the multi-billion dollar international arms trade --." The treaty would only take effect after 50 countries ratify it by their own governments. Then it will depend which governments ratify it, and, "how stringently it is implemented." Nothing comes easy! Don't hold your breath.

United Nations Commentary

Morison in *Oxford History of the American People* gives the overview, "The charter of the United Nations established an international body measurably stronger than the League of Nations. But it had the same defect of giving the Big Five on the top - the United States, Britain, Russia, France and China, a veto on every decision."

When the United Nations had to ask the Security Council to authorize military action in Syria in 2013, and the Security Council members (Russia and China) refused, then it is certainly inadequate policing.

In 1945, Reves put it simply in *Anatomy of Peace,* "When the police have to ask permission of the guilty to act, you have no police. When peace depends on the willingness of any one nation to keep it, war has not been ended." What is, and has been, needed is a United Nations military force strong enough to separate disagreeing nations. Needed, of course, is the veto elimination.

Free Inquiry Magazine, 2007, "A goal of world improvement would seek to develop cooperative efforts among the segments of the world to deal with common problems."

Anne M. Rombeau, Pioneer female aviator 1952, wrote in *This I Believe,* "I see arising, a unity of people, regardless of race or creed.

This convinces me that world peace is an achievable, practical idea through the United Nations. To me the Principle of Life is universal and I believe that as an individual we control our destinies. So we can in turn control the destiny of the world. The bottom line is the courage to make the change." Her wonderful comment did not take into account the fragility of treaties and the implication of international versus global organization.

Emery Reves, *The Anatomy of Peace,* "History demonstrates indisputably, that there is only one method to make man accept moral principles and standards of social conduct. That method is *LAW*."

Linus Pauling is quoted in *Force of Nature* by Thomas Hager, "The time has now come for morality to take its proper place in the conduct of world affairs; the time has now come for the nations of the world to submit to the just regulation of their conduct by international law." Gloria Faizi outlines clearly where we are at! *The Bahai Faith,* "Mankind - has passed through the stages of forming the tribe, the city state, and the nation. The time has come for the establishment of a world commonwealth."

In early Greek and Roman history, cities were sovereign entities. The next step was the collaborative one of small states cooperating to form a major state or country. About 1870, both Germany and Italy consolidated their small states into a national country. Great Britain did the same with Scotland, England, Wales and Northern Ireland. The United States, Canada and Mexico did the same with their regional entities. The natural progression is to a unified one-world state. Albert Einstein, 1932, *Ideas and Opinions,* "Anybody that really wants to abolish war must resolutely declare himself in favor of his country resigning a portion of its sovereignty in favor of international institutions; he must be ready to make his own country amenable, in case of dispute, to the award of an international court (*law*), and unless military and aggressively patriotic education is abolished, we cannot hope for peace." Einstein was dealing with his current situation which desperately needed internationalism. In our current situation, over 80 years later, we still don't have "sovereignty resignation," as evidenced by the veto of the UN Security Council. Universalism was discussed by him on other later occasions, but his 1932 concept, was complete internationalism.

Albert Einstein, *Ideas and Opinions* 1951, "So, as a *modest beginning* of international order, the United Nations was founded," - "Furthermore U.N. decisions do not have binding force (law) on any national government, nor do any concrete means exist by which decisions can be enforced."

Mahatma Gandhi, in *The Great Quotations* states, "My nationalism is intense internationalism. I am sick of the strife between nations and religions." That is a superb comment, before the discussions about universalism arose. He then commented that "India must conquer her so-called conquerors by love. For us patriotism is the love of humanity." He looked on the domineering British government with love! That was his non-violent philosophy in action.

Howard Zinn wrote in *The Peoples History of the American People,* "The creation of the United Nations, during the war, was presented to the world as international cooperation to prevent wars. But the U.N. was dominated by the WWII major countries (the Big-Five). Senator Arthur Vandenberg wrote in his diary that it certainly was not an "internationalist dream of a world state." He was impressed that Cordell Hull (U.S. Secretary of State) (during UN formation negotiations) was "carefully guarding our American veto in the scheme of things."

The others: Russia, the UK, France and China, were doing the same. The representatives of each country doubtless arrived with very specific instructions to vote to retain their nation's veto. I am certain that each one knew of the shortcomings of League of Nations. The news of the forthcoming allowance of the Security Council veto would have caused my professor, Mr. Elliot, and Emery Reves, author of *Anatomy of Peace,* to instantaneously anguish at the lost opportunity. Robert Maynard Hutchins (described in the chapter on Universalism), and his visionary friends, were not listened to by anyone in the State Department. Currently in 2012 to 2015, I think of the daily loss of lives in Syria alone!

PERSPECTIVE

Leo Cherne wrote in the introduction to the 1963 edition of *The Anatomy of Peace,* "This book was completed in 1945 before the United Nations was formed, and it took insight and courage to look at the fresh ink of the (already published) Charter, and then say, as Emery Reves did, "This is not the answer. We have only gathered together many sovereignties, and there will be no peace until there is but one sovereignty that of a "World Order." He continued "The pacifist and peace-by-hardware extreme are too simplistic. The notion that all men will have peace if some men merely lay down their arms is a perennial. It has followed every peace and preceded every war. And, the "hard" peace-by-hardware people think that power grows out of the muzzle of a gun. But it remains there, unrelated to ideas, politics, economics or any of the other subtleties of modern international relations. In our world the hardest truth to live with, is the recognition that only sovereign international power can guarantee peace. It is unbearable precisely because that supreme power does not exist, and it is unbearable because no great nation is leading the difficult (efforts) to organize that supranational authority." Those words written when the UN had been studied, and was opening for action, but still true. The United Nations did not, and does not, have "sovereign international power."

Le Cherne continues, "Tragically, as it turned out, the UN became the guardian of the burgeoning national sovereignties rather than the *supranational* power which exists beyond all of them." The laws of the new UN only offered protection to existing membership countries. "Law, and only law, can bring peace among men; treaties never can."

Emery Reves, *The Anatomy of Peace,* 1945- Emery Reves begins his book saying: "Nothing can distort the true picture of conditions and events in this world more than to regard one's own country as the center of the universe, and to view all things solely in their relationship to this fixed point. Yet this is the only method admitted and used by seventy or eighty (193 in 2013) national governments of our world, by our legislators and diplomats, press and radio."

Reves is speaking of his current world, as it was in 1944-5. "We are living in a geocentric world of nation states. We look upon economic, social and political problems as "national" problems. No matter in which country we live, the center of our political universe is our own nation. In our outlook, the immovable point around which all other nations, all the problems and events outside our nation, the rest of the world supposedly rotate, is - our nation. This is our fundamental and basic dogma. According to this nation-centric conception of the world of world affairs, we can solve political, economic and social problems within our nation, the fixed immutable center, in one way - through law and government and in the circumambient world around us, in our relations with the people of other nations, these problems should be treated by other means by "policy" and "diplomats." We must search for the truth about peace. Treaties between nations can never produce peace." He makes clear that one has to eliminate from one's mind, the "center of the universe" concept, and adapt a global outlook. A postscript at the end of the book said: "A few weeks after the publication of this book the first atomic bomb exploded over the city of Hiroshima." One comment being made was that the immensity of the bomb would make it probable that it would never be used between nations. Seventy years later, it has never been used. However, follow through his comment.

"The mutual distrust of the Soviet Union and the United States makes nuclear war thinkable, not unthinkable! What does that mean? It means that as long as there are humans on either side making the decisions the use of nuclear weapons is possible. It means that no atomic bomb, no weapon that the genius of man can conceive, is dangerous in itself. That is the argument that the National Rifle Association would love. "Weapons are only dangerous when they are in the hands of "others" (sovereign states other than our own). It follows that the ultimate source of danger is not the atomic energy, but the sovereign nation-state (country)." Think of the unpredictable bluster of North Korean dictator Kim Jung Un.

Instantly, we think of a nation-state other than our own. He brought us very, very close! Today it is terrorists! "The problem is not technical; it is purely political." So what can the world do for the still- existing problem? In my opinion, in the future, transfer national allegiance to "Universalism" - global allegiance!

Emery Reves continues, "Existing anarchy in international relations, due to absolute international sovereignty, must be superseded by universal statutory law, enacted by a duly elected legislative body. Such universal law must take the place of the utterly fallacious, ineffective and precarious rule of unenforceable treaty obligations, entered into by sovereign nation states and disregarded by them whenever it suits their purpose." Four years earlier, in 1941, Reyes had seen the disregard, by Hitler, of the 1939 Moscow/Berlin Treaty, resulting in millions of deaths.

James Carroll in *House of War* writes, "The United Nations - had been intended - as an alternative to war, but that dream was dispelled in the chill of the Cold War. While world leaders gave lip service to the idea of eliminating nuclear weapons, the United States and the Soviet Union were hell-bent on stock-piling them."

S.E. Morison, *Oxford History of the American People,* "At its first session the U.N. General Assembly appointed a twelve-member Atomic Energy Commission," to decide how to handle the new destructive atomic bomb. Paraphrased*:* Bernard Baruch, the U.S. representative, made the wonderful proposal to abolish all American nuclear weapons and internationally control the use of atomic energy for peaceful purposes only. The U.S. knew that their proposal would be vetoed by paranoid Russia, as they would expect inspections would be used to allow spies into their country. If accepted, it would also have frozen Soviet bomb development, while the U.S. already had theirs. It is a parallel situation to the current bilateral paranoia in the Iran negotiations. They knew that the Soviet refusal of such a benign gesture by the U.S. would give the Russians a very negative image in the eyes of the world. International political intrigue! Power! Politics! What a wonderful humanitarian opportunity missed by Soviet paranoia!

Consequently, for all the years since, the hand of the symbolic clock of the *Bulletin of Atomic Scientists* has hovered a few short minutes before the midnight of nuclear holocaust. Leaving a copy of the current issue of the magazine in my office waiting room, visually illustrated the concept to my 1960s California patients. In those years they did not need much further commentary, as they were much more aware of the nuclear threat hanging over the world, than the public's complacent acceptance of the same threat today.

Bernard Kouchner, one of the founders of Doctors Without Borders wrote in the *LA Times* Oct 18th 1999, "Now it is necessary to take the further step of using the right to intervention as a preventative measure to stop wars before they start."

UN Secretary-General Kofi Annan, July 16th 1997, quoted in newsletter of Campaign for UN Reform, "An effective security can only (be) said to exist, if the UN Security Council can rapidly dispatch military forces with the requisite predictability and reliability."

Walter Cronkite, World Federalists Association 2001, "- the UN created in 1945 is not what the world needs today."

Will the United Nations Change? Yes. World progress is agonizingly slow, but I think it must. Change is inevitable. The concept of this is-where-I-am-at-now applies here. The United Nations only appears to be frozen-in-time. The only thing unchangeable is that there will always be change. It must come, and it will come. In 2015, we have only waited 70 years! As I see it, the United Nations may require restructuring, certainly elimination of the veto. That will be the most difficult. The nation-states are immovably jealous of their veto prerogative. But, in time (maybe much time), internationalism will be globalized. I only dread that it might take another world conflagration to make the existing global conservatives, and the United States populace, desperate enough to face the truth.

Free Inquiry magazine, Aug-Sept 2005, "Perhaps the most important reform to be achieved on the international level is an appreciation for international ethics. I submit that the world needs to develop transnational institutions that bond people together. Some of these institutions are: expanded UN Security Council; international court of justice; an environmental enforcement agency; and universal taxation." The Security Council has expanded to, I think, nine. However, the original 5 nations are still the only ones able to use the veto. Good recommendations to patch up our inadequate international model.

Edna Williams-Meakes said it very clearly in *The Quest for World Peace and an Alternative to War,* "The United Nations must be freed from the domination of the powerful. The planet - must be protected in total. Since war is man-made, it is possible to prevent war."

Universalism

Socrates, *The Great Quotations,* "I am not an Athenian, not a Greek. I am a citizen of the world." He was an ancient Universalist!

Alfred Lord Tennyson, 1809-1892, English Poet, *Yahoo,* "Til the war-drum throbbed no longer, and the battle flags were furled, in the Parliament of Man, the Federation of the World." He was another early Universalist.

President Jack Kennedy In an *American University* address, said "For in the final analysis, our most basic common link is that we all inhabit the same planet. We all breathe the same air. We all cherish our children's future. And we are all mortal."

As a post WWII, Chicago student I was employed as a salesman and was taught to always, "lead with the store's best product," usually because that made more profit for my employer. Because I view the concept of world federation as not too far-out to be considered, I will lead with what I believe is the best product and is certain, in time, to occur. *The inexorable progression of the international political affairs of the world will lead to the end goal of global federation.* It will probably need much time.

Many of the philosophical comments made regarding the United Nations, apply also to the concept of Universalism or Global government. However, the concept changes from *inter*-nationalism to globalism or universalism. The goal is unity of all nations and their peoples, but *NOT* uniformity. Every individual is unique and distinct from every other. That quality will always be retained.

This concept may sound utopian to some, but it was not too farout to many of the intellectuals of the late 1940s. Having, in the recent past, undergone the largest, bloodiest, most destructive world war in history, realistic legislation was being considered. In 1949, the U.S. Congress was much less polarized, and much more progressive than today.

Harry Ashmore in *Unseasonable Truths* described how legislation was produced that called on the United States to "support and strengthen the United Nations and to seek its development into a world federation open to all nations with defined and limited powers, adequate to preserve peace and prevent aggression through the enactment, interpretation and enforcement of World Law." The resolution was backed by *133 sponsors from both houses of Congress."* Such a wonderful chunk of convinced legislators! A good beginning! That could have been the leading edge of progressive change. It was on the table! It just needed a majority! Sixty-five years ago! Disillusionment! There was not a majority. Patience was, and is, necessary! Progress is imperceptibly slow!

Realistically, the day will come when all countries will have to face that moment of nation-surrender to globalism, when patriotism becomes global. Currently and realistically, the United States wields major influence in world leadership, and yet I think the United States will be among the last to give up to universalism. However, I am inflexible in my belief that the latent intelligence of the citizenry of the nation, and the world, will resurface and will resume the march to universalism, along with fellow-globalists of other countries. There is a rhythm to the progress of the history of the world. The current (2014) international, reign of ISIS barbarism, I hope, has to be the maximum pendulum-swing to such regressive beliefs of the middle ages. Now, in early October 2014, President Obama appears to have achieved a modicum of international cooperation that bodes well for the future. Unfortunately, though he dreamed differently, it currently appears to continue to be a militaristic future.

Dr. Max T. Krone, 1952 Dean of the Institute of Arts, University of Southern California wrote in *This, I Believe,* "Thinking of visions of this earth from a far off star said, "What I would see from afar is what I too often cannot see at close quarters - that "earth is fair and all her folk be one."

Isaiah 2:14 and Micah 4:3 *The Bible,* "And they will hammer their swords into plow shears, and their spears into pruning hooks. Nation will not lift up sword against nation. And never again will they learn war." Learn from the ancient wisdom of the Bible, but please, disregard the theological dogma.

Clinton Lee Scott, *Religion Can Make Sense,* "The Jewish prophet Malachi, more than five centuries before Jesus, (500 BC) asked his generation, "Have we not all one father? Hath not God created us?" "To Jesus, the heart of religion was the oneness of mankind. The problems that vex the men of all nations will not be solved until they are dealt with in the light of common humanity, living in one world with one destiny, and with one supreme task of learning how to live decently together. Universalism's genius is in the fact that, while other denominations have set their faces toward a past that is gone, or a world to come after this world, universalism is faith in the capacity of man to make this life a fraternity of free men."

Julian Huxley, *Knowledge Morality and Destiny* 1957, "What the United States and other great powers should aim at, is to succeed in providing leadership and in facilitating right development in the world at large; and this it can do if it successfully provides good will (The Golden Rule) and expert assistance in the creative process of developments, whereby the universe as a whole can realize more of its' potentialities in richer and greater fulfillment."

Adlai Stevenson, *Putting First Things First,* "World order will come not through the purity of the human heart, nor the purge of the human soul, but will come from a thousand common ventures that are possible and imperative." Those actions through the aegis of the United Nations will grow into a global brotherhood-of-man government. It'll take time! Stevenson continues, "Science has given us the knowledge and technology, and common sense has given us the wit (wisdom) to perceive that common interest impels us to common enterprise. The will to peace cannot be legislated. It must be developed by organized, patient effort. The laws and the institutions of international cooperation have to evolve out of a combination of the common aspirations and experiences of the peoples of the world. In an independent world there is no longer any demarcation between social and political problems. The solution of one depends on how well we understand the other, and to the extent to which we succeed in doing both."

Thomas Hager in *Force of Nature* relates that in the late 1930s, Clarence Streit, an American political journalist, wrote a book named *Union Now,* which advocated "consolidation of the world's democracies into a federation modeled on the union of American states. Streit's book, with its appealing idea of extending the basics of the U.S. Constitution to the entire world, became a mini-phenomenon, spawning a Union Now movement." In 1940, Linus Pauling, *Force of Nature* gave his first political speeches, and his topic was the Union Now movement. "He ended his speeches with a stirring vision of a planet at peace, organized and run by a stable, democratic world government."

The biggest hurdle to world government (Universalism, Globalism), lies in developing the necessary ability to transfer patriotism from one's country to the world and all its peoples. *"Them" or "They" must be included in "Us".* We, by tradition, are imbued with our national pride and a visceral love for our own country, and so we must each contend with that urge to view ourselves as a little different to others, and instead, sublimate our nationalism for globalism.

LA Times May 8th 1967, "Engaging in a lively dialogue at Caltech's Beckman Auditorium, two of the western world's most noted historians (Allan Nevins and Arnold Toynbee) agreed that a world government or world authority would be the key to world-wide problem-solving and that the force behind this would be "religious" in nature. Established religions would not be the driving force, but rather the feeling of brotherhood overcoming national boundaries." It is evident that they viewed the slow drift of world opinion as so aimless, that only the inherent dynamism of a religious concept would seize the imagination of the world, thus securing global agreement. I think the "brotherhood" of all of the worlds' peoples, would certainly qualify as that incentive.

Edward Bellamy in his book *Looking Backward* 1883, "You must understand that we all look forward to an eventual unification of the world as one nation. That no doubt, will be the ultimate form of societ*y."*

Gloria Faizi in *The Bahai Belief* 1971 wrote, "The world is but one country, and mankind its citizens." She then comments that the ideal man "is a man who, today, dedicates himself to the service of the entire human race."

Martin Luther King 1967, *Where do we go from here?* "The call for a world-wide good neighbor policy is more than an ephemeral shibboleth, it is a call to a way of life which will transform our imminent cosmic elegy into a psalm of creative fulfillment." Soaring language! It means the same thing! I looked it up!

President Grover Cleveland, 1893, *The Great Quotations,* "I believe that our Great Maker is preparing the world, in his own good time, to become one nation, speaking one language." The universal language had been created in 1887 six years before, with the invention of "Esperanto," and was said to be a topic of deep interest by Winston Churchill.

Margaret Mead, American anthropologist 1952, *The Great Quotations,* 'I believe that human life is given meaning --. Today it means taking upon ourselves the task of creating one world in such a way that we both keep the future safe and leave the future free."

Sidney Harris, Los Angeles Times, Aug 1960, "Patriotism is a "brotherly" feeling of loving your own country. However, that same brotherly feeling should be must be transferred to loving the world."

Senator Alan Cranston, *The Killing of the Peace,* "There must not be a, "balance of power," but a, "community of power." In other words:

"balance" doesn't preclude war, but a "world community of power," would be a globalization of power, and so could maintain peace.

Sir Norman Angell, Writer 1933, *The Great Quotations,* "The root problem is very simply stated: if there were no sovereign independent states, if the states of the civilized world were organized in some sort of federalism, as the states of the American Union for instance are organized, there would be no international war as we know it - The main obstacle is nationalism."

Sigmund Freud, Psychoanalyst, in a 1932 letter to Albert Einstein in *The Great* Quotations: "There is but one sure way of ending war, and that is the establishment, by common consent, of a central control which shall have the last word on every conflict of interests. For this, two things are needed: first, the creation of such a supreme court of jurisdiction. Secondly: its investment with adequate executive force. Unless the second requirement is fulfilled, the first is unavailing." Freud knew that the League lacked executive force during the League Nations, but his advice was not heeded at the formation of the United Nations.

Albert Einstein, *Ideas and Opinions* 1950, "A world federation presupposes a new kind of loyalty on the part of man, a sense of responsibility that does not stop at national boundaries. Each country will have their history as a monument to the world's progress but National patriotism should be replaced by World Patriotism (*OUR)* world. I can visualize a new kind of loyalty on the part of man, a sense of responsibility that does not stop at the national boundaries. To be truly effective, such loyalty must embrace more than purely political ideas." Possibly moderated by WWII, his opinion about international cooperation had moved to that of a global federation.

Einstein continues, "Do I fear the tyranny of world government? Of course I do. But a world government is preferable to the far greater evil of wars, particularly with their intensified destructiveness. If such a world government is not established by a process of agreement, I believe it will come anyway, and in a much more dangerous form. For war, or wars, will end in one power being supreme and dominating the rest of the world, by its overwhelming military strength. But I also believe that world government is certain to come in time. It will come, I believe, even if there is another world war, though after such a war, if it is won, it would be world government established by the victor's military power, and thus to be maintained permanently only through the permanent militarization of the human race." The U.S. has that permanent militarization already. His clear-sighted premonition of one remaining victor, a super-power, a world-cop and a permanent world's arms race is the hegemony striven for by the United States of today.

Albert Einstein *Ideas and Opinions,* "I also believe that world government, and peace, can come through agreement and through the force of persuasion alone, hence at low cost. But if it is to come in this way it will not be enough to appeal to reason. Unless the cause of peace gathers behind it the force of a religion, it hardly can hope to succeed." We are a long way from that point at this time. Public knowledge, or even just an awareness of the concept of global government, is at an abysmally low level. It needs to be reintroduced to school and college curriculums; advocated by educators; promoted by articulate statesmen and politicians; and discussed in depth at public forums. Though I see only the few, who are in world federation organizations, currently speaking out, I remain optimistic in the long term.

Einstein is not saying the lack of religiosity of the people of the world would make its occurrence any less likely. He is saying that World Government would have to become *THE* religion. The absence of world-wide interest in world government contributes significantly to my disillusionment. Perhaps it will be another world peril, similar to the nuclear bomb of those panic-filled years, to have that world-government-feeling rise again. Nuclear War? World-wide famine? Space encounters? Perish the thoughts!

A superb current effort to establish Universalism comes in the growing popularity of the NBC organization with web address of, mnbc.com global citizen.

PERSPECTIVE

Please pay special attention to the next six pages probably this book's most important. They are dominated by two outstanding personalities, Emery Reves and Robert Maynard Hutchins.

As WWII and its savage, revolting daily news were becoming history, Emery Reves was publishing one of the most thought provoking books in history *Anatomy of Peace.* Emery Reves was born of Jewish parents in Hungary in 1904; was educated in universities in Berlin, Zurich and Paris; became literary agent and friend of Winston Churchill, and authored *Anatomy of Peace in 1945.*

Albert Einstein wrote, pointedly and humbly, in *Ideas and Opinions,* "I myself do not have the gift of explanation with which I am able to persuade large numbers of people of the urgency of the problems the human race now faces. Hence I should like to commend someone who has this gift of explanation. Emery Reves, whose book, *The Anatomy of Peace* is intelligent, clear, brief, and, - dynamic on the topic of war and need for world government." The wisest of men are said to be humble. Albert Einstein shows his humbleness, having read *The Anatomy of Peace.* Read it!

His book found immediate national and international acclaim. Leo Cherne, Executive Director of the Research Institute of America, wrote the Introduction to the 1963 edition of *Anatomy of Peace* and said, "The book was completed before the United Nations was formed (the text was complete but not yet approved and adopted), and it took insight and courage to say, as he did, 'This is *NOT* the answer; we have only gathered together many sovereignties, and there will be no peace until there is but one sovereignty - that of World Order.'"

Cherne continues, "Certainly there was no lack of agreement then that only a world authority could dissolve the terrible threats raised by nuclear bombs. Albert Einstein, whose efforts made the bombs possible, said *The Anatomy of Peace was the answer to the political questions created by the bombs.* His judgment was echoed by scores of sophisticated voices."

Cherne continues, "Statesmen throughout the world hurried to join their voices to his. Newspapers and wire services applied superlatives. United States Supreme Court Justice Owen J. Roberts assembled a group of the world's most illustrious literary, political and diplomatic figures, to urge on the American people the importance of the Reves' analysis. The Reader's Digest published the first three-part condensation in its publishing history. Twenty-three thousand discussion groups throughout the United States discussed and debated the Reves conception." What a tremendous impact! What a calamity that the impetus was never sustained! Its timing was in that progressive window of time in post WWII. Disillusionment!

Now follow his reasoning. Emery Reves, *Anatomy of Peace,* 1945, "Logical thinking and historical empiricism agree that there is a way to solve this problem and prevent wars between the nations once and for all. But with equal clarity they also reveal that there is one way, and one way alone, to achieve this end: *The integration of the scattered conflicting national sovereignties into one higher sovereignty, capable of creating a legal order within which all people may enjoy equal security, equal obligations and equal rights under the law."* Reves continues, *"Peace among men can only be achieved by a legal order; by a sovereign source of law; by a democratically controlled government with independent executive, legislative and judicial bodies. The same on a global level, as on the U.S. governmental level. A legal order is a plan laid down by common consent of man to make their individual lives, their families and their nation secure."*

Reves continues, "The road to world sovereignty and government is a long, hard, steep and stony road, guided by reason. We may have to follow it for a century. We may have to recreate it to be followed by another century. If we want to build this (global) cathedral, and live as free men in security let us bear in mind the profound words of Francis Bacon in his "Novum Organum" 'It is idle to expect any great advancement in sciences by the super-inducing, engrafting of new things on old. We must begin anew from the very foundation, unless we would revolve forever in a circle with mean and contemptible progress.'" In the interim, continue to improve the United Nations.

Reves continues, "No conception is more erroneous than to believe that man must first be united in religion, culture, political outlook, economic methods, before he can be politically united in a state, a federation or any unified legal order. In fact, those variations are the rich cultural differences that must be retained. There is no first step to world government. World government is the first step. Integrated social relations regulated by law - which is peace - have been possible only within social units of indivisible sovereignty, with one single source of law, irrespective of the size, territory, population, race, religion and degree of complexity of such social units. It has never been possible between such social units, even if they were composed of populations of the same race, the same religion, the same language, the same culture, the same degree of civilization." Individual countries agree to disagree. Reves continues, "The term international sounds comprehensive, as it relates to the countries of the world. However, internationalism means exactly what it says. It expresses *inter*-nationalism. It does not, and never has, opposed nationalism and the evil effects of the nation-state structure. We have played long enough with the toy of internationalism. The problem we are facing is not a problem between nationalisms. It is the problem of a crisis in human society, caused by nationalism, and which consequently nationalism or internationalism can never solve. What is needed is Universalism." The limitation of the League of Nations and the United Nations lay in the fact that they viewed the world as a world-wide group of nations and not as a global entity.

Emery Reyes, *Anatomy of Peace* 1945, "Five steps (to peace) are clearly visible on the road from idea (of world government) to realization:

1. Conception of idea; proclamation of principle.
2. Spread the doctrine.
3. Elect representatives.
4. Those representatives organize world government, debate programs, fight out details, compromise and arrive at solutions even if imperfect.
5. Develop programs."

The same as our own federal government there will be an ongoing, never-static, always-improving, evolutionary process to improve the initial world-government format.

When planning his speech at the seventh anniversary of Israel, and seven days before his death, Albert Einstein in *Ideas and Opinions,* "urged the creation of world government." At his bedside April 17th, 1955, when he died was the (speech) manuscript with his beginning words to the future Israeli anniversary, "I speak to you today not as an American citizen, and not as a Jew, but as a human being."

Another superior intellect, also focused on world federation, was Robert Maynard Hutchins. Born in Brooklyn, Wikipedia records that "although both his father and grandfather were Presbyterian ministers, Hutchins became one of the most influential members of the school of secular perennialism." (re-occurring).

Only if a description of who, "Hutchins" was, is now presented, will the following quotations be appreciated. Robert Maynard Hutchins, 1899-1977, was described by Harry Ashmore in *Unseasonable Truths,* "as precocious, brilliant, and endowed with the will, energy, and presence to promote his convictions. During his long career as a legal scholar, political philosopher, educational reformer, and civil libertarian, he became the dean of Yale Law School by age 27; the president of the University of Chicago by age 31 (remained president for 20 years); Chairman of the Board of Directors of the Encyclopedia Britannica; editor of The Great Books of the Western World; Associate director of the Ford Foundation. In 1959 he co-founded, with Mortimer Adler, the Center for the Study of Democratic Institutions in Santa Barbara, California. Later as president of The Fund for the Republic he led the counter-attack that is given the primary credit for putting an end to the dismal era of McCarthyism."

About 1958, when I joined the *United World Federalists* and Sane, (*Sane Nuclear Policy),* and started to read about him, I came to appreciate Hutchins leadership and wisdom. I became a member of the Center for the Study of Democratic Solutions, Santa Barbara, California and received *The Center Magazine.* I purchased the Great Books of the

Western World, of which he was initially editor. Dictionaries research words and encyclopedias research places, events and things. The Great Books of the Western World researched ideas. They comprised around 54 books, all written prior to 1900. Their topics included the entire writings of writers such as Socrates, Aristotle, Plato, Marx and many more. Other topics were war, peace, religion, philosophy, government and many similar categories. As mentioned elsewhere, a negative thinking episode impelled me to give them away at my age of 75 years, thinking that I wouldn't be likely to find a use for them again. I think that I thought that was "positive thinking!" It was not!

The following quotations are all taken from the book, *Unseasonable Truths* written by Harry S. Ashmore, who as a member of the board of directors of the Fund for the Republic developed a long, and intimate, association with Robert Maynard Hutchins. "The words peace, cooperation, community and charity have fallen out of our vocabulary. They are, in fact, regarded as a sign of weakness and as showing that one who uses them is guilty of the capital crime of modern times, lack of realism."

"The right wing *Chicago Tribune* was ready to pounce when the committee to frame a World Constitution circulated a confidential copy of its draft charter to 350 experts on constitutional law, inviting their comment prior to its scheduled publication March 1948. "WORLD STATE'S SUPER-SECRET CONSTITUTION the newspaper blared, when a copy fell into their hands. PLAN SPONSORED BY HUTCHINS, BARED."

"The implication of conspiracy was far-fetched, since the document was designed to bring into focus the already widespread discussions of the perceived need for some form of supranational organization to preserve peace in the atomic era. A number of organizations with grassroots support were advocating the surrender of a degree of national sovereignty to the powerless United Nations. If the Hutchins group took the most advanced position among those world federalists, it could hardly be called militant."

"A foreword to the constitution signed by Robert Maynard Hutchins and G. A. Borgese stated: "The problems of world government are hard and intricate. The Committee felt that these problems can best be clarified in a Constitutional design, intended as a concrete picture to show what a Federal Republic of the World, under certain conceivable circumstances might look like. That the "conceivable circumstances" for the rise of World Government are not at hand, the Committee knows full well." However, the circumstances of the late 1940s did allow this kind of discussion and planning. In the unimaginative U.S. political climate of 2013 there is no such possibility. The innate intelligence of our leaders (maybe global leaders) will in time, force the return of progressive thought. The idealism of President Hutchins, never flagged, but realities confined him to the practical progressive steps that he could continue to take, which my politician-brother Frank referred to as, "Politics being the art of the possible."

"If what our Western World Federalists have in mind is a world union with no binding commitment toward the dismantlement of colonialism, outlawry of racial discrimination, provision for social security these three being the acid test of any world thinking - if that is the case, our western world federalists may talk to one another for years and decades to come. Those millions inside our border and those hundreds of millions abroad, who do not care much for liberty without bread, who do not have anything to feel secure about, who do not remember any blessings of peace or war - will laugh."

"Hutchins never considered this (world government) an immediate prospect, but he was convinced that the mutation of extant governments into a world government was as historically inevitable as had been the merger of city-states and nation-states into empires." The cooperative union of Europe, with its 'Euro' was later evidence of that trend, but still lay in his future. "The issue was urgent, he felt, for only movement toward world government offered a way out of the Cold War confrontation between East and West."

"However, the framework of World Government was proposed on paper. A Federal Convention made up of delegates chosen by votes; a President elected by the Committee for a six-year term; a 99 member unicameral (one legislative body) legislature called the World Council; a president-appointed cabinet; a sixty-member Supreme Court; a military Chamber of Guardians; a department to defend human rights. All departments subject to control or dismissal by the World Council."

A policy statement: *"The four elements of life: earth, water, air and energy - are the common properties of the human race.* The management and use of such portions thereof as are vested in or assigned to particular ownership, private or corporate, or national or regional, of definite or indefinite tenure, of individual or collectivist economy, shall be subordinated in each and all cases to the interest of the common good." In countries with Socialist administrations, those four elements are usually communally owned, administered and shielded from private exploitation.

In 1976, speaking to a Santa Barbara audience, and commenting on his prior involvement with the Committee to frame a World Constitution, "he conceded that, 'it was a most unacceptable proposal and it was buried almost immediately by the Cold War.' His, and Justice (Supreme Court William O. Douglas) Douglas's, campaign for world law had enjoyed no greater success." We have to hang on to the United Nations because it's all we have." but it would continue to be an exercise in futility so long as it remained a league of sovereign states. He asserted, as he always had, that the survival of civilization would require a new world order, but this was no call to action. He closed with a somber quotation from Mathew Arnold's "Dover Beach":

And we are here as on a darkling plain,
Swept with confused alarms of struggle and flight,
Where ignorant armies, clash by night.

"Many people think, and I (Ashmore) am one of them, that we cannot have world peace without world government. But if the world is to last, it must rest on world community. Such a community would arise if men were persuaded by Aristotle's Ethics."

"No man could do that without religious faith, and he (Hutchins) therefore concluded that it was not possible to speak of the brotherhood of man, as proponents of world government were wont to do, without conceding the fatherhood of God."

Hutchins said "I have not found it necessary to concern myself on questions of religious faith." However, to a student's convocation the influence of his Presbyterian minister father showed when he said "The brotherhood of man must rest on the fatherhood of God." The World Constitution had been offered by its framers as a "proposal to history."

Education

Malala Yousafzai, 2013 Nobel Peace prize winner, *The Arizona Republic.* The Pakistani teen, shot by the Taliban for advocating girls' education, addressing the United Nations said, "Let us pick up our books and our pens. They are our most powerful weapons. One child, one teacher, one book and one pen, can change the world. Education is the only solution." Accurate words from an already experienced teenager!

Marie Curie Polish-French Scientist, in *The Arizona Republic,* "You cannot hope to build a better world, without improving the individual. To that end each of us must work for his improvement and at the same time share a general responsibility for all humanity." That should be the aim of all education.

Education is the key to everyone's personal future. Education is the key to solving every problem that faces society - poverty, ill health, failing government, and war. Education will be necessary to attain the desired solutions. It is even more true to say that the future of the world also depends on education. *The Arizona Republic* printed the wise words of "President James Madison the father of our Constitution, who explained in Federalist 55 that the moral character of a people, molded through education, is most essential in a nation where the people rule." More wise words came from President Jefferson when he referred to a democratic nation needing an, "educated, and informed electorate."

Even, in the infant phase of the Republic, they knew that the, "equal vote," meant that each vote still carried with it only the political awareness of the voter. Each vote also carried with it the bigotry, prejudices, false opinions and *absence* of information on which to make an informed vote. Carl Sagan wrote in *A Demon-Haunted World* that "our species needs, and deserves, a citizenry with minds wide awake and who have a basic understanding of how the world works." So the "informed" vote is the one that will lead to a better society. The electorate are not dumb, just uninformed. It is why I wrote President Johnson (see my Vietnam War letters - July 25th 1966, and Sept 1966, "Please, just give the American people the truthful facts and they will support you." Public sentiment can lead to war, or to avoidance of war. With the absence of convincing facts, President George W Bush strove mightily to achieve favorable public opinion, leading up to the Iraq War. A better-informed electorate could well have helped us to avoid a disastrous and baseless war.

Michael Tariff, *Los Angeles Times,* November 11th 2003 (2 months post 9/11), "- if a war depends for its support on the citizenry's ignorance, as the Pentagon and White House evidently believe this one does, that war does not merit support." How can you make a wise decision without the facts? Probably the most informed of the top echelon of our lawmakers are still uninformed in many ways. That is why they have committees to look for the facts of any situation, so that they (Congress) can vote intelligently. That is basic. You already know it. I see myself as also uninformed, having had a shallow general education, and by not later taking the necessary steps to inform myself.

I thought of my professional education (Podiatry), as providing me with the knowledge necessary to solve my patient's foot problems while, hopefully, making a reasonable living for myself (a traditional entrepreneur). My professional education was focused on medical knowledge but nothing on the important problems which we are faced with all through life. Somewhere "along the line," I came to feel that my education was a hollow empty one, and that, though I had achieved officer-level in the military services, and achieved a "doctorate" in my profession, that I was, nevertheless an uninformed voter. And I was slowly coming to understand why professional schools prefer students who have a BA degree, or something similar, before they study their "major" profession. After about a dozen years of practice life I found the narrowness of my education was "bugging me."

A mile from my office, in the early 1960s, North High School in Torrance, California, was offering adult evening classes that would provide the basis for a BA degree, to be later completed in university classes. I briefly considered it; despaired on how evening classes would affect the Golden Rule in my home life; how it would affect others around me; decided instead to purchase the previously-mentioned *Great Books of the Western World* which, with home study, could lead to the same result.

The stresses of everyday life, my lack of dedicated application and my sporadic usage of the books, doomed the idea from the beginning. It did provide me with a revealing peak into the possibilities of an expanded mind; and then, suffering from a delusion that I was too old to ever need them again, I mistakenly gave the books away in 1997. This story is related to illustrate what I have come to realize would have provided one basis for an "informed vote." I am not saying that only with that level of education would an informed vote be possible, but wish only to emphasize my view that appropriate education is the primary answer to all problems, including the informed vote.

Henry Peter Broughman comments in *The Great Quotations,* "Education makes people easy to lead, but difficult to drive; easy to govern but impossible to enslave."

My feeling of a "hollow" education was not, of course, unique. *The Great Books of the Western World* had been utilized for teaching, and Q&A sessions, by Robert Maynard Hutchins and Mortimer Adler, were conducted at the University of Chicago.

These stimulating sessions were remembered nostalgically by photojournalist John Godfrey Morris, in *Unseasonable Truths,* "Mr.

Hutchins continued to disturb me after graduation. I was (necessarily) engaged in the great American game of Getting Ahead. But - Getting Ahead to What? Why? Right ends, first principles - these kept haunting me. What did they have to do with my weekly paycheck?

The money came uneasy to my palm. The suspicion grew that I had only begun my education. I went back to the books, great ones and little ones. I sought the forgotten passages in the works of the philosopher, historian and novelist. I found, too, that words which were once wasted on me in the classroom now had a meaning derived from life." For many, the profession-based education, proved to be unsatisfying and inadequate.

In his book, *Ideas and Opinions* Albert Einstein reflects on educational standards, "No event of the past few years reflect such disgrace on the leading countries of the world, as the failure of the disarmament conferences so far; for this failure is due not to the intrigues of ambitious and unscrupulous politicians, but also to the indifference and slackness of the public in all countries." In that last sentence Einstein is lamenting the uninformed electorate by referring to it as "indifference and slackness." The deeper thoughtfulness needed for the informed electorate can only come through improved appropriate education. I refer to appropriate education because the biases of teacher and institution, will affect the end result. Also, as stated by Einstein, "unless military and aggressively patriotic education is abolished, we cannot hope for peace."

Speaking of the United Nations and of future world government, Einstein said, "Where can the strength in such a process come from? Only from those who have had the chance in early years to fortify their minds and broaden their outlook through *study.* Thus, we of the older generation look to you and hope that you will arrive with all your' might and achieve what was denied to us." Eighty years later I fervently echo his words!

In 1958, when I first arrived in California, their educational system, from kindergarten, through university, was free to the student. For California it was the Golden Years of Education. What is it that has happened that the university students of today graduate with enormous debt obligations which restrict their financial plans for years to come? There should be a return to those earlier days. The future of the country depends upon an educated work force. Summer 2013 bulletin of the *Democratic Socialists of America,* "We believe that education is a right, not a privilege, and this crisis is unnecessary. There is enough wealth in this country to easily provide universal, publicly funded higher education for all at no cost to students. Other industrialized countries are moving in that direction, while the U.S. goes the opposite way."

Winston Churchill hints at scholastic deficiency in *Brilliant Thoughts,* "The best argument against democracy is a five-minute conversation with the average voter." Should we despair? No! Society has not yet devised the level of education needed. It will come. Listen to the logical, futuristic words of Robert Hutchins.

Harry Ashmore regarding Robert Hutchins, President University of Chicago, in *Unseasonable Truths,* "Hutchins faith in the future universal education, to guide human beliefs and actions is clear. His own faith was grounded in the conviction that a form of education could be devised, that would sharpen men's intellectual capacity so that they would be able to identify the basic ideas of their times, think dispassionately about them, and arrive at rational courses of action. Logic, dictated the first priority in the nuclear age must be prevention of war. Other civilizations were destroyed by barbarians from without - we breed our own." Yes, indeed! Many of our machismo-laden militarists qualify as barbarians.

Albert Einstein, 1945, *Ideas and Opinions,* "Unless the cause of peace based on law, gathers behind it the force and zeal of a religion, it can hardly hope to succeed. Those to whom the moral teaching of the human race is entrusted, surely have a great duty and a great opportunity. The atomic scientists, I think, have become convinced that they can arouse the American people at the truth of the error by logic alone. There must be added that deep power of emotion which is the basic ingredient of religion. It is to be hoped that not only the churches, but the schools and colleges, and the leading organs of public opinion, will acquit themselves well of their unique responsibility in this regard."

John Henry Newman on Nov 21st, 1953, in the *Saturday (Review?) of Literature* wrote, "A liberal education is the education which gives a man, a clear conscious view of his own opinions and judgments; a truth in developing them; eloquence in expressing them; and a force in urging them. It teaches him to see things as they are, to go right to the point, to disentangle a skein of thought, to detect what is sophistical, and to disregard what is irrelevant --. He is at home in any society, he has common ground with every class; he knows when to speak and when to remain silent." That, of course, is the ideal. How many currently have the time or the money for such an education? It is probably not possible to state the situation more incisively, clearly and understandably than one of our nations most trusted personalities Walter Cronkite.

Verne Gay in the *LATimes Magazine*, Jan 21st 1996, Walter Cronkite on the *Dearth of Trust*, "So where has trust gone? To Cronkite's thinking, several factors have contributed, linked by a single theme: *a less educated citizenry*." Cronkite speaks forcibly of how demagogues, "use this ignorance to further their ends. - important debates (such as) the national budget, welfare, health care, law enforcement, tax law, nuclear energy, environmental issues, are reduced to battlegrounds of meaningless rhetoric. Because most Americans are not educated in the minutiae of these subjects, cynicism is born, he says. And from cynicism springs distrust." *"But loss of trust begins with the question of education, which lies at the very bottom of every problem that we have. If the people were truly well-informed, were truly philosophical, were truly aware of our associations with one another {then}presumably our dialogue and our reporting would be considerably better than it is. But the tragedy is we aren't educated to any degree. Education levels are so low that the public does not have a capability of making an informed judgment as to how trustworthy these people should be, so we're handicapped from the beginning."*

Echoing my point about my "hollow education" Cronkite said that it is not only the inner cities but even "those with Harvard degrees are uneducated in a general philosophy that I find so important, which is the understanding of civil dialogue, the understanding of the other fellow's point of viewpoint, and an attempt to moderate or mediate between the two." Cronkite then comments that this deficiency comes in our "self-proclaimed Information Age, where more pure knowledge is more available than ever before." More knowledge available than ever before, but less wisdom on the things that really matter.

Bewailing the lack of opportunity for such a broad-based education, I belatedly, recently and embarrassingly, became aware of the *United World College,* a bright beacon for the future that is now fifty years old. *Time Magazine,* June 3rd 2013, "UWC believes that to achieve peace and a sustainable future, the values it promotes are crucial: They are:

1. international and intercultural understanding;
2. celebration of difference;
3. personal responsibility and integrity, mutual responsibility and respect;
4. compassion and service;
5. respect for the environment;
6. sense of idealism;
4. personal challenge and action and personal responsibility.

Celebrating their 50th anniversary they now have world-wide locations in the United Kingdom, Bosnia-Herzegovina, Canada, Costa Rica, Hong Kong, India, Italy, The Netherlands, Norway, Singapore, Swaziland, and since 1983, the United States.

How wonderfully that fills my hopes and dreams. I again, find myself speaking of the present steps to a bright future. What a wonderful fulfilling future a participating, idealistic teen could have! The new vision has to be of hundreds of such colleges within the next century. I trust that this is not another illusion to be shattered. I will cover the United World College in more depth under the heading of "Global Education."

www.uwc.org/time/
1721 Emerald St, London, WGIN 3QN United Kingdom.
State Route 65, Montezuma, N. M. 87731

PART SIX

United States Re-entry 1958 to 2015

The intent of *Perspective* is to describe what I view as the moral bankruptcy of war, causing the fiscal bankruptcy of the nations (particularly the United States), and doing so by using my own personal narrative as a framework on which to attach history and commentary. To maintain an awareness of my personal continuity, I will insert the following non- military time line, a brief non-military oriented summary of the first five years in the United States.

Peggy, Michael (age- 2 years) and I entered the United States on permanent residence visas on July 18th 1958, at Port Huron, Michigan; drove west on highway #2 to Edmunds, Washington where Peggy and Mike stayed with our sponsoring friends, Aurelio (Ray) and Muryl (Mu) Medina while I continued to Gardena, California where I stayed with my Chicago classmate, Dr. Sherwood Alan Van Dyke and his wife Ardyce (Ardy); worked painting houses with John Hayes for 6 weeks. August 11th at Dr. Van Dykes recommendation, though available in LA County, I took 2 days to drive to Berkeley to get a signature from Dr. Ralph S. Minor on the Validation Certificate for the California Board of Medical Examiners; later in August 1958 drove to San Francisco to get Peggy and Mike; moved to a Gardena apartment; was soon notified that my application to take California State Board podiatry examinations in September was being side-lined for "review"; in late August 1958, secured a construction job with Anderson Bros Paving Co of Culver City, California; to retain the job I joined the "Laborers and Hod-carriers "Union, LA Local 300; moved to a rented house in Long Beach, California in spring of 1959; took the State board exams in March 1959; California Board of Medical Examiners issued a "certificate to practice Podiatry," on May 6th 1959; rented office space and purchased office equipment; in July 1959 announced opening of office for, "the practice of General Chiropody (old name for Podiatry), foot orthopedics, foot surgery and child foot care," at 4537 W Redondo Beach Blvd, Lawndale, California; continued working at Anderson Bros full time; took office appointments only in the evening and Saturday; after 13 months, the Anderson job was terminated October 1st 1959; secured a job with Los Angeles Yellow Cab Company on October 2nd, having to first sign a "declaration of intention," to become a United States citizen; took patients from 8 AM to 3 PM; then each day I drove to Yellow Cab Co near down-town LA and drove 4 PM to 2 AM shift; about early January 1960, left Yellow Cab and accepted a 40 hour per week, "podiatric internship" at the Harbor General Hospital in Torrance, California; which involved directing the volunteer Podiatry Clinic; which paid a "token" wage of $21.36 per 40-hour week ("gas-money"); took patients only after 4 Pm at my office; financial crisis engulfed Los Angeles County about July 1960 so my fulltime status at the clinic ended; continued as volunteer clinic director for about 4 more years; in July 1962 moved office to Knoll Crest Medical Building, 18402 Hawthorne Blvd, Torrance, California; in May 1963 faced the 5-year U.S. residence decision point for U.S. citizenship; sold my practice in March 1979; continued a part time house-call and nursing home practice until 1992. I have lived in Redondo Beach, Long Beach, Paramount, and Laguna Hills, California and Mesa Arizona 1958 to 2015.

At my five year U.S. residence point in 1963, at age 41, it had been 23 years since I had left home for WWII, and I was intensely aware of the old adage, "A rolling stone carries no moss." This, I knew, should continue to be my final move. It was.

Tormenting Reality

Our five year U.S. period of residence brought a period of deep reflection about U.S. citizenship. The United States that I had studied and worked in during the late 1940s had changed. The post-war euphoria had dissipated. The hopeful future of progressive political change had dissipated. The USA was now Cold War-stressed. The Soviet-USA emotional stew of fear, mistrust and animosity had been simmering for a dozen years, and had already cooked up the Korean War. Occasionally, in the 1958 news, there would be a reference to Ho Chi Minh, the leader of the remote country of Vietnam, winning still another battle against France, his colonial master. The U.S. foreign policy analysts were concerned, as, in their view, it was fulfilling the menacing world domination aim of the global Communist leaders; that each lost battle or newly formed Communist nation would lead to another tumbling domino; triggering the next one; the final expected result being Communist domination of the world.

It was planned that our five-year incubation period would result in the automatic creation of two shiny, freshly minted, U.S. citizens. My three year (1947 to 1949) residence in Chicago (on a student visa), could not be used toward permanent residence.

By 1963, we had become disappointed in the Cold War society in which we found ourselves. I will quote from my unpublished manuscript, *American Citizenship Reconsidered.*

"When we arrived in California from Canada in 1958, we had come from a more psychologically placid Canadian political scene, and from a distinctly non-militaristic nation which was supporting the United Nations unreservedly. Canada was already into their then-eighteen-year-old policy of sending a contingent of Canadian soldiers under the U.N. flag to any trouble spot in any part of the globe. This has now become a seventy-year policy, unequalled by any other nation. We had found a marked contrast in the frenetic, anti-Communist, political ferment of the Cold War, with its (UNAC) Un-American Activities Committee, its Senator Joe McCarthy inquisitions, and the generalized anti-Soviet paranoia. Whatever the degree of anti-Communist hysteria existing in Canada, it could have been multiplied by ten in California."

Nuclear Nightmares

"Your personal bomb shelter was the topic of market bulletin boards and newspapers, radio and TV ads. There were newspaper articles detailing construction of your own bomb shelter, and then articles about what should be stocked in them for survival. There were articles on wilderness-survival techniques, if that became necessary. There was a map in the paper suggesting what would be the best evacuation route for people living in various locations of Los Angeles County. (Los Angeles was boxed-in by ocean, mountains with minimal canyon exits from the area). Movies and TV tapped into the paranoia with apocalyptic movies like, "On the Beach," and Dr. Strangelove."

"The Soviets had tested their first hydrogen bomb six or seven years earlier and the United States the U-bomb in 1953. At 11 AM every Friday morning the long piercing wail of the air raid alarm put the neighborhood nerves 'on edge.' We used a centrally-placed linen closet in our rented house to store 14 gallons of water and many canned and packaged food, in case of Soviet attack, (subbing as earthquake preparedness as well).

"Applications at Desmond's Shoe Store, the Yellow Cab Company, and many others, asked if you had ever been a member of the Communist Party. The Soviet threat was a common topic of concerned discussions with neighbors. CBS Journalist Eric Sevareid's White Paper reported that the U.S. had enormous numbers of military bases, installations and outposts circling the world. The news reports were heavy on IBMs, Inter-continental ballistic missiles (ICBMs), Titan missiles, the Dew Line, testing of nuclear warheads in the Nevada Desert, skulking Soviet submarines in questionable locations, discussions about what the Soviet space ships contained, concern about how U.S. educational standards had allowed the Soviets to get the Sputnik-jump on the U.S., and, that the U.S. air-force maintained loaded long-range bombers in the air, twenty-four hours every day."

A menacing nuclear threat enveloped the U.S. The threatening peril of nuclear holocaust was world-wide, because nuclear war threatens the total planet. The world-wide psychological stress was intensified because other nations felt they were unavoidably captive to the irreconcilable rancor of the USSR and the U.S. Recent intensity of negotiations leading to the Iranian nuclear treaty signed in June 2015, illustrates the worlds continuing concern over nuclear control. However, after over fifty years of successful nuclear control, we have ceased to have that gut-level tension of the early 1960s, when the new, mysterious technology threatened our existence. Consider those tense years. *American Citizenship Reconsidered.* "The threat of nuclear war hung menacingly over everyone for our first years in the United States. From the development of the atomic bomb in 1945, the hydrogen bomb in 1949 and the U-bomb (nuclear bomb) in 1953; testing in the atmosphere had never stopped, primarily by the U.S., the Soviets and the French. A panel of experts, were convened in Geneva in July 1958 (our month of U.S. arrival), and by late-August had decided that it was technically possible to detect a nuclear explosion anywhere in the world, whether in the atmosphere, under water, or under the ground. Up until that time, the hawks in the Eisenhower administration, and in the U.S. military, had viewed efforts towards a nuclear bomb *test ban, as Communist subversion.* Physicist Edward Teller and the Atomic Energy Commission had pushed for continued testing. Great Britain and the USA had just completed a series of tests, and then stated that they were ready for a one-year test ban, if the Soviets were. The Soviets agreed."

From the book *Force of Nature* by Thomas Hager: "The Geneva Test Ban talks were slated to start on the last day of October 1958, a date when it was then expected that an informal halt in testing would begin as well. In preparation, all parties concerned rushed ahead with what might be called the last bomb tests possible for some time. The United States called its series, "Operation Deadline." In the first three weeks of October alone, the Soviets set off fourteen bombs, spewing clouds of fallout that sent the radiation readings in Los Angeles soaring, "to 120 times normal rates," the highest ever recorded outside the nuclear test ranges. By the time Halloween had arrived, the three nuclear powers had tested sixty-three bombs in 1958, one third of the total number tested since World War II, all in the space of ten months. At the same time, a UN expert committee, after reviewing all the evidence, supported (scientist Linus) Pauling's finding, by concluding that bomb tests probably caused between four hundred and two thousand cases of Leukemia per year, and that even the smallest amount of radiation was likely to cause deleterious genetic effects."

Dr. Linus Pauling's words were given added power by the fallout that continued (in 1959) to drift down from the previous fall's frenzied bomb testing. The headlines brought the issue into people's homes almost daily: "Jetliner found coated with radioactivity after U.S. flight;" "Strontium 90 in Minnesota wheat beyond permissible limits;" "Strontium 90 levels rise rapidly in milk and children's bones;" "Strontium 90 levels in New York double in four years."

The Geneva Test Ban talks dragged on through 1959, but collapsed at year's end, largely due to the opposition of one man 'hawk' scientist Edward Teller. The French tested their first atomic bomb in January 1960; the secret U.S. spy plane U-2 was shot down in May 1960, scuttling the imminent Paris peace talks.

Thomas Hager writes in his book *Force of Nature,* Page 532, "Between Sept 1961 and the end of November, the Soviets indulged in the greatest orgy of nuclear testing the world has ever seen. One test alone measured an enormous fifty-eight megatons, the largest man-made explosion ever created, three thousand times more powerful than the Hiroshima blast. By the time the testing frenzy ended in late November, the Soviet Union had tested fifty bombs, roughly one explosion every two days. Pauling estimated that the resulting radiation would create 160,000 birth defects, and that increase in Carbon 14 alone would cause 4 million aborted pregnancies, still births, and birth defects over the next several score generations."

Hager continues, "In April 1962, President Kennedy approved the resumption of atmospheric testing. The one bright spot was the partial test ban treaty (still allowing underground testing), signed by Kennedy and Kruschev, June 1963." Then JFK was assassinated Nov 22nd 1963. With major world issues at stake, no wonder conspiracy theories abounded. The dismal nuclear warfare scene; the angry, insulting Soviet/U.S. rhetoric; and the smoggy, Strontium 90 laden Los Angeles atmosphere made us feel we were living at "Ground Zero." Compared with the laid-back military attitude of the Canadian government, I was coming to realize, that like it or not, the USA was a militaristic nation. The daily drum-beat of threatening war was keeping the nation perpetually tense, and it was also keeping MIPUGU happy. War production soared. And there have been minimal moments of progressive hope ever since. Though the nuclear terror should have ended with the 1990 collapse of the Soviet Union, that never happened.

Some *LA Times* headlines, Sept 1997 to Feb 2003:

- *Cost of Keeping Nuclear Arms Rises U.S. Says." ($45 billion over ten years)*

- *Ban Nukes And Start Here at Home*
- *The Loser Will Be the Human Race If Comprehensive Test Ban Treaty Fails*
- *A More Dangerous Place.* This was about the rejection of the test-ban treaty by the GOP Senate leadership;
- *Disarmament's Glacial Pace.* Another editorial regarding the slowness of decommissioning of nuclear warheads;
- *Death of Admiral Eugene Carroll Jr., Age 79.* Admiral who urged nuclear disarmament;
- *U.S. Plan to Build Nuclear Stockpile Advances*
- *The G.W. Bush Administration Plans to Repair and Renew Nuclear Inventory*

My Space White House Style, Oct 21st 2006, *Tribune* editorial. That editorial criticized President George W. Bush for his harsh language in saying that the U.S. will operate, "unfettered" in space, and will sign no treaty restricting U.S. space activity. This while restricting all others. To other nations, this was not peaceful.

Associated Press 2013 headline, *Bloated Nuclear Spending Gets Bashed by Government Critics.* "- refurbishing 400 of the country's B61 bombs has grown from $1.5 billion dollars to $10 billion." Just a fixer-up program for an extra 8.5 billion dollars! "The Department of Energy has fewer than 16,000 employees but more than 92,000 contractors." "The nuclear program has turned into a massive jobs program with duplicative functions."

The Nation magazine in Feb 1998 filled the major part of the magazine with articles calling for international abolition of nuclear weapons. On Feb 19th 1998 I wrote to President Clinton, and asked him to read the magazine. I wrote, "The sterility of the concept of, "nuclear deterrence" is clearly illumined by (Jonathan) Schell and the others. Though currently quiescent, the global problem remains, in the form of the continuing archaic deterrence concept in the minds of many, and in the expensive ageing, monstrous, nuclear relics stored in large numbers in this country and in other countries. The first far-sighted steps in a long process are needed. Please be the progressive leader to take those steps. Your name will be enshrined in the annals of the worldwide search towards a permanent peace." I received no answer. As I understand it, in 2015, there are currently 8 nations that have nuclear capability. Our multi-nation discussions ending in an agreement with Iran in June 2015, is an attempt by the 5 signatories (The U.N.'s Big Five) to *maintain a partial monopoly in nuclear military technology, but also to stop the spread of nuclear technology.* It is a worthwhile goal that has to be tried.

On August 2nd 2015, the TV program *Sixty Minutes* on CBS, detailed the status of the current, highly-secret, space military technology. The United States is very active but it is China that is presented as the leader and as an ominous threat to the rest of the world. I assume that the U.S. arms industry has long ago cranked up their massive, fearinduced, sales-driven rhetoric against our new nemesis China. Now is the time for Good Will and preventative negotiation.

Politics by Assassination: JFK, MLK, RFK

The American public was wrenched by three political assassinations between 1963 and 1968. Believing in political progress by the ballot box, it came as a major shock to suddenly have political calculations dictated by bullets. Within a five-year period, John Fitzgerald Kennedy (JFK), Robert Francis Kennedy (RFK), and Martin Luther King, (MLK), three of America's most progressive personalities, were abruptly removed from political consideration by guns. Other reasons were mooted, but all three could have been directly related to their individual stands on the Vietnam War.

My nebulous hopes for a progressive America were shattered. In my life time they were the only three public figures for whom I literally shed tears. Each of them, in their own way had captured my admiration, trust and love. I was shattered. Disillusionment spiked Big-Time! Making a country-changing move; coming from a more placid society; bringing moderately progressive opinions; nursing an incipient Podiatry practice; I found my American citizenship aspirations were considerably dampened by my developing disillusionment. Who says that a bullet doesn't affect politics? The United States would be a different country today if even one of the three survived his assassin.

It is easy in our comfortable, hazy memories to *THINK that we remember,* that the assassinations were all solved and that justice prevailed. After all, after many contending conspiracy theories, Lee Harvey Oswald remains the officially identified lone gunman who killed JFK, and Jack Ruby killed him within forty-eight hours. Had justice prevailed? Had Jack Ruby's vigilante justice conveniently removed Oswald, our key to ever knowing the truth? Palestinian Sirhan Sirhan, said to have a visceral hatred of Presidential-aspirant Robert F. Kennedy's support of Israel, was widely seen via TV, to have been the only *apparent* assassin of RFK, and he remains in prison to this day. Did justice prevail? James Earl Ray was *found guilty* of the criminal assassination of Martin Luther King and died in prison many years later. But, how about the 'King-family' civil trial results, 32 years later?

Assassination of President Jack Fitzgerald Kennedy.

Samuel Eliot Morison, *Oxford American History,* "With the death of John Fitzgerald Kennedy something seemed to die in each one of us. Yet the memory of that bright, vivid personality, that great gentleman who's every act and appearance, appealed to our pride and gave us fresh confidence in ourselves and our country will live in us for a long, long time."

About 11 Am, Nov 22nd 1963, I was on my day of house calls in the cities of Lawndale and Hermosa Beach, California, when a scream came from the car radio: "President Kennedy has been shot." Unbelievable!

Reaction 1: An elderly white lady in a modest, clean home gave the expected response, crying, "What is happening to the United States? I am a Republican and disliked President Kennedy, but who would do this? This is a disaster for our country!"

Reaction 2: The unexpected response came from a 50-year-old, barefoot, unemployed, white, Arkansas-born male, living with his elderly mother in a junk-laden patio of a modest house, "What other way could you get rid of the son of a bitch?" I guessed this was a prejudiced response to the Kennedy support for the black freedom movement.

My brother Frank was in a political caucus, in the legislature in Regina Saskatchewan Canada, and he said the meeting ended abruptly, with he and several members shedding tears. JFK had been internationally loved. Except for our own anguish, I remember mainly the suffering of those who were interviewed on TV that day.

The new president, Lyndon B. Johnson was faced with the history of the assassination of President Abraham Lincoln. Author Jim Bishop in *The Day Lincoln was shot* said, "The story of the assassination, in time, became so interlarded with fiction that the principal assassin, J. Booth, became a minor character. After years of reading and making notes, I found that I had as many as four versions each at variance with the others - of what happened in any one hour." President LBJ's quandary was instantaneous. To soothe the country, and the world, a suspicion-free investigation must begin immediately.

In the Kennedy assassination, the deluge of conspiratorial commentary immediately spread world-wide. Several investigations were mounted. Several suggested assassins were mooted. Immediate suspicions were: Was it the Soviets? Was it the Cubans? Was it the Mafia? Was it an anti-Roman Catholic movement? Was it the vociferous elements of the Republican party who detested JFK? Some people even suspected Vice President L. B. Johnson, who now became President! The killing of Lee Harvey Oswald by Jack Ruby (Rubinstein), and his own subsequent death (said to be of cancer) took away intriguing possible lines of inquiry, and increased conspiracy suspicions.

The 718-page *Report of the Warren Commission on the Assassination of President Kennedy* was intended to be comprehensive. It took over 10 months for the 7 "distinguished public citizen-members" commission, and their staff of 26, to compile and print it. LA Times, Oct 6th 1964, "The FBI conducted 25,000 interviews the FBI submitted 2300 reports; the Secret Service conducted over 1500 interviews." It was not the only investigation. Harrison E. Salisbury in the introduction to the

Warren Report wrote, "The case has attracted dozens of independent investigators of varying degrees of competence."

There was considerable distrust of the *Warren Report,* as itself being a "rushed, potentially untrue investigation, designed to allay the concerns of the country and the world." Because of universal, concerned expectancy, the Administration wanted the *Report* to be disseminated as soon as possible. With a staff of 150, working around the clock, Bantam Books had published the first printing only 80 hours after the release of the *Report.* The editor wrote in the preface, "Since President Johnson thought that it was of vital importance that the whole truth about President Kennedy's death be given to the world as quickly as possible, special arrangements were made to airlift the books all over the world. Thus, the Warren Commission Report in this edition will be read in London, Paris, Tokyo, Melbourne and other cities throughout the world almost as soon as it appeared in Los Angeles."

It was made available from the Supt. of Documents, Government Printing Office, Washington DC, - the cost, $2.25 soft cover and $3.25 cloth cover. In my case it was hard back, and free, but from the *History Book Club,* and only with purchase of the following month special. You didn't have to read the book just the first two sentences. *"The assassination of President Kennedy was the work of one man, Lee Harvey Oswald. There was no conspiracy, foreign or domestic."* The administration's goal was accomplished, though it never seemed to lessen the public's distrust. My trusting, non-conspiracy oriented mind, accepted the simplistic report as probably true. I still think so, though I will explain after the account of the MLK assassination, why I still have abundant reason to wonder.

Assassination of Dr. Martin Luther King Jr.

April 4th 1968 - The FBI very quickly identified James Earl Ray as a prime suspect in the death of MLK; he was located and imprisoned; he confessed; retracted his confession 3 days later; tried for over 3 decades to have a trial so he could prove his innocence; and died in prison 31 years later. Did justice prevail? *OR* - did justice prevail over three decades after his death, when, *LA Times,* Dec 8th, 1999, reported that a Memphis jury, hearing a civil suit decided that King was a victim, not of a lone racist gunman but of a vast conspiracy? That dramatic event needs relating.

Martin Luther King had a strong premonition that he was going to be killed, years before it happened. Vituperative attacks by: -some parts of the media; -some portions of the clergy (the white fundamentalists); -some of the "establishment" (especially J. Edgar Hoover and FBI); - and the traditionally prejudiced whites. After the assassination of JFK, he told Coretta, his wife, "That is what is going to happen to me also. I keep telling you this is a sick society."

Tavis Smiley in, *Death of a King.* His plane to Memphis on April 3rd had been delayed because of a bomb threat. Addressing that, in his last speech on April 4th he said, "But it (a threat) doesn't bother me now because I've been to the mountain top. And I don't mind. Like anybody, I would like to live a long life. Longevity has its place. But I'm not concerned about that now. I just want to do God's will. And he has allowed me to go to the mountaintop. And I've looked over. And, I've seen the 'promised land'. I may not get there with you." Prescient remarks! "But I want you to know tonight that we, as a people, will get to the 'promised land'! And I am so happy tonight. I'm not worried about anything. I'm not fearing any man! Mine eyes have seen the glory of the coming of the Lord!"

Robert F. Kennedy was flying to Indianapolis when told of MLK's death. The Indianapolis Chief of Police advised RFK not to speak of the news as it was dangerous, and could cause a riot (riots were already starting in many places) and the Chief couldn't provide protection. (RFK's own assassination would come within two months). He disregarded the Chief. He acknowledged to the audience that many would be filled with anger. "For those of you who are black and are tempted to be filled with hatred and mistrust of such an act against all white people. I would only say that I can feel in my own heart the same kind of feeling. I had a member of my own family killed, but he was killed by a white man." RFK went on to say that the country needs and wants only unity between black and white and asked the audience, to "pray for the King family and the country." "The speech was credited, in part, with preventing post-assassination rioting in Indianapolis where it was given, though there were riots in many other parts of the country. It is widely considered one of the greatest speeches in American history."

The single bullet that killed Martin Luther King while he stood on the balcony of the Lorraine Motel in Memphis Tennessee May 4th 1967, came from the bathroom of an apartment about 300 feet away.

The group of witnesses with King, saw that fact, but did not see the assassin.

James Earl Ray, who from prison, in 1992, wrote the book *Who Killed Martin Luther King,* naturally presents his own explanation of events, of which I would normally be wary. However, (related later in this account), as much of his point of view was validated by the 1999, "King Family" civil trial, I will use his book to help give a simple timeline account.

Ray referred to himself as a, "2-bit career criminal," which appears accurate, as he had an early record of robbery, burglary, violence, and jail time in Leavenworth, etc. The concept for his actual innocence is strengthened by the fact that his petty criminal background presented the ideal personality needed for someone from a higher echelon of crime endeavor, who wished to use him to be the fall guy on a *big* job, the MLK assassination.

In 1967 my wife Peggy, my son Mike, and I attended the Montreal 'EXPO', celebrating Canada's 100 years of independence. Crooks are said to migrate to events where major crowds congregate so maybe that is why "Raoul," the recruiter for that *big* job entered Ray's life when they met in a bar in Montreal during EXPO They soon found themselves to be kindred spirits in crime, and so for the next 9 months they successfully shared in some gun running and drug smuggling at both the Windsor/Detroit border point, and at Laredo, Mexico. They had two cars, but Raoul always did the planning (what job, location, time, etc.).

In the last few days before the assassination, several actions by Raoul appear to indicate that he was preparing for the murder. At 3 PM on April 4th 1968 Raoul told Ray that he had arranged to "meet some gun runners" (the reality was assassination planning not guns), at Jim's Grill in Memphis, Tennessee (across the street from the Loraine Motel - the assassination site). Raoul suggested that Ray rent an apartment upstairs which he did. Thus, after the assassination, the apartment contained incriminating, fingerprint-laden items, including a rifle. As it appears from this account that Raoul intended to be the actual assassin, he didn't really care if Ray was there or not, as long as the finger prints etc. indicated that Ray was there.

Paraphrase. "Ray went out for tire repair and as he was returning to Jim's Grill he saw a police car parked nearby. With his crime record, Ray instinctively turned away; heard on the car radio that MLK had been killed; drove to Atlanta; took a bus to Toronto; detailed in the book how he was able to get a bogus Canadian passport by May 2nd; flew to Lisbon, Portugal on May 6th; flew to London on May 16th; and on June 8th 1968, trying to make connections to go to Nigeria, Africa he went to Heathrow airport, where, on presentation of his bogus passport he was taken into custody. That was the day of the funeral of Robert J. Kennedy who had been assassinated on June 5th.

Back on April 19th, the FBI had announced that they had evidence that James Earl Ray was the assassin, mainly through a statement by Charles Q. Stephens, who lived in the adjacent apartment and said that he had seen Ray leaving the murder scene. However, Grace Walden Stephens, his wife contradicted him. Attorney Mark Lane in his preface to Ray's book said, "According to Mrs. Stephens on April 4th 1968, her husband was drunk. He pounded on the locked bathroom door to no avail (where the gunman was), and stumbled downstairs to urinate in the bushes behind the rooming house. Then she heard a shot, and almost immediately after that she saw the killer as he walked with a package in his hand, past her door." She said Charles returned completely unaware of any happenings.

Lane continues, "When photographs of James Earl Ray were shown to her she unequivocally stated that he was not the man who had emerged from the bathroom just after the shot was fired. She was threatened by FBI agents and local police and told to cooperate. She was offered a substantial, "reward" if she would identify Ray. She said she would be, "glad to cooperate, and, if they ever caught the right man she would readily identify him."

"In violation of the laws of Tennessee Mrs. Stephens was surreptitiously sent to a mental institution. She had never before been to such an institution, and had no history of mental illness. She was illegally incarcerated there for ten years until I (Mark Lane) was able to organize a public campaign to seek her freedom. The campaign included active participation from black and white religious leaders in Memphis, led by Reverend James Lawson, a close friend and colleague of MLK. That movement, together with motions filed in court, secured her transfer to a half-way house in Memphis. From there, at her request, I spirited her out of that city to Los Angeles, where she resided with my family. I returned to Memphis and challenged authorities to take action against me they declined." However, offering $100,000 reward, they had accepted the testimony of husband Charles Q. Stephens.

Ray said in his book that his defense was to be financed by William Bradford Huie, a writer, who would provide whatever "publicity, "the lawyer, Arthur Hanes Sr., or Ray, wanted, in return for having a legal contract stating that he be the sole author of a final book on the trial. One clause of that agreement affected the unrestricted ability of Hanes to represent Ray, by requiring that Hanes could not allow Ray to be cross-examined when on trial, because, that would put Ray's story into the public domain of the media, and consequently depreciate the "news value" of his later book.

The ballistics test from Ray's rifle would have been conclusive evidence but, "The FBI decided not to conduct a ballistics test on the rifle claiming that the fatal bullet was misshapen." Photos make it appear that this could be true. However, some experts say there should still have been sufficient identifiable features to be able to do so.

Jesse Jackson, Preface, *Who Killed Martin Luther King: 1992,* "Over a decade ago Congressman Louis Stokes (D. Ohio) chaired the House Select Committee in Assassinations, which investigated the death of MLK Jr. In its report which was released in 1979, the committee concluded that James Earl Ray fired the shot that killed Dr. King. It should be noted that its conclusions were not based on ballistic evidence since the rifle allegedly used in the shooting was not test-fired. However, on the basis of circumstantial evidence available to it, the Committee also concluded that there was a likelihood that the assassination of Dr. King was the result of a conspiracy." Note that that was the Committee opinion.

However, Jesse Jackson said in the foreword to *Who killed Martin Luther King?,* "I have never ruled out the government's direct involvement because there were many in the government, J. Edgar Hoover among them, who had an intense, visceral and deep hatred and fear of Dr. King."

LA Times, August 30th 1997, Judge Joseph D. Brown, requesting another attempt at ballistics tests was overruled by a Tennessee appeals court which said: "A judge is a fair and impartial adjudicator, not an investigator," and that they were, "disturbed by the trial judge's handling of these procedures." I'm obviously unable to question this ruling but the same disturbing thought arises: If someone wanted to cover up a conspiracy and maintain Ray as the sole assassin, it would be in their interest *NOT* to allow further testing of the bullet. Ray's lawyers in their brief to the appeals court said, "What the local district attorney might fear is the fact that ultimate testing might eliminate the alleged murder weapon as the weapon that killed Dr. Martin Luther King Jr." Ray's account of the reason he pled guilty, was that Percy Forman, the public defender, recommended that he should do so because:

1. Life magazine and Reader's Digest had already found him guilty.
2. If he went to trial, the court clerk would steer the jury to angry blacks.
3. Charles Q. Stephens, the drunk would get his $100,000, even though his wife said he wasn't in the building.
4. Most importantly, because he (Ray), *would not* be given the death penalty if he pled guilty.

So he pled guilty, though it appears that Ray realized after a short time, that he had a good chance of proving the "conspiracy." So he recanted his confession three days later and spent the rest of his life, unsuccessfully, trying to secure the trial he never had. *Without a trial,* and regardless of recanting his confession, he was found guilty and was given a 99-year sentence.

James Earl Ray died in prison, April 23rd 1998. The next day, the LA Times, April 24th 1998, editorialized. Headline: *Open The Files On King Killing.* "The federal committee concluded that Ray was the killer but he might have received help from others. The records of that investigation have been sealed by Congress until the year 2029, ostensibly to protect the innocent from possible defamation. But is there no way to protect them while also giving Americans the facts they deserve to know? The slaying was not only a crime but a key event in the civil rights movement, and American history. Why wait so long? The secrecy only compounds speculation."

A year and a half after the death of James Earl Ray the *LA Times,* December 9th 1999 reported that, "More than three decades after the Rev. Martin Luther King was assassinated, a Memphis jury hearing a lawsuit brought by his wife and children, found Wednesday that King was the victim not of a lone racist gunman but of a vast conspiracy." So there you have it! *Conspiracy!* "The jury awarded the King family, which sought only a token sum, $100 wrongful death suit, against Loyd Jowers, the ailing former owner of a Memphis restaurant (Jim's Grill), who six years ago, claimed he hired King's assassin as a favor to a Mafia friend. He never named the accused shooter." From him they could have found out who "Raoul" was. In 2029 we may find they did.

Loyd Jowers was said to have got late-life religious concerns about his after-life celestial status, and, desiring to improve his odds with the future divine court, he felt a marked urge to confess to the temporal authorities about all that he knew. The King family, and attorney William F. Pepper, took the opportunity to sue him, and used his testimony, to demonstrate that there was a conspiracy by the federal government in the assassination of MLK. Imagine the same lawsuit *directly* against the federal government. Financially impossible! But the point was made by using Jowers.

The Federal government must have been very apprehensive about what the trial would divulge. They placed restrictions on who could be in the court room, on the media, and on national magazine and newspaper coverage. By limiting trial access and muzzling the media, what should have been a transparent, "public" trial, became a shadowy trial shrouded by unanswered questions. I think their efforts were successful with me. I have subscribed to a daily newspaper my entire life. The *Los Angeles Times* is a superb newspaper and would not miss anything so newsworthy. I could certainly have been inattentive, and my present memory is certainly less than perfect. However, public discussion was muted, or limited by agreement. So my end result is that I remember only my one clipping regarding the trial. The trial was against Jowers, but the federal government understood clearly *that it was also* "on trial." I am now curious about the pre-tria*l* coverage to which I was exposed. The record seems to indicate there was little or none. My uncertain memory doesn't tell me that there was any, either.

Who Killed Martin Luther King? April 7th 2002, prosecuting attorney, William F. Pepper: "So far as we are concerned the truth about the assassination was fully revealed in court, under oath, over a month long trial in late 1999 in Memphis. *In King v. Jowers, et al, some 70 witnesses completely set out the details and the range of the conspiracy which was coordinated by the U.S. Government with the assistance of state and local officials and on the site implementation of local organized crime representatives."* All in one sentence!

April 7th, 2002-William F. Pepper (to a friend), "I am disappointed, but not surprised, that one as knowledgeable as yourself does not appear to be aware of the details of the trial. It was blacked out by all of the mainstream - network and cable - media. Court TV promised to cover it live, but their team was ordered to stay in the hallway outside of the courtroom and only enter when Mrs. King or members of her family took the stand. My final book on the case is finished and it includes a critical analysis of the AG's investigation and all of the government's publicists over the 34-year history of the case." - "Even the *New York Times,* in a front page piece (never again mentioned by their local reporter), acknowledged that members of the jury were quoted as saying that the evidence never before seen or heard or tested under oath was overwhelming."

Author, activist and Christian theologian, Jim Douglass, who attended the trial, commented in the *Fellowship of Reconciliation Magazine,* "The historic trial was so ignored by the media that apart from the courtroom participants, I was the only person who attended it from beginning to end. What I experienced in that courtroom ranged from inspiration at the courage of the Kings, their lawyer-investigator William F. Pepper and the witnesses, to amazement at the governments plot to kill Dr. King. The seriousness with which intelligence agencies planned the murder of Martin Luther King Jr. speaks eloquently of the threat of King and nonviolence represented to the powers that be in the spring of 1968."

Jesse Jackson, 1992, Foreword, *Who killed Martin Luther King?,* "Dr. King was projected by Director Hoover as a threat to our national security. Mr. Hoover felt that Dr. King threatened the interests of the military-industrial complex and the ideology and mentality of the Cold War."

April 7th 2002, William F. Pepper, "Your analysis is correct. This type of claim distracts us from the overall coordinating role of Government and powerful economic interests which decided that

MLK had to be removed from the scene, because of his increasingly effective opposition to the war, and, perhaps, more significantly, his commitment to bring 500,000 of the wretched of America to Washington, not to march but to encamp and daily visit their elected representatives to demand the restoration of the social welfare/ health and educational programs which had been severely, even terminally, cut in deference to the military budgetary increases. The army knew that their demands would not be met; realized that the massive assemblage would likely become enraged; and emerge as a revolutionary force in the nations' capitol the very belly of the beast and were fully aware that they did not have the troops available to put down the rebellion. - Remember, at the time, General Westmorland wanted another 200,000 (soldiers) for Vietnam, and those were also not available."

An admission: "In 1993, *The Memphis Commercial Appeal* reported that the military had frequently spied on King and on the day of his death an eight-man team of Army Green Berets was in town. The army defended *(not denied)* it's spying on King saying that the civil protests of the era had grown too numerous for the FBI to handle."

Mark Lane, "Hence, MLK had to be stopped. He would never be allowed to bring that alienated mass to Washington. A logistics officer in charge of troop movements and truck allocations at Fort Meade passed word to me that on the morning of the assassination he was put on alert, and told to bring the National Guard and other troops to Washington that afternoon. Martin Luther King was shot at 6.01 PM. The troops were already on the move in anticipation of the rioting which was certain to break out when the news reached the capitol." From that statement it is clear that someone in Washington knew the assassination was to come later in the day, and was preparing the military to be ready.

Statement by Mrs. Martin Luther King Jr (Coretta): "There is abundant evidence of a major high level conspiracy in the assassination of my husband, Martin Luther King Jr. And the civil court's unanimous verdict has validated our belief. I wholeheartedly applaud the verdict of the jury and I feel that justice has been well served in their deliberations. This verdict is not only a great victory for my family, but a great victory for America. It is a great victory for truth itself. It is important to know that this was a SWIFT verdict, delivered after about an hour of jury deliberation." "The jury was clearly convinced by the extensive evidence that was presented during the trial that, in addition to Mr. Jowers, the conspiracy of the Mafia, local, state, and federal government agencies were deeply involved in the assassination of my husband. The jury also affirmed overwhelming evidence that identified someone else, not James Earl Ray, as the shooter, and that Mr. Ray was set up to take the blame."

Wikipedia Following the King family trial, "Responding to a reporter's comment that the conspirators were nameless, Dexter King (son of MLK) said, 'No, he (Mr. Loyd Jowers) named the shooter.' The shooter was Memphis police officer Lt. Earl Clark who he named as the killer. Once again, beyond that, you had credible witnesses that named members of a Special Forces team, who didn't have to act because the contract killer succeeded, with plausible denial, a Mafia contracted killer." So, it appears that the mysterious Raoul was possibly Earl Clark. And that James Earl Ray was innocent! And, that justice did *NOT* prevail!

Obviously the establishment had to respond to the verdict. *LA Times, June* 10th 2000. "After 18 months, a Justice Department investigation rejected allegations that conspirators aided or framed James Earl Ray in the 1968 assassination of civil rights leader Martin Luther King Jr. It recommended against further investigation."

In his foreword to *Who killed Martin Luther King?* Rev. Jesse Jackson speaks of the threat that MLK presented to both J. Edgar Hoover the FBI director; to President Johnson and to the military-industrial complex. Being intimately involved in my own small Pacific Unitarian Church corner of opposition to the Vietnam War, it was automatic to listen for those public voices who commented in the daily news. We were aware that the eloquence and obvious integrity of MLK was quickly making its mark. He wrote his four books in nine years and I acquired each one as they were published. The first three were philosophical and religious, including description of his belief and practice of non-violent protest etc. Dr. King had not yet taken major opposition to the Vietnam War.

In 1967, in *Where Do We Go From Here?,* he really started to criticize the inadequacies of the American governmental and social institutions and the administration and its handling of the Vietnam War. The following quotations illustrate his eloquent command of the language; the importance of his observations and his distress at the lack of morality in the U.S. military stance in Vietnam. In my view this book alone could be viewed with fear by the administration, and that is why a few quotations follow. It gives strength to the conspiracy discussion only because of its eloquence and the forcefulness of its arguments. The administration could easily visualize individuals and groups, who, using these quotations, would develop organized defiance.

Two quotations from *Where Do We Go From Here?:* "There were twice as many negroes as whites in combat in Vietnam at the beginning of 1967, and twice as many negro soldiers died in action (20.6%) in proportion to their numbers in the population."

"The Black Power advocates are disenchanted with the inconsistencies in the military posture of our government. Over the last decade they have seen Americans applauding non-violence whenever the Negroes have practiced it. They have watched it being praised in the sit-in movements of 1960, the Freedom rides of 1961, in the Albany movement of 1962, in the Birmingham movement of 1963 and in the Selma movement of 1965. But then these same black young men and women have watched as America sends black young men to burn Vietnamese with napalm, to slaughter men, women and children, and, they wonder what kind of a nation it is that applauds non-violence whenever Negroes face white people in the streets of United States but then applauds violence and burning and death when those same Negroes are sent to the field of Vietnam."

Imagine the impact of these eloquent words on the jobless, the hopeless, and the hungry: "All of this represents disappointment lifted to astronomical proportions. It is disappointment with timid white moderates who feel that they can set the timetable for the Negro's freedom. It is the disappointment with a federal administration that seems to be more concerned about winning an ill-considered war in Vietnam than about winning the war against poverty here at home. It is the disappointment with white legislators who pass laws on behalf of Negro rights that they never intend to implement. It is disappointment with the Christian church that it appears to be more white than Christian, and with many white clergymen who prefer to maintain silence behind the security of stained-glass windows. It is the disappointment with some Negro clergymen who are more concerned about the size of the wheel-base of their automobiles than about the quality of their service to the Negro community. It is disappointment with the Negro middle class who has sailed or struggled out of the muddy ponds into the relatively fresh flowing waters of the mainstream, and in the process have forgotten the stench of the backwaters where their brothers are still drowning."

"In the wasteland of war, the expenditure of resources knows no restraints; here our abundance is fully recognized and enthusiastically squandered."

"The Washington Post has calculated that we spend $332.000 for each enemy we kill. It challenges the imagination to contemplate what lives we could transform if we were to cease killing. The security we profess to seek in foreign adventures we will lose in our decaying cities. The bombs in Vietnam explode at home; they destroy the hopes and possibilities for a decent America."

How aptly phrased and how prophetically he described what has happened to our schools, national infrastructure etc. Look at our present-day gigantic national debt, the failing schools, the crumbling infrastructure, and citizen trust of government of *less* than 10%! What a wonderful nation this would now be if the wisdom of Dr. Martin Luther King had won the national dialogue of 1967!

Read carefully these quotations of MLK and consider that to J. Edgar Hoover, they sounded revolutionary. MLK was clearly advocating government change akin to democratic socialism, which to Hoover was identical to Communism. MLK was also challenging the strategic militaristic plans of the United States. MLK's foreign policy was to be as non-violent as his domestic policy. In the previous few years public respect for him, and for his opinions, had soared. To J. Edgar Hoover, he was an ENEMY.

MLK, "In the days ahead we must not consider it unpatriotic to raise certain basic questions about our national character. We must begin to ask "Why are there forty million poor people in a nation overflowing with such unbelievable affluence?" Why has our nation placed itself in being God's military agent on earth and intervened recklessly in Vietnam and the Dominican Republic? Why have we substituted the arrogant undertaking of policing the whole world for the high task of putting our own house in order?"

MLK, "All these questions remind us that there is a need for a radical restructuring of American society, for its very survival's sake. America must re-examine old presuppositions and release itself from many things that for centuries have been held sacred. For the evils of racism, militarism and poverty to die, a new set of values must be born. Our economy must become more person-centered than property and profit-centered. Our government must depend more on its moral power than on its military power."

MLK, "So when in this day I see the leaders of nations talking peace while preparing for war, I take fearful pause. When I see our country today intervening in what is basically a civil war, mutilating hundreds of thousands of children with napalm, burning villages and fields at random, painting the valleys of that small Asian country red with human blood, leaving broken bodies in countless ditches and sending home half-men mutilated mentally and physically; when I see the unwillingness of our government to create the atmosphere for a negotiated settlement of this awful conflict by halting bombing in the North and agreeing to talk unequivocally with the Vietcong and all of this in the name of pursuing the goal of peace, I tremble for our world."

MLK, "The stability of the large world house which is ours will involve a revolution of values to accompany the scientific and freedom revolutions engulfing the earth. We must rapidly begin the shift from a "thing" oriented society to a "person" oriented society. When machines and computers, profit motives and property rights, are considered more important than people, the giant triplets of racism, materialism and militarism are incapable of being conquered. A civilization can flounder as readily in the face of moral and spiritual bankruptcy as through financial bankruptcy."

Where, Do We Go From Here?, published one year earlier, had made it clear to President Johnson that, if the blacks listened to Dr. King, that he (LBJ) could not count on automatic, black, political support. Johnson's progressive, domestic *l*egislation, including Medicare and Medic-Aid, had great public approval, including black support. But, on the international stage, the Vietnam War had become his own personal, well-deserved, catastrophic millstone. Rising from his job as a Texas rural school teacher, to the Presidency of the nation, had taken finely-honed political instincts. As speaker of the House in earlier years, he had been known as a consummate, arm-twisting, marvel at getting legislation passed. But he was said to be apprehensive of Martin Luther King and that the new, militant MLK, was stirring a larger national Vietnam debate than he could handle. Though President Johnson had been battered into announcing on March 31, four days before MLKs assassination, that he was not going to run for re-election, martyred MLK was still a threat to the administration

The Assassination of Congressman Robert F. Kennedy

June 4th 1968. My entire night became sleepless when near midnight the TV brought the news that Robert Kennedy had been shot at the Los Angeles Ambassador Hotel. On the road to becoming the Democratic, Presidential nominee, he had just won the electoral vote-heavy, California presidential primary election. He was transferred to the Hospital of the Good Samaritan where several hours of surgery took place before he died. The shooting took place with television, radio, and reporter coverage and it was very evident that the assassin was Sirhan Sirhan, but there always remained a question as to whether there was a second gunman. Sirhan Sirhan's gun, had a capacity of eight bullets and they had all been used. As recently as 2007, an analysis of some of the audio of that night, stated that there were thirteen shots and that two shots were too close together to have been possible from one gun. There was a report of a girl "in a polka-dotted skirt running from the hotel saying, "We got the one in Dallas and now this bastard." Truth? Fabrication? Distortion?

The combination of Sirhan's diaries where he stated he wanted to kill RFK; that he hated RFK because of his support for Israel; and the photographic evidence made the trial a "slam-dunk" for the prosecution of Sirhan Sirhan, who has now spent over 46 years in prison. But conspiratorial theories remain.

It had been thought that RFK would win the majority of the Democratic presidential primary voters over his rival Hubert Humphrey, but with Bob Kennedy gone, Humphrey won the primary and then lost the popular vote in the general election to Richard Nixon 43.7% to 44.4%; and lost in that imprecise relic of the past the electoral vote, by 191 delegates to Nixon's 301. Such different margins alone, demonstrate the absurdity of the electoral system. Robert Kennedy might still have lost the election but could so easily have won. Politics by assassination!

The conspiracy involvement in the assassination of Martin Luther King, having been legally established, it should have become mandatory to review the assassinations of the Kennedy brothers. Investigations of both could prove revealing. Consider the audio evidence of a second gunman in the RFK assassination. Someone was involved in changing the route of the election entourage so that it passed through the kitchen. Might that be *the-same-somebody* who first found, and recruited, a genuine RFK-hater, Sirhan Sirhan? And Sirhan Sirhan could be even living his life in jail, considering himself as being the sole planner of the assassination, when someone may have carefully facilitated his opportunity. Unlike Ray's imprisonment,

Sirhan's has had minimal media attention. I wonder how much psychological, psychiatric, and just plain historical debriefing he has received over the years. Certainly, in the light of the conspiratorial background uncovered in the MLK case, there should have, by now, been a more careful review of all of the details in the RFK case.

It *is now established* by the civil King-family trial *that there was a United States government conspiracy in Martin Luther King's death*; it is now established that President Jack Kennedy planned the withdrawal of U.S. troops from Vietnam by 1965; Robert F. Kennedy had spoken out passionately against the Vietnam War and had just won the California primary in his race for the Democratic presidential candidacy which, to me, all suggests the possibility that the same conspirators of the MLK assassination 2 months earlier, could have been on the loose again? It seems that only "us lefties" cried at all these funerals! Somehow there should be someone who still has this combined affair on the front burner of investigation. I hope so! I wish I could still be around when the files to the King trial are released in 2029! It has become a reasonable bet that the guilty verdict of James Earl Ray will be declared a miscarriage of justice. Also that J. Edgar Hoover will be found to have been involved in at least MLKs death.

I do not recall a specific moment, or year, at which time I decided I would defer seeking American citizenship. I do remember intensively re-considering it during this three-assassination period. President L. B. Johnson, the effective, progressive president in social and domestic affairs, was waging an immoral, illegal, cruel war in Vietnam. The USA no longer appeared to be a democracy that was keeping their citizenry contented. The massive, nation-wide, anti-war demonstrations were confrontational, angry, violent, at times deadly, and routinely suppressed by the police. The desperate, agonizing black riots raging in big cities, revealed the shallow façade of American democracy. The moral, articulate beacons of hope (JFK, MLK and RFK) were being assassinated by what *MUST* be right wing political forces! I was beginning to consider conspiracy. To me, Canada's brand of democracy, even with its deficiencies, was much more free, than the United States; was more tranquil; less confrontational; more cooperative and more pleasant for both observer and participant.

Canada's foreign policy was, and is, independent. It has only occasionally said "Me too" to a U.S. venture. I continued to find myself opposing most of the United States international policy decisions, most especially where it involved war. I was bothered by the necessity of pledging allegiance to the United States, when much of the time I would prefer to be objecting to U.S. foreign policy decisions. So the decision kept being deferred until - one day the deferral became the decision. So it is to this day!

The Vietnam War

"If America's soul becomes totally poisoned, part of the autopsy must read *Vietnam*," wrote Dr. Martin Luther King in, *Where Do We Go From Here?*

"We were wrong, terribly wrong. We owe it to future generations to explain why," said Robert S. McNamara, former secretary of Defense in 1996, in *In Retrospect.* Describing the current contemporary military scene in 1962 (my fourth year in the U.S. and the approximate beginning of the Vietnam War), Neil Sheehan in *A Bright Shining Lie* describes, "- the American largest empire in history United States had 850,000 military men and civilian officials serving overseas in 106 countries." With the added, "Sixth Fleet, the listening posts along the Soviet frontier in Turkey and Iran, the diplomats from the State Dept., the agents from the CIA, and other officials and their wives and families, the USA had 1.4 million overseas." To me, the USA qualified as a militarist nation.

Written for the Iraq War, but applicable to the Vietnam War is the following quote. Walter Laqueur, in a book review in the *LA Times* June 13th 2003 speaking of President G. W. Bush and his neo-con advisors wrote, "Their weakness was also their belief in American particularism that their country stood for certain superior principles and that this gave them the right, if need be, to act unilaterally in foreign affairs." The U.S. received very little help from other nations for the Vietnam War or the Iraq War.

This entire *Perspective* narrative/historical commentary is dedicated to reviewing my war concerns of those years. The daily chronicle of bloody news from the obviously immoral Vietnam War had soon become the abortive force in my plans for American citizenship. As such, I must include it in this account. And as such, I must include selected material from my resulting unpublished manuscript *American Citizenship Reconsidered.*

In 1989 Professor Walter Capps of the University of California in Santa Barbara appeared on the, "60 Minutes" program on CBS. He described the course on The Vietnam War which he said he was teaching to young students who (only 16 years post-war) had no memory of the war. So, to aid him, I donated to the University of California in Santa Barbara, what remained of my books, and all of my original letters regarding the Vietnam War. I shall quote in limited detail from my *American Citizenship Reconsidered,* an unpublished manuscript, which I donated in 1997, to The University of California in Santa Barbara. There has been minimal change in my perspective since 1997, so there should be very little need for additional commentary in this mini-history.

We now know that President Jack Kennedy was planning to bring the U.S. military home from Vietnam by 1964-5. *The Baltimore Sun* on Dec 23rd 1997 headlined that declassified documents indicated he had "a plan to bring the troops home in 1965." In an interview on CNN on Nov 22nd, 2013, the 50th anniversary of his assassination, his nephew Robert F. Kennedy said, "President Kennedy had already made official plans to withdraw all American troops from Vietnam by the end of 1965." However, he was assassinated soon after my fifth U.S. residential year point, and, President L.B. Johnson, after promising "no American boots on the ground in Asia," promptly upped the U.S. military presence in Vietnam, from Kennedy's 15,000 advisors, to a July 1965 figure of around 175,000. It appears President Kennedy's assassination, followed by President L. B. Johnson's decisions, were what led to most of the deaths of 57,000 American soldiers. LBJ's towering progressive home legislation (Medicare, Medicaid) was unfortunately blighted by his abysmal Vietnam War decisions.

From my *American Citizenship Reconsidered,* "Not being an American citizen, I felt reluctant to join in physical opposition to what I viewed as an American political problem. However, as the human cost grew, the immoral dimensions of the conflict became dominant, and the political objectives became transparently false. I finally realized that personal moral conviction outweighed any other considerations."

"The theme of morality, or the lack of it, will pervade this entire account, including my letters to the Presidents. It became obvious that the U.S. administrations' arguments and reasons for being in Vietnam were so obviously erroneous that the loss of life and resources on both sides could not be justified." Several years later, in 1971, the *Pentagon Papers* released by Daniel Ellsburg, confirmed our entire anti-war argument, and in late 1995 Secretary of Defense Robert McNamara, in his book *Retrospect* acknowledged that immorality."

"It is logical that in any professional practice one shouldn't discuss politics, religion or their peripheral issues. I knew it! I believed it! But the Vietnam War frequently forced me to override the rule. Most important was the fact that doing in "real time" what was the moral thing, brought with it peace of mind and an ease in living with oneself later. I progressed through concern, through preoccupation, to passionate fixation in opposition to the war. I placed reading materials such as *Ramparts Magazine, the I. F. Stone news-letter, the Bulletin of the Atomic Scientists Magazine, Commentary magazine, and the Bulletin of the Committee of Responsibility (*MD's medical war reports) in the reception room. They were all in opposition to the war. The best was a superb, small, concise booklet issued by the American Friends Service Committee, authored by Margaret Hoffman and titled *Vietnam Viewpoints.* I underlined in red all the historical details about Vietnam, the former French experience there, the U.S. position there - facts that the public were not being told. These frequently sparked comment, a lot of questioning, a moderate amount of which was antagonistic."

My *American Citizenship Reconsidered,* "I had some pre-war concerns that intensified my Vietnam War anxieties. With minimal elaboration, they were:

1. "A humanity-based morality instilled by my parents."
2. "My five-year WWII exposure to the "wastefulness of human life and material resources."
3. My visceral dislike of, "Winston Churchill's 1946 Fulton Missouri speech coining the disillusioning term *Iron Curtain.* It seemed brutally dismissive of the millions of Russian lives lost when fighting the Nazis as our ally of the previous year. The words were doubtless true, as a respected world authority he seemed to be setting the stage for later divisive political discourse, or war.
4. "My repugnance of UNAC and Senator Joe McCarthy."
5. "I.F. Stone in his book, *The Hidden History of the Korean War,* "High level U.S. Administration officials (thirteen names listed), giving opinions that the U.S. military in South Korea should be maintained even if peace came. General Van Fleet of the U.S. 8th Army said in December 1952, "Korea has been a blessing. There had to be a Korea here or somewhere else in the world". Startling! General Eisenhower said at the time (paraphrased), "speaking of peace in Korea will make the U.S. public less worried about the Communist threat in Europe." Sixty years later the U.S. still maintains over 30,000 servicemen in South Korea!
6. "James Forrestal, U.S. Secretary of Defense, predicted there would have to be over 40 years of increased military defense of the U.S. How did he calculate that?"
7. "President Eisenhower warned the U.S. of the "military-industrial complex." Colonel David Hackworth (America's most decorated soldier) in his book *About Face* wrote, "This

incestuous relationship has got to stop." He was speaking of the second-career types, the Colonels, Generals and other "Brass," who leave the military and go and work for the defense contractors in their second careers." *I would say that it is the expensive drain of tax-payer dollars and of natural resources that have gone into the military in the past 50 years that has left the U.S. with an immense multi-trillion-dollar deficit, a much deteriorated infrastructure, and a very distrusting electorate.* And as to the *lives lost* - speaking only of American servicemen: WWI --116,000 killed; WWII - 405,000; The Korean War - 54,000; The Vietnam War - 58,250." Also around 150,000 wounded.

8. "The threat of nuclear war and the deleterious effects of continued testing."
9. Disillusionment in the inefficiency of the United Nations.
10. The pervasive, intensive public concern over the Communist threat."
11. "A review of my reoccurring desire to move out of the U.S. again."

"The bucket of pre-Vietnamese War concerns, that I have described, could not help but influence my decisions including the one about citizenship. In July 1963, it was 5 years since we had arrived in California, which was the required time of residence before one could become a citizen. Decision time had arrived. My "declaration of intent," to become a U.S. citizen was dated Oct 1st 1959."

"It could be said that if I was politically conscious enough that I should have taken American citizenship and then fought for what I believed. However, pledging allegiance comes first and the voting and advocating of one's beliefs come later. Disregarding my personal reasons for being in the U.S., I had lived in 3 other countries long enough to know that there were good alternatives to living in the U.S. I know very well what I have missed by not becoming a citizen of the country in which I lived. The trade-off has been acceptable as my political integrity and my peace-of-mind have been maintained."

"A patient of mine told me about the "very active" Vietnam-War studies group in the Social Concerns Committee of the Pacific Unitarian Church in Palos Verdes. For that reason, I joined, recording my first check October 14th, 1964, just before the L. B. Johnson election and not thinking that it would be almost 9 years later before the agony of Vietnam would be over for the United States, and 11 years for the wrap-up of the Vietnamese Civil War."

"Attending the weekly committee meetings in the church was an exhilarating experience. The traditional Unitarian concern over the "here and now," rather than the "here-after," made their concern over the Vietnam War inevitable. The 10 to 12 committee members were an organized, articulate, dedicated, and active group. We delegated weekly projects, resulting in getting an abundance of study materials, books, the administration's 'White papers,' "Administration Position Statements," and Depts. of State and Defense "position papers." We printed leaflets, sent out mailings, attended protests, and most importantly, we exchanged information both historical and contemporary to answer our questions and to inform each other's views. Each evening there, I learned immeasurably more about South East Asia, about Vietnam, the past French involvement, and the current U.S. involvement, than I did in months of TV, radio, magazines, and newspapers. That was, of course, because we were getting comprehensive, balanced, and indepth information - not TV sound bites, or the administration's usual filtered information.

We gave regular cogent, synoptic reports to the Sunday congregation and to Reverend Al Hendricksen. It helped him to aim many Sunday sermons at the immorality of U.S. involvement in Vietnam. One memorable sermon was on the delusion that the U.S. exhibited when "judging other countries by their actions; not judging itself by its own actions, but instead by, "its own ideals." Thus, the U.S. government overlooked their own provocative or unjust actions, "because the administration said it's, "intentions were pure."

"There were an abundance of arguments against U.S. involvement in the Vietnam War and the reasons were historic, geographic, economic, military, political and social. But they were all secondary - to the *moral* one. You will find morality, or the lack of it, at the core of almost every letter I sent the Presidents. However, because the administration used a political argument as the basis for being there, many of my letters attempted to give the legal reasons why we shouldn't be there. I think the immorality of the U.S. position in Vietnam, is what made the anti-Vietnam War movement such a gut-level, passionate crusade."

"Many other governmental actions, inactions and scandals have increased the distrust of the U.S. citizenry in recent years. However, the assassination of President Kennedy in 1963 and the Vietnam War could be said to be the beginning of the increase in the belief that the U.S. government could not be believed. In 1995 Walter Cronkite quoted a 1964 poll, the question being asked: "Is the federal government run by big interests looking out for themselves? 64% said "No" and 36% said "Yes." In 1994 the same poll was taken. The answers were 81% "Yes" and 19% "No." A drop in government confidence of 45% in 30 years! A poll reported this week (early June, 2013) that only 10% now trust the government. You can't go much lower! Now 54% lower confidence level than 49 years ago!

"As the deaths of U.S. servicemen and the killing of Vietnamese non-combatants increased, the U.S. public distrust increased. My discontent was always tempered by not being a U.S. citizen. In reality, I probably didn't have a right to have any input on the war. I was an alien and felt like an alien, because I was being alienated by the actions of the U.S. government. U.S. citizenship seemed alien to me. Pledging allegiance to such a government seemed alien, and inconceivable to me. Many U.S. citizens felt similarly and gave up their citizenship to live in other countries."

"I felt angry because I was being placed in the uncertain, uncomfortable and difficult position of feeling morally that I must protest, but at the same time feeling that I didn't have a legal right to have any right to protest. I felt insecure because though I was a legal alien, I was none-the-less - an alien." Physically, I protested infrequently. I went to the Park Plaza hotel once, when President Nixon came to town. I went to the Los Angeles Sports Arena on one occasion when the keynote speaker was Dr. Benjamin Spock. "The Committee of Social Justice of the first Unitarian Church in Los Angeles pledged that for the duration of the war, they would hold a daily 12 Noon to 1PM "vigil" in front of the Federal Building in downtown Los Angeles. On a periodic basis, when my schedule allowed, I drove the 30 mile return trip to join them. We carried placards, marched the 4 blocks around the building, or stood on the sidewalk in front of the main door, engaging anyone who wished - in argument or agreement."

"About 1966, Florence Beaumont, a middle aged lady, in anti-Vietnam War protest, burned herself to death on the steps of the Federal Building in downtown Los Angeles. A few days later I attended the memorial service held on the same steps. In the crowd I saw my close friend, Dr. Sol Balkin and his wife Janelle. He later used my agonizing dilemma regarding citizenship, as an example of the disillusionment that many would-be citizens were undergoing. They were formerly Jewish, but through them, I subsequently, periodically attended the 1st Unitarian Church in LA." The church frequently had anti-Vietnam War speakers of national prominence, including Dr. Linus Pauling (Twice Nobel Prize winner), and Bishop James Pike of LA. It was during my time there that Nixon's ill-fated Vice-President, Spiro Agnew, referred to the war-protestors as "nattering nabobs of negativism;" as "pusillanimous pussy-footers;" and as "an effete corps of impudent snobs." Someone in the church had a quantity of 3-inch lapel buttons made up - one saying, "nattering negative nabob, and the other one "effete snob."

I decided "I could be most helpful, and hopefully most effective in information gathering and exchanging, and in letters of opposition and support. So that is where I placed my major effort."

"Many organizations voiced opposition to the war and I sent letters of support and/or small checks. I joined the ACLU (American

Civil Liberties Union), as they proved to be a real thorn in the side of the administration. Many U.S. administration actions skirted the Constitution, national laws and international laws, and the ACLU challenged the legal status of every shaky procedure, every statement, and every policy or position, that was being used in pursuit of the war. The United World Federalists voiced opposition to the war so I joined and acted as usher and "gofer" at an annual national convention that they held in Los Angeles on November 19th 1966. I was offered free admission because I was helping, but fearing my name would not be recorded as a member, I insisted on paying admission. Actor Paul Newman was featured. Standing at the entrance, I took the opportunity to shake hands with California Senator Alan Cranston, (author of *The Killing of the Peace* and former president of the *United World Federalists*)."

United World Federalists are now named *World Federalist Movement, Institute for Global Policy.* In their 2013 statement of aims they say the following:

- To work towards world federation" (government similar to U.S.).
- To define, and develop, the concept of world citizenship.
- To clarify world political issues. (Paraphrased).
- To implement, if possible, all majority decisions by its Congress.
- To support the current agencies of the United Nations. (paraphrased).
- The association, while supporting the efforts of the United Nations shall work to transform it by fundamental amendment into a world federation." These aims, of course, irritated the ultra-patriotic fundamentalist in every country. The individual who swore, "*my* country right or wrong," automatically rebelled.

I joined the "*Individuals, Against the* ***Crime of Silence,"*** which stated the following:

I have declared my name to the office of the Secretary General of the United Nations to be on record with the above declaration: A declaration to our fellow citizens of the United States.to the peoples of the world and to future generations:

1. We are appalled and angered by the conduct of our country in Vietnam.
2. In the name of liberty, we have unleashed the awesome arsenal of the greatest military power in the world upon a small agricultural nation, killing, burning and mutilating its people. In the name of peace, we are creating a desert. In the name of security, we are inviting world conflagration.
3. We, the signers of this declaration, believe this war to be immoral. We believe it to be illegal. We must oppose it.
4. At Nuremberg, after World War II, we tried, convicted and executed men for the serious crime of *OBEYING* their government, when that government demanded of them crimes against humanity. Millions more, who were not tried, were still guilty of the *crime of silence.*
5. We have a commitment to the laws and principles we carefully forged in the AMERICAN CONSTITUTION, at the NUREMBERG TRIALS, and in the UNITED NATIONS CHARTER. And our own deep democratic traditions and our dedication to the ideal of human decency among men demand that we speak out. We therefore wish to declare our names to the office of the Secretary General of the United Nations, both as permanent witness to our opposition to the war in Vietnam and as a demonstration that the conscience of America is not dead.

"Some other organizations that declared opposition to the war, that I joined were: *National Committee for a Sane Nuclear Policy ("SANE"); The Peace Action Council; The United Nations Association; National Conference for New Politics; and the "Peace and Freedom Party."*

"Those who approved the war, such as our California Senators, Tom Kuchel and former Hollywood actor George Murphy, got letters of argument and disapproval. Some peripheral organizations such as magazines, minority groups, and churches spoke out against the war, and I sent many letters of approval."

"The following is a list of checks that I sent because of some linkage to the Vietnam War; opposition to it; for printed information or argument regarding it." (My records of post 1970 had already been discarded). There are 68 names of individuals and organizations listed. Then there is a list of 57 names (mostly political figures) (followed by an addendum list of 44 names) - totaling 101 political figures, to whom I sent letters (without check) to approve or disapprove of their stand. Not included because of length. When I wrote this account in 1997, I added: "I remember, but have no record, of writing to journalist, Howard K. Smith, Eric Sevareid, and author, Felix Greene. I also wrote to actor, Robert Vaughn, approving his public disapproval of the war, but received no reply."

"In the early 1980s I gave about 18 books on Vietnam, to the Paramount, California Public Library. Along with them was a 3-book set on Chinese History, in each of which there were historical notes on Vietnamese relations. As there was no U.S. diplomatic relations with China, current information was murky, and there had been a great deal of political discussion as to what degree China supported Vietnam; China's concern for war on her border; and for a potential anti-Chinese political entity on her border. Our committee felt the need to explore that historical relationship."

"In 1987, the CBS program, "60 Minutes" had a segment on Professor Walter Capps of the University of California in Santa Barbara (UCSB), and the university course he was teaching about the Vietnam War. It was fourteen years after the United States had been defeated and had withdrawn from Vietnam, and Professor Capps had become aware that many of his students had misconceptions of the war because they had little recollection or understanding of what the Vietnam War was about."

"I suddenly realized that there could be some value in my Vietnam War letters, records etc. I contacted him, and eventually sent him the residual portion of written materials, government 'White Papers', books, etc. for him to use in his course. I planned on sending him photocopies of the carbon copies of my letters, but my photocopier was mal-functioning, and photocopies are not ideal for study purposes in any case, so I sent him the original letters of reply to my letters sent to the Presidents, Senators, etc. There could be a small treasure trove of the original signatures of some notables there. I still retain a readable, but poor, set of the photocopies. In his last communication in, July 1996, (before he died), he stated that "the materials will fit into a permanent research collection."

"I originally wrote letters spontaneously, kept no carbon copies, and turned my answers over to the Pacific Unitarian Study group. However, they urged me to keep a copy of my letters to compare with the answers, and to keep them as a record for follow-up, reference, and study. My first recorded letter to President Johnson (LBJ) was May 11th 1966, and my last recorded letter to President Richard Nixon was Feb. 23rd, 1973. In the total of 36 recorded letters (plus 4 known but not recorded) to them, the dominant theme was morality or the lack of it. To the 20 recorded letters to President Johnson I received 22 replies, indicating at least two letters which I failed to record. In contrast to the LBJ acknowledgements to apparently every letter, there were only two replies to 15 recorded letters to President Nixon, and one reply to an unrecorded letter. Though the letters were addressed to the President, most answers were "form letters" or "boiler-plate" letters and they came from the Department of State. Some letters seem to have stimulated White House awareness and response." Though all letters and replies are recorded in *American Citizenship, Reconsidered,* I will limit to only five those reproduced here.

For the benefit of those historically interested individuals I feel I should describe our anti-Vietnam war position. The following communication will do that. In 1965, I had been asked by Don Jameson, chairman of our committee to write about the immorality of the war, but to emphasize the legality of our anti-Vietnam War position in answer to "Elmer," who had written a pro-war opinion for a local paper. Don Jameson was an engineer and executive with, a utility, Southern California Edison Company.

"To: Don Jameson, Chairman, Vietnam Seminar, Pacific Unitarian Church, Palos Verdes Peninsula, California.

Dear Don: I feel it mandatory to respond to the militant views expressed in Issue #25 of Focus, voicing support for the administration's escalating war in Vietnam.

I shall attempt to take Elmer's comments point by point. It is suggested that "full time experts in Washington know what they are doing." That should be a bigger concern than thinking that they don't know what they are doing! That anyone could knowingly pursue this brutal conflict in aid of the series of corrupt, puppet, Saigon regimes, and against the aspirations of the majority of the people of Vietnam is frightening. President Eisenhower estimated this majority at 80% in 1955.

The war is not a civil war through, "subversion and outside instigation" by the Communists. It *IS* a civil war because *Vietnam is one country.* In 1954 the Geneva Agreements decided on approximately the 17th parallel as a *temporary* dividing line and stated, "the military demarcation line is provisional and *should not* in any way be interpreted as constituting a political or territorial border." It was also explicitly promised in both the armistice agreement and the Geneva Agreements that a national election would be held within two years to unify the country. It would appear that *our,* "subversion and instigation" is promoting and militarily supporting Diem, an American Catholic protégé, (in a population about 11% Catholic/89% Buddhist). We are supporting his refusal to hold elections, against the 80% majority, which means that we *contravened* our own unilateral declaration of support for the Geneva Agreements.

Every year from 1955 through 1959, Ho Chi Minh (Communist leader of "North" Vietnam) appealed for elections and was *refused.* This accounts for the formation of the National Liberation Front in 1960, and for the step-up in guerilla activity. Our State Departments, "White Paper" in March 1955, intended to prove to us the basis for our actions against North Vietnam could, even then, only list 6 Northern-born Vietnamese guerillas. The fact that the NLF continues to successfully oppose our limitless, sophisticated bombing, artillery, napalm and shelling, mainly with their shoulder arms and grenades, shows that they have extensive local support, not to speak of courage, conviction, and stamina. They are clearly indigenous, but doubtless with northern support. Ho Chi Minh would be bound to have influence in the NLF as it was him that President Eisenhower's (estimated) 80% would have voted for in 1956. However, the NLF has their own leaders and a seven-year old, 10-point program for running the country. Our reluctance to negotiate with them, suggests that we don't want to admit that they exist. If President, I would:

1. Un-conditionally cease bombing of North Vietnam.
2. Cease all aggressive military activities.
3. Give public assurance of our immediate willingness to negotiate with the NLF.
4. Urge military cessation on the other side, and, as talks continue.

It is implied that we have an alliance with South Vietnam. There were only two documents:

1. Letter from President Eisenhower to Diem in October 1954 stating that we were giving aid to his government to help it build "a strong viable state, capable of resisting attempted subversion or aggression through military means." This was clearly specified as for only a Diem government, and was to be subject to his responsiveness in carrying out reforms that reflected the aspirations of his people. He was not responsive, and is now dead, so this letter has only historical significance.

2. The SEATO (South East Asia Treaty Organization) agreement involved no pledge of assistance to South Vietnam, as South Vietnam did not, and could not, be a signatory (*It was not, and is not, a country.).* It only agreed with those signing it, to consult with them in cases of subversion, and to deal with aggression, "by each, acting according to its constitutional processes." This is not a guarantee of assistance.

Yes! It is the responsibility of our government to prevent destruction of our country and to prevent the fighting of wars on our soil. However, our administrations concern about a belligerent China appears to be greatly overdrawn. Consider the following:

- China has no military personnel outside its borders. (Our automated military complex of men, equipment and bases circles the globe and semi-circles China). China engulfed Tibet because for over 1,000 years it had been an integral part of China, even voting as an example, in the 1946 and 1948 elections for Chiang Kai Check. However, I do deplore the forcible squelching of Tibet's Buddhist beliefs in this process.
- The India border dispute has been a continuing source of dissension between India and China ever since the indefinite "McMahon Line" was drawn in the Himalayan peaks over a century ago. It was, and is, a border with arguable uncertainties.
- China's internal problems in the last 18 years should have made it obvious to us that her bluster was protective, rather than aggressive, or expansionist. To this we have reacted with our own suspicious and apprehensive response. It follows that the Vietnamese venture is not necessary on this score either. (Thinking of the Vietnam War as being promoted by the U.S. so as to provide a buffer, or a base, against China).

We also:

- Contravene the Geneva Agreements to which we had agreed by our independent declaration of support.
- Contravene our own constitution in waging an undeclared war.
- Contravene the United Nations Charter, Article 33 with reference to the settlement of disputes.

Finally, I cannot, in good conscience keep submissively quiet, while we ruin an entire country, its villages, its farm lands, its jungles; wreck its economy; subvert and, "puppetize" its government; and kill and maim its peoples. Elmer callously dismisses this as an, "Outpost." In his view this permits us to do all this as a "legitimate, anti-Communist action." We lack faith in our system if we must export it by force, instead of by persuasion, reason and example. I would submit that Elmer needs to consider The Golden Rule in relation to our actions with the Vietnamese people.

I would also suggest that the long history of Unitarian liberal activists, would deny Elmer his platitude that liberals only talk, and do not act. The free discussion demonstrated by this Social Concerns Bulletin, will allow all points of view to be considered and thus reasoned and responsible actions will more likely ensue. Sincerely yours - Dave

The following is a 1966 work sheet assembling historical facts, not a letter, but which could be later used by any of us in spontaneously writing to the administration etc. *Follow this carefully and you will have an understanding of the illegality of the Vietnam War.* "Whereas; History has shown that wars do not settle international problems - countless innocent people including children are being maimed, orphaned and killed.

Therefore, we oppose on moral grounds the U.S. participation in the Vietnam War because we oppose war as a means of settling international disputes."

The premise of the U.S. administration was that the U.S. was not interfering in a civil war in Vietnam because it was not a civil war. They construed the Geneva Agreements as having formed two countries North and South Vietnam. The easy-to-follow dozen historical facts refute the U.S. point of view.

- The French from about 1885, had occupied the Vietnam region as *ONE unit,* under the name of Indo-China, until they withdrew when the pre-WWII occupation by the Japanese took place.
- The Japanese allowed the French Vichy authorities to administer Vietnam as *ONE* unit from 1941 to 1945.
- In March 1945 the Japanese (who occupied Vietnam) put up Bao Dai as emperor of *ALL* of Vietnam.
- In Sept 1945 after the Japanese surrender, Ho Chi Minh was chosen President of *ALL* of Vietnam, with Bao Dai as "Counselor of State".
- In 1946 the French returned to re-assert their control over nationalism in ALL of Vietnam.
- In 1949 the French brought Bao Dai back and the same as the Japanese had done, they made him emperor of *ALL* of Vietnam. The bloody "French" Vietnam War took place, until the French, being defeated, left in 1954.
- The Geneva Convention of 1954 continued to define Vietnam as *ONE* nation stating that "the military line (the line dividing north and south) *IS PROVISIONAL AND SHOULD NOT IN WAY BE INTERPRETED AS CONSTITUTING A POLITICAL TERRITORIAL BOUNDARY.*
- The Geneva agreement further decreed that the line was provisional *until GENERAL ELECTIONS* would be held in July 1956, 2 years later, and that this election would then be supervised by an "International Supervisory Commission."
- The *unilateral* statement issued by the *U.S. accepted* this view of Vietnam as *ONE* nation, referring to it as such.
- *2013 commentary:* President Eisenhower commented that the 1956 election would produce an 80% vote for Ho Chi Minh

in that election. What happened to our support for the right of self-determination? There doubtless would have been no Vietnam War and (ultimately) 58,000 Americans and countless Vietnamese would still be alive if that election had been allowed. But the specter of "spreading Communism" intervened.

- The United States directed that that election would *not* be allowed to take place. We lacked faith in our own guiding light."
- The U.S. opposed self-determination of Vietnam, *AS A WHOLE* by giving unqualified support to Diem in his refusal to allow South Vietnam to participate in these elections.
- The Geneva Agreement specifically stated that *neither side* could accept military bases, supplies, etc. yet the United States aided the Diem government with 250 million dollars each year (1956-1957) of which 160 million dollars was for military assistance.

2013 Commentary: That is an illustration that the United Nations is inadequate when international agreements are flouted at will. We point at other countries who disregard international treaties but we do the same! If the U.S. had abided by the international Geneva Agreement, Vietnam would probably have "gone" Communist, *because when we lost the war it "went" (or remained) Communist anyway, and forty years later, STILL is Communist.* But there would not have been the futile expensive agony of the Vietnam War and 58,250 of our own servicemen would still be alive. The only clear answer for *ignored* international treaties is World Government, so treaties are not necessary.

By thus helping to set up *a separate* political unit in South Vietnam the U.S. was *defying* the Geneva accords.

Ho Chi Minh, once having been President of *ALL* of Vietnam; having led and won the war of independence against the French; and having kept his side of the Geneva Agreement; and having watched the other side defy the agreement; cannot help but feel (1966) that Vietnam is still *ONE country!*

Continued work-notes:

To quote Eric Sevareid, June 1st 1966, "When men, speaking the same language, living within the same cultural context, raised in the same cities and villages fight each other by the thousands that, is civil war. When men of the north, including Prime Minister Ky, are part of the government of the South, and vice versa, that is civil war." My 2013 Commentary - Ky, was born in North Vietnam; was a South Vietnamese fighter pilot; had been made prime minister of South Vietnam; and managed a liquor store in Orange County, California after the Vietnam war ended.

"-The U.S. continues to refer to aggression from the North even though the above listed *facts* show that it is not aggression but *CIVIL WAR.* Thus we are interfering in the internal affairs of another country. Therefore, we feel that there is no legal background in being in Vietnam; that we should de-escalate, with the intention of eventually leaving Vietnam."

President Kennedy's view in his words was, "In the final analysis it's their war. They're the ones who have to win it or lose it. We can help them, give them equipment, we can send our men over there as advisors, but they have to win it."

2013 commentary: In the paranoid atmosphere of the time, Kennedy appeared to be accepting the threat of international Communism as valid, but, as has been said elsewhere, he was not planning U.S. involvement in the future conflict. There were approximately 15,000 U.S. "advisers" in Vietnam at the time of his assassination. Kennedy's assumed position was (unintentionally) stated by General Volney F. Warner in 1983 in *Dereliction of Duty,* "In retrospect, I'm absolutely convinced that we lost the war wrong. We should have fought that war in an advisory mode and remained in that mode. When the South Vietnamese failed to come up and meet the mark at the advisory level, then we never should have committed U.S. forces. We should have failed at the advisory effort and withdrawn." It has more recently been confirmed that there are documents in the Kennedy Library that confirm his planned withdrawal. "Assuming, as records have shown, that Kennedy was strongly considering withdrawing the U.S. forces from Vietnam - an assassin's bullet may have cost the United States 58,000 servicemen's lives! Politics by assassination!"

Work sheet: "THUS WE HAVE NO COMMITMENT IN VIETNAM. It is further illegal within our country as under Article 1, Section 8 of our Constitution, war must be declared by the Congress. President Johnson admits we are in a war, and yet the administration hasn't even asked for a debate by the Congress on the subject of a declaration of war! We are violating the charter of the United Nations and the American involvement in Vietnam cannot be justified under it. Thus we are not taking a positive stand in having the United Nations take any action in Vietnam, as you know that our position could not withstand examination by the United Nations." End of work notes.

My letters to the President were typed on my professional letterhead and were usually influenced by the latest news of the current events in Vietnam. Some were short because I was sure that the recipient in Washington was more interested in numbers, for or against, than in the content of the letter - and anyway that was what my available time allowed. I quickly found that my letters seldom reached the President as they were received at the State Department, and a form letter was returned to me saying that it was appreciated; the President is always interested; or "the President has asked me to reply"; and usually included a one-page policy statement. A different, explanatory and longer letter, Oct 12th 1966, from Dixon Donnely, Asst. Secretary said "President Johnson has asked me to thank you for your letter to him, and to see that your views are brought to the attention of responsible officers of this department." Two others were, "read at the White House" instead of the usual, repetitive form-letter from the State Department.

I will include about 5 letters, though they are longer, because they more clearly outline for the reader, and the President - my views.

July 25th 1966
President L. B. Johnson
White House
Washington, DC

Dear Sir: I realize that you inherited a terrible problem in Vietnam and that there had to be tremendous decisions taken. I know that that you feel you are right and that you have done everything in your power to seek an honorable peace. However, I am totally and unequivocally against your Asian policies, but most particularly the Vietnam portion of it. I feel that there are definite actions that can be taken that will carry you down in history as the greatest of all AMERICAN PRESIDENTS. These I will enumerate at the end of this letter. I cannot make these points without my reasoning which goes as follows:

Article 6 of the Geneva Agreement in 1954 stated, and I quote: "The conference recognizes that the essential purpose of the agreement relating to Vietnam is to settle questions with a view to ending hostilities and that THE MILITARY LINE IS PROVISIONAL AND SHOULD NOT IN ANY WAY BE INTERPRETED AS CONSTITUTING A POLITICAL OR TERRITORIAL BOUNDARY." End quote. The USA supported this view in our unilateral statement which said Quote: "In the case of NATIONS NOW DIVIDED AGAINST THEIR WILL, we shall continue to seek to achieve unity through elections supervised by the United Nations to insure that they are conducted fairly." Thus WE spoke of one nation - *not* two. Thus Ho Chi Minh certainly thought of it as one not two. Thus his subsequent actions are clearly a problem of their own national concern, as it is clearly a civil war. Before the Geneva agreement Ho Chi Minh controlled ¾ of the country south of the existing dividing line. Yet he withdrew in accordance with the Geneva agreement and with full expectation of an election. Then Diem, with our support, would not allow the election to take place. In helping Diem to set up a separate state in

South Vietnam we deliberately defied the Geneva agreement. Thus as these FACTS show: this was, and is, a civil war. *Thus there is no aggression involved.* Thus we are interfering in the internal affairs of Vietnam. We are not allowing self-determination of the country as a whole, to take place, as it did in our nation at the time of our own civil war.

You have spoken of the, "Chinese threat" so many times yet it only appears to exist in our worried minds. Tibet being swallowed up by China was the first aggression (you) referred to, yet, Tibet has been a part of China for over 700 years. Tibet participated in the 1946 and 1948 elections, when Chiang Kai-Shek was still in power. So even Nationalist China, (the Chiang-Kai-shek government), considered Tibet as part of China. This appears somewhat inaccurate to be considered "aggression." The border dispute in the Himalayan region has never been considered settled at any time in the past. The region was remote and there has been genuine disagreement before.

There has been no public evidence of Chinese military forces being involved anywhere outside their boundaries (except the above-mentioned Himalayan dispute). How many countries have our military forces (bases), and how close to our adversaries' borders are our forces, I might ask? Certainly the aggressiveness appears to be most evident on our part. Even at the time of the State Department's White Paper of 1½ years ago, there were only a small handful of Chinese weapons found on the Viet-Cong (not to speak of the American and French weapons also found). Thus I once again question the, "Chinese threat," as except for verbal belligerence (in response to our belligerence) they have not spread beyond their borders, whereas our military forces circle the globe.

The actions I feel that are indicated very clearly are as follows:

1. Immediate de-escalation of the war, stopping bombing of both the north and south portions of Vietnam; cease "search-and- destroy" missions; cease troop build-ups.
2. Unequivocal and clear announcements of our intention to

reach a settlement which will include early withdrawal of our troops, and dismantling of our military bases. Also state very clearly our intention to sign and support international agreements, regarding this settlement.

3. Unless the National Liberation Front is allowed an opportunity to enter into negotiations and subsequent elections, there can be no negotiated end to the war. So negotiate directly with the NLF.
4. Tell the Ky government junta, or their successors, that the U.S. will withdraw support if they refuse to negotiate in good faith.

Mr. President, the course I have outlined is one which will require strong leadership, direct and incisive action (to demonstrate our sincerity) and an immediate program to present the historical realities of our position there, to the American people. I know that their understanding would be immediate and responsive to your leadership. You would gain the gratitude of the American people, the Asian peoples, and the peoples of the entire world if you but seize this initiative. Our greatness as a nation in facing up to our legal, moral and humanitarian ideals would be enhanced. I trust that you will give these suggestions serious consideration.

Sincerely,
David Meakes, DSC.
(My degree DSC, Doctor of Surgical Chiropody had not yet been changed to DPM, Doctor of Podiatric Medicine.)

August 4th 1966
Department of State, Washington, D. C.
18402 Hawthorne Blvd,
Torrance. California, 90504

Dear Dr. Meakes:

President Johnson has asked me to reply to your recent communication regarding Vietnam.

The President always appreciates the helpful interest of his fellow citizens in making their views known to him. You may be sure that your comments have been fully noted.

Sincerely yours,
Dixon Donnelly
Assistant Secretary

That letter of reply was normal boiler-plate. That was the identical "stock" answer to most of the letters. My letters usually reflected the news of that date, so they were of both approval and disapproval. At that early stage of my letters I probably visualized some-one sitting down, actually reading them, and, dreaming that maybe someone was being influenced by them. The stream of "stock" answers soon brought realization that there would be miniscule attention to my letters, by anyone of significance in Washington. The State Dept. periodically sent enclosures as their position shifted on different situations.

Oct 18th 1966
President L. B. Johnson,
White House, Washington DC

Dear Sir: The Los Angeles Times reported this morning, with banner headlines that you had predicted the eventual overthrow of the Red Chinese government. I would question how one can expect any possible ameliorating of the existing tensions with this challenging comment. I would respectfully urge every conciliatory action possible be taken, to encourage Red China to enter into normal international relationships, beginning with our support of her acceptance into the United Nations. Her degree of international alienation would probably make her spurn the UN at this time; she would probably also prove distrustful, obstructive and argumentative if she did enter; but in the long run the results could not help but be beneficial to the world. Not the least would be our improved stature in the eyes of the rest of the world.

I base the above recommendations on the clear and evident fact that they are not as militarily aggressive as our State department appears to think they are:

1. There are presently no known military forces outside of their own borders. I cannot refrain from noting that ours are spread around the entire world, including large numbers near their own borders.
2. Tibet has been pointed to as evidence of their military aggressiveness. However, it has been administered by China for over 1,000 years, voted in Chinese elections, and was considered by previous governments, including Chiang's, as being part of China.
3. The Indian border dispute was one of long standing, drawn in an area of great possible error (due to its extreme Himalayan inaccessibility). It was also testified before the Committee on Foreign Relations that the Indians were the first to move forward.
4. Their diplomatic aggressiveness has been rebuffed around the world - as in Africa, Cuba, and Indonesia, etc.

Again, I would state, that we have far less need to fear them as members of the United Nations than we do as isolated outcasts. Their long, 4,000-year-old history as a proud and great civilization is one where all other nations dealt with her with great respect. This, plus their over-700 million population, must tell them that they are a force to be reckoned with in a dignified and circumspect manner in world affairs. I submit that it is our place to take positive action to bring her into world affairs and not to further alienate her.

Sincerely,
David Meakes, DSC

Nixon and Kissinger did that only a few years later. There were three similar "thank you" letters in seven days, one from the "Office of Public Services" and two from the Department of State.

October 31st 1966
Department of State Washington, DC.

Dear Dr. Meakes:

President Johnson has asked me to reply to your recent communication. We appreciate receiving comments and suggestions from the American people on the subject of our foreign relations. Your communication has been read with interest by officials at the Department of State.

Sincerely yours, Dixon Donnelly
Assistant Secretary of State

March 3rd 1968
President L. B. Johnson
The White House Washington, DC

Dear Mr. President:

If ever you had a chance for greatness, and for securing your place in history as the greatest of all American presidents, it is right NOW.

Your White House Commission on Civil Disorders has told you of the doubling in population of the segregated, disadvantaged and low or, - no income in the ghettos of our nation's cities. The Commission has also told you of the profound frustrations and abject despair of these people. As you requested them to, they have spelled out the needs, in fact the dire necessities that they, (the commission) see as essential. The basic financial necessity is for 24 billion dollars for the program of jobs, education and housing. The commission emphasizes that no country can live half free and half slave, and that this country is rapidly polarizing into a black and white America.

On the other hand we are fighting an immoral, illegal, unjust, unwinnable, and brutal war in Vietnam; being held there to support a militaristic, unpopular and corrupt South Vietnamese government; are destroying their forests, the food-producing areas, the villages, the cities, the economy, the culture, and the people of BOTH North and South Vietnam; have lost the respect and admiration of the other countries of the world; are taking the lives of our own boys at the rate of 1,000 a month (over 1800 last month), and this not to speak of the wounded; pouring our resources and money at the rate of 30 billion dollars a year into the abyss. And NOW you are said to be considering up to 100,000 military reinforcements.

I submit that logic can only dictate one sane course - total and early withdrawal from Vietnam. This would include cessation of bombing of North Vietnam, discussions with the National Liberation Front, and preparation for an immediate, but phased, withdrawal. We cannot win the Vietnam War by eliminating the "Rebellious War" in our cities at home because of the lack of money and the time needed. But we can eliminate the "Home War" by eliminating the Vietnam War. Bringing our boys home, with 24 billion of the 30 billion being spent there, would give the cash for these absolutely essential home needs. The remaining 6 billion dollars can be used in a positive manner to rebuild the economy and the people of all Vietnam, and to assuage some of the terrible wounds we have inflicted there. Our home problems and our Vietnam problems would then be on the road to correction and the love and respect of our friends, would in time be restored. I know that you face a likely deficit of over 20 billion dollars; that you face a penny-pinching Congress; that you face an election year in which money-programs are not popular (however, this is a transfer of money from one "project" to another). I urge you to seize this opportunity and to courageously demonstrate your ability to achieve greatness in this - the greatest of emergencies that our nation has ever faced. Please do not fail us. Please lead the people and the Congress towards a solution such as I have outlined. Your name will live through-out the annals of history for your vision and leadership if you but respond to this challenge in a positive manner.

But it must be NOW. In a very short time, as little as a few weeks, or months, it will be too late.

Sincerely,
David Meakes, DSC

The answer came from the White House in *"The White House"* envelope.

March 11th 1968
The White House Washington, DC

Dear Dr. Meakes:

On behalf of President Johnson, I should like to acknowledge your letter. Please be sure that your comments have been fully noted.

Sincerely,
Whitney Shoemaker
Assistant to the President

In the interim, one week later, on March 10th, 1968, I lost my reasoned patience and sent of another short letter.

President L.B. Johnson
The White House Washington, DC

Dear President Johnson:

How much longer will you allow yourself to be kept captive by the American military in your un-deflectable position of allowing the brutal Vietnamese carnage to continue? I realize that for you, the easiest course is to fight on, but in reality the logical and most moral decision is the hardest decision to make - that of withdrawing from Vietnam militarily. It must be obvious to you by now, that history will record you as not being able to face the stark reality of the failure of the Vietnamese venture. Time is on the side of the Viet Cong. When you started the bombing of Vietnam over three years ago, in 1965, the Pentagon estimated the North Vietnamese as being approximately 400 in number in the Viet Cong. Now the estimate is set at 110,000 North Vietnamese infiltrators - and this a month after the "Tet offensive," where your administration speaks of 40,000 of the "enemy" being killed! These numbers alone, show the failure of your policy.

As stated at the beginning of this letter, the imperative action you must take to avoid the inescapable judgment of history is to withdraw *NOW.*

Sincerely,
David Meakes, DSC

March 26th 1968
Department of State Washington, DC

Dear Dr. Meakes,

President Johnson has asked that I reply to your recent letter on Vietnam which was read at the White House and forwarded to the Department of State for our consideration." He finishes the letter with the standard repetitive stock-letter.

Signed by
Dixon Donnelly
Assistant Secretary of Public Affairs

Was President Johnson paying attention? Does one letter shift a President's policy? Of course not! It was the thousands of letters he got saying the same thing, plus, facing political and military reality. *However, it was only five days after that last letter, "on March 31st, 1968, President Johnson announced that bombing would cease for most of North Vietnam, that he was offering peace talks, and that he would not run for re-election."*

On April 1st 1968 I sent him a letter requesting that he cease the bombing of *all* of North Vietnam; that he "make concessions" to" demonstrate integrity of purpose" and that "my thanks and support go to you."

On April 13th 1968, mailed from the White House, came a specially printed card with presidential seal, signed by Lyndon B. Johnson: "Mrs. Johnson and I shall never forget your thoughtfulness at this time. Each of us must share a purpose - to move the world ever closer to the day when peace and justice prevail for all men. With reason and good will, we shall succeed."

I had written President Nixon on Jan 7th 1972, commending him for his proposed trip to Communist China., and I had written to him 16 times regarding the war. However, it was now nearly nine years since I had joined the Vietnam War study group; the bloody chaos continued; the harsh rhetoric continued; and the bloody chaos in Vietnam continued. My last two letters follow.

December 28th 1972
President R. M. Nixon
The White House Washington, DC

Dear President Nixon:

Your savage, brutal handiwork in the murderous bombing of Hanoi and Haiphong will show you and the acquiescent American public to the world as the savage Ghengis Khan of this century. The image of a benevolent, humanitarian America was gone in any case, but this action erases any pretenses we might have had to our espoused pious platitudes of morality. Your name will take its besmirched place in history as a cruel militarist. Please cease the bombing immediately as all history of war shows that this only hardens the enemy's resolution.

Sincerely,
David Meakes, DSC

I received no reply. My last letter follows. The unification of Vietnam didn't come for two more years so my letter still refers to North and South as separate entities.

Feb 23rd 1973
President R. M. Nixon
The White House Washington, DC

Dear President Nixon:

My complete unequivocal support goes to you in your recommendation that we help to rebuild North Vietnam. In addition, I would like to see constructive, non-military help to South Vietnam. These measures will help to maintain peace in South Eastern Asia and are the humanitarian, decent and responsible thing to do. I would be happy to pay my portion of the taxes for actions such as these.

Sincerely David Meakes

The offer to help rebuild North Vietnam was never brought to fruition. The "Watergate" break-in participants had been arrested June 17th 1972.The last American troops left Vietnam March 29th 1973. The Watergate scandal forced President Nixon to resign on August 9th 1973. The Vietnamese had defeated the United States. Saigon fell to the "North" Vietnamese April 29th 1975, and in humiliation, the American Embassy was hastily evacuated by helicopter. The Vietnamese had unified north and south.

I record about 40 letters from Senators or Congressmen to whom I wrote. I wrote to some other leaders including Prime Minister Lester B. Pearson of Canada, Secretary General U Thant of the United Nations, Martin Luther King Sr., Arthur Goldberg U.S. Ambassador to the United Nations. Most sent personal replies but a few were obviously preprinted routine answers. A representative group of those who were supportive follow:

Senator Frank Church, Washington D.C., May 1967: *You, and many others who have expressed similar feelings, lead me to believe that there is developing and articulate force in this country for a realistic foreign policy. Where once there were thousands, now there are millions; where once there a handful in Congress, now there are scores. I hope you will continue to make yourself heard --.*

Senator Joseph Clark, Washington D.C., May 25th 1967: *Thank you very much for your comments on the grave situation in Vietnam. Escalation has brought us no closer to a peaceful solution and I have once again proposed a cease-fire in order to create a more favorable climate for a negotiated settlement of the tragic and costly war.*

Senator Alan Cranston, Washington D.C. (3 replies) March 25th 1969: *Thank you for advising me of your opposition to President Nixon's decision to proceed with an ABM system. I consider it a grave error to undertake the ABM deployment before every effort has been made to negotiate with the Soviet Union a reduction of the burdens and dangers of the arms race.*

Senator Mark Hatfield, Washington D.C. May 9th 1967: *Your thoughtfulness of writing of your concern, with the problems facing us in Vietnam, is deeply appreciated. The possible consequences of our involvement there are of such significance that I would hope that all Americans would share your concern.*

Senator Robert F. Kennedy, Washington, D.C. (2 replies), March 19th 1968 (2½ months before his assassination.): *I just wanted to let you know how much I appreciated your kind words in support of my views on the war in Vietnam. As you know, the conduct of the war is a matter of deep concern to me, as it is to all Americans. I was therefore especially pleased to hear from you, and I want you to know that I shall continue to speak out whenever it seems necessary or helpful to do so.*

Senator Eugene McCarthy, Washington D.C. (2 replies): *I appreciate your concern over the situation in Vietnam and am pleased to know of your support for my efforts.*

Senator George McGovern, Washington D.C., May 3rd 1967: *Thank you for your support of my position regarding our involvement in the Vietnam War.*

Senator Wayne Morris, Washington D.C. (2 replies) June 1967: *Your letter was one of many thousands received from all over the country.*

Senator Thurston Morton, Washington D.C., Oct 5th 1967: *It was indeed kind of you to commend me for my recent comments in regard to Vietnam, and I deeply appreciate your thoughtfulness.*

Prime Minister L. Pearson, Ottawa Canada. May 30 1967: *My letter had appealed to him, as a Nobel Peace Prize recipient, and as a good friend to the United States, to stop the "independent, hands-off attitude which is not a positive step towards peace." and that, instead, to utilize the, "hard words of a good friend" - which would be a "moral necessity" at that time. I urged that he "allow history to record him in the positive action - by speaking out publicly and refusing in any way to support the United States role in Vietnam.*

No personal response could be expected of a national leader of a nation to a foreign individual. From his secretary: "The Prime Minister has taken note of your views on the Canadian Government's policy relating to the conflict in Vietnam, and has asked me to forward the attached documents which clearly set out the Canadian position on the matter." I sent all documents of this kind to the University of California in Santa Barbara.

Congressman Thomas W. Rees, California March 16th 1967: *Thank you very much for your kind letter in support of my recent statements and votes with regard to our Vietnam involvement. The knowledge that concerned individuals in my district are in agreement with my stand on this extremely vital issue is very reassuring.*

Governor George Romney (father of 2012 presidential aspirant Mitt Romney), Michigan, October 23rd 1967 (2 replies): *Thank you for your recent letter concerning my comments on the urgent need for honesty and candor between the Government and the people of America. Your expression of support for my position on this critical issue is appreciated.*

I am convinced this country cannot realize its greatness, nor solve the domestic and international problems it faces unless our leaders tell us the truth, and I believe the time has come to speak out clearly about it.

Governor Romney was a Republican, who, having been exposed to administration and defense department promotional tours, said that he had been, "brain washed." Routine use of that phrase had predominately referred to American soldiers, who, as prisoners of war, had been indoctrinated into enemy beliefs, by their captors. Romney had the courage to say (in effect) that the Department of Defense was "brainwashing" him. His fellow-Republicans were especially critical. Using that one phrase lowered his standing in the polls regarding his run for the presidency. I do not have a copy of my letter to him but his answer here is evidently directed toward my reference to that topic.

> *"I believe it was a tragic mistake for us to become involved in what is principally our land war in Southeast Asia, and that our involvement there on the present large scale was not desirable or necessary in terms of our national interest."*

Governor Romney then listed things he had or hadn't said about Communism, consequently making it clear he was not speaking favorably about Communism, but only criticizing the arguments of the U.S. war promoters.

Secretary-General of the United Nations, U Thant, Date unknown. Maybe April, 1967: *The Secretary-General of the United Nations has received your recent letter on the subject of Vietnam. He is grateful to you for your assurance of support in his efforts to help towards a peaceful solution to the problem.*

Congressman Jerome R. Waldie, California, October 5th 1967: *I appreciate your letter approving my recent change of position in regard to the Vietnam War. - I deeply hope the President will review this policy and adopt a more constructive course of action. Adlai Stevenson stated the problem in a concise manner. "Where we have erred let there be no denial. Where we have wronged the public trust, let there be no excuses. Self- criticism is the secret weapon of democracy, and candor and confession are good for the political soul.*

Vietnam War: Commentary

My disillusionment at the lack of moral integrity of the United States government, as evidenced by its conduct in the Vietnam War, has always been the primary reason why I could not in good conscience apply for United States citizenship. The Iraq War reinforced my opinion. Consequently, the following Vietnam War commentary becomes necessary as it provides justification for my opinion and my decision.

The decade-long, United States-immersed, agonizing, bloody, brutal, futile war was at-last over. As a sort of time-line this Vietnam War account is adequate - but not nearly to the completeness of my *American Citizenship Reconsidered* from which it was taken. For the history student the post-war analysis is invaluable. So the following review of the mistakes made, is very important in avoiding future wars. Please read the following, and then ask yourself if (in the "light" of 2013) how much have our leaders really learned?

American Citizenship Reconsidered continued: One of the purposes of our Vietnam War Committee at the Pacific Unitarian Church was to have the White House and the State Department record large numbers of protest-letters, telegrams, etc. Though I frequently sent post cards, it seemed inadequate to me not to use persuasion, and so, many of my letters were longer in the hope that someone could be moved by a cogent argument. I know that even now, in late 1997, there will be those who will question some of the statements, arguments, and conclusions in my letters. I would urge those to read just a few more pages of post-war revelations, conclusions and comment by authoritative analysts. First, some almost pre-war comments by President Johnson.

In Feb.1997 some of President Johnson's phone conversation tapes were released. *These comments were made in May 1964*, and preceded the *Tonkin Gulf* episode by 2 months, preceded his 1964 re-election by over four months, and preceded the 1965 build-up of U.S. troops in Vietnam by almost a year. These comments occurred when there were only about 15,000 U.S. troops in Vietnam - that figure increasing to 540,000 by late 1968. The following comments were made to Senator Richard Russell of the Senate Armed Services Committee. President Johnson, "It's the biggest damn mess I ever saw." "They'd impeach a president though, that would run out, wouldn't they?" Speaking of a Sergeant who worked in his house he said "Think about sending the father of six kids in there and what the hell are we going to get out of him doing it? It just makes the chills run up my back."

Minutes later President LBJ said to National Security Advisor McGeorge Bundy and speaking of the sergeant again, "What in the hell am I ordering him out there for? What the hell is Vietnam worth to me? What the hell is Laos worth to me? What is it worth to this country? It looks to me like we are getting into another Korea. It just worries the hell out of me. I don't know (when) we can ever hope to get out of there once we're committed. - I don't think it is worth fighting for, and I don't think we can get out, just the biggest damn mess."

So why did President Johnson, *later* commit the nation to the "mess"? In the LA Times, March 25th 1997, Robert Scheer comments, "Yet despite seeing no value in the war, Johnson soon ordered a massive escalation of the conflict that left 58,000 Americans dead, and more than a million mostly adult civilian Vietnamese dead, and his own nation divided as it had not been since the Civil War. So in the end, Johnson sent a half-million troops to Vietnam and carpet bombed the country with more explosives than were used in World War II because he wanted to deprive the Republicans of their one issue and feared even Congress would turn against him if he withdrew.

But kids got killed in Indo-China. Mines turn up in the rice paddies, to be stumbled upon by innocent children. These deaths are a regular reminder of the young Americans and the far larger number of Vietnamese, Cambodians and Laotians who were sacrificed on the altar of political ambition."

Robert Scheer, *Los Angeles Times,* May 2nd 2000: Yes, we, a decent, educated and free people, did something enormously vicious and stupid. But we can't admit to its full dimension because to do so would call into question that assumption of national virtue, our most revered but corrosive characteristic. Even now the war must be viewed as a "mistake", a "quagmire", a "bad compromise", but never acknowledging the descent into barbarism. For such behavior is reserved only for those who live under a flag different from our own."

Robert D. Schlesinger in his book *A Time for War* concluded that the Vietnam War was never about Vietnam for the United States. Its genesis was a belief that everything that happened everywhere was somehow connected to the Sino-Russian threat. Its conduct was shaped by the rhythms of American domestic politics. In other words: worldwide Communism and domestic politics.

America's most decorated soldier (over 20 medals including seven Purple Hearts) Colonel David Hackworth, in his book *About Face,* quotes George Kennan, one of the original authors of the U.S. containment policy which started the Cold War and who, much later reappraised his position saying," The lessons of Vietnam are few and plain: not to be hypnotized by the word "Communism," and not to mess in other people's civil wars where there is no substantial American strategic interest at stake." For Kennan that was a momentous reversal of his earlier opinions. As one of the architects of the Cold War, his opinion carried immense weight.

Brief commentary from *Dereliction of Duty,* Subtitled*: Lyndon Johnson, Robert McNamara, the Joint Chiefs of Staff, and the lies that led* *to Vietnam*, 1997, authored by H. R. McMaster. From the book cover, "The book traces, on a day-to-day basis, the interactions of President Johnson, Robert McNamara, other Administration figures and the Joint Chiefs of Staff, It is a damning account of deliberate lies, primarily by President Johnson; his lack of integrity and candor in communicating with the American public; arrogance and disregard of the Military Services by Robert McNamara; marked inter-service rivalry between the Joint Chiefs of Staff; and the inexcusable failure of the Joint Chiefs of Staff to challenge military decisions (often based on political considerations), by President Johnson, and by their civilian boss Robert McNamara, Secretary of Defense."

Further quotation from the book cover: "The book also reveals for the first time how the virtual exclusion of the Joint Chiefs of Staff from the decision making process exacerbated the problem. Based on dramatic and irrefutable evidence, *Dereliction of Duty* proves that the war in Vietnam was NOT lost in the field, on the front pages of the New York Times, or on the college campuses. It was lost in Washington D.C., even before the U.S. military assumed *sole responsibility* for the fighting in 1965, and before Congress and the American people realized the country was at war, indeed, even before the first American units were deployed." "The roles played by the President's closest advisers in the decisions to escalate American involvement in the war are central to the story. And the reasons behind those decisions - now exposed - challenge McNamara's claim that American policy makers were prisoners of the ideology of the containment of Communism and therefore should be absolved of responsibility for the final outcome."

H.R. McMaster, *Dereliction of Duty* quoted Robert S. McNamara in 1964, "I don't object to it being called McNamara's War. I think it is a very important war and I am pleased to be identified with it and do whatever I can to win it."

In 1996, twenty-seven years after his administration-exit, the "brilliant genius" and the most authoritative critic of the multitude of Vietnam War critics, turned out to be its primary architect! Robert McNamara published his book *In Retrospect.* It was big news and especially surprising because of his major condemnation of himself, though usually phrased as "we", or "our", etc. For one who searches for the WHY, the book is a *must.* It validated my 30 years of angry exasperation. I could not write the foregoing without transcribing the following from my unpublished manuscript *American Citizenship Reconsidered.*

McNamara's quotations are copied in turn from *In Retrospect.* Unless specified otherwise, the following is from Robert McNamara's book.

Unpublished manuscript *American Citizenship Reconsidered By David Meakes,* "Robert McNamara was Secretary of Defense from June 1961 to February 1968, being the prime adviser and CEO of the Vietnam War in all of the Kennedy administration and 4 out of the 5 years of the Johnson administration. His book *In Retrospect,* published in 1995, gives a definitive inside look at the planning and execution of the war. What really brought an avalanche of world-wide commentary was the amazing degree to which he acknowledged the faulty concepts and reasoning that enmeshed the U.S. in the war in the first place, and the abject failure in planning and execution of the war, once it was under way. In his 1996 soft cover edition he has included, *an extra 141 pages of comment and analysis by* others, about the war but also *about his 1995 edition.* His own comments are profuse and a representative group are included here, their impact magnified because of his status as the highest official in the Department of Defense of that time.

Page 179, "We, as a government, failed to address the fundamental issues, or how to solve the problem (how to, where to, or if to, fight the war)."

Page 62, "-our position (on neutralization of Vietnam), was replete with inconsistencies and incongruities."

Pages 444-445, "It has been confirmed that President Kennedy was planning to withdraw the American forces by the end of 1965." McNamara says there is a tape in the Kennedy Presidential Library in Boston," that is accessible only through the Kennedy family that makes that fact clear." *An assassin's bullet DOES change history!*

Page 147, Before the 1964 election, and a year after Kennedy's assassination, President Johnson said publicly in August 1964, "Some others are eager to enlarge the conflict. They call upon us to supply American boys to do the job the Asian boys should do --. Such an action would offer no solution at all to the real problem in Vietnam. Yet McNamara says that one day after the Kennedy assassination, President Johnson was already telling members of his cabinet to "Win the War!" Page 169, "During the fateful period January to July 1965 (President LBJ's first six months post-election), Johnson instituted bombing of North Vietnam and committed U.S. ground forces to South Vietnam, raising the total U.S. troop strength from 23,000 to 175,000 with the likelihood of another 100,000 in 1966, and perhaps more later. All this occurred without adequate public disclosure or debate, planting the seeds of an eventually debilitating credibility gap." This statement by the *TOP* man in the Defense Department!

Page 232, "Over and over again - we failed to address the fundamental principles."

Page 107, "-how limited and shallow our discussions of the alternatives to our existing policy in Vietnam had been, i.e. Neutralization or withdrawal? But we never carefully debated what U.S. force would ultimately be required; what our chances of success would be; or what the political, military, financial and human costs would be, if we provided it. Indeed, these basic questions went unanswered."

Page 48, "The U.S. commanders, as I did, misunderstood the nature of the conflict. They viewed it as primarily a military operation, when in fact, it was a highly complex, nationalistic and internecine struggle." A civil war! That had been the first fact established, and then emphasized by our Unitarian study group.

Page 112, "-we still did not recognize the North Vietnamese and Viet Cong struggle as nationalistic, in nature." Once again, a civil war! How come the Defense Department didn't know that, when our little study-group knew it? By these statements about civil war, he indirectly acknowledges the political nature of the DMZ (demilitarized zone) dividing North and South Vietnam (as he then viewed it), was not a realistic one, *as both parties* were fighting for their national unity. Note that McNamara frequently still refers to South Vietnam as a country, as distinct from North Vietnam, which of course, in President Johnson's mind, during that period, it was. The DMZ "*had been declared as provisional, and should not in any way be interpreted as constituting a permanent, political or territorial boundary.*"

Yet nowhere in his book does he acknowledge the validity of the prior Geneva Agreement, making "the line provisional, and not in any way be interpreted as constituting a permanent, political or territorial line." He acknowledged so much else so why would did he not acknowledge the actual law (the Geneva Agreements).

Page 23, "But the North Vietnamese had chosen where, when, and how long, to fight."

Page 261, "- military force, especially when wielded by an outside power - just cannot bring order to a country (South Vietnam) that cannot govern itself." That is another argument that South Vietnam was really not a country. The administration never realistically assessed the U.S. supported, South Vietnam, puppet government as essentially impotent.

Page 333, "- hindsight proves us wrong. We both over-estimated the effect of South Vietnam's loss on the security of the West - if the South Vietnamese were to be saved, they had to win the war themselves."

Page 253, "What disturbed me the most (about University protests) was that opposition to Administration Vietnamese policy, increased with the institution's prestige and the educational attainment of its students." Rather than just "being disturbed," McNamara, might have realized that there was a thoughtful *educated reason* for those protests.

Page 421, "- a young Quaker named Norman R. Morrison, father of three and an officer of the Stony Run Friends Meeting in Baltimore, burned himself to death within forty feet of my Pentagon window, - his wife issued a statement - "Norman Morrison (gave) his life to express his concern over the great loss of life and human suffering caused by the war in Vietnam. He was protesting our Government's deep military involvement in the war. He felt that all citizens must speak their convictions about our country's actions." That was an echo of Florence Beaumont in Los Angeles and, of a large group of Saigon Buddhist monks who did the same. McNamara continues, saying that, "I knew that Marg. and our three children shared many of Morrison's feelings about the war, as did the wives and children of several of my cabinet colleagues. And I believed I shared and understood some of his thoughts. There was much that Marg. and I and the children should have talked about, yet at moments like this I often turn inwards instead. It is a grave weakness. The episode created tension at home that only deepened as dissent and criticism of the war continued to grow."

Page 411, Craig McNamara, son of Robert McNamara said "I consider it immoral to fight in Vietnam and kill people."

Page 164, Robert McNamara, "It is clear that disengagement was the course we should have chosen." Many of my letters to LBJ asked for withdrawal.

Page 321, McNamara presents a chart indicating six major points in time, at which withdrawal could have, and should have, taken place. Page 219, "- totally incorrect appraisal of the "Chinese threat," that pervaded our thinking. Among other shortcomings they took no account of the centuries of hostility between China and Vietnam, which flared up again, once the U.S. withdrew from the region. - here again the lack of expertise and historical knowledge seriously undermined policy." How come our little Pacific Unitarian study group knew about it? Because, all that we had to do, was to look in the index of my soft-back 3-volume Chinese history set - for "Vietnam!" Pentagon research lacked simplicity!

Page 358, Comment by Richard Draper, New York review of Books on May 11th, 1995, "That there were deep differences between the Chinese and Vietnamese never seems to have been considered by the (Administration) leaders."

Page 352, Theodore Draper, "The Pentagon and Stated Department had no senior officials with intimate knowledge of South

East Asia, because the top East Asian and Chinese experts in the State Department had been driven out during the McCarthy years of the 1950s."

In middle 1964 there had not yet been a U.S. Congressional Authorization allowing the Johnson administration to legally go to war. Then, Johnson seized an opportunity, when a supposed North Vietnamese aggressive action took place in the Tonkin Gulf.

July 30th 1964, South Vietnamese patrol boats attacked two North Vietnamese islands in the Tonkin Gulf.

July 31st 1964, The U.S. destroyer *Maddox* entered the Tonkin Gulf.

Incident 1, August 2nd 1964 - Two North Vietnamese high speed patrol boats attacked the *Maddox* with torpedoes and automatic fire.

August 3rd 1964, *South Vietnamese* boats attacked the North Vietnamese coast. The U.S. sent destroyer Turner Joy into the Tonkin Gulf.

August 4th 1964, Low clouds and thunderstorms brought low visibility.

August 4th 1964, The two destroyers sent reports of "torpedo wakes", "cockpit lights", "search light illumination," "automatic weapons fire," and radar and sonar. *None of this ever happened.*

Incident 2, About 5 hours later, at 1.27 PM, on August 4th, Captain John Herrick, patrol commander on the Maddox sent this "flash" message to Honolulu and Washington: "Review of action makes many reported contacts and torpedoes fired appear doubtful. Freak weather effects on radar and over-eager sonar men may have accounted for many reports. No actual visual sightings by the Maddox. *Suggest complete evaluation before any further action taken."* The confusing and conflicting reports left the sense that the attack may never have occurred. The U.S. ships had been in the northern coastal gulf of North Vietnam in any case. But, regardless, the administration used the shaky episode to go before Congress to pass the, "Tonkin Gulf Resolution," which allowed the appropriation of the money that was necessary for the buildup of troops, *thus avoiding asking Congress for a formal declaration of war.* A highly questionable ruse to get appropriations without declaring war!

The only change in the main body of the 1996 edition of *In Retrospect,* from that of the 1995 edition, is that on November 9th, 1995, McNamara conferred with the North Vietnamese general who had been in charge, General Vo Nguyen Giap. *He said that no attack had taken place by the North Vietnamese on August 4th 1964!*

Pages 127 to 129, "Congress did not conceive The Tonkin Gulf resolution as a declaration of war, and did not intend it to be used, as it was, *as authorization for an enormous expansion of U.S. forces in Vietnam from 16,000 military advisers to 550,000 combat troops.* Securing a declaration of war and specific authorization for the introduction of combat forces in years might well have been impossible, but not seeking it was clearly wrong." This is the illegality, or part of it, that was referred to in part of my letters, - only *now, in those words,* it comes from the then-Secretary of Defense!

Page 129, Continued McNamara comment, "-was the Johnson administration justified in basing its subsequent military actions in Vietnam - including enormous expansion of force levels - on the Tonkin Gulf Resolution? The answer was absolutely not!" Once again it was *illegal.*

Page 367, Theodore Draper, "- it should have still been necessary for the Johnson administration to come back to Congress for further authorization to expand U.S. forces in the war." Same page, Statement by President Johnson to McNamara: "We know ourselves in our own conscience, that when we asked for the Tonkin Gulf Resolution, we had no intention of committing this many - ground troops. And we are doing so now and we know it is going to be bad, and the question (is) do we just want to on a limb by ourselves?" Draper continues: "So President Johnson knew that he "was going out a limb constitutionally by resting on the Tonkin Gulf Resolution. In fact, both President Johnson and the Congress acted cravenly during the Vietnamese War." End of Draper quote.

Page 247, McNamara, "(Our) efforts to stimulate movement to a negotiated settlement continued, but they were amateurish and ineffectual."

Page 247-248, "In 1966 and 1967 there were several strong leads towards negotiations. These were through Lester B. Pearson, Canadian Prime Minister; Janusz Lewandoski, International Control Commission Polish representative; Prime Minister Harold Wilson of Great Britain; and through Soviet Premier Alexei Kosygin." Each time, as the crucial meeting dates arrived, the leads fell through because President Johnson stepped up the bombing, rather than show good will. This was exactly what had been done in the Korean War by Generals McArthur, Ridgeway and Van Fleet.

Page 174, "-sustained bombing of North Vietnam, kept secret from the American public, finally began on March 2nd, 1965. On that day 100 aircraft launched from carriers in the South China Sea and airbases in South Vietnam struck ammunition dumps in North Vietnam. Operation Rolling Thunder, as the air program came to be known, had begun. It would continue for three years and drop more bombs on Vietnam than had been dropped on all of Europe in WWII." Note that his comment does not include the bombs dropped by the U.S. in Vietnam from 1968 to 1973, in the last years of the war (the Nixon administration war). Note also that North Vietnam had no air-force so they dropped no bombs at all on U.S. forces.

Page 243, "between 1965 and 1967 U. S. and South Vietnamese air-force dropped over a million tons of bombs on the *South,* more than twice the tonnage dropped on North Vietnam. Fighting produced more and more civilian casualties and squalid refugee camps. The increasing destruction and misery brought on the country we were supposed to be helping troubled me greatly." So he says 30 years later. He still calls it a "country."

Page 244, "U.S. intelligence estimated, that infiltration increased from about 35,000 in 1965, to as many as 90,000 in 1967, while Hanoi's will to carry on the fight, remained firm." See my letter March 10th 1968 Page 307.

Page 245, "All of this, led me to conclude that no amount of bombing of the North, - short of genocidal destruction, which no-one contemplated - could end the war."

Page 165, "- the conclusion of U.S. Consul General Ricco in Hong Kong, and Sir Robert Thompson in Malaysia that Rolling Thunder had strengthened rather than diminished Hanoi's will."

Page 237, "-the entire evidence showed that our adversaries - through a combination of recruitment in the South and infiltration from the North - expanded their numbers substantially. Viet Cong and North Vietnamese forces increased in size through 1966 and into 1967."

Page 228, "Dick Helms, of the CIA, told President Johnson on June 22 1966, "Increased bombing in the North could not stop movement of supplies to the South." It should be remembered that transportation, and provision of supplies, between North Vietnam and the Viet Cong in South Vietnam, took place along canopied jungle trails and on the backs and bicycles of the guerillas, and that they had elaborate tunnel complexes along the way, intended for rest and supply depot purposes. U.S. military technological expertise could not stage effective bombing. Bombing was eventually deemed futile.

Page 238, "CIA analysts stated on May 23rd 1967, "Despite increasingly effective "search and destroy" operations - the Vietnamese Communists have continued to expand their main forces, both by infiltration and by local recruitment --. It appears the Communists can continue to sustain their overall strength during the coming year."

Page 291-2, "CIA director Dick Helms reported to President Johnson on August 29th 1967, that since March of 1967, we had flown over 10,000 bombing sorties *per month* against North Vietnam - over a 55% increase, over the same period in 1966. Despite this escalation and despite the increasing hardships, economic losses and mounting problems in management and logistics by the air war - Hanoi continues to supply its own needs and to support its aggression in South Vietnam. Essential military and economic traffic continue to move."

Over 30 of my recorded letters to Presidents Johnson and Nixon asked for bombing cessation or withdrawal (and thus bombing cessation).

Page 252, "- We failed miserably to integrate and coordinate our diplomatic and military actions as we searched for an end to the war." Page 280, "- we had failed. Why, this failure?" In June 1967 McNamara, having asked himself this question, started 36 researchers collecting all relevant documents from all source to provide a framework for future analysis. One of these researchers was Daniel Ellsberg, who, 4 years later in 1971, leaked the papers to the New York Times, who christened them "The Pentagon Papers". The papers literally confirmed all that our Pacific Unitarian Church study group had long before concluded - and much more.

Page 321 - Robert McNamara lists 11 causes of the war in Vietnam:

1. We misjudged the geopolitical intentions of the North Vietnamese and the Viet Cong - and exaggerated the danger to the U.S.
2. We totally misjudged the political forces within Vietnam.
3. We underestimated the power of nationalism.
4. We were profoundly ignorant of the history, politics, and culture of the people of the area and also the personalities and habits of their leaders.
5. We failed to recognize the limitations of modern, high technology military equipment, forces and doctrine in confronting unconventional highly motivated people's movements. We failed in winning the minds and hearts of the people.
6. We failed to involve Congress or the American people by discussion and debate, prior to taking action.
7. We failed to maintain support of the American public, because we failed to explain fully as things developed. (That

was the point I made in my letters to Johnson about the need of telling the American people the facts).

8. We do not have the God-given right to shape every nation in our image or as we choose.
9. We did not hold to the principle that U.S. military action (except for security) should be carried out with multinational forces.
10. We failed to recognize that in international affairs, there may be problems for which there is no solution.
11. We failed to organize the top echelons of the executive branch to cover all aspects of the management of the war.

The book *In Retrospect* covers only up to the point of McNamara's resignation in Feb. 1968, and does not cover any of the 5 years of the war (the Nixon era) after he left."

In the book *The Living and the Dead,* by Paul Hendrickson (1996), the author quoting Shakespeare's Hamlet in referring to Robert McNamara says "This above all, to thine own self be true - "and he (McNamara) wasn't. I think those of our Pacific Unitarian Church, and others who protested the war, for the moral reasons, were true to themselves and also those who, for the right reasons, fled the country.

In the book *Our War* by David Harris, blame is also brought to the American public. Quotation: "Having made lying an acceptable government function, our government is now overrun with liars - having refused to live up to their own values, we are now increasingly without values at all." In his view "the war exposed the U.S. as the world's greatest fraud, a country who took their civics lessons from Hollywood. Laid bare, America then shunned introspection in favor of the serviceable consensus that the war had been a "mistake." Thus in polite company the listener can choose whether he thinks it had been 'villainy, geopolitical miscalculation, or just being fire-power-light.' Americans have learned to "stand-tall" again, without ever understanding how Vietnam laid us low." End of Harris quotation.

In McNamara's book *In Retrospect,* Page 353 (1996 Soft back) there is a cogently articulate editorial from the April 12th 1995, *New York Times,* thought to have been written by Editorial page editor Howell Raines. "Comes now Robert McNamara with the announcement that in the fullness of time (he has) grasped realities that seemed readily apparent to millions of Americans throughout the Vietnamese War. At times he appeared to be helping an obsessed President prosecute a war of no real consequence to the security of the United States. Millions of loyal citizens concluded that the war was a militarily unnecessary and politically futile effort to prop up a corrupt government that could neither reform nor defend itself."

New York Times: "Through all the bloody years, those were the facts as they appeared on the surface. Therefore, only one argument could be advanced to clear President Johnson and Mr. McNamara, of the charge of wasting lives atrociously. That was the theory that they possessed superior knowledge, not available to the public; that the collapse of South Vietnam would lead to regional and perhaps world domination by the Communists; and moreover, that their superior knowledge was so compelling it rendered unreliable and untrue the apparent facts available to even the most expert opponents to the war."

New York Times: "With a few throw-away lines in his new book *In Retrospect,* Mr. McNamara admits that *such knowledge never existed.* Indeed, as they made the first fateful steps toward heavier fighting in late 1963 and 1964, Mr. Johnson and his cabinet, 'had not truly investigated what was essentially at stake and important to us.' As for checking their public position that only a wider war would avail in the circumstances, "we never stopped to explore fully whether there were other routes to our destination."

New York Times: "Such sentences break the heart while making it clear that Mr. McNamara must not escape the lasting moral condemnation of his country."

New York Times: "Mr. McNamara wants us to know that he, too, realized by 1967 that the dissidents were right, that the war had to be stopped to avoid "a major national disaster." Even so, he wants us to grant that his delicate sense of protocol excused him from any obligation to join the national debate over whether American troops should continue to die at the rate of hundreds per week in a war he knew was futile. Mr. McNamara believes that retired Cabinet members should not criticize the Presidents they served no matter how much the American people need to know the truth. In Mr. McNamara's view the President can never become so steeped in a misguided war that patriotic duty would compel a statement."

New York Times: "Perhaps the only value in *In Retrospect* is to remind us never to forget these were men who, in the full hubristic glow of their power, would not listen to logical warning or ethical appeal. When senior figures talked sense to Mr. Johnson and Mr. McNamara, they were ignored or dismissed from government. When young people in the ranks brought that message, they were court marshaled. When young people in the streets shouted it, they were hounded from the country."

New York Times: "It is important to remember how fate dispensed rewards and punishment for Mr. McNamara's thousands of days of error. Three million Vietnamese died. Fifty-eight thousand Americans got to come home in body bags. Mr. McNamara, while tormented by his role in the war, got a sinecure at the World Bank and summers at the Vineyard."

"So much has changed since those horrendous times. The nation has belatedly recognized the heroism of the American troops who served in good faith because they, in their innocence, could not fathom the mendacity of their elders. But another set of heroes - thousands of students who returned the nation to sanity by chanting, "Hell no, we won't go" - is under attack from a band of politicians who sat out the war on student deferments. In that sense we are still living in the wreckage created by the Cabinet in which Mr. McNamara served." *New York Times:* "His regret cannot be huge enough to balance the books for our dead soldiers. The ghosts of those unlived lives circle close around Mr. McNamara. Surely he must in every quiet and prosperous moment hear the ceaseless whispers of those poor boys in the infantry, dying in the tall grass, platoon by platoon, for no purpose. What he took from them cannot be repaid by prime-time apology and stale tears, three decades late." "Mr. McNamara says he weeps easily and has strong feelings when he visits the Vietnam Memorial. But he says he will not speak of those feelings. Yet someone must, for that black wall is wide with the names of people who died in a war that he did not, at first, carefully research nor, in the end, believe to be necessary."

The Week magazine May 20th 2005: 'Sometimes, it is better to lose', said Robert Scheer in *thenation.com.* Thirty years ago last month, the last helicopter lifted off from a Saigon rooftop, marking the end of the U.S.' disastrous, misadventure while devastating Vietnam. And, it left our nation bitterly divided and humiliated. And for what? Three presidents ignored the lessons of history in trying to crush the Communist revolution in Vietnam. No foreign power, no matter how mighty, can outlast a committed nationalist insurgency. Yet a generation after our ignoble departure, it turns out that a communist Vietnam isn't so bad after all. Today the country strongly resembles the one that the Kennedy, Johnson, and Nixon Administrations unsuccessfully tried to create by bombing it back to the Stone Age. Stable and peaceful, Vietnam has a growing middle class and a falling poverty rate, and threatens none of its neighbors. Though it is still an "avowedly communist" nation, Vietnam's economy, like China's, is an unlikely "mix of Karl Marx and Adam Smith." In Ho Chi Minh City, Vietnam's leaders are calling for corporate investment, not world revolution. The U.S. has become a major trading partner, and American Express and Master Card placed ads on parade floats marking the glorious anniversary of the fall of Saigon. It would be comical, except for the terrible price so many people paid for the lesson."

McNamara's book, followed by the *NY Times* editorial, and finally Robert Scheer's historical commentary, has helped to validate the intensive efforts of the Pacific Unitarian Vietnam War Study Committee and to assuage my decades of disillusionment of U.S. foreign policy.

Perspective Recap

Random Comments: During my adult years of 1939 to 2014, there have been a series of wars, greater in number for Americans, as they were involved in all of them. As a medic in WW11, it was required that I be involved where the wounds were the freshest and bloodiest, so inevitably, I soon developed a gut-level hatred of war. My naïve conviction that future wars would be avoided, collapsed at the failure of the idealistic United Nations to either prevent or intercede in the series of wars. Striving to avoid public criticism over the deaths of civilian women and children, the military spokesmen have cloaked their reports in euphemisms such as, "precision bombing", "surgical strike" and "collateral damage." It was immediately clear that this was military obfuscation in action. Just more lobbyist lingo aimed at keeping the American public thinking that we were too benevolent to be torturing or unnecessarily injuring civilians and to keep us from knowing accurately what was happening. Think *Mai Lai,* and Abu Ghraib.

For the purposes of this account, in 2013, with national and public trust in the U.S. government eroded to "less than 10%", we must take the initiative to search for permanent global answers to our global problems, but do it with maximum transparency, maximum educational input, maximum public participation, and ASAP. The dissipated confidence *MUST* be restored. Or progress will be stymied.

Our analysis has shown that some of the causes of war listed are: Fear and Insecurity; Religion and Patriotism; Money and Power; Acquisition of territory; Paranoia; the Media; and failure to Negotiate. We have discussed the future of the *Big Three: World peace, World government and the Brotherhood of men,* and their relationship to the elimination of war. It has already been made very clear that, in my opinion education is the answer to the world's problems. Not just any education, but "Global Education," is necessary for the development of what I view as the idealistic, symbiotic, and *essential Big Three.*

Global Education

Though presentation will differ, I will be, apologetically, repeating some of the basics of some of my educational concept, such as the Golden Rule. The primary thrust of everything I wish to say here is regarding EDUCATION and I wish to say at the outset, that no concept here is unalterable. Anything that I propose is changeable. I seek help from every source. If it is a worthy goal, then it needs full discussion and free, unlimited input by all. For example, when I say "teach, the Golden Rule through to university level," and later scientists in education determine that by high school is sufficient, then so-be-it. The bottom line, *I* think, is that *the bed-rock reflex must be there for the Golden Rule to "kick in." It must be automatic to be effective. Bring your good ideas. And the time is NOW. Not involving me. My longevity has been great, but cannot be anything but limited. So if you, at any level, feel motivated, do so and do so in some new direction.*

A teacher, I'm not. An educational scientist, if there is such a category, I'm not. I am just a guy with some ideas which, *I* think, might be of use in building a framework for the global education which is integral to our global future soon or later. Those ideas are currently under the title, "The Big Three," and the three headings:

1. The Golden Rule.
2. Global Education
3. World Federation.

It was Chicago in Feb. 1947 and Mr. 'B' the manager of the local Chicago store, one in the Maling chain of the region's most economical shoe stores, was emphasizing to the neophyte shoe salesman (me) that the most desirable product (our most expensive shoe $7.95) was the one to present to the customer first. "It is our preferred sale because there is more profit for the store."

In this current topic it is crystal clear that my preferred product is where the profit to the people of the world is greater, and that is with our triple header. So the triple symbiosis - world government, world peace and the brotherhood of man are presented as though but one entity. And, Yes! It is the best product! I know of nothing else to consider! There are smarter people who may know of better ideas. Welcome! Develop them. Present them. Fight for them. I personally hope that they involve The Big Three. The Golden Rule recommendation is repeated here, with World Federation in mind.

The Golden Rule: In my view, comprehensive changes and innovations in education must take place. If the over-all concept of world government is proven to be a valid one, then the educational scientists will develop an educational program based on an awareness of the successes and failures of the past, but, also importantly, based on the expected global view of the future. It would be an educational program designed and developed by scientists and engineers in each specialty. It would then be distributed and taught in all regions of the world, concentrating most specifically on children from their earliest age of learning ability. I emphasize children first, because, in my view, the greater the numbers of the world's children who have been impregnated with the Golden Rule concept, the more successful will be the educational impact of the early programs. Some will say, "What is so different? The Golden Rule is taught to kids now." Yes! It is taught, ***BUT***, - usually in church settings; only in a few minutes;

in a perfunctory manner; not to all children; and is usually buried in unrelated religious dogma. In the past, emphasis has primarily been placed on the dogma. The dogma was the moral lesson, not the Golden Rule. Golden Rule teaching should predominate.

What I am urging is that educationalists develop a substantial secular course, embellishing, and emphasizing, the Golden Rule concept, and I am urging maximum emphasis over all the years from kindergarten to university. The course content would be appropriate to the level of student comprehension in psychology, and in the myriad of relationships in personal lives, family, sexual, marital, play, organizations, corporations, and in international relations. I recommend that the curriculum include an interest in the needs, desires, capabilities and talents of the *individual.* This would promote the well-being, the needs, the happiness and the fulfillment of the individual. Establish friendships. Establish sharing. Avoid confrontation. Thus fulfill the concept of the "pursuit of happiness."

Regarding the teaching of the Golden Rule my 1996 quotation, "As a universally accepted concept, it seems to me there would be no disagreement by religious organizations, school authorities, teachers' unions, and individuals. In time, probably several generations, there would be a positive influence on all families and their home lives. Gradually this should permeate, through school teaching, to even the most dysfunctional families. That will lead to greater sympathy and respect for all others; greater appreciation for the richness of all peoples and cultures, thus edging toward a time where the "brotherhood of man," would be real, and not simply an empty platitude." End of 1996 quotation.

I think that deep indoctrination would, in time, result in amicable, gracious solutions in personal affairs, business affairs, military affairs indeed, all aspects of life. Simplistic? Overstated? Utopian? Maybe. But, I implicitly believe it will occur sometime in the future. I believe it because, that state of mind is what is necessary for world peace, world government and the brotherhood of men. They are interdependent. They are synergistic. And they await only the global intelligence to get action underway. Their symbiotic relationship results in each one aiding and developing the others. If you secure one, you will, simultaneously, secure the other two.

It is of interesting, but idle, conjecture to wonder what the world would be like if the Golden Rule was a prevailing element in human nature to start with. Was it because of the saber-toothed tiger syndrome that the human race had developed in a more distrusting direction? Maybe it was because of some crafty fellow-Neanderthal? I think that our world, founded on the Golden Rule, would have been an exceedingly more pleasant, people-oriented society, and, being on a sort of auto-pilot, the religionists and I, wouldn't feel the need to push the Golden Rule; and I would have looked for another subtitle, or, more importantly, not even feel the need to write this book. Just an abstract reverie!

I can visualize considerable derision by many, who will be saying that I am talking about a lightweight, "Mickey Mouse" aspect of psychology that cannot possibly have the result that I am suggesting. Think again! It is practical. It is not coincidental that twenty-four out of the 30 examples of the Golden Rule previously mentioned came from religions, from all parts of the world and - over thousands of years. The other six came from philosophers. They were all advising use of the Golden Rule for practical reasons. The sources of these independently-arrived-at thoughts were the thoughtful intelligentsia of the millennia. The universally accepted, intrinsic value in the Golden Rule would make our current days more pleasant, and would be an important, essential component in daily life in that utopian future.

To repeat still again: Alfred Adler, Austrian psychoanalyst, 1870-1937, *The Arizona Republic*, "There is a Law that man should love his neighbor as himself. In a few hundred years it should be as natural to mankind as breathing or the upright gait; but if he does not learn it he shall perish." Dr. Adler's words accurately reflect my thoughts. Who knows the number of years? As I view it, the necessary slow impaction and accumulation rate of every act of good will, reinforcing previous ones, would incrementally produce the same kind of foundational, molecular solidity and strength that the eons of development produce in the limestone stalactites and stalagmites. The accumulation of centuries of Golden Rule and good will teaching would have built an immense base of stability. Teaching the Golden Rule intensively would provide a softening of the psychological climate necessary for success in further global changes. This minor step to future change seems infinitesimal and so it seems to be irrelevant. But it is not irrelevant. It is the massive repetition that counts. If you're teaching it, what would graduation reached be like? It would imperceptible. You would already by then, possess that amiable relationship with others that would signify past success. Our world would be a more pleasant world. That happy state of affairs would be graduation.

It is clear that the knowledge that is required to build a house will probably include architecture, carpentry, plumbing, and electricity. Also that long experience, new techniques, new materials will improve the result. Much the same comments will be true when building, or operating, a factory; building and running a community or city; and every other human venture, including building a Golden Rule world society.

If one envisions the myriad of problems to be solved when building a future, unique, evolving society, it is clear that it can only come with the aid of a new body of questing thought. I would assume that the psychological sciences would need to be a major source. Being evolutionary in nature I would expect progress in this process to be exceedingly slow, even millennial. That would make the end result impregnable.

However, initial steps should start *NOW!* There must be individuals who can see the value of early planning and would take the first steps, possibly through organizations etc. I recollect the story of the old French general whose servant wished to defer to the afternoon, the planting of a tree that would not mature for sixty-five years. The general said, "No! It is all the more important to start this morning." Teachers and educators should start on their own, and then seek senior departmental direction.

Robert Maynard Hutchins would certainly have qualified as a scientist in global education. A short recap of his accomplishments. He was Dean of Yale Law School at age; president of the University of Chicago at 31 (remained 20 years as president); chairman of the board of directors of the Encyclopedia Britannica; associated director of the Ford Foundation; Co-founder and initially editor of the Great Books of the Western World; co-founder of Center for the Study of Democratic Institutions; and president of the Fund for the Republic.

Harry Ashmore, *Unseasonable Truths,* "His (Maynard Hutchins) own faith was grounded on the conviction that a form of education could be devised that would sharpen men's intellectual capacity so that they would be available to identify the basic ideas of their times, think dispassionately, and arrive at a rational course of action." That sounds superb for an adult like Thomas Jefferson himself. But, is it applicable to children? "He (Mortimer Adler) and Hutchins had always agreed that any child of normal intelligence was capable of learning, and if properly taught, could be equipped to master the kind of education required of citizens, charged with governing themselves. Schooling of this sort was not only the right of every child as a means of self-improvement, but a necessity in the democratic republic envisioned by the American Constitution." "At eighty-six, Adler was still in the lists, pushing his "Paideia Proposal," which called for the reorganization of the first twelve grades of school to provide a single track for all children. He had formed a national committee made up of prominent educators committed to the principle enunciated by Hutchins - *"The best education for the best is the best education for all."*

"The system he envisioned would include the beginning of a liberal education in the last nine grades of elementary and secondary school. This would provide the means to improve the intellectual skills of those who would go onto college and to encourage the others to recognize that learning should be a lifelong process and was not limited to an institutional setting."

The concept of, "sharpening one's intellectual capacity" is what seems to me, to be necessary to secure the informed electorate which

Jefferson wished. His, own education was comprehensive and classical, doubtless studying all aspects of the available knowledge of the time. How could the maximum number of registered voters of our day (or his day) ever be expected to achieve that high level of education that he and Robert Hutchins desired?

Contemporary community standards of education require that 100% of the children of the public be required to have the minimal education required to function in today's society. For the last few generations that minimal level has been rising from High School graduation to university level. Further education, as happened to me, then gets channeled into some specialty, and, to improve your skill, all further study takes place inside that bubble. You improve your specialized knowledge, but further growth in generalized education is over unless you choose to study further. Because the super-intellectual and super-educator, Robert Maynard Hutchins believed that men's "intellectual capacity can be sharpened," it brings serious hope to the electorates - and I find myself encouraged and eagerly listening. That is the sort of education I think would be necessary for "global education." Hutchins has made me able to think positively about global education. It has brought optimism to this effort. Hutchins and Adler's planning for a world constitution are inspiring to contemplate, but fruition appears so much more remote now, then when being promoted some 75 years ago. My *disillusionment!*

When that welcome moment of renewed interest reappears, as I think it must, the plans will only need dusting off. As a professional educator, Robert Maynard Hutchins may have known that Kurt Hahn was, at that time, also studying education on a Universalist level. Global education is the key to every problem of the world, or of its people. The human intellect producing the current rolling tide of new technology, new social and governmental innovations will eventually bring with them the answers we seek; and wonders now impossible will grace our future global utopia. Believe me! My adult years have brought to fruition many of the "impossible" fantasies of prior years. It will continue to happen. But the educational thrust must be global;

must be comprehensive; must be gender-neutral, ethnicity-neutral, religiously-neutral and geographically-neutral. The potential exists in everyone. Our innate abilities will not be equal, but for each of us there should be a matching fulfilling occupation to serve the functional needs of our cooperative society. Everyone's social, medical, educational and emotional needs would be fulfilled by the automatic, cooperative services of others. High levels of service and accomplishment would be recognized, celebrated and rewarded. This is possible in a *national* cooperative society, but in a *global* brotherhood, it would be our utopia.

How do we promote these ideas? The traditional, direct way is to write, phone, visit with, and lobby our congressional representatives. Acquaint them, and also UN delegates, with the attempt made 67 years ago at establishing global laws and constitution. The fact that the congressional approval stood at 133 votes demonstrates that what was once possible, is possible and desired again. A more appropriate time maybe coming.

The United World College

My unfocussed amateurism showed when I realized that I must have been residing, blindly, under the proverbial rock, and so I never heard of the United World College, until they celebrated their 50th anniversary. Time magazine, on June 3rd 2013 brought me the 'news.'

In 1963, Kurt Hahn, a German educationalist, developed a vision based on his post WWII experience at the NATO Defense College where he had observed discussion and collaboration between former enemies. He wanted to "transmit a spirit of mutual understanding to young people to help them overcome prejudice and antagonism through living and working together." He founded the *United World College,* headquartered in Great Britain. The UWC philosophy was triggered by a thought, voiced by Lester B. Pearson, Prime Minister of Canada, "How can there be peace without people understanding each other, and how can they understand each other if they don't know each other."

The United World College - Envisioned by Hahn, the goal of the college was to, "transmit a spirit of mutual understanding to young people to help them overcome prejudice and antagonism through living and working together." "UWC believes that to achieve peace and a sustainable future, the values it promotes are crucial:

- International and intercultural understanding.
- celebration of the difference.
- personal responsibility and integrity.
- compassion and service.
- respect for the environment.
- sense of idealism.
- personal challenge, and action and personal responsibility."

These are obviously admirable values that would fit into a, "global education," and would broaden one's outlook on life, culture, global environment, etc.

"United World College was founded in 1963 with the vision of bringing together young people, whose experience was of the political conflict of the cold war era, offering an educational experience, based on shared learning, collaboration, and understanding, so that the students would act as champions of peace." Consequently, many of the colleges have been built in countries were revolutions have occurred and very carefully selected students from both sides of the conflict are chosen. Thus the aim is to insert political and cultural compatibility into the areas of greatest need, and where probably the greatest future disagreement would take place. In other words, putting UWC establishments directly into the region of past political or military turmoil would be like sowing seeds of healing and cooperative understanding in advance of possible renewed dissension.

In the 50 years since the formation of the London, England headquarters, they have built twelve colleges in twelve countries, and two more are being opened in 2014. The Pearson College in Victoria, Canada was built over forty years ago in 1973, and the United States College in New Mexico in 1983. In the 2013 and 2014 classes, there are 219 students listed in the United States UWC student roster; forty-three from the United States, ten from China, 1 to 6 students from 74 other countries. About 1000 students per year are graduated worldwide. Funding is from individual donations, fund-raising clubs and societies. There is no financial support from corporate interests, government or national interests and for-profit enterprises, including universities. Thus growth has not been rapid, but it has probably been the most solid kind of development possible. Most important, pure untainted, uninfluenced, student education, should result in superb world-citizen graduates.

"We welcome students from a deliberately diverse range of backgrounds and experiences. At UWC, diversity extends to differences in socio-economic background, culture, race and religion, as well as nationality. UWC students are united in their commitment to positive social action to build a more equitable and fairer world." That commitment continues through their adult lives.

Two of the colleges, begin teaching students as early as two years of age. "We believe that you can educate the younger students in such a way that it insures prejudices do not develop, they care about the environment, they show respect for other people and wish to help those who are less privileged than themselves."

"The B Diploma is one of the well regarded and widely known secondary school qualifications in the world and is recognized by the world's leading universities."

At the Sept 2011 Clinton Global Initiative meeting, "UWC attended and launched a new scholarship and mentoring program for young women from conflict and post-conflict affected countries."

The following is the list of principles of the United World College, which I unsuccessfully attempted to render into a clarified, paraphrased translation. I finally realized that they state so clearly the difference of the UWC education from the routine education, that it was necessary to leave them as they were, and duplicate them in their entirety. With my lack of professional educational insight, I have been unable to definitively state what I mean when I refer to "global education." I think that UWC does it for me, and it also articulates the primary aim of this book: the apparent road to a world free of war; one where the Golden Rule becomes dominantly integral, (automatic); one where a democratic, cooperative global governmental entity is inevitable. This statement of principles I believe to be the "Holy Grail" of my quest and the most important page in the book.

The Principles:

UWC schools and colleges offer life-defining experiences for young people enabling them to discover the possibility of change through courageous action, personal example, and selfless leadership. A UWC education enshrines a commitment to the balanced development of the whole person and encourages an integrated development of human potential across a range of different dimensions, including the intellectual, moral, aesthetic, emotional, social, spiritual and physical.

All schools and colleges share UWC's missions and values, and each school and college responds to the UWC mission statement within the context of its location which recreate distinctive identities based upon local resources and opportunities." UWC's guiding principles are founded on seven educational principles inspired by Kurt Hahn. Though set within the context of Hahn's thought, it reflects experience gathered from our fifty- year history as well as current educational thinking. Underpinning these principles is the pursuit of peace and justice as the founding arm of UWC. These are the seven basic principles from which the practice of education at UWC schools and colleges is derived:

1. *That, the education should take place in a diverse college community. The selection of students should ensure representation from regions and social groups that reflect the wide range of tensions among and between peoples.*
2. *That this education requires active promotion of intercultural understanding and the development of genuine concern for others founded on shared life experiences, and cooperative and collaborative living. This includes reflective dialogue on global issues and critical and courageous engagement in the pursuit of peace.*
3. *That physical fitness and a healthy lifestyle are integral to the*

balanced development of the whole person. Unhealthy lifestyles limit human potential and limit progress in all dimensions of development.

4. *That community interaction is placed at the heart of college/school life. This requires the full and active participation of all members of the school or college.*
5. *That students are able to engage in continuing positive action toward issues of sustainability, on both an institutional and individual level.*
6. *That opportunities, for students to practice personal initiative, self-discipline and responsibility, manage risk, and embrace challenge must be provided. Where appropriate, these opportunities are supported by a reassuring adult presence.*
7. *That recognition is given to the fact that each individual possesses unique talents and abilities. Programs should exist in each college which will enable all sel*ected students to fulfill their potential.

Elimination of War

This book grew out of a lifetime of frustration over the inability of our contemporary political systems to eliminate the squandering of our world's wealth and resources, and the blood of her youth, in the pursuit of national security, corporate profits, full employment, power, territory, nationalistic pride (patriotism), religious beliefs and paranoia. That frustration remains! The necessity for the governments of the world, to squelch this voracious appetite for "blood money" remains! My earnest hope is that *someone*, somewhere, may grab the spark of the anti-war movement and carry it to new heights. When the ingrained political, religious and nationalistic hatreds of the individuals and cultures are replaced by deep seated convictions of love (The Golden Rule), then our dream of a cooperative society of perfection would be at hand. Human nature, would still call for argumentative discussions over methods and objectives.

Repeat, Alfred Lord Tennyson on Yahoo, "Til the war-drum throbbed no longer, and the battle flags were furled, in the Parliament of Man, the Federation of the World." The elimination of war would be a monstrously huge task, but as I have faith in the long term intelligence of the people of the world, I know that it is not only possible, but think that it is inevitable. Mahatma Gandhi, said, "We must not lose faith in humanity." There is an abundance of further quotations to the effect that what can be imagined, can also be achieved. So if it is imagined, possible and inevitable, then let us also make it mandatory to start *immediately!*

Repeat again the vision of, "Alfred Adler, Austrian psychoanalyst (1870 1937) "There is a law that man should love his neighbor as himself. In a few hundred years it should be as natural to mankind as breathing or the upright gait, but if he does not learn it he must perish." Those words summarize this entire account. The Golden Rule applied to each cause of war previously described, would, in time, resolve the issue. This concept is so very, very important that I would ask you to override your automatic feelings of doubt. This is not just a play-on words. Of course it is idealistic and simplistic! But that does not make it wrong. Reducing the concept to its most simple form, when there is a point of contention between two entities, *EACH* adversary should feel that their concerns have been fully respected, considered and accommodated. It is mutually doing unto others as you would have them do to you.

Teaching the Golden Rule as a moral obligation, and teaching it so deeply that it becomes the primary response in all situations, *must* be the world-wide imperative educational goal. That sentence is the fundamental message I would wish the reader to take from this entire effort! In times of war and of emergency many anecdotes have portrayed this humanitarian impulse. That spontaneity has occurred because the basic Golden Rule principle had been implanted so deeply that it was an instantaneous, instinctive, visceral impulse at the moment of usage. At the recent Boston Marathon bombing a man's legs were blown off, and the Costa Rican immigrant, Carlos Arredondo, applied a tourniquet and went with him on the ambulance to the hospital. He demonstrated one of those gut-driven actions *that can also exist* in corporate boardrooms and national governments. It only needs that deep implantation and understanding of the Golden Rule - inculcated into *ALL* (world-wide) children at their earliest moments of awareness and carried through to adulthood. Carlos' wife said that the teaching had come from Carlos' mother. Idealistically it would permeate all of life's situations.

World peace is impossible without a global organization reflective of the input of the world's countries. My contention is that *ONLY* with that deeply-ingrained, altruistic, good-will centered, view of our relationships with others, can those causes of war be overcome. The affairs of a nation are carried on by humans. So it is a matter of the national leaders applying those humanitarian points of view to international affairs. Early in this account I spoke of teaching the Golden Rule at all levels of education. I am sure that Dr. Adler had that in mind when he referred to, "a few hundred years" as a reasonable estimate of the necessary teaching and development time, for his concept to develop into Alfred Tennyson's, "world parliament and brotherhood of man." I have lived most of the first century of his estimate, and it appears to me that in the cacophony of world voices, Dr. Adler's idealistic words have not been heard. However, I am optimistic that his, "few hundred years," could still be appropriate.

Our ailing globe contains a swarming mass of about 7 billion of us, each one of us being different to every other, and each one deserving to have a global, institutional, humanitarian concern for their welfare. The term *welfare* would include the physical and mental needs of all ages, but, for the young, a fulfilling globally-oriented education. For that to happen it is necessary to have a global federation. I inflexibly believe that the future of the world's people depends upon the eventual disappearance of all national entities (countries) and, in their place, the formation, and administration, of a democratic, cooperative global organization representing equally all peoples of the earth, and taking care of their needs without deference to color, ethnic origins, religious or regional factors.

In all countries there are idealistic, progressive thinkers who would be ready for constructive, progressive action but, at this time, the nationalistic opinions of much of the populations of long-established nations, especially the U.S., makes this opinion idealistically utopian. It may surprise many that there was that post-WWII period, I described, during which world confederation was being seriously debated. If it was that important at that time, then it is even more so now. One must have a goal, if still distant in time. That was my dream when, over 50 years ago, I joined the *United World Federalists.* The dream of world federation is still a necessity for world peace to become possible. To construct a new successful, universal, global organization we must first re-study and understand the successes and failures of the past. It *will* come.

Addendum, Sept 16th 2015.

Astonishing! An indescribably wonderful letter has arrived from an excited organization, Citizens for Global Solutions (CGS), linked to United World Federalists - Institute for Global Policy! Thrilling news! My futuristic hope that deep-in-the-future, maybe centuries, the world might again consider world federation, - has been reduced to five years! At least the first steps. The location is The Hague, Capitol of the Netherlands, which is the center of many international organizations, including the International Criminal Court of the United Nations. In June 2015, a report by The Hague Commission on Global Security, Justice and Governance, issued a short list of recommendations for improvement of the United Nations. The Hague Commission's report calls for a five-year dialogue on its recommendations culminating in 2020 the 75th anniversary of the end of WWII, the dawn of the atomic age, and the birth of the United Nations in a "World Conference on Global Institutions." Remarkably, they have even opened the door to the possibility of amending the United Nations Charter if necessary to effect the positive changes needed to meet 21st century challenges. Obviously, strengthened policing powers and the elimination of the veto will dominate discussions of change.

It is marvelous to see actual progress in what has been the apparently futile, utopian, academic pursuit of world federation. It has been this 'American-Canadian's' 50 year 'Citizens for Global Solutions' dream. I have lived long enough to see my four and a half years of effort in authoring this book validated.

Bibliography

Adler, Bill. *Wit and Wisdom of Jimmy Carter.* Secaucus, NJ: Citadel Publishing, 1994.

Albom, Mitch. *Tuesday's with Morrie. New York, NY:* Doubleday, 1997.

Anderson, Peggy. *Great Quotations from Great Leaders.* Naperville, IL: Simple Truths, 2007.

Asad, Muhammad. *Road to Mecca.* New York, NY: Simon & Schuster, 1954.

Ashmore, Harry. *Unseasonable Truths.* Toronto, Canada: Little, Brown and Company, 1989.

Ayres, Alex. *Wit and Wisdom of Abraham Lincoln.* London, England: Penguin Books, 1952.

Batty, Peter. *House of Krupp.* New York, NY: Stein & Day, Dorset Press Publishers, 1996.

Beebe, John. *Integrity in Depth.* New York, NY: Fromm International Publishing Co, 1995.

Bellamy, Edward. *Looking Backward 1883.* Reprint. New York, NY: New American Library of World Literature Inc, 1960.

Berton, Pierre. *The Great Depression: 1929 1939.* Toronto, Canada: McClelland & Stewart, 1990.

Borkin, Joseph. *The Crime and Punishment* of *I.G. Farben.* New York, NY: Simon & Schuster, 1978.

Braithwaite, Rodric. *Moscow 1941.* New York, NY: Alfred Knopf, Random House Publishing, 2006.

Burleigh, Michael. *Moral Combat.* New York, NY: Harper Collins Publishers, 2011

Byfield, Ted. *Alberta in the Twentieth Century.* Edmonton, Alberta: United Western Communications Ltd, 1998.

Carey, John. *Eyewitness to History.* Cambridge, MA: Harvard University Press, 1987.

Carroll, James. *House of War.* New York, NY: Houghton Mifflin Company, 2006

Chase, M.E. *Life and Language in the Old Testament.* New York, NY: W.W. Norton & Company, 1955.

Chavez, President Hugo. *Understanding the Venezuelan Revolution.* New York, NY: Monthly Review Press, 2005.

Chawla, Navin. *Mother Theresa.* Rockport, ME: Element Books, Inc., 1992

Chi, Lui Wu. *Confucius.* New York, N. Y.: Philosophical Library, 1955.

Churchill, Winston. *Painting, as a Pastime.* New York, NY: Corner Library, 1932.

---. *Memoirs of the Second World War.* Boston, MA: Houghton-Mifflin Company, 1959.

Clark, Grenville & Sohn, Louis B. *World Peace through World Law.*

Cambridge, MA: Harvard University Press, 1958.

Coldwell, M. J. *Left Turn, Canada.* London, England: Victor Gollancz Ltd, 1945.

Comfort, W.W. *Just Among Friends.* Philadelphia, PA: American Friends Service Committee, 1959.

Couch, William T. Editor. *Colliers Encyclopedia. Chicago, IL:* The Crowell-Colliers Publishing Co, 1955.

Cousins, Norman - *Albert Schweitzer.* New York, NY: W. W. Norton Inc., 1985.

Cranston, Alan. *Killing of the Peace.* New York, NY: Viking Press, 1945.

Davies, J.C. *History of Borlase School.* Aylesbury Buckinghamshire, England: G. T. De Fraine & Co Ltd, 1932.

Dawkins, Richard. *The God Delusion.* New York, NY: Bantam Publishing, Trans-world Publishing, 2006.

Dorsey, Larry - *Healing Words.* New York, NY: Harpers Collins Publishers, 1993

Durant, John and Alice. *Pictorial History of American Presidents.* New York, NY: A.S. Barnes & Co, Inc, 1955.

Durant, Will. *The Story of Philosophy. New York, NY:* Simon & Schuster, Inc, 1953.

Eban, Abba. *Personal Witness.* New York, NY: G. P. Putnam Sons, 1992. Einstein, Albert - *Ideas and Opinions.* New York, NY: Wings Books Random House Inc, 1954.

Faizi, Gloria. *Bahai Belief.* Willamette, IL: Bahai Publishing Trust, 1971.

Ferm, Vergilius. *Encyclopedia of Religion.* New York, NY: Philosophical Library, 1945.

Friedrich, Erich. *War against War.* Seattle WA*:* The Real Comet Press, 1987 edition, Douglas Kellner, 1924.

Fromkin, David. *A Peace to End all Peace.* New York, NY: Avon Books, Hearst Corp, 1989.

Galland, Adolf. *The First and the Last.* New York, NY: Ballantine Books Inc, 1954.

Gandhi, Mohandas. *Gandhi: An Autobiography The Story of My Experiments with Truth.* New York, NY: Dover Publications, 1948.

Gaskin, Margaret. *Blitz.* Orlando, FL*:* Harcourt, Inc., 2006.

Glubb, Sir John. *Muhammad.* New York, NY: Stein & Day Publishers, 1970.

'God'. *The Bible.* Chicago, IL: The Moody Bible Institute, 1400 BC to 100AD.

Gorresio, Vittorio. *The New Mission of Pope John XXIII.* New York, NY: Funk & Wagnalls, Reader's Digest, 1970.

Gourfinkel, Nina. *Gorky.* New York, NY: Grove Press, Inc, 1960. Grossman, Lt. Col. Dave. *Stop Teaching our Kids to Kill.* New York, NY: Crown Publishers, 1999.

Hackworth, Col. David H. *About Face.* New York, NY: Simon & Schuster, 1989.

Hager, Thomas. *Force of Nature: The Life of Linus Pauling.* New York, NY: Simon & Schuster, 1995.

Harris, Whitney B. *Tyranny on Trial.* Dallas, TX: Southern Methodist University Press, 1954.

Higham, Charles. *Trading with the Enemy.* New York NY: Barnes & Noble Arrangement with Lowenstein Associates, Inc, 1983.

Hillman, James. *A Terrible Love of War* New York, NY: The Penguin Press, 2004

Hiss, Alger. *Recollections of a life.* New York, NY: Arcade Publishing Inc. (Little Brown), 1988.

Hitler, Adolf. *Mein Kampf.* Boston, MA: Houghton Mifflin & Co., 1939

Hodgson, Lynn-Philip. *Inside Camp X. Fort Henry, Ontario:* Blake Book Distribution, 1999.

Hoskins, Lotte. *I Have a Dream. The Quotations of Martin Luther King, Jr.* New York, NY: Grosset and Dunlap, 1968.

Humes, James C. *The Wit and Wisdom of Winston Churchill.* New York, NY: Harper & Collins Publishers, 1994.

Huxley, Julian. *Knowledge, Morality and Destiny.* New York NY: American Library, Harper Bros, 1958.

Isaacson, Walter. *Einstein.* New York, NY: Simon & Schuster, 2007.

Jack, Homer. *Religion and Peace.* New York, NY: The Bobbs-Merrill Co Inc, 1966.

Johnson, David. *The London Blitz.* New York NY: Stein and Day Publishers/Scarborough House, 1980.

Josephus, Flavius. *The Life and Works of Flavius Josephus.* Translation by Whiston, William. New York, NY: Holt, Rinehart & Whiston, date unknown.

Karolevitz, Robert F. *Challenge, The South Dakota Story.* Sioux, SD: The Brevet Press, 1975.

Kemp, Peter. *Convoy: Drama in Arctic Waters.* Edison, NJ: Castle Books, Book Sales Inc. 2004.

---. *Decision at Sea: The Convoy Escort.* New York NY: E. P. Dalton, 1978.
King, Martin Luther Jr. *Strength to Love.* New York NY: Harper and Rowe Pocket Books Inc, 1963.
---. *Stride to Freedom.* New York, NY: Ballantine Books, Inc, 1963
---. *Why We Can't Wait.* New York NY: Harper and Rowe, 1963-1964
---. *Where Do We Go from Here?* New York NY: Harper and Rowe, 1967
Hanna, Edward and Hicks, Henry and Koppel, Ted (compiled) HANNA. *Wit and Wisdom of Adlai Stevenson.* New York NY: Hawthorne Books, Inc, 1965.
Kraybill, Donald B. *The Puzzle of Amish Life.* Intercourse, PA: Good Books, 1990.
Kurtz, Paul. *Free Inquiry Magazine- Bimonthly.* New York NY: Council for Secular Humanism, 2005.
Lalonde, Emerson Hughes. *Thy Neighbor as Thyself.* Boston, MA: The Universalist Publishing House, 1959.
Lamont, Corliss. *Philosophy of Humanism.* New York, NY: Frederick Ungar Publishing Co, 1949.
Langfeldt, Gabriel. *Albert Schweitzer.* London, England: George Allen & Unwin, Ltd, 1981.
Lawrence, T. E. (of Arabia). *Seven Pillars of Wisdom.* New York, NY: Dell Publishing, 1927.
Leasor, James. *Green Beach.* New York, NY: William Moore & Co. Inc., 1975.
Leonard, Wolfgang. *Betrayal.* New York, NY: St Martin's Press, 1986.
Lestock Historical Society. *Memories of Lestock.* Lestock, Saskatchewan: 1980.
Lewis, John. *Socialism and the Individual.* New York, NY: International Publishers Co Inc, 1961.
Liddle, Verle A. and Theron C. *A Thought for Today.* Salt Lake City, UT: Liddle Enterprises Inc, 1965.
Low, Marie Ann. *Dustbowl Diary: 1927-1937.* Lincoln, NE: University of Nebraska, 1984.
Lukacs, John. *June 1941: Hitler and Stalin.* New Haven CT: Yale University Press, 2006.

Manchester, William - *The Last Lion.* New York, NY: Little Brown & Co Publishers, 1983.

McClaren, Brian D. *A Search for what Makes Sense.* Grand Rapids, Michigan: Zondervan, 2007.

McIlwraith, Naomi. *Kiyâm.* Edmonton, Alberta: Athabaska University Press, 2012.

McMaster, H. R. *Dereliction of Duty.* New York, NY: Harper Collins Publishers, 1997.

McNamara, Robert S. *In Retrospect.* New York, NY: Vintage Books Random House, Inc, 1996.

Miller, Francis Trevelyan - *The Complete History of World War II.* Chicago, IL: Reader's Service Bureau, 1945.

Miller, Merle. *Plain Speaking, an Oral Biography of Harry S. Truman.* New York, NY: Berkley Publishing Corporation, 1973.

Moore, Michael. *Dude, Where's My Country?* New York, NY: Warner Books, Inc, 2003.

Morison, Samuel Eliot - *Oxford History of the American People.* New York, NY: Oxford University Press, 1965.

Morrison, Toni. *Brilliant Thoughts.* Lincolnwood, IL: West Side Publications, 1973.

Moyers, Bill. *World of Ideas.* New York, NY: Doubleday Dell Publishing Group, Inc, 1989.

Mowat, Farley. *Eastern Passage.* Toronto, Canada: McClelland and Stewart, 2010.

Murrow, Edward R. *This, I Believe.* New York, NY: Schuster & Schuster Inc, 1952

Nehru, Jawaharlal. *India's Freedom.* New York, NY: Barnes & Noble, Inc, 1936

Nissenthal, Jack. *Winning the Radar War.* New York, NY: St Martin's Press, 1987

Overy, Richard. *1939: Countdown to War.* New York, NY: Viking Penguin Group Inc, 2010.

Pearsall, Paul PhD - *Pleasure Prescription.* Alameda, CA: Hunter House Inc, 1996.

Phillips, Derek. *Towards a Just Order.* Princeton, NJ: Princeton University Press, 1986.

Philosophical Library. *Wisdom of Tolstoy.* New York, NY: Philosophical Library, 1968.

Prouse, A. Robert. *Ticket to Hell via Dieppe.* Scarborough, Ontario: Van Nostrand Reinhold Publishers, 1982.

Raban, Jonathan. *Bad Land.* New York, NY: Vintage Books, Division of Random House Inc, 1996.

Ray, James Earl - *Who killed Martin Luther King?* Bethesda, MD: National Press Books, Inc, 1992

Remarque, Erich Maria. *All Quiet on the Western Front* New York, NY: Ballantine Books, Random House, 1928.

Reves, Emery. *Anatomy of Peace.* New York, NY: The Viking Press Inc., 1945.

Riaznov, David. *Karl Marx and Friedrich Engels.* New York, NY: Monthly Review Press, 1973.

Robertson, Terence. *Shame and the Glory.* Toronto, Ontario: McClellan & Stewart, Ltd, 1963

Rosen, Lee. *Religion in America.* New York, NY: Simon & Schuster Inc, 1963

Roth, John L. *A Quiet and Peaceful Life.* Intercourse, PA: Great Books, 1979.

Sagan, Carl. *Demon Haunted World.* New York, NY: Ballantine Books Random House, Inc, 1996.

Schweitzer, Dr. Albert - *The Light within us.* New York, NY: The Philosophical Library, Inc, 1958.

Scott, Clinton Lee. *Religion Can Make Sense.* Boston, MA: Universalist Publishing House, 1949.

Seeley, Charles S. *Modern Materialism.* New York, NY: Philosophical library Inc., 1960.

Seldes, George. *The Great Quotations.* New York, NY: Pocket Books, Simon & Schuster, 1960.

Shanks, Herschell. *Biblical Archaeology Review Magazine.* Washington, DC: Biblical Archaeology Society, 1977-2012.

Sheehan, Neil. *A Bright Shining Lie.* New York, NY: Random House, 1988.

Smiley, Tavis. *Death of a King.* New York, NY: Little, Brown and Company, 2014.

Smith, Hedrick. *The Power Game.* New York, NY. Random House Inc, 1988.

Stevenson, Adlai. *Putting First Things First.* New York, NY: Random House, 1960.

Stevenson, William. *A Man called Intrepid.* New York, NY: Ballantine Books, Division of Random House, Inc, 1976.

Stone, I. F. *Hidden History of the Korean War.* New York, NY: Monthly Review Press, 1952.

Taylor, A.J.P. *The Origins of World War II.* New York, NY: Schuster & Schuster, 1961.

Terkel, Studs - *The Great Divide.* New York & Toronto: Pantheon Books Random House Inc, 1988.

Terraine, John. *Life and Times of Lord Mountbatten.* New York, NY: Holt, Rinehart & Winston, 1968.

Toynbee, Arnold. *A Study of History.* New York, NY: Oxford University Press, 1946-58.

Verle, A. and Liddle T. C. *A Thought for Today.* Salt Lake City, UT: Liddle Enterprises, Inc, 1965.

Villa, Brian Loring. *Unauthorized Action.* Ontario, Canada: Oxford University Press, 1989.

Warren, Chief Justice Earl. *The Warren Commission Report: The Official Report on the Assassination of President John F. Kennedy.* New York NY: McGraw Hill Book Company, 1963.

Wells, H. G. *The Outline of History.* New York, NY: Garden City Books, Doubleday and Co Garden City, 1920 & 1949.

Whitaker, Brigadier General Denis. *Dieppe: Tragedy To Triumph.* Toronto, Ontario: McGraw Hill, 1992.

Wilkerson, John. *Jerusalem as Jesus Knew It.* New York, NY: Thames and Hudson, 1978.

Williams-Meakes, Edna. *A Quest for Peace and Alternatives to War.* Ottawa, Ontario: Humanist Association of Canada, 1994.

Wishart-Bank End Historical Society. *Emerald, Past in Prose, Poetry & Pictures.* Wishart, Saskatchewan, Canada: The Wishart-Bank End Historical Society, 1980.

Wood, Edward W., Jr. *Worshipping the Myths of World War II.* Dulles, VA: Potomac Books, Inc., 2006.

Woodward, Bob & Bernstein, Carl. *The Final Days.* New York, NY: Simon & Schuster, 1976.

Woodward, Bob. *Veil: The Secret Wars of the CIA., 1981-1987.* New York, NY: Simon & Schuster, 1987.

Zinn, Howard. *The People's History.* New York, NY: Harper Collins Publishers, 1980.

CPSIA information can be obtained
at www.ICGtesting.com
Printed in the USA
FSHW02n2327300418
47467FS